AF600400

GOD MADE WORD

An Archaeology of Mystic Discourse in Early Modern Spain

God Made Word

An Archaeology of Mystic Discourse in Early Modern Spain

DALE SHUGER

UNIVERSITY OF TORONTO PRESS
Toronto Buffalo London

Toronto Buffalo London
utorontopress.com

ISBN 978-1-4875-2880-5 (cloth)
ISBN 978-1-4875-2882-9 (EPUB)
ISBN 978-1-4875-2881-2 (PDF)

Toronto Iberic

Library and Archives Canada Cataloguing in Publication

Title: God made word : an archaeology of mystic discourse in early modern Spain / Dale Shuger.
Names: Shuger, Dale, author.
Series: Toronto Iberic ; 71.
Description: Series statement: Toronto Iberic ; 71 | Includes bibliographical references and index.
Identifiers: Canadiana (print) 20210252219 | Canadiana (ebook) 20210252340 | ISBN 9781487528805 (cloth) | ISBN 9781487528829 (EPUB) | ISBN 9781487528812 (PDF)
Subjects: LCSH: Spanish literature – Classical period, 1500–1700 – History and criticism. | LCSH: Mysticism in literature. | LCSH: Mysticism and literature – Spain – History. | LCSH: Mysticism – Spain – History.
Classification: LCC PQ6046.M9 S58 2022 | DDC 860.9/353 – dc23

We wish to acknowledge the land on which the University of Toronto Press operates. This land is the traditional territory of the Wendat, the Anishnaabeg, the Haudenosaunee, the Métis, and the Mississaugas of the Credit First Nation.

University of Toronto Press acknowledges the financial support of the Government of Canada, the Canada Council for the Arts, and the Ontario Arts Council, an agency of the Government of Ontario, for its publishing activities.

Canada Council for the Arts
Conseil des Arts du Canada

Funded by the Government of Canada
Financé par le gouvernement du Canada

Contents

Acknowledgments

The ideas that would come to form this book first entered into the world in a job talk I gave in spring 2013 at Tulane University. I am immensely grateful to Tulane for offering me the position and to the warm, supportive environment I have found in the Spanish and Portuguese department. From the financial support of the administration to the mentorship of senior faculty to the academic exchange and friendships of my colleagues, I could not have asked for a better academic home. I would particularly like to thank Chairs Jean Dangler and Christopher Dunn, Deans Carole Haber and Brian Edwards of the Tulane School of Liberal Arts, and my colleagues Linell Ajello, John Charles, Antonio Gómez, Tatjana Pavlovic, Rachel Stein, and Henry Sullivan. My other academic home is my local café, and I would like to thank all the baristas at the Freret Starbucks.

Portions of this book were researched at the Newberry Library in Chicago, the Biblioteca Nacional de España, and the Archivo Histórico Nacional in Madrid; thank you to all the archivists and librarians, and particularly to the heroes of the Interlibrary Loan office at Tulane's Howard-Tilton Memorial Library. I presented portions of this book at the Newberry Library Symposium on Latin America in the Early Colonial Period and at the annual conferences of the Modern Language Association, the Sixteenth Century Society, the Renaissance Society of America (RSA), and the Grupo de Estudios de la Mujer en España y Latinoamérica, and I thank all the organizers, co-presenters, and respondents who gave me feedback and encouragement. I am indebted to Louise Burkhart and David Tavárez for their assistance with chapter six, which led me far from my comfort zone. Ever since I proposed this project to Suzanne Rancourt at RSA, she and the entire team at the University of Toronto Press have been supportive, patient, efficient, and everything a scholar could wish for in a publisher.

I know it is commonplace to thank one's parents, but in my case, I owe more to my mother than most. Thank you, mom, for the sounding boards, the proofreading, and the genetic predisposition for early modern studies. My dogs Chip and Baxter have provided very little in the way of concrete feedback, but insofar as mysticism is about a pure, ineffable love, they have been my teachers.

Finally, an acknowledgment of a different sort. I edited this book during a global pandemic. None of our present-day concerns enter directly into the scholarship of this book, but I would be remiss if I did not take a moment to recognize the immense loss, sacrifice, and suffering that marked 2020 and beyond.

GOD MADE WORD

An Archaeology of Mystic Discourse
in Early Modern Spain

Introduction

Working on Spanish mysticism in my university library provides good exercise. The books that interest me are divided into two sections: the great Spanish mystic poets San Juan de la Cruz, Santa Teresa de Jesús, and Luis de León reside in the literature section on the second floor, along with plays that staged their lives, while early modern prose about mystic prayer, or secondary works about mysticism itself, are housed two floors up, in the religion section. Even here there is a division: those authors whose spiritual credentials were recognized in their own time reside in the sections dedicated to their various orders, a few call letters away from those who only become legible to history because the Spanish Inquisition judged their mysticism to be false. Yet when one begins to look at the words and ideas espoused in mystic poems, theological treatises, and Inquisition depositions, one finds considerable overlap: of people, of concepts, of strategies for expressing the ineffable. The division is not entirely arbitrary, for it was precisely during the early modern period that the generic and institutional conventions that mark the difference between a poem and a prayer manual, or an approved practice and a condemned one, are formed. Such divisions emerge from a complex interplay of factors both extrinsic and intrinsic to the texts themselves. Contexts of enunciation – the spaces in which discourses are produced – are informed by a variety of factors that inevitably shape the discourses produced there, and at the same time, the discourses themselves compel changes in the spaces where they are produced and received. During periods of particular instability and change, these processes accelerate and intensify.

Given the extreme religious, political, and social instability and change that marked the sixteenth century, it would be remarkable if we did *not* find such an accelerated and intensified restructuring of the language of man's relationship with God during that period. Theology, politics, and literature have always mutually influenced each other in a never-ending and never-beginning cycle, but the ruptures occasioned by the invention of the printing press, the discovery of the Americas, and the Reformation (these three themselves all related, of course) set in motion a process of discursive shift whose repercussions are still being felt and that are reflected in the divisions of my library. It is hardly breaking news that the Renaissance ushered in an era of great change, but there is a tendency to focus *either* on the changes in institutions *or* on the changes in literary expressions. Historically, a teleological focus on the *modernity* of the early modern period led to an emphasis on the emergence of secular, capitalist, individualist structures; the residual elements of culture, to use Raymond Williams's term, would not seem to require study or theorization, as they could be defined precisely as that-which-did-not-change.[1] Insofar as the Counter-Reformation Church was the object of study, condemnation often took the place of comprehension. Williams's formulation of the essential interplay between residual, dominant, and emergent cultures gave rise to new focus on institutions and forms that Burkhardt and his followers would have seen as "anachronistic" or unmodern, thus leading to renewed focus on the Counter-Reformation, and the religious institutions inherited, at least superficially, from the medieval period.

Yet studies focused on institutions, particularly those with a Marxist orientation, provide an uncomfortable lens through which to view religious movements, given that the Marxist worldview is not only secular but antagonistic to religion, assuming *a priori* that religion is a human construction meant to naturalize or obscure human goals. By the same token, Marxist literary critique, while abundant, does not really focus on language itself but is instead interested in how signifiers reveal and obscure the signification of power. This has created a split between historical studies, generally centred on institutions and even in their most archival turns reading exclusively for meaning, and literary studies, usually focused on single authors, reading with close attention to language but with less interest in how words shape *praxis* and institutions. Furthermore, literary studies tend to focus exclusively on textual objects that have been *a priori* designated as *literary*. In the case of the Spanish mystics, this is almost always understood to refer to poetry, and until the groundbreaking work of Stacy Schlau and Electa Arenal opened the canon to a few other female authors, to the poetry of Santa Teresa de Ávila, San Juan de la Cruz, and Fray Luis de León. Theology, oral testimony or depositions, confessors' manuals, and other forms of discourse produced primarily for functional ends or as a byproduct of institutional procedures, were excluded from language-based study.

This designation of "historical" and "literary" texts, and the subsequent delimitation of the tools through which to analyse each, is problematic because, as this book will argue, language and ideas circulated between poetry, theology, theatre, speech, and other discourses, and indeed it is only by studying this circulation that we can see how the "historical" and the "literary" began to separate, at least with respect to mystic discourse.

Before examining the factors behind this anachronistic separation of mystic poetry from its historical context, we should clarify the operant use of the term *mystic* for this study. There is no single definition of "mysticism," and religious scholars disagree about the precise contours of the term. There are mystical forms of almost all religions, and indeed some scholars have argued that non-religious experiences (drug-induced states or neurological disturbances) can be mystical as well. William James, the father of the academic study of mysticism, set out in his *The Varieties of Religious Experience*[2] a quartet of fundamental characteristics of mystic experience: the mystic state is noetic (i.e., it provides a higher truth than can be achieved through "normal" modes of consciousness), transient, passive, and ineffable. Later scholars have quibbled with one or another of these terms, but insofar as they share a presupposition that *all* mystical experience can be defined and analysed as homologous, they can all be grouped as part of a "perennialist" school. For a believer, the noetic quality of mysticism – an experience that transcends time, place, and subjectivity – comes directly from the timeless, universal, transcendent nature of God. Among secular academics, this characteristic points to a structural similarity across mystical traditions and thus lends itself to an academic analysis that also transcends (or ignores) historical context. It is this possibility, I would argue, that prompted the interest in the Golden Age mystics among secular literary scholars, liberals, non-Spaniards in the nineteenth and twentieth centuries. It seemed possible to divorce these poets from the Counter-Reformation Catholic ideologies and institutions from which they emerged.

A more contemporary trend in the study of mysticism, largely pioneered by Steven Katz, rejects any "noetic" essence of mysticism. According to Katz, the mystic experience may *seem* (and be represented) as outside of human constructs of space, time, and culture, but this itself is a cultural construction. All experience, for Katz, is produced within a cultural matrix: "There are NO pure (i.e. unmediated) experiences. Neither mystical experience nor more ordinary forms of experience give any indication, or any grounds for believing, that they are unmediated. That is to say, all experience is processed through and organised by, and makes itself available to us in extremely complex epistemological ways" (26).[3] This approach requires returning mystic literature to its theological, ideological, and historical matrix. Because this implies a return to the domain of historians, at least as far as history and literature have been delimited in modern academia, this has shifted the focus of enquiry away from language. What tends to get lost, then, between the perennialist and contextualist approaches, is a *contextualized, historically specific study of mystic language*, particularly of discourse produced by mystics (and would-be mystics) whose works were never admitted into a literary canon.[4]

It would be contradictory to propose a contextualized, historically specific study of mystic language in general, and it is probably true that, in many contexts, mystic language has little impact on larger socio-historical trends. This book is concerned with one historical context – Spanish Catholic mysticism of the sixteenth and seventeenth centuries –because, this book will argue, the representation of mystic experience occupies a central role in developments that might otherwise seem discrete, unrelated. It should be clear, then, that this book is not concerned with the totality of mystic experience or the formal similarities across mystical traditions. It is also agnostic as to the relative legitimacy of one or another professed mystic, or the value (in either aesthetic or theological terms) of one or another expression of the mystic experience. It is, instead, concerned with how individuals and institutions judged value and legitimacy in their own time and how the language of mysticism and the language of judgment mutually influenced each other.

Why emphasize language over other aspects of mystic experience and representation? The central argument of this book is that the struggle to represent an ineffable interior experience is fundamental to many of the social and artistic developments we associate with the Golden Age of Spain, developments that do not on their surface seem to have much to do with mysticism or with each other. Mysticism in early modern Spain, as we shall see, differs from medieval mystic movements in the unusual preoccupation with questions of language. The advent of print and proto-national institutions meant that language spread far beyond the local, communal bounds that characterize most medieval communities that dedicated themselves to cultivation of mystic union. The great mystic *texts* of the medieval period are mostly written in Latin and/or had limited readership; the mass mystic *movements*, on the other hand, did not encourage individuals to write or dictate accounts of their experiences. Early modern Spanish practitioners of mystic contemplation (known in the period by various terms, including *oración mental* and *recogimiento*) were *textually* linked in ways that go beyond those of any medieval mystic movement; writing or conveying in language the mystic experience became not just a byproduct but instead an essential component of interior spirituality itself.

Interior spirituality need not be written. The experience of divine union *cannot* be written because knowledge of God transcends human reason and language,[5] and thus it cannot be represented directly and fully in language. The desire or compulsion to approximate in words the mystic experience is not unique to early modern Spain, but the breadth and diversity of reasons for such representation is, as well as the innovation in forms that such representations take. The fundamental motor of innovation is the tension between a desire to disrupt (to make new) and a desire to make known. If the mystic experience itself is the tree that falls in the forest when no one is around, mystic discourse is the attempt to describe the sound that was made. Michel de Certeau, whose *Mystic Fable* represents the main exception to the previously cited dearth of historically contextualized language-based studies of mysticism, makes a crucial distinction between mystic experience (beyond representation), mystic discourse (the paradoxical attempt to represent that which transcends representation) and a third element, mysticism, which represents the codification of such attempts into a stable signifying system (83–4).[6] This distinction – and the constant push and pull between the three possibilities – will be crucial to this study and thus is worth elaborating in more detail.

Following de Certeau, mystic discourse is inherently paradoxical because the discourse must at the same time attempt to describe in human terms the experience and convey the insufficiency of those terms, the *otherness* of the event. Mystic writers have used various strategies to convey this otherness: paradox, negation, neologism, symbolism. Because, as the fifteenth-century Italian humanist Lorenzo Valla put it, "a new reality requires new words" (qtd. in de Certeau 83), the search for a proper expression of this experience tends to produce new terminology, new metaphors, new symbols, new literary forms. The representation of the changes in the human interior produces "transmutations performed within the vocabulary borrowed from standard language that operate in the interior of words" (144).[7] Mysticism for de Certeau is fundamentally disruptive, transgressive. This does not, however, mean that all mystics were revolutionaries or explicitly opposed to the dominant ideologies and institutions of their day. The levels of disruption are varied, and it was de Certeau's insight to see that the primary level of disruption occurs at the level of the signifier, that mysticism is "a manner of using received language *differently*" that *then* "becomes objectified in a set of delimitations and processes" (16). These disruptions of language ripple out to form practices, and these in turn shape lives, ideas, and institutions. However, the primacy of language in early modern mysticism means that any study that focuses solely on lives, ideas, and institutions will be partial and disjointed, like a study of the human body that leaves out the brain.

De Certeau elaborates a further paradox inherent to mystic discourse. Disruption provokes a response. Mystic discourse disrupts other discourses, those associated with prevailing ideologies and institutions, and inevitably these institutions respond. The responses need not be strictly oppositional or subject to a simple logic of adoption or censorship. However, the very act of taking the language of mystics and subjecting it to non-mystic modes of analysis in order to determine the proper response affects the transgressive power of the mystic's language, dependent as it is on newness, strangeness, otherness. For de Certeau, mystic language displaces and de-naturalizes.[8] Institutional discourse repeats, resignifies, and ultimately seeks to put these mystic expressions "back into place" (to locate them, to naturalize them). Mystic expressions become clichés, their meaning stable. As de Certeau puts it, mystic discourse, which he associates with *lo místico* (mystic as an adjective) ceases to be mystic in the moment it codifies into *misticismo* (mysticism as a noun). An intriguing extension of this identification of *lo místico* with a disruptive language of interiority is that it need not be tied to any given genre or even to religion. Indeed, de Certeau argues that by the end of the seventeenth century, "in the place once occupied by *mystics*, there remained only: stockpiles of psychic or somatic phenomena, soon to be subjugated by psychology or pathology; 'exercises' of meaning, colonized by theology, which transformed them into practical 'applications'; and radical questions, forgotten since then or taken up by philosophy" (77). Later, it "reappears in the gaps within scientific certainty, as if ever returning to its birthplace" (77–8). Mysticism emerges in the cracks of stable discourses of knowledge about the self, whether this discourse be labelled religion, psychology, or neuroscience.

The Mystic Fable is more of a collection of essays on individual mystic figures or figures of speech than a single narrative. What gets lost in the jumps between chapters is a close analysis of how this displacement and replacement occurs. De Certeau's arguments are either broadly theoretical or focused on particular, and predominantly French, texts. The missing links are the non-mystic institutions or spaces of enunciation and the ways that their own discourse and praxis changes in response to the mystic interruption. Furthermore, while I believe de Certeau's identification of language at the heart of *lo místico* in the early modern period applies equally to Spain and his main area of focus, France, the story of the two nations' responses to *lo místico* differs markedly. Mysticism bleeds into Spanish missionary efforts in the New World, the *comedia*, and the Inquisition, institutions which are distinct to Spain during this period. This study then seeks to fill in the gaps in the process that takes *lo místico* to *misticismo*, to tell the story of how religious discourse was disrupted by a mystic language and how it re-settled and sent *lo místico* elsewhere to other discourses of knowledge. A recurring theme throughout the chapters is this constant, cyclical, and multi-directional process of revitalization and condensation: a constant movement between adjective and noun, transgression and system.

As should be apparent from the title of this book, in addition to Michel de Certeau, the other theorist whose ideas gird my approach is Michel Foucault. I am not concerned with Foucault's work on the early modern period but instead on the theory, suggested in *The Order of Things* and fully laid out in *The Archaeology of Knowledge*, of the way that disciplines and discourses form. To understand this method, it is useful to review some of Foucault's terminology as set out in that work. Like Foucault, I begin by questioning "those divisions or groupings with which we have become so familiar":

> Can one accept, as such, the distinction between the major types of discourse, or that between such forms or genres as science, literature, philosophy, religion, history, fiction, etc., and which tend to create certain great historical individualities? We are not even sure of ourselves when we use these distinctions in our own world of discourse, let alone when we are analysing groups of statements which, when first formulated, were distributed, divided, and characterized in a quite different way: after all, 'literature' and 'politics' are recent categories, which can be applied to medieval culture, or even classical culture, only by a retrospective hypothesis, and by an interplay of formal analogies or semantic resemblances; but neither literature, nor politics, nor philosophy and the sciences articulated the field of discourse, in the seventeenth or eighteenth century, as they did in the nineteenth century. In any case, these divisions - whether our own, or those contemporary with the discourse under examination - are always themselves reflexive categories, principles of classification, normative rules, institutionalized types: they, in turn, are facts of discourse that deserve to be analysed beside others; of course, they also have complex relations with each other, but they are not intrinsic, autochthonous, and universally recognizable characteristics. (21)

Like Foucault, I am interested in the "complex relations" between the "reflexive categories, principles of classification, normative rules, institutionalized types" that subsequent scholarship and my own library inscribes and perpetuates; like Foucault, I believe that the first step towards understanding the principles behind such a division of knowledge lies not in searching for a pre-discursive essence but instead in seeing how discursive formations arise and change. Foucault defines the discursive formation as a subset within the set of intelligible expressions for which "one can define a regularity (an order, correlations, positions and functionings, transformations) ... between objects, types of statement, concepts, or thematic choices." He elaborates that "the conditions to which the elements of this division (objects, mode of statement, concepts, thematic choices) are subjected we shall call the rules of formation. The rules of formation are conditions of existence (but also of coexistence, maintenance, modification, and disappearance) in a given discursive division" (38). To paraphrase, a discursive formation is a set of statements about a given object, concept, or theme (often defined only within or according to that discourse itself), which is understood according to a shared set of interpretative rules. To give an example, we might think of the discourse around psychological trauma. Presumably, people have been having terrible experiences and adapting poorly since the beginning of time, but in the nineteenth century there emerged a specific discourse that named such reactions as trauma and traced them to childhood and sexual dynamics. This discourse was enunciated by educated men who defined their new branch of knowledge as psychology and applied it mostly to women. In the 1970s, a different approach and language of trauma emerged, largely in the wake of the return of Vietnam War veterans to the United States. That generation saw a narrative model of trauma (treated by talking) progressively replaced by a neurological one (treated with medication or therapies designed to rewire the brain). The scope of the term PTSD (post-traumatic stress disorder) has, in the twenty-first century, expanded from the limited use by professionals to mainstream culture and particularly college campuses (the call for "trigger warnings" before any disturbing content on a syllabus). The word "trauma" carries through the three moments, but the three moments have little else in common; the word is not applied by the same authorities, to the same symptoms, or in the same terms.

It is beyond the scope of this book to attempt to explain how this change happened, but clearly such an explanation would require an analysis of how this limited discursive formation came into contact with other discursive formations. The shift in the 1970s is clearly related to the Vietnam War, the 1960s counterculture, and advances in neuroscience, and presumably the discourses around all three played a role in the re-shaping of the discourse around trauma. Similarly, the current dilution of trauma is clearly tied to the Internet and social media. Nor is influence unidirectional; the discourse of PTSD has changed how we wage and speak about war; the discourse about trigger warnings has changed the nature of academic discourse, etc. Discursive formations are not precisely delineated masses and they are never static; in fact, if we speak about any given "discourse" it is probably because it is in flux. The true sign of a stable discursive formation is that it seems natural and thus invisible, a given unity rather than a subjective connection of dots that could just as easily be connected in different configurations. When a discourse begins to move – when sentences that had once seemed limited to a certain interpretative regime, within a set circle of interpreters, become redistributed or re-signified – they inevitably call into question not just the immediate objects of those sentences but adjacent discourses and the social spaces of their enunciation. Thus, a study of a shifting discourse is hardly a dry exercise in semiotics but instead provides a key to broader social changes. Paradigm shifts begin with words.

The Archaeology of Knowledge represents Foucault's only strictly theoretical/methodological work, his attempt to distil a method from the work he had done with regard to specific discourses in his previous books (psychopathology, political economics, grammar). The result, as is to be expected from the project itself, is rather lifeless; Foucault is so concerned with stripping away any appeal to biographies or intentions that he gives the impression of a history that operates entirely without them. My book applies the methodology of an archaeology to mystic discourse in early modern Spain, but it also recognizes that archives (the discursive formations that compose them), institutions, and "spaces" are all constructs that *people* (for the most part intentionally) create, circulate, modify, and interpret. This book hopes to thread a line between the traditional biography-based study and the cold, dry approach of semiotics: privileging discourse as the "object" but only to better understand the lives and experiences of once-living people.

Even in a study focused on circular networks of discourse, one must inevitably mark off a narrative frame: choose an originary moment and identify a first shift away from that moment. As I argued with respect to the example of discourse about trauma, not every moment is equal, and the isolation of any given period as a privileged one for revealing discursive (and by extension social) change, requires a justification. Christian mysticism was hardly born in Spain in 1500.[9] Much of the vocabulary of mysticism has its origins in the writing of pseudo-Dionysius, whose

Mystical Theology and other works are largely considered the foundation of Christian mysticism. Dionysius's focus is on the unknowability and unrepresentability of God and is thus considered a *negative* or *apophatic* mysticism. "Dionysius" is a pseudonym; we know nothing about the author or his mystic experience, but the writing does not suggest a first-person or empirical experience of God. The approach is strictly philosophical-intellectual. It would not be until the high Middle Ages that Christian mystics shifted towards a *cataphatic* or *positive* theology: adding to the impossibility of knowing God through reason or language a possibility of *experiencing* God through love.[10] The period from 1200 to 1350 presents many interesting parallels with the period of study of this book, and indeed scholars refer to a "twelfth century Renaissance," which would place the flourishing of mysticism in the thirteenth century in an interesting and suggestive parallel with the sixteenth century: a moment just subsequent to the height of a period of intellectual and scientific innovation. The twelfth-century Renaissance often is marked as ending in 1215, with the Fourth Lateran Council's imposition of mandatory aural confession;[11] similarly, the Renaissance in Catholic Spain can be seen as giving way to the Baroque around the Council of Trent and the imposition of a regimen of "confessionalization." Further development of such connections is beyond the scope of this book, but it is essential to note the direct influence of the strengthening of the Roman Catholic Church and the creation/expansion of monastic orders on this earlier mystical moment. Almost all of the medieval mystic writers were associated with monastic orders: Hildegard of Bingen (Benedictine), Bernard Clairvaux (Cistercian), Francis of Assisi (Franciscan), Bonaventure (Franciscan), Meister Eckhart (Dominican), Hugh and Richard of St. Victor (Augustinians), Henry Suso (Dominican), et al. This coupling of institutional entrenchment and individual mystic practice is also fundamental in early modern Spain. The thirteenth century also saw the spread of mysticism from an individual and exceptional practice within cloistered walls to popular movements, most notably with the Beguines and Beghards in Northern Europe, and gave rise to institutions (medieval inquisitions) dedicated to policing the border between piety and heresy. This phenomenon too will be repeated in the period under study in this book.

Yet despite the importance of medieval mysticism and the existence of medieval inquisitions across continental Europe, the phenomenon largely stopped at the Pyrenees. The only Iberian Christian figure who might fall into the category of a medieval mystic was the Franciscan polymath Ramón Llull; like pseudo-Dionysius, his work centres on the (im)possibility of knowing and representing God and frequently recurs to a similar language of paradox and negativity. However, Llull's most important contributions were scientific and philosophical, rather than affective or devotional. "Despite the nondeductive character of his works, Lull's [*sic*] thought is deeply rational. Only seldom in his mystical writings does love eclipse the intellect or obscure its powers" (Hillgarth 610).[12] There was a medieval inquisition in Aragon, but it was largely inactive after the thirteenth century.[13] By and large, the military instability that characterized central Spain in the twelfth and thirteenth centuries impeded the establishment of contemplative monasteries; in Castilian universities, Thomism prevailed, and in general Castilian Catholicism during this period was practical and didactic rather than scholarly. The instability became even more pronounced during the second half of the fourteenth century, in Castile marked by civil war in which both sides appealed to a militant and often violently anti-Semitic Catholicism to motivate their supporters.

There was a rich mystical tradition in medieval Spain, but it was not a Christian one. Islamic mysticism, or Sufism, flourished in Muslim Spain during the twelfth and thirteenth centuries (the *reino de taifas*). Miguel Asín Palacios was the first to suggest a direct influence of Andalusi Sufí mysticism on San Juan de la Cruz and other Golden Age mystic poets, a theory that remains contested but is now accepted by numerous scholars.[14] While there are striking similarities between the works of Andalusian Sufi and Castilian Christian mystics, the difficulty in making the argument of direct influence lies in the gap of several hundred years between the two and the dearth of any material evidence of manuscripts or printed translations of Arabic poetry to Castilian (or of Castilian Christian mystics familiar with Arabic). Cynthia Robinson has offered the most compelling "solution" to this gap thus far, which finds continuity through a small and previously unstudied corpus of fourteenth-century Castilian manuscripts (most prominently, a *Vita Christi* by the Catalan Franciscan Francesc Eiximenis, written in Latin in 1400 and translated into Castilian around 1430), and which bears "many motifs or topoi common both to the Shādhilīs and well-known Andalusi mystics such as Ibn 'Arabi" and also to San Juan de la Cruz, to the point that, in Robinson's judgment, "it is almost impossible to avoid reaching conclusions concerning interaction" (114).[15] It is still, however "impossible … to argue that direct contact with Arabic texts 'influenced' Eiximenis" or that the seventeenth-century mystics were familiar with Eixemenis's work. Robinson concedes as much: "Rather, it is likely that many of the ideas that seem, to modern scholars to offer evidence of the 'Islamic influence' were exchanged and debated in an oral context that is, for the most part, lost to us, at least in its particulars" (113). If such transmission did take place, it would also seem to have been lost to its sixteenth-century recipients, who, if they inherited "motifs or topoi" common to Sufi mysticism, did not recognize them as such. Without then rejecting the possibility of such influence, we may still say that, overall, the legacy of medieval mysticism – autochthonous or imported – on Iberian Christians was minimal until roughly 1500 and thus that it is legitimate to begin our narrative at the turn of the sixteenth century, when a series of factors favoured a renewed focus on an interior life.

More or less at the turn of the sixteenth century, there emerged a variety of movements seeking to reform the Catholic Church by turning to a more personal, spiritualized experience of God. Eventually, some of these would be embraced, some classified as Catholic heterodoxies (Erasmism, *alumbradismo*, etc.), and some condemned entirely as heresy (Lutheranism, and later Calvinism). The process of parsing out these movements was a slow, tendentious, and often inconsistent one.[16] What is important is that the difficulty of distinguishing renewal, reform, and rupture created a crisis within the Catholic Church, one that led to the creation and imposition of new forms of observation and control of interior religious experience. There are important parallels with the changes introduced in the Church in the thirteenth century, also in part in response to new, private devotional practices: the sacramental requirement of confession and the constitution of inquisitions to investigate and prosecute heresy. Yet geopolitical, social, and technological changes in the Renaissance meant that the mechanisms for circulating, practicing, and controlling spirituality were quite different than two hundred years prior.

By far the greatest change, and it could be argued the root of all the ensuing changes, was the invention of the printing press. Medieval mystic treatises were limited first by their being written in Latin and second by the limited circulation possible in a manuscript culture. The possibilities of print, the rise in literacy among the laity, and the adoption of the vernacular for spiritual texts are all inseparable cultural phenomena that made the spiritual landscape of late fifteenth-century Spain very different from that of thirteenth-century France or Sweden, even when many of the doctrines themselves might be similar.[17] The ease of mass printing and increased use of the vernacular obviously increased the possible audience for spiritual works, but other social trends of the late fifteenth and early sixteenth centuries also facilitated a circulation of mystic writings far beyond what was possible in the medieval period. Cardinal Cisneros, archbishop of Toledo and the most important religious figure in Spain during the reign of Isabel and Fernando, spearheaded the printing of devotional materials in the vernacular as well as in Latin. Among the works published under his direction were several that promoted a more interiorized spirituality, and as well as volumes recounting the visions of late medieval women, mostly of a prophetic nature.[18] He also focused on education, and literacy rates rose dramatically in Spain (as in the rest of Europe). There has been debate over the exact level of literacy,[19] but it is undoubtable that rates rose dramatically between the late medieval and Renaissance periods. In Spain in particular there was, after the expulsion of 1492, a community of *conversos* who had the financial means and the education to read Scripture and devotional literature. It is difficult to measure exactly how the *converso*'s ancestry affected their approach to Christian doctrine, but Stefania Pastore, among others, has made the argument that a "converso sensibility" gave this group a fresh perspective on staid ideas, and it is undeniable that *conversos* were over-represented among the sixteenth-century Spanish mystics, both those who were ultimately celebrated by the Church (Teresa de Jesús, Juan de Ávila) and the early *alumbrados*, examined in chapter four. The *conversos* were almost all concentrated in urban centres, and the rapid urbanization of Spain and Spain's religious communities is another social factor that led to an increased spread of ideas that had once been associated with remote, ascetic communities. Because of Spain's role as the first European imperial power, urbanization occurred sooner, to a greater extent, and earlier than in other European nations. In 1502, Sevilla was named the only authorized port to and from the Indies and quickly drew a massive permanent and transient population, similar to what occurred in Madrid, after the court moved there in 1561. The "discovery" of the Americas led to an exodus of men, and the resulting imbalance led many women, unable to find husbands, either to enter convents or, since there remained a limited number of spaces in these and entrance in most still required a major economic investment, to become *beatas*: a status that encompassed a wide variety of extra-conventual religious professions and was a constant source of preoccupation to Church authorities. While some ecclesiastical authorities discouraged these tendencies, others celebrated the growth of spirituality among the laity, seeing it as a bulwark against the incursion of Protestant heresy, materialism, and corruption. All of these factors led to contexts in which ideas about spirituality spread quickly – in print or through other forms of transmission – and were adopted and adapted by diverse publics, religious and lay, male and female, educated and not. The effects of such transmission are the subject of this book.

As might be expected, the first movements towards an interior spirituality enter discourse in the form of theological treatises written by clerics. Chapter one considers a corpus of works of vernacular treatises of interior prayer. Melquíades Andrés Martín was fundamental in drawing scholarly attention to these mostly forgotten works and to the impact of the genre as a whole. However, his readings of individual works in the corpus tend to focus on their theology (heterodox or orthodox) or their formal classifications as belonging to one or another spiritual movement. While Andrés's scholarly contributions are undeniable, he was also an ordained priest, and his readings retain a defense of the *truth* of the methods espoused in one or another text, a question outside the scope of academic study.[20] There has been some study of certain texts of this corpus from a secular or agnostic perspective, but here the overwhelming focus has still been on classification, with the binary of "medieval" versus "modern" substituting for the heresy/orthodoxy lens. The debate becomes a question of whether these texts that emerged at the dawn of the "early modern period" are more "early" or more "modern": do they represent a residual strand of medieval culture against the dominant trend of secularizing Renaissance humanism, or instead reveal an emergent humanist sensibility? The question is usually answered by pointing to the origins of one or another idea within the work, and both arguments can be sustained: the most important works of interior prayer both draw from medieval knowledge, or even copy directly from medieval mystic texts, and add contemporary insights and styles.

My study of these works separates itself from the teleology of the modern by focusing instead on innovation: *new* and *modern* are not synonyms, and innovation can just as easily originate in the re-ordering and re-signification of old sources as the *ab nihilo* creation of new ideas or forms. This gradual revitalization of a genre is, I argue, what we see in this corpus of guides to interior spirituality. Many of the works in this corpus are adaptations, if not direct translations, of the 1441 *Imitatio Christi*, generally attributed to Thomas à Kempis, and the titles alone give a sense of a homogeneous and imitative genre. If the widespread popularity of the *Imitatio* and *Vita Christi* represent a new affective and individual spirituality in contrast to the early Thomist paradigms, there is within the corpus of Spanish *Imitatio* imitations further development of a truly *mystic* discourse. This chapter analyses how a relatively small and homogenous group of theologians, particularly Franciscans, moved beyond the *Imitatio* model and constructed a new discourse of interiority. The chapter examines this process in a close reading of two of its most canonical and influential texts, Francisco de Osuna's

Abecedarios and Bernardino de Laredo's *Subida del monte Sión*. Each one provides evidence of the elevation of language from a means to an end, and the degree to which words become not just a means for *representing* the divine but also signs with the power to reveal and create divine union. Whereas the *Vita* and *Imitatio* prioritized the imitation of God made flesh, these authors return to a God whose essence is language (God made Word). They do so not at the expense of the body but through a triangulation, in which the possibility of achieving divine union becomes a matter of the proper representation of divine union – God in Flesh – through words. The question of names, etymologies, descriptions, and structures becomes a matter of primary importance. The importance of words brings the contemplative treatises into the terrain of the poetic, while the importance of precision requires the assimilation of discourses of anatomy, empiric science, and etymology. These discourses, reassembled in new configurations and grafted onto the traditional structures of scholastic theology, become something new, what de Certeau calls "a body marked by transplanted concepts and metaphorized words, tattooed with implicit or explicit quotations" (119).

Throughout these works we find tension between the authors' roles as theologians and as spiritual directors: the former seeks to represent the mystery of union, the latter aims to de-mystify the steps towards union so they might be traversed by members of a spiritual community. The Franciscans wrote in the early days of print, before a formal bureaucracy of censorship had been instituted, and without seeming to comprehend the speed and distance that printed works would travel. In many ways, they retained the authorial expectations of the pre-print era. Although writing at the same time, Ignacio de Loyola's contemplative guide, the *Spiritual Exercises,* was directed towards a much wider public and, while sharing some of the linguistic strategies of the Franciscans, it represents already a shift in the trend towards systematization of contemplative practice and hence a dilution of the mystic elements, what de Certeau termed a shift from *lo místico* to *la mística*. This shift becomes even more stark when the *Exercises* are compared with a little-read spiritual diary that Loyola kept in the months prior to the founding of the Jesuit Order, in which he tested out the *Exercises* on himself and recorded the spiritual effects. The result was a hermetic, hybrid, mysterious private text whose formal difference from the *Exercises* provides insight into the role played by horizons of reception in the development of mystic language and formal innovation.

Chapter two turns to the genre of poetry, often considered the mystic genre *par excellence* and (at least until recent attention turned towards the spiritual autobiography) the only form of mystic expression studied specifically for its use of language. This book makes the argument that the distinction between mystic poetry and other forms of mystic expression is anachronistic because mystic language circulates in many genres and spaces in early modern Spain. Still, it is worth spending some time on the question of the relationship of mysticism and poetry: what we mean by "mystic poetry" to begin with and what the relationship is between mystic poetry and mystic language more broadly. I argue that the imposition of Inquisition censorship changed this relationship; whereas the pre-censorship contemplation manuals, although written in prose, are rich in ambiguous, figurative, poetic language, the censors demanded clarity, rejecting any experimentation in form or substance. However, Inquisition censorship was limited to print, and thus the valence of lyric poetry, long associated with orality and manuscript transmission, changed; what had seemed like a limitation in the early decades of print (limited circulation, formal elements that limited creative freedom) became an advantage. This chapter considers a wide variety of poems and poetic fragments, canonical and anonymous, integrating close reading of the poems themselves with a consideration of how the mystic poem becomes a discrete discursive landscape within/against other forms of writing. The chapter focuses on the paradigmatic mystic poet San Juan de la Cruz, but instead of exclusively reading his works as singular textual unities, I consider his "Cántico" and "Noche oscura" in a discursive landscape, co-existing (cross-pollinating) with his own prose commentaries and, with surprising frequency, appearing in the letters and spiritual autobiographies of female mystics across Spain. The different modes of transmission and contextualization reveal how gender, genre, and networks of circulation can make identical words have different effects.

One of the chief features of lyric poetry is the relative dissociation of the author's identity as biographical and juridical subject from the poetic voice. This is often exaggerated in mystic poetry because the mystic experience destabilizes identities and subjectivity. Yet authorities, secular and ecclesiastic, only act on individuals, not free-floating souls. Chapters three and four deal with how literary forms and social institutions emerged to discern, guide, and discipline the individual mystic. In the third chapter, I analyse the genre of the spiritual autobiography *por mandato*, the first-person accounts of spiritual graces that confessors required/requested of their mystic penitents. As Alison Weber and others have argued,[21] the order to write was not necessarily an antagonistic, censoring one; many confessors were open to legitimate mystic experience among even lay, female penitents, but in order to determine whether a particular confessant was on the right path and also whether individual visions were divine, demonic, or delusional, these visions had to be made legible. The criteria for discernment, as formulated in a burgeoning genre of discernment manuals,[22] depended on criteria internal and external to the visions, and thus the would-be mystics were asked to write not just the events of their interior life but also the relevant facts of their biography and daily activities. This need to integrate and represent a biographical and spiritual life results in the new genre of the spiritual autobiography, distinct from the ostensible model of Augustine's *Confessions*. I analyse the tensions manifest in this genre between a hierarchical system that demands clarity and accountability, and a literary form that offers an unprecedented space for expressive freedom, particularly for *female* self-expression. While Teresa de Ávila's *Libro de la vida* was the model for this genre, a closer look at her would-be imitators, particularly those who never achieved success as writers or spiritual authorities, gives an idea of the possibilities and limits afforded by the mystic lexicon for understanding and representing the self.

While it was the confessor's duty to monitor the spiritual activities of his flock, at times individuals disobeyed or ignored confessors' commands or the confessor himself was suspected of encouraging a false (either fraudulent or demonic) spirituality. Prior to the Council of Trent, spiritual heterodoxy had been an ecclesiastical matter, but the fear of interior spiritualities tied to Protestantism led to the Inquisition being tasked with policing would-be mystics. The fourth chapter looks at the discourse produced when it is the juridical, rather than the penitential, subject whose inner spiritual experiences must be diagnosed and disciplined. Historians have conducted important studies of the *alumbrados*,[23] in truth a heterogeneous group of practitioners of heterodox interior spirituality, and their archival legacy, but with almost no attention to their language, or the discursive conflict that arises in the record of Inquisition *procesos*. In my chapter four, I apply the tools of literary analysis to the diverse, polyphonic documents in a *proceso*. Unlike the confessor–confessant relationship, which develops over time and in which both participants usually draw on a shared discourse, the law requires a single and definitive judgment, and the juridical framework was ill-equipped to admit a language of metaphor and ambiguity. A close analysis of language shows the Inquisitional interrogations foundering on precisely the status of language: on the inability of the law to deal with poetic language and interpretation. Unlike most of the earlier Inquisition trials against Judaizers and *moriscos*, these cases go in circles and end either inconclusively or with relatively minor punishments, leading, I argue, to the weakening of the Inquisition as an institution.

This argument supposes a re-thinking of the traditional, Enlightenment narrative of the decline of the Inquisition and the retreat of religious experience from the domain of public justice.

Chapter five builds on a term coined by Álvaro Huerga in his monumental study of *alumbradismo*. He divides *alumbradismo* intro three categories: *alumbradismo radical*, *sensual*, and the third and chronologically latest, *alumbradismo teatral*. He uses the term rather vaguely and does not suggest any connection with actual theatrical practice at the time, but this seventeenth-century phenomenon does coincide, both geographically and temporally, with the high point of Baroque religious theatre, principally in *autos sacramentales* and *comedias de santos*. In this chapter, I consider the ways that playwrights staged the mystic encounter; given that much of the ambiguity of mystic discourse resides in the status of the vision-described-in-words, playwrights and directors, who were able to add actual visual elements, had to imagine a different distribution of the "real" and the perceptible. While the *autos sacramentales* frequently employed mystic poetry, the language was divorced from a subjective experience of union. In the *comedia*, on the other hand, which did emphasize human lives and religious experience, playwrights generally avoided the representation of interiorized spirituality, sticking closely to biblical narratives or approved hagiographies. Still, the canonization of several relatively contemporary, contemplative saints in the early seventeenth century meant playwrights would have to stage mystic contemplation. I focus on Lope de Vega's plays staging the lives of Saint Augustine and Santa Teresa, as well as Agustín Moreto's *Santa Rosa del Perú* and Tirso de Molina's *Santa Juana* trilogy to show how these playwrights, rather than use the interplay of word and image, light and sound, to further develop the possibilities of suggesting the mystic encounter, use these same elements to erase it. Even when Lope or Tirso incorporate mystic language into the scripts, they uses the scenic elements to erase the doubt, ambiguity, and subjectivity in the words. I also consider how these strategies might have been received among the audience, suggesting that perhaps, if this was a strategy to forestall any audience identification with the staged saints' direct communications with God, it may have backfired. The requirements of theatre and the conventions of staging required the actors and actresses to exaggerate with physical movement any experience of divine or demonic possession. This exaggerated physicality is what characterizes the *alumbrados teatrales*, extending even into the interior of their visionary life, with visions that move away from the intimacy of earlier examples and become spectacular. Rather than prevent audience identification with mystic saints by setting their lives in a world of spectacular exteriority, the plays may have given audience members a new model to imitate, both with their bodies and within the visionary plane. The substitution of the ineffable with the spectacular would signify the ultimate dissolution of mystic discourse as an experiment in language and thus the end of our study. The language of the ineffable and the experience of the divine would become two separate discourses, a discursive unity dissolved.

Yet in a book focused on circulation, it seems inappropriate to suggest such a linear trajectory. Instead, I end by circling around to the beginning, reconsidering the story we told in chapter one of the origins of a new mystic discursive formation. In my final chapter, I wish to suggest a second narrative, not to replace the first but to exist alongside it in a state of co-possibility. In addition to representing a break from the general chronological progression of the first five chapters, this chapter also marks a break from my own field of expertise. In chapter one, I identified the Franciscans as the key order in the composition of the first contemplative prayer manuals. I did not mention their role as the first order active in missionary efforts in the newly "discovered" Mexico. Chapter six suggests that these two phenomena might be related. De Certeau begins his theorization of a "new" language of mysticism by citing fifteenth-century humanist Lorenzo de Valla's call for "new words" to describe a "new reality" (qtd. in de Certeau 83). Lorenzo de Valla died in 1457, nearly half a century before the "discovery" of a much more radically "new" reality on the other side of the globe would make his words prophetic. The creation of an indigenous-language Christianity was a "new reality" that didn't just need "new words"; it required a new language. In the final chapter, I propose we invert the typical direction of transatlantic religious studies, which look at the influence of Christian ideas on indigenous communities, and consider the possibility that the encounter with Nahuatl, Nahuatl poetry, and indigenous Mexican religion caused the early Franciscans to re-think their own language and categories for spirituality. I examine competing translations of "el Coloquio de los doce" (the first "dialogue" between the first Franciscans missionaries and native Mexicans), early Nahuatl-Spanish dictionary entries on "soul" and "heart," and a never-published Nahuatl translation of the *Imitatio Cristi* to argue a possible connection with the linguistic destabilization that underlies the mystic movement in Spain.

Sadly, I have not benefitted from any moment of transcendent revelation in the course of research and writing, but in its own way, this study seeks to, as de Certeau says of mystic discourse, achieve a "communication between disparate sites (or 'experiences') … to overcome that diversity, to bind its elements together" in a narrative that, while it does not aspire to recreate a lost unity, at least "combines a number of acts and places into a unified textual sequence, that is, an order (chronological, cosmological, etc.) capable of interrelating and classifying these operations and their original sites" (119–20). Not a revelation, but a new way of seeing.

Chapter One

Prayer Manuals

In the introduction to his study *Poesía y mística,* Emilio Orozco Díaz writes that "instinctively and inevitably, the mystic's language diverges from common or natural language, the language of knowledge or of the theologian, and merges and identifies with that of the poet" (76).[1] This separation of mystics from theologians denies the possibility of a mystic theology. Yet the poetry of Santa Teresa, San Juan, and Fray Luis de León does not emerge *ab nihilo* from a world of rote catechisms and colloquial speech, but instead separates itself from a body of mystic discourse that had been flourishing in Spain since the turn of the sixteenth century. The "Cántico" and the other great mystic poems, all dating from the 1560s or later, would have been impossible had the authors not been steeped in the literature of contemplation, a prose genre that emerged in the age of religious reform. As Armando Pego Puigbó affirms, the "prayer manuals constitute the spinal column of Spanish spiritual literature of the sixteenth century. One cannot understand the development of mysticism in the second half [of the century] without the precedent of the discussions regarding prayer that these manuals made reference to and to which they decisively contributed" (201).

The roots of the shift towards an individualized, interiorized, affective relationship with Christ lie in the late medieval period and are widespread across Europe. Seminal in this movement were the *Vita Christi* – commentaries and collections of meditations on the life, and especially the death, of Christ, which aided their readers in an affective identification with Jesus. These texts, and the devotional communities dedicated to their reading and realization, did not reach Spain until the late fifteenth century. Indeed, as Cynthia Robinson writes, there is a "striking scarcity in Castile of devotional literature to which Christ's humanity and passion are central, literature that is by contrast plentiful in most European contexts ... Likewise, the importation of these texts was roundly rejected by Castilian Christians, old and new" (10). This changed under Cardinal Cisneros, chief primate of Spain under Queen Isabela and sponsor of a broad program of translation and publication of medieval devotional works: Saint Bonaventure's *Lignum vitae*, Ludolph of Saxony's *Vita Christi*, Thomas à Kempis's *Imitatio Christi*,[2] as well as hagiographies and the visionary accounts of Italian mystics Catherine of Siena and Angela of Foligno, who will be discussed in more depth in chapter three. Of all the devotional titles, the *Imitatio* had the greatest impact and influence; it was first translated into Spanish by 1488, with two editions in Castilian and in Catalan, and countless (what would now be considered) plagiarisms in the successive decades, the best known being Fray Luis de Granada's version published in 1536.[3] This shift was part of the "humus" (to use Andrés Martín's term) from which Catholic reform, the Protestant Reformation, *alumbradismo*, and "authorized" mysticism arose. In Spain, even when first Luther and then Erasmus's ideas had been condemned, the *Imitatio* remained a best-seller (its success largely due to its appropriation by Jesuits) and an orthodox example of Catholic piety.[4]

The *Imitatio* is not, by and large, a mystic treatise. Secondary scholarship may characterize it as "inward-looking" or "characterized by a profound interiority" (von Habsburg 23) but this must be qualified. The *Imitatio* emphasizes mental prayer and contemplation and critiques empty dependence on external symbols, but there is no suggestion that words or images are insufficient for representation of internal processes. Even book two, dedicated to "The Inner Life," understands "inner" in opposition to worldly or secular, rather than "occurring in an interior space." The reader is advised to meditate and to ignore worldly goods, but there is no suggestion that traditional prayer methods are insufficient for meditation. When, in book three, the author turns to "Inner comfort" and the interior conversation with Christ, the dialogue is represented as a clear exchange of humility and counsel, with the voice of Christ either taken directly from Scripture or offering simple lessons in the basic virtues of patience and humility: "Fear nothing, abhor and run from nothing, as much as from your own sins; they should displease you more than the loss of any possession you may have." (59; bk. 3 ch. 4); "My friend, I must be your supreme and final end if you wish to be truly blessed. If I am, your love will be purified and not be twisted back on yourself and on the things of this world, as it so often is." (66; bk. 3 ch. 9). Similarly, the disciple's side of the conversation is clear, consistent, and almost entirely lacking in figurative language. In keeping with the Platonic dialogic model, this is not meant to represent a conversation with any degree of realism, nor are the interlocutors mean to be psychologically verisimilar. Each speaker enunciates a moral or philosophical position, and while the speaker of inferior status (the student, the sinner) is given space to voice his doubts and objections, there is never any doubt that the master or superior moral voice will ultimately overcome them. The very clarity of the student's questions or objections makes them entirely unbelievable as authentic expressions of doubt or inner struggle. At the beginning of the journey, the disciple has not achieved the ideal spiritual or moral plane of the master, but he is always already an ideal: an ideal learner, an ideal Christian. Thus, despite the intimacy of the dialogic form and the call to "internal" consolation, the *Imitatio* remains principally a book of doctrine, with some mystical influence.[5]

Several Spanish authors writing in the pre-Trent period invert this tendency. These authors follow the doctrine of the *Imitatio* – rejection of worldly vanity and self-importance, cultivation of solitude and meditative prayer, emphasis on Christ's love and sacrifice – but the question of the space of inner prayer, as opposed to the fact of its existence, is expanded and becomes the focal point of the treatise. Instead of clearly instructing the reader on the proper subjects upon which to meditate, essentially filling the space of the imagination with images and words, these books reject the validity of images and words to convey the divine, and thus the focus shifts from the signified to the signifier.

The foregrounding of the signified occurs gradually within the genre. Two works published in 1500, Gómez García's *Carro de dos vidas* and the *Exercitatorio de la vida espiritual* by García de Cisneros, are generally recognized as the first Castilian works in the genre of interior prayer. Both works have a coherent structure throughout. The *Exercitatio* in particular reveals a scholastic enthusiasm for minute systematization: the three stages of mystic union (illuminative, purgative, unitive) are broken down into progressively smaller steps, each step accompanied by a program of meditations. The *Carro* is more abstract but also more laden with extended quotes of scriptural and patristic authorities. In both works, the authorial tone is consistent and authoritative, although there are moments where the reader has a sense of an author pushing to make words do new things.[6] In the two texts to which I dedicate the majority of this chapter, Francisco de Osuna's *Abecedarios espirituales* and Bernardino de Laredo's *Subida al Monte Sión*, these moments multiply and overtake the systems and hierarchies that still by and large prevail in Gómez García and García Cisneros. In the *Abecedarios* and the *Subida*, the mystic struggle with language becomes, or at least threatens to become, the essence of the text's mysticism, rather than a difficulty to be overcome in the presentation of doctrine or method. Through an examination of these two influential guides to mental prayer from pre-Trent Spain, I show how the goals of structure and rupture coexist in their texts, how a struggle for "new words" for interior processes organizes (and disorganizes) the goal of communicating theology or spiritual practice.[7] I then turn to two works by Ignacio de Loyola, the *Spiritual Exercises* and the never-published *Diario*, to see how the mystic and the pedagogic split apart in the post-Trent era.[8]

Francisco de Osuna and the Mystic Alphabets

The prominence of language is foregrounded in the very title of the most important mystic works of the pre-Trent period: Francisco de Osuna's *Abecedarios*. The *Abecedarios* have only a loose alphabetical structure; most, but not all, of the *Tratados* in the six *Abecedarios* are glosses on a series of distiches in alphabetical order, but only within the fourth *Abecedario* do we find an *abecedario strictu sensu*, with a list of attributes of divine love beginning with each letter of the alphabet. For reasons that are still not entirely clear, the *Abecedarios* were published out of order: the third in 1527, followed by the first in 1528, then the second and fourth in 1530, and the last two posthumously (with possible contributions from other authors).[9] However, Osuna explains in the prologue to the *First Alphabet* that the original project was a series of alphabetic distiches, with the glosses and commentaries added later. Ironically, then, a work that (as we will see) urges readers to see beyond the *letra* to the *sentido interior*, began with *letras exteriores*. In any case, what is clear is the fundamentally linguistic nature of Osuna's mysticism. Even as he writes in a "lengua vulgar," Osuna takes pains to argue for the non-arbitrary, meaningful nature of letters and words. As he explains, "Cosa es manifiesta que los nombres han de ser tales que convengan a las cosas que se imponen, según lo usan los sabios, cuyas ciencias están en gran parte sabidas, entendidos los términos y vocablos de ellas, lo cual es porque importan mucho de las mismas ciencias y declaran muchas propriedades de ellas" (*Tercer Abecedario* VI.1.199–200) ("As is customary among wise men, names clearly must suit what they describe, for if we understand the terms and vocabulary, much of the learning will already be apparent. Because terms evoke a great deal of the information itself and explain many qualities, it is appropriate for those wishing to be instructed in a discipline or science to insist on effective language, for understanding the thrust of language and why a term is used for a thing being discussed is an auspicious start to learning" [160]).[10] However, Osuna's operation is the reverse of those who study "ciencias" by analysing the "términos y vocablos de ellas." Osuna is *constructing* a science via a circular procedure: he gives it a "término y vocablo" (*recogimiento*), and he finds within Scripture resonances of the term, employed in diverse contexts, which he then reads as biblical evidence of the practice. He is at pains to prove that he is not inventing anything new but merely uncovering a latent meaning under the surface of the words and stories of the Bible, awaiting allegorical exegesis. Rather than justifying allegorical reading through evidence in the text, Osuna converts allegorical exegesis into a sacred, mystical practice in itself, since the word *mística* is connected to *misterio*, "que quiere decir escondida." But whereas medieval mystics focused principally on the hidden meanings of words,[11] Osuna connects the intellectual practice of allegory to the *human* interior: "quiere decir escondida, porque en el secreto escondimiento del corazón la enseña el buen maestro Jesús" (VI.2.198) ("Some call it mystical theology, which means hidden, because the good teacher Jesus imparts it in the secret hiding place of the heart" [160]). With this phrase, Osuna signals the difference between medieval, philosophical-intellectual mysticism (à la Dionisio) and the modern contemplative mystic *practice*, experienced in the body.[12]

Osuna's justification of the importance of names is not only based on their qualities ("propriedades"). Quantity matters too. "Hay algunas cosas de tanta excelencia y de tan notables propriedades, que aun muchos vocablos no bastan para las declarar, como vemos en los grandes señores, que, cuantos mas ditados tienen, mas vocablos añaden y títulos y armas, para que sean sus señorías traídas a noticia de todos" (VI.1.199) ("Some things have such excellent, notable qualities that even a multitude of terms is insufficient to describe them. This is evident among eminent lords who, the more they rise in rank, the greater number of words, titles and coats of arms they add to bring their dominance to everyone's attention" [160]). Thus to show the value of la *teología mística*, Osuna is at pains to accumulate synonyms: "Llámase tambien esta manera de oración sabiduría"; "llámase también esta manera de orar arte de amor"; "llámase también de unión"; "Llamase también este ejercicio profundidad" (VI.2.202–3). ("This kind of prayer is also called wisdom"; "this kind of prayer is also called the art of love"; "It is also called union"; "This exercise is known as profundity" [163–5]). Chapters two and three consist of pages upon pages of synonyms or alternate names. Even when Osuna interjects "¿Para qué diré más?" (VI.3)[13] ("Why say more?"), he continues to offer more, including: escondimiento, abstinencia (del pensamiento), allegamiento, encendimiento, recibimiento, consentimiento, redaño y grosura, atraimiento, prohijamiento, advenimiento, alteza, amistad, abrazamiento, ascensión, cautividad, and cielo tercero (VI.3.203–6) ("concealment, abstinence [from thought], drawing near, enkindling, a welcome, consent, the marrow and fat, attraction, adoption, arrival, height, friendship, opening of the devout heart, spiritual ascension, captivity, and the third heaven" [165–7]). The rhythm of his prose accelerates as the synonyms accumulate; for the early terms, he provides a careful exegetical explanation, while at the end he merely offers a list of metonymic associations:

> es un silencio que en el cielo de nuestra ánima se hace, aunque breve y no tan durable como el justo desea; es un servicio que a solo Dios hacemos, adorando su sola Majestad; es silla que le tenemos aparejada para que se detenga en nuestra casa interior; es tienda de campo para andar por el desierto; es torre fortísima de nuestro amparo, desde do hemos de atalayar las cosas celestiales, y vaso de oro para guardar el maná en el área de nuestro pecho; es valle en que abunda el trigo que tiene grosura y redaño, y es victoria que vence el mundo menor, sujetándolo enteramente a Dios; es viña que hemos de guardar con vigilancia y sombra del que deseamos, do gustamos de su fruto; es unción enseñadora del Espíritu Santo, y huerto por todas partes cerrado, del cual damos la llave a sólo Dios, que entre cuando quisiere. (VI.3.206)

> It is … the silence, albeit brief and not as lasting as the just may wish, that reigns within the heaven of the soul. It is a service we render for Him so He will visit our interior house; a field tent for travelling through the desert; a sturdy, protective tower where we survey heavenly things; a vessel of gold to hold manna in the ark of our breasts. It is a valley abundant in wheat, which has fat and marrow; and it is the victor that conquers the lesser world, subjecting it entirely to God; the vineyard we ought guard with vigilance and where in the shade of the One we love we taste His fruits; and it is the anointing doctrine of the Holy Spirit and a garden enclosed on all sides, the key to which we give to God alone so He may enter as He pleases. (168)

This methodical exegesis further evolves into poetry, echoing the overflow of meaning and the bounds of logic that, as Osuna has just explained, separates mystic theology from scholastic (or speculative) theology. Indeed, he has just explained the difference between the two methods by analogy with a container of a liquid which, when heated, "se calienta en el vaso do está; empero, cuando hierve y bulle, parece en alguna manera no caber en sí, mas exceder a sí mismo el licor, que antes estaba seguro y ser llevado sobre sí por la virtud del calor" (VI.2.201–2) ("begins to bubble and boil, it seems as if it cannot be held in the container but by virtue of the heat surely will spill over itself and be carried beyond itself" [163]). Scholastic or speculative theology is akin to the vessel that "contiene en sí misma dentro en sí," whereas "cuando concibe el espíritu del amor en fervor del corazón, en alguna manera sale de sí misma saltando de sí o volando sobre sí" (VI.2.202) ("is self-contained, but when the spirit of love is conceived in the fervor of the heart, in some way the soul goes jumping outside of itself or flying above itself" [163]). The prose in the following pages begins with a controlled explanation and grows, "herviendo y bulliendo," with a seemingly uncontrolled overflow of synonyms that is checked not with a conclusion but with the sudden "¿Para qué diré más?" This movement echoes the transition from speculative to mystic theology itself.

After offering his litany of synonyms and metonyms, Osuna concludes that the best term for his mystic practice is *recogimiento* (recollection), and the text moves from the proposal of different words to a justification of the single chosen word, drawing out the various senses of "recoger" and applying them to the practice of mystic union. "Se llama recogimiento ... porque recoge los hombres que lo usan haciéndolos de un corazón y amor"; "recoge el mismo hombre a sí mismo, hablando de lo exterior"; "este ejercicio recoge la sensualidad"; "lo cuarto que recoge este ejercicio es convidar al mismo que lo tiene a que se aparte a lugares secretos"; "hace que se recojan los sentidos" etc. etc. (VI.4.208–9) ("This devotion is called recollection because it gathers together those who practice it and ... makes them of one heart and love"; "it gathers together the exterior person within himself"; "this devotion recollects sensuality"; "the fourth way this exercise recollects us is by inviting the one who enjoys it to go off to secret places"; "it calms [*recoge*] the senses" etc. [169–71]). More than a rigorous justification of the importance of *recogimiento* in Christian life, and certainly more than a practical manual for the contemplative, Osuna's theology is poetic: he gathers (*recoge*) interiorities. He takes the "surface" or exterior of the Bible and uncovers (creates) depths, interiorities, and mysteries. The result is essentially a prose poem, a lexical archipelago of words associated with depth:

> Llámase también este ejercicio profundidad, la cual contiene oscuridad y hondura; porque este ejercicio se funda en la hondura y profundo corazón del hombre, el cual debe estar oscuro; esto es, privado de humano conocimiento, para que de esta manera estando [en] tinieblas, sobre él venga el espíritu de Dios sobre las aguas de sus deseos a decir que se haga luz divina." (VI.2.203)

> This exercise is known as profundity with respect to the depth and darkness of the devotion, for it originates in the depths of man's heart, which are dark because human understanding has been deprived of light. Seeing the heart plunged into shadows, the spirit of God comes over the heart on the waters of desire to proclaim his divine light. (165)

This revelation (creation) and mapping of interior spaces is particularly notable in his allegorical reading of the Old Testament. Here Osuna applies a standard scholastic practice – finding point-by-point allegorical correspondence between the Law of Moses and the Law of Christ, but the meanings he finds latent in the Old Testament are distinct from the ones drawn out by scholastics.[14] Where the medieval scholars drew out the promise of a future redemption, Church, and Last Judgment – an epic narrative of cosmic events – Osuna reads each of his selected passages as a narrative of interiority, of the invisible events that occur within the human mind and soul. For example, he reads the Old Testament story of the dispersal of the sons of Joshua as an allegory of the danger of distracted thoughts. He cites the prophecy in Isaiah 11:12–13 that "God will signal the nations and gather together the exiles of Israel, and from the four corners of the earth he will bring together [*recogerá*] the scattered ones of Judea" (I.3.101), but instead of the promise of a Christian kingdom to come, he reads the chapter as an allegory of the importance of inward prayer. In this interpretation, the exiles of Israel are "las vagabundos pensamientos del que quiere aparejar su corazón al Señor" (I.3.102) and his "señal" is the faith, by which he alerts "las interiores naciones e inclinaciones nuestras" (I.3.101–2) ("the errant thoughts of the one who wishes to prepare his heart for the Lord"; "the interior nations and our affections" [55]). Instead of reading outwards – from the past to the future, from the history of one man to the history of all men – he allegorizes inwards, from the "mundo mayor" to the "mundo menor, que es el hombre" (I.3.102) and, even further, from a man's outer self to his interior.

In Osuna, almost any biblical text can be taken out of its narrative context and converted into an allegory of the "mundo menor." Ezekiel 1:15, "There appeared over the world by the animals a wheel with four faces," becomes another warning about the distractions of the human heart, since "Rueda se llama el corazón por el poco sosiego que tiene volviéndose y estando casi siempre en continua mutabilidad" (I.3.103) ("the heart is this wheel, restlessly revolving round and round, almost always changing" [56]).[15] Osuna returns again and again to the Old Testament stories with even the slightest mention of interior spaces, especially the temple of Solomon (with its "patio interior") and, from the

Song of Songs, the "bodega secreta del vino cálido del amor divinal" (*Cuarto abecedario* 242) ("secret cellar of wine warm with divine love").[16] Some of these interiorized readings (and there are many more[17]) are not original to Osuna (he draws particularly on Richard of St. Victor[18]), but the singular focus with which he interiorizes the Old Testament is unique. He is not occasionally citing biblical passages to illustrate a larger point; the interiorization of the Bible *is* the point. "Poco sabrosa es la lección de la letra exterior si no tomare del corazón la glosa y el sentido interior" (*Tercer abecedario* V.3.187) ("the mere reading of the letter will be tasteless and of little benefit if we do not take to heart the commentary on the exterior letter and its interior meaning" [147]); "el acto interior es raíz de todo el merecimiento principal" (*Cuarto abecedario* 341) ("the interior act is the root of all principal merit").

He makes this explicit in the prologue to the *Cuarto Abecedario* in an extended allegorical reading of Deuteronomy 22:6: "If a bird's nest chance to be before thee in the way in any tree, or on the ground, whether they be young ones, or eggs, and the dam sitting upon the young, or upon the eggs, thou shalt not take the dam with the young." Osuna explains that "La madre que hallarás en el nido, que es el libro presente, es la letra de la Sagrada Escritura; los pollos de ella son los diversos sentidos y declaraciones espirituales de que me entiendo servir dejando la madre en paz" (229–30) ("The mother you find in the nest, which is this book before you, is the letter of the Holy Scripture; her chicks are the diverse meanings and spiritual statements of which I intend to make use, leaving the mother in peace"). The "verdaderos israelitas" ("true Israelites") he goes on to say, are those who "están *dentro* de la letra de la Escritura" ("are *within* the letter of Scripture") (emphasis mine), and his job will be to draw out these "pollos" ("chicks") from the "huevo cerrado" ("sealed egg") of the Testament, not just by drawing out an interior meaning, as all exegetes do, but by showing that the entire meaning *is* interiority. He looks at chickens and finds eggs.

Osuna frequently uses terms or concepts inherited from medieval theologians, whose language for interiority drew on a fairly set lexicon inherited from Saint Augustine (himself Christianizing the ideas of Plato) to describe interior states.[19] The soul had three "potencias": memory, will, and intellect. The passions (what we would today call emotions), and sense operations were also identified, classified, and explained in medieval scientific terms.[20] Osuna, as we saw in the passage above relating the four winds to the four passions, draws on this system, but since he defines mystic theology in opposition to scholastic theology, he is also at pains to create a new and distinct language of interiority. The paradox here, as with all mysticism, is the need to systematize that which transcends any rational system, to name that which transcends language. This is the paradox of a "ciencia mística": a science based in something that is beyond human reason, knowledge, and language. As Osuna frames it early in the *Cuarto abecedario*, "nos es necesario tener en nosotros muy ordenada la ley del amor y los grados de él, no sacaremos poco aviso si miramos en el presente capítulo la orden que tuvo Dios en amar; ca, si la imitamos, podremos decir: Metióme el Rey en la bodega del vino y ordenó en mí la caridad. Entremos, pues, con mucho tiento a la bodega secreta del vino cálido del amor divinal, para nos ordenar y regir por él" (242) ("it is necessary for us to keep the law of love and its stages very well-ordered within ourselves, we would be well-advised to examine in this present chapter the order of God's love; for, if we imitate it, we will be able to say: The Lord placed me in his wine cellar and ordered charity in me. Let us then enter, with much caution, into the secret cellar of wine warm with divine love, so that we may be ordered and ruled by it"). The contradiction is patent: how can a graded, orderly system be born of a secret, drunken love?[21]

The question is ultimately unanswerable; the attempt to answer it produces the mystic treatise, with its alternations between science and poetry. For example, in a section of the *Cuarto Abecedario* dedicated to understanding whether God's "ley de amor" is equal for all, Osuna writes that such an "inner love" is infinite, but to explain how this infinite love can be contained in a single person, "cosa finita y poca" ("a small and finite thing"), he proposes an example from geometry:

> Si hubiese una circunferencia de compás que hiciese un cerco infinito en grandeza, mayor que el cerco del cielo, y en medio dieses un punto, claro está que podrías traer infinitas líneas de la circunferencia al punto, pequeñito; y podrás barruntar la proporción de la ley de amor que el Señor tuvo ab aeterno con cada uno de los escogidos; y el que profundamente imaginare esto con atención, verá venir sobre sí la mar del amor divinal y será opreso y derribado con su gloria. (243)

> If a compass could draw a circumference that was infinite in size, greater than the enclosure of the heavens, and you put a dot in the centre, clearly you could draw an infinite number of lines from the circumference to that tiny point; and you can begin to grasp the proportion of the Law of Love that God has had, *ab aeterno*, with each of his chosen people; and he who thinks deeply on this, paying close attention, will see the sea of divine love come upon him and will be oppressed and toppled by His glory.

Unlike the scholastic metaphor, which brings the unknown into focus by proposing a comparison to the known world, here the metaphor depends on mathematical impossibilities and resides at the limits of the imagination. Furthermore, the end result of the mathematical example is not to produce rational comprehension but to "derribar" and "oprimir" the reader's rational capacities with an excess of affect. As a scientific metaphor, then, the "ejemplo" is a failure, but as a *mystic* metaphor, one that exemplifies the very impossibility inherent to mystic representation, this failure is a success.

While here Osuna makes a comparison between interior and exterior worlds, in many instances he intertwines the two in single description, describing interior experience with the language of natural processes, particularly those associated with vessels (filling, emptying) and heat (burning, melting). A section of "Ley de amor" explains why the Holy Spirit is referred to as the sun in the Gospels, registering seven effects produced by both: *secar, derretir, reglar, alumbrar*, etc. (*Cuarto abecedario* 501) ("to dry, to melt, to regulate, to illuminate"). While the point-by-point identification of allegorical correspondences is a typical scholastic form of argumentation, we can already see in the nature of the comparison – between the sun's effects on the natural world and the Holy Spirit's effect on the soul of the individual – a shift towards interiority. Similarly, a list of "vessel"-related metaphors and allegories for the heart draw from diverse books of the Bible and natural images, but each unite at the description of an interior space:

> es lámpara de la virgen prudente, que es tu ánima, en que cuando saliere a recibir a su esposo, ha de llevar olio de misericordia y lumbre de fe; … y es consistorio divino donde Él trata sus secretos; y es el forcaz donde el ángel del gran consejo desciende a refrigerar los que dentro en Él andan; y es cámara pequeña del verdadero Heliseo; y es vaso de oro lleno del maná de la gracia celestial, puesto en el arca de tu pecho; es incensario con que se perfuma Dios; pesebre angosto donde nasce el niño Jesús; cama florida suya; huerto del rey Asuero, donde por su mano injiere diversas virtudes; es arco de la amistad de Dios, puesto en las nubes de las lágrimas para que se acuerde cómo nos ama; ciudad pequeña de Dios que es alegrada con el ímpetu de gracia; libro de la vida por do has de ser juzgado; santo sepulcro del cuerpo de Cristo; altar donde sacrificamos a Dios nuestros deseos; paraíso donde Dios y sus amigos se comunican y deleitan; brasero de oro del templo de Dios. (366)[22]

> it [the heart] is a lamp to the prudent virgin of your soul that when she goes out to greet her husband she may carry the oil of mercy and light

> of faith ... The heart is God's tribunal where he conducts his secrets, the furnace where the angel of great counsel descends to refresh the ones who go about in him; it is the intimate chamber of the true Eliseus, a gold vessel placed in the ark of your breast, overflowing with the manna of heavenly grace, the incensory with which God perfumes himself, the narrow manger where the child Jesus is born, his flowery bed, the garden of King Assuerus where he plants by hand a variety of virtues. And the heart is the rainbow of friendship with God set in a cloud of tears to remind us how much he loves us; it is a small city of God gladdened by the influx of grace; the book of life where you are to be judged; the holy tomb for Christ's body; the altar on which we sacrifice our desires to God; the paradise where God and his friends commune and take pleasure; the golden brazier of God's temple. (135)

With each example, the historical and apocalyptic books of the Bible, and finally the Bible ("libro de la vida") itself, are repurposed, made intimate and interior.

Osuna often creates the interior space by rearranging and repurposing the exterior human body. Osuna is, among the Spanish mystics, unusually open to the literal participation of the body in the mystic experience, and this non-dualist attitude leads him to embrace the use of corporeal language in his metaphorical description of spiritual experience.[23] Early in the *Tercer Abecedario,* he cites San Bernardo in identifying four ways to love: "amar la carne carnalmente y el espíritu carnalmente, la carne espiritualmente y el espíritu espiritualmente" (*Prólogo* 91) ("to love the flesh carnally, the spirit carnally, the flesh spiritually, and the spirit spiritually" [43]), and he clarifies that while there is a hierarchy within these four steps, it is appropriate for man to seek to ascend to pure spiritual love via the flesh. "Debemos, empero, parar mientes que el amor que dice carnal no es malo, ni se toma en el mal sentido que comúnmente lo solemos entender, porque en estas cuatro maneras de amar no ha hecho sino distinguir entre mas y mas acendrado amor" (92) ("We should consider carefully, however, that so-called carnal love is not bad and should not be understood in the bad sense that commonly prevails, for the four ways of loving are only distinctions among increasingly pure forms of love that reveal how we are to love Christ Our Lord more purely" [43]). In the "Ley de amor," there is a rather spectacular praise poem in which Osuna declares the love of each part of the body for God, not just the heart or eyes but "muslos," "pechos," "dedos," and "narices" ("thighs," "breasts," "fingers," and "nostrils") and even proclaims that "ámante mis miembros secretos cuando por ti se apartan de todo deleite carnal" (433) ("my secret members love you even when for you they have turned away from any carnal pleasure"). Just as the body has a role in spiritual love, bodily language can be used to write of spiritual love. To understand the spirit, one must ascend via the body.[24]

Almost all mystic writers employ the concepts of an "ojo interior" or "oído interior," a corporeal counterpart to the doctrine of "spiritual senses" that had been used since Origen of Alexandria to describe divine union.[25] Osuna takes the by-then commonplace phrase and shakes it up, adding details, mixing metaphors. "Cerrando los sentidos corporales y exteriores ... abriésemos los interiores del ánima" (*Tercer Abecedario* III.1.141) ("by closing the corporeal and exterior senses, let us open the soul's interior ones" [97]),[26] he exhorts, but then he continues, comparing human understanding of divine matters to the owl and bat in the face of the sun, "al cual no pueden conocer ni mirar siquiera sus rayos, por la improporción y poca lumbre que tienen, siendo sus ojos muy oscuros, menester es que como aquellas aves de poca vista nos escondamos" (III.1.141) ("which [they] cannot know or even look at the rays of the sun because the capacity of their small eyes to receive light is disproportionate to the sun's brightness. So, too is our capacity to look upon God's splendor limited, and so too we must hide ourselves like those birds" [97]). These dimly seeing eyes are interposed between the "sentidos corporales" (bodily senses) and the "ojos interiores del ánima" in a somewhat unclear position: it would seem that the essential function of the comparison, more important than the exact identification of correspondences, is to repeat the *hidden* ("nos escondamos") and dark ("ojos muy escuros") nature of mystic experience and mystic theology, in contrast with the clarity of scholasticism and most medieval theology.

The above-cited passage concludes by promising that in the world beyond we will be able to see God's face "sin pestanear" (III.1.141) ("without blinking") and thus implicitly seeing with eyes. In the *Cuarto abecedario,* however, Osuna explains:

> has de saber que el ánima no se servirá de los ojos corporales para ver la Divinidad; porque como entonces estará suelta y libre en sus operaciones, aunque podrá ver por las uñas y por todo el cuerpo, que será más claro que un cristal, no verá por él como ahora que está atada a órganos determinados; sino ella, por sí, será toda ojos de sí misma, como el sol, que él es ojos de sí mismo. De manera que el ánima verá por todas partes, tan enteramente por la espalda como por la cara. (380)

> You must know that the soul will not make use of the eyes of the body to see the Divinity; since at that time it will be free and untethered in its

> operations, although it will be able to see through your nails and through your whole body, which will be clearer than glass, it will not then see as it does now, through designated organs, but instead the soul, on its own, will be all its own eyes, like the sun, which is also all its own eyes. In this way, the soul will see through all your body parts, as fully through the back as the face.

Lest spiritual eyes seem too comprehensible, Osuna forces his reader to contemplate the relation between body and sight, soul and body. More than the ultimate image evoked, the comparison demonstrates the struggle to describe perception without a body. He proposes that it is "suelta y libre" from the body, yet he immediately re-assigns it fingernails, a back, "todo el cuerpo" (and in other passages he speaks of the soul's hair [*Cuarto Abecedario* 394] and the heart's arms and wings [*Tercer Abecedario* III.2.144]). In the fragment cited, it is ultimately the use of the reflexive pronoun that can best convey the otherness of the divine sensory experience: "ojos de sí misma." This play with pronouns and prepositions is frequent in mystic writing. Unlike the metaphorical comparison to a comprehensible noun, which must immediately be rejected or modified to emphasize that in fact the mystical experience is like nothing else, the pronoun and preposition are more abstract and can more easily evoke difference that is not tied to something known. The reflexive pronoun in particular can create *interior* division between the self and the self at the same time that its latent sense of circularity parallels the exegete's (and Osuna's in particular) reading of all levels of the cosmos as part of the constant "synergy"[27] between interior and exterior spirituality.

In her chapter on the *ánima* in Osuna, Laura Calvert notes that the term seems to fluctuate in its connotations and valences across and even within the *Tratados*, particularly in its relation to other interior faculties and functions. She is largely interested in reconciling these differences and identifying their sources, but I prefer to read what seems like inconsistency as a push against any settled, pre-existing linguistic or conceptual form. To express the transcendence of divine union, Osuna must imagine a new geometry that acknowledges known models for the relations of insides to outsides only to disrupt them.[28] Not even a paradox, such as the phrase "fuera de sí," can be allowed to settle into cliché. Is it correct to say that during divine ecstasy we are "fuera de sí"? What exactly is "outside" of what in this construction? Osuna writes:

> No hay necesidad que digamos estar los espíritus humanos fuera de sí cuando por divino don se apartan de los sentidos lodosos, porque San

> Pablo, en su arrebatamiento, dice que del todo ignora si estaba en el cuerpo o fuera de él; pero preguntas que dónde están. Están en lo que está de dentro de él, ca profundo es el corazón del hombre y no escudriñable; y también que el hombre es tan secreto a sí mismo, que sólo él conozca lo que tiene dentro. Así que no son sacados, sino traídos los espíritus en aquel cenáculo interior; y también que allí se juntan con el amado por castísimo abrazamiento, más secreta y seguramente cerradas de fuera las puertas de los sentidos. [*Cuarto abecedario* 460]

> It is unnecessary to say that the human spirits are *fuera de sí* [literally outside themselves, figuratively transported, in rapture] when by divine grace they move away from the dirty, earthly senses, since Saint Paul, in his rapture, says that he was entirely unaware if he was in his body or outside it. But they, you may ask, where are they? They are within what is within him, because the heart of man is deep and inscrutable, and man is such a secret to himself that only He knows what he holds inside. And so his spirits are not taken out, but rather drawn in to that inner conclave; and is there too that they join with the Beloved in the most chaste of embraces, but with the doors of the senses secret and securely closed from without.

This is a science that can only be described in poetry, through proposing new configurations of nouns and verbs ("no sacados, sino traídos"), or of literal and figurative language. Typical theological treatises feature a "yo" instructing a "tú" on the subject of "Dios" through reason and appeal to the senses, yet the mystic experience blurs and denies these frontiers. The heart is knowable and not knowable, the spirit is drawn out ("arrebatado") and brought in, the Beloved is within, the self is without. This love that Osuna defines in opposition to "amor intelectual" requires "una participación de naturales inclinaciones y sentimientos, aplicando a sí mismo las fuerzas del corazón" (290) ("the participation of natural tendencies and feelings, applying the heart's forces to itself"). How can "love," and particularly a love that is defined in opposition to reason, "apply" something, much less apply it to another abstract interior entity – "las fuerzas del corazón"? Love and the soul have a new configuration later in the work, when he proposes that "el amor sea medianero y solicitador entre el ánima y Dios, cuando ella quiere vacar a él sólo y gozar de él secretamente, sin que otro alguno entienda en ello, sino el solo amor entrañal y la bienquerencia del corazón" (430) ("love be the intermediary and petitioner between the soul and God, when she [the soul] wishes to devote herself entirely to Him alone and take pleasure in Him in secret, without anyone else but the innermost love and the heart's good will becoming involved").

Love, the soul, the heart, and "otro alguno" (most likely referring to the rational, conscious faculties) are all part of a single self, and at the same time separate entities capable of action, or at least capable of assuming verbs.

In other sections, Osuna relies particularly on reflexive verbs and indirect objects to reorient the relationships between God, the soul, the internal faculties, etc. (For example, the virtues "cuasi hacen dar de sí al corazón, que es como guante, porque untado con buenos aceites y calzándoselo da de si" [394] ["almost make the heart, which is like a glove, stretch (but literally, "give of itself"), because, greased with good oils and placing it on, it stretches (gives of itself)"]; "No te maravilles porque he dicho que, cuando te humillas, se te humilla Dios; porque tal se dará Dios a ti cual tú te dieras a Él, y con la medida que lo midieres te medirá, estimarte ha en lo que lo estimares y hará de ti la cuenta que hicieres de Él" [484] ["Do not wonder that I have said that when you humble yourself, God humbles himself to you; because God will give Himself to you as you give yourself to Him, and with the measure that you measure Him, He will measure you, He will esteem you insofar as you esteem Him, and He will render the account of you that you render of Him"].) In the tension identified by de Certeau between *lo místico* and *la mística* – between a transgressive description and a normative system – Osuna almost always remains in the terrain of the former. The *Abecedarios* are structured (somewhat) systematically, but the system is alphabetic-mnemonic, with no relationship to a systematic practice of mystical union. In individual passages, Osuna may offer practical advice conducive to contemplation, but whenever he seems to offer a clear or static definition of the interior space itself where this union is to occur, he negates or complicates some aspect of this apparent clarity. In general, his focus, befitting the alphabetic structure, is linguistic: the *Abecedarios* are best described as a constant metonymic siege on the ineffable, an attempt via metaphor, paradox, citation, etc. to describe the mystic experience. The system that is proposed, insofar as there is one, is poetic, rather than theological. For instance, we can look at the passage, mentioned previously, in which Osuna cites seven similarities between the effects of the sun and the effects of the Holy Spirit. Each parallel is drawn out with a multiplication of correspondences that occur only in the realm of language. For example:

> El sexto efecto del sol es alumbrar, lo cual hace en el ánima el Espíritu Santo mediante el don del entendimiento, del cual se puede decir El sol que alumbra, por todas las cosas mira, esto es, hace que todas las veamos ... Este sol resplandece en los escudos dorados, que son los sabios

entendimientos, y los montes son las dignidades de la Iglesia. (*Cuarto abecedario* 502)

> The sixth effect of the soul is to illuminate, which the Holy Spirit achieves in the soul by means of the grace of understanding, from which we can say that the Sun that illuminates, gazes on all things: that is to say, it allows us to see them … This sun shines on the golden *escudos* [literally a shield, but also a coin], which is our wise understanding, and the mountains are the dignitaries of the Church.

Rather than a progressive rhetorical argument that proves a point or a methodical guide to achieving the seven desired effects of the Holy Spirit, this is fundamentally an exercise in metaphor.[29] In general, Osuna's advice for the would-be mystic seems best summed up in his recommendation, given directly to the reader in the *Tercer Abecedario*, that when they feel "alguna gracia" in their soul, they should not stop and "escudriñar" (interrogate) its exact source and nature, but instead open their hearts and have faith. "No cures de saber qué cosas son aquellas que pasan por ti o que se obran en ti, sino confía; porque si esto no haces y quieres mirar y remirar, perderás la gracia que entonces obra" (V.4.194) ("Do not be anxious about what is happening but trust in God. If you act otherwise and try to analyse and reanalyse you will lose the grace that is at work" [155]). Osuna assumes the best of intentions among his readers and thus, not preoccupied with weeding out heretics or frauds, he advocates openness over discernment.

This confidence came from the origins of the Franciscan recollection movement, organized in "small communities, hermitages, and houses of prayer," where "following an old Franciscan custom, the friars in these houses lived a life of silence, strict asceticism, poverty and intensive prayer" (McGinn *Mysticism in the Golden Age of Spain* 25).[30] Osuna's stated intent was to spread the practice of *recogimiento* beyond this public, and at times he explicitly insists on the suitability of some degree of contemplative prayer for all. However, at least in the early versions of the *Abecedarios*, he seems to have naively assumed that all Christians would respond in a predictable way, akin to what he had observed amongst his fellow friars. The majority of the work is clearly written before the outbreak of *alumbradismo* made "alumbrar" a suspect word. In later works, Osuna was forced to recognize the *alumbrado* heresy and distance his *recogimiento* from their *dejamiento*, but the *Tercer Abecedario* represents a strident defense of even possibly extreme manifestations or interpretations of mystical union. While acknowledging the delicacy of the subject and the diversity of opinions from respected authorities about the degree to which spiritual ecstasy should be manifested in the body (*arrobos, gritos,* etc.) and in the presence of others, or the relative weight of the *ley de amor* over all the other *mandamientos,* Osuna defends the positions that Alonso de la Fuente and other persecutors of *alumbrados* would identify as heretical.[31] He notes that "bien sabemos que Santo Domingo y San Francisco y muchos de sus compañeros tuvieron cosas que no pudieron encubrir sin dar voces y gritos y tener otros movimientos no acostumbrados; y pues que ellos los tuvieron, no es mucho que ahora los tengan otras personas devotas" (V.2.185) ("We know for a fact that when Saint Dominic and Saint Francis and many of their companions experienced things they could not conceal, they uttered sounds and cries and acted in unusual ways. If this happened to them, it is not extraordinary for devout people nowadays to experience similar phenomena" [145]). Osuna assumes a reader who models his life on Saint Francis or Dominic; while we know that he shared his early manuscripts of the *Tercer Abecedario* with laypeople while studying theology in Alcalá (Pacho 412), it is clear from the text that his imagined reader still shares the subjectivity of a Franciscan friar or Dominican monk. In the *Tercer Abecedario,* Osuna only briefly acknowledges the existence of any other type of response, when he warns of "ignorantes devotos, que por una poca de lumbre que han recibido de Dios, o por algunas revelaciones a que dan más crédito que debían, se extienden en el hablar de Dios mucho más de lo que deben" (III.2.147) ("ignorant devout people who, because they absorb a little light from God, or because they have had a few revelations on which they place more importance than they ought, their revelations, rush on talking about God far more than they should" [104][32]), but even here his "ignorantes" are assumed to be "devotos" and their "lumbre" from God. The possibility of heretics, malicious *embusteros,* or demoniacs is never contemplated.

Indeed, perhaps the most striking characteristic of the *Abecedarios,* in contrast with later mystic treatises and works that will be examined in chapters 3–5 of this book, is the almost complete absence of the devil. The only section dedicated exclusively to the question of demonic imposture comes near the end of the *Cuarto abecedario,* in a chapter titled "De cómo el demonio se trabaja por falsarnos la ley del amor para enseñorearse de los que por amor habían de estar sujetos a Dios" ("How the devil labors to counterfeit the law of love to gain power over those who ought to be subject to God through love"). Even here, however, Osuna emphasizes the limited powers of the devil, "cuán poco puede el demonio contra tu amor" (625–6) ("how little the devil can achieve against your love"). As important as the insistence here on the power of free will ("pues Dios no te puede forzar ni constreñir, menos lo podrá hacer el demonio, pues que tu voluntad es tan libre que de ninguno puede padecer violencia" [626] ["since God can neither force nor constrain you, the devil can hardly do so, since your will is so free that it cannot be forced by anyone"]) is the assumption by Osuna that his readers have already dedicated their free will to pious, virtuous, love of God.

While at times in the *Abecedarios* Osuna expresses a desire to spread *oración mental* beyond the monastery, it is clear that he never truly contemplated a diverse, heterogeneous interpretive community, one that might include recent converts or non-cloistered, uneducated women. Yet the scandal of *alumbradismo* forced Osuna to recognize that this had occurred and to distance himself from the *alumbrados* in the prologue to the *Primer Abecedario*. His defense rests on the problem of circulation: a treatise, intended for like-minded Franciscans, was taken and circulated beyond his control: "tomándomela, comunicáronla (triste de mí) a otros sin yo saberlo: y así vino de mano en mano lo que yo tenía secreto" (*Primer Abecedario* 126) ("they took it from me, they shared it [to my great sadness] with others without my knowledge, and thus what I had held as secret was passed along from person to person"). The "secreto" here is not Osuna's mind but the intimate community of the monastery, which can act as a single body. As Armando Pego Puigbó notes, "the 'to my great sadness' comes from having to negotiate the principle of the 'non-negotiability of a common meaning' that is the underlying condition for the existence of a community" (161).[33] The prologue does not concede any doctrinal terrain, but rather doubles down on the validity of the doctrine among a given readership. The problem becomes not one of theology but of society: how to control the appropriation of doctrines by those who will, willfully or accidentally, misinterpret them. This is, Osuna implies, a problem for bishops and Inquisitors, not for theologians. In the 1530s, this was still a sustainable distinction.

Bernardino de Laredo and the Mystic Body

Osuna's treatises share many elements with another Franciscan treatise cited by both Teresa and San Juan de la Cruz: Berardino de Laredo's *Subida al monte Sión*. Laredo, a physician as well as a Franciscan friar, wrote the *Subida* between 1535 and 1538 and, like Osuna, imagined a readership of like-minded Franciscans who aspired to begin or progress in their practice of interior prayer. Laredo's advocacy of frequent communion, interior over vocal prayer, and mysticism over scholasticism, all escaped censure because he wrote while the assumption of such a limited readership was still tenable, before the great "outbreaks" of *alumbradismo* and the codification of the *alumbrado* heresy.[34]

Unlike the mnemonic structure of the *Abecedarios*, the *Subida* is divided into three parts that correspond to the three stages of mystic union: purgation, illumination, union. This also corresponds to a progression from an audience of beginners in the practice of mystic prayer to the more advanced reader.[35] As with Osuna, the declaration of an organizing system at the outset is undermined by the progressively abstract and poetic content, as we shall see. The *Subida* begins as a manual, presenting a series of "reglas" for each of the three books, corresponding to the three stages of mystic ascent. The first two stages are presented together in list form, each stage divided into a weekly calendar with distinct meditations for each day. The first week assigns a different question to each day (e.g., "Lunes. Quén soy. Martes. De dónde vengo. Miércoles. Por dónde vine") and the second a different fragment of Christ's Passion ("Lunes. De Getsemaní a Caifás. Martes. De Caifás a la columna" etc.) (I, "Ordinario de las ebdomadas" 29) ("Monday. Who I am. Tuesday. Where I come from. Wednesday. How I came" "Monday. From Gethsemane to Caiaphas. Tuesday. From Caiaphas to the column").

Instead of proceeding immediately to the third stage, Laredo interjects, with respect to the second, that "tantas veces se multiplica esta semana segunda, o digo la segunda parte de este libro, cuantos capítulos hay en él multiplicados" (29) ("this second week, or rather the second part of this book, can be repeated as many times as there are chapters within it") and adds that the reader may dedicate a day to each chapter or spend a whole day on a line, or a single word, as he pleases. Already, then, the seeming clarity and rigidity of the system is complicated; the linear transparency of a week-by-week program becomes a Zeno-like paradox, with time expanding infinitely as the reader/practitioner dedicates his day to smaller and smaller fragments of the text. Laredo seems hesitant to introduce the third, theologically thornier, section, adding another warning about the possibilities for *sequedad* and delayed results in the practice of the first two stages, citing the anecdote of a friar he knew who had suffered for three months before he finally "comenzó a sentir – aunque muy de cuando en cuando – qué cosa es el gusto de la oración" (30) ("began to feel – although very infrequently – the pleasure of prayer"). With a final praise to God, he sets out the program for the third stage, whose programmatic topics are more diverse, less clearly aligned in a progression:

Lunes Donde hay caridad y amor está Dios.

Martes Engrandeced a Dios conmigo y levantemos su nombre hasta él mismo.

Miércoles En el principio crió Dios el cielo y la tierra.

Jueves El ánima que a Dios se allega es un espíritu con Él.

Viernes Cristo padeció. Cómo se ha esto de sentir por quietud intelectual.

Sábado Recibimos en medio de vuestro templo las misericordias vuestras, dice el ánima a su Dios.

Domingo Ninguno conoce al Padre sino el Hijo; ni al Hijo conoce otro que su Eterno Padre. (30)

Monday Where there is charity and love there is God.

Tuesday Magnify God with me and let us lift His name to Himself.

Wednesday In the beginning God created the heavens and the earth.

Thursday The soul that draws near to God is a spirit with Him.

Friday Christ suffered. How this can be felt through intellectual quietude.

Saturday We receive your mercies in the midst of your temple, says the soul to its God.

Sunday No one knows the Father without the Son; he who knows the Son knows none other than his Eternal Father.

The system is made even more precise with an assignment of different stages to different times of day: "Hase de notar que la aniquilación tiene lugar o tiempo señalado, dende rezados maitines hasta prima. Los misterios de Cristo, dende prima a nona" (31) ("Note that the annihilation has a designated time or place, from the matins to primes. Christ's mysteries, from prime to nones"). Internal thoughts can also be coordinated to external rituals or actions so that each meal is a memory of Christ's last supper, each chiming of the clock corresponds to a strike of the hammer into the nails, "y así, contando las horas, cuente el ánima los golpes en el secreto interior" (32) ("and thus, counting the hours, the soul counts the blows in its inner secret/secret interior"). However, a caveat once again offers room for variation. His "reglas," he clarifies, should only be a guide ("norte"):

por donde se rige el ánima principiante para despertarse a andar dentro en sí; mas si alguna vez o veces se hallare en los tiempos señalados ocupada en otra cosa de lo que aquí se señala, hase de quietar en ella y tenerla por mejor, porque lo que se le ofrece, siempre le conviene más que lo que ella buscar puede con su pobre diligencia. (31)

to direct the beginner's soul in order to awaken and walk within itself; but if at some time or times it should find itself occupied in something other than what is indicated here, it should be calm there and prefer it, because that which offers itself to the soul is always more suitable than what the poor soul must diligently seek out.

The contradiction of the systematizing of the transcendent is made patent in this last phrase: a step-by-step guideline that ends by declaring that "lo que se ofrece" is always superior to what is achieved with diligent method. And this is particularly true in the third stage since "las cosas del espíritu no se pueden escribir muy a la clara" (37) ("matters of the spirit cannot be written with much clarity"). Inevitably, then, his book will contain "cosas oscuras entre muy muchas muy claras" ("amidst the many very clear things, other obscure ones") and the reader who comes up against

> puntos que no los entienda bien, no se congoje por esto, ni los pregunte a las *Glosas* ni a quien entienda mejor, hasta que él por sí, una vez y muchas veces, aun digo un día y muchos días, las tales oscuridades rumie él solo por sí en la mental oración, en el secreto escondido del ánima, dentro en sí misma, donde se suelen hallar en el libro de la vida, que es Cristo, y es su doctrina, las ciertas declaraciones con que se sabe en el ánima entender, por Mística Teología, qué es a lo que sabe Dios. (36)

> points he does not understand well should not be distressed, nor should he seek answers in the Glosses or from someone with more understanding, until, on his own and many times – for a day, and many days – he meditates on his own and for himself in mental prayer, in the secret hidden within the soul itself, where in the Book of Life which is Christ and his doctrine, one usually finds the true statements through which the soul knows how to understand, through mystic theology, what it is to *taste/ know* God.[36]

The difficulties of the highest stages of mental prayer can only be clarified through mental prayer; there is no exterior referent for the mystic experience. Laredo's opening structure of rules and timetables seems to announce a much more methodical, scientific approach than we find in Osuna, but from the outset the system undermines itself. The initial framework of a method that can be supported via scriptural and rational exegesis never disappears entirely but largely gives way to a spirituality that can never be defined and can only be affirmed from within, only approximated via a language of affect, excess, neologism, and paradox. Even the general movement from system to anti-system across the three volumes implies a consistency and coherency beyond that which we actually find in the volumes. The text is heterogeneous, and even in the third book, dedicated to the most elevated state of union, "aquello que ella [el alma] entiende no entiende cómo lo entiende; sábelo sin saber cómo lo sabe; sabe que conoce a Dios, pero porque aquél que conoce es incomprehensible no sabe conocer comprehendiendo" (II, 11, 470) [37] ("that which the soul understands, she does not understand how she understands it; she knows it without knowing how she knows; she knows that she knows God, but because what she knows is incomprehensible, she does not know how to know with comprehension") also promises intermittently to provide "con reglas autorizadas, la manera para poder hacer oración atenta" (III, 30, 536) ("our whole purpose here is to show, by authoritative precepts, the manner wherein the soul can make attentive prayer" [188]). In contrast to Gomez García's *Carro de dos vidas*, there is no steady *subida* along a single path, but instead a series of diagonal and curving approaches.

At the beginning of book one, Laredo sets out the paradox of a method that should eventually lead to anti-method. At the advanced stages of prayer, Laredo says, no preparation is necessary. "El ánima aprovechada, en pocos años acierta el lugar de la oración y pocas veces le pierde de vista; y, como cama portátil, la lleva de camino y la asienta adondequiera que le vaga reposar" (I, X, 65) ("The diligent soul, within a few years identifies the place of prayer and rarely loses sight of it; like a portable bed, he carries it as he goes and sets it down wherever he seeks to rest"). However, to reach the stage where method is dispensable, the novice will need to learn methodically. Unlike in the prologue, Laredo now frames this in first person; he is teaching from his own experience. "Pero los que de nuevo comienzan, paréceme a mí que les daría la manera que yo tuve en mi principio, como me la dió mi Dios de balde cuando quiso su bondad" (65) ("It seems to me that for those who are just starting, I will give them the method I used when I was beginning, since God gave it to me for free when, out of his goodness, He so wished"). The "manera" consists of beginning each session of prayer with "aquesta protestación: ¡O muy soberano Rey, incomprehensible Dios y universal Señor nuestro, ante cuya majestad se abrasan en amor los serafines y tremen los poderíos de los cielos" (65) ("this cry: "Oh most sovereign King, incomprehensible God and our universal Lord, before whose Majesty the angels burn with fire and the powers of the heavens tremble"), and it continues for a full folio, filled with exclamations and excesses of affect. As the penitent speaks in the first person ("yo, pecador miserable … os pido, mi Dios" [65–6] [I, miserable sinner … I beg of you, my God"]),[38] it is not clear if Laredo is writing a script for some other "yo" to repeat or if he seeks to recreate his own spiritual experience on the page. This latter interpretation is strengthened by the sudden interruption of another voice into the prayer: "Y luego, dentro de sí, dé el ánima una gran voz, tal que penetre los cielos y no se sienta en la tierra, y diga así: – ¡A hombre!, ¿quién eres? – Soy tierra, y aun bien astrosa. – ¿De dónde vienes? – Responda: De la tierra arenosa" (66) ("And then, from within, let the soul emit a great voice, such that it penetrates the heavens and is not heard on the earth, and let it say: 'Ah, man! Who are you?' 'I am earth, and quite dirty still.' 'Where do you come from?' The response: From the sandy soil"). The "dialogue" continues in a series of six cryptic questions and answers, which Laredo goes on to interpret allegorically. The methodology is typical of medieval allegory, but, as in Osuna, the allegory is turned inwards: "Y estas seis respuestas y seis preguntas son los seis obreros que se ha dicho que han de *ahondar* la zanja en el templo que a Dios se ha de edificar; y son las seis gradas por donde se dijo que ha de descender el ánima para *entrar* en su cama primera" (67, emphasis mine) ("And these six answers and six questions are the six workers who, it is said, will *dig the deep trench* in the temple that shall be erected to God; and they are the six steps by which it is said that the soul will descend to *enter into* its first bed"). This pattern continues throughout the volumes, with each allegory pointing inwards. Not only are objects and relationships in the natural world interpreted as symbols of interior experiences, but the whole of Christian history, the story of Christ in the Bible, or Christ made Word, is ultimately projected into the interior space of the contemplative. He recommends the contemplation of the symbol of Saint Atanasio, which, he claims, his readers ought "traer con vivo fuego esculpido muy dentro en el corazón" ("carry this holy Symbol sculpted in living fire very deep within their heart") because "sin intrincaciones muestra a conocer a Dios altísimo, increado y humanado, y tiene en sí un no sé qué entretallado en sus versos, que, si toma hábito en las entrañas del ánima, ya no ha menester pensar en él para traerle a la continua con su firmeza ingerido fuertemente en las entrañas" (II, 12, 245) ("without convolutions it lets us know God on High, never created and made man, and it has within a certain something carved into its verses such that, if it becomes a custom within the core of the soul, itis no longer necessary to think about it in order to have it continually present, with its strength, ingested firmly within the interior"). In this phrase, Laredo moves back and forth – more accurately, he erases the borders between – internal and external bodies, signifiers and signifieds. God is carved ("entretallado") into words but also into single symbols, themselves sculpted in fire in the contemplatives' heart and soul, where, deeply "ingerido," they "toma hábito."

This passage from book two initiates a section of guided meditations that join together the intellectual (meditation itself) with the affective and visceral to an unprecedented degree.[39] Jessica Boon has shown that "of all the authors in the first generation of Franciscan recollection mystics, Laredo's medical understanding of the body heightened his awareness that the spiritual could only be reached through the corporeal" (143). Yet his reader is not encouraged to imitate the physical pains inflicted upon Christ's body that he describes in such vivid detail through flagellation or penitence, but instead to meditate upon them. The corporeality is always already understood as interiorized in the mind, soul, and heart. Whereas the penitent who physically imitates the Passion is limited by laws of matter and flesh in what and how he can recreate Christ's suffering, the contemplative is limited only by what language can evoke. Thus, Laredo can suggest parallels and correspondences that exceed physical possibility, asking his reader, as Boon catalogues, to "imagine his or her heart as the column to which Jesus is tied under torture … Alternatively, Laredo recommends that the mystic's heart becomes the material base of the cross, inundated with the blood dripping from Christ's wounds" (81). The passion meditations in Laredo are, as Boon notes, written "in apparent opposition to the beginnings of public Holy Week processions by confraternities that followed a *via crucis* mapped onto the streets of Seville" (81), substituting a physical journey with a mental one. However, where Boon sees the emphasis in Laredo on the body as evidence that he rejected any mystic model that moved away from or aspired to transcend the body, I see the meditations on bodily suffering as insisting on the power of language to reconfigure all earthly, physical knowledge, beginning with the body. The meditations do not narrate a visual image or narrative; they produce relationships that have no physical, real referent to relationships on earth. It is only through the power of language that such correspondences can be made, and made known.

A few examples of Laredo's Passion meditations should suffice to show the degree to which language intervenes not to paint a picture or tell a story but to re-orient the relationship between the contemplative and the contemplated. In chapter XIII, Laredo tells his reader:

> si piensas en la coronación, sea tu corazón la silla, o sea la púrpura, y no haya alguna espina que no toque y lastime o te ensangriente los ojos, pues que la sangre sagrada aun por ellos y la boca reventaba y por el rostro corría. Y si piensas en la cruz, sea tu corazón la piedra en que fue hincada y aun lo más tierno e interior sea el agujero de ella, de manera que la sangre que corría por el madero lave tu dura substancia y se entre en el cordial agujero y nunca salga de allí. Y así en todos los misterios. (II, 13, 253)

> If you think about the coronation, let your heart be the throne, that is to say the purple robe, and let there be no thorn that does not touch or

> wound you, or bloody your eyes, since his holy blood poured even from there, and burst from his mouth and ran down his face. And if you think of the cross, let your heart be the stone into which it was driven, and let the most tender and inner part be the hole, in such a way that the blood that ran down the wood cleans your hard substance and enters into the kind hole and never leaves, and so forth in all of the mysteries.

Because body parts are only interior/imagined here, they can be infinitely re-combined and re-interpreted: the heart can be a seat and a stone, the heart can have eyes, interiorities can always be opened up to contain further interiorities, and blood can circulate throughout, at times representing pain, at times representing purification.[40]

Laredo's extensive discussion of anatomical terminology in the section dedicated to Luke's description of Christ seemingly sweating blood in Gethsemane belies his medical education but weds it to a faith in a prelapsarian power of language to create reality, even mystic reality. The title of the chapter and first sentences frame the topic of the chapter as one of language rather than anatomy:

> es de notar que *dice* el evangelista en este paso "casi gotas de sangre." Y si *esta dición* "quasi," referimos a las gotas, de manera que entendamos *querer decir* "casi gotas," podémoslo así sentir, que aun es conforme a *la letra*; pero si *decimos* "gotas casi de sangre" o "de casi sangre" aun tendrá más consonancia ... (II, 17, 263, emphasis mine)

> it should be noted that the Evangelist *says* at this point "almost drops of blood," and this expression "almost" we apply to the drops in such a way that we understand *he meant to say* that they were "almost drops"; we can take it this way, which is according *to the letter*, but if we *say* "drops almost of blood" or "of almost blood," it would be even more appropriate.

Why should it matter whether the "almost" modifies drops or blood, or, as Laredo interprets the difference, whether the substance that Christ emitted came from the skin or the veins? On one level, it matters to Laredo because "la sangre, cuando está dentro en las venas, no está tan purificada, tan pura, ni tan digesta como ya salida de ellas por vía de porosa resudación," ("blood, when it is within our veins, is not as purified, as pure and digested as that which has left them by means of sweat through the pores") and thus, because Christ's "sudación" should be of the purest possible form, it is important to determine what form that would be (264). But the process of determining is entirely circular, drawing not on any known physical properties of blood but on the power of language, of metaphor, to create new categories in order to affirm them as realities. Sweat *seems* more "presta a movimiento" ("quick to move") and thus "los doctores médicos la comparan al rocío que está en las hojas de los árboles" (264) ("medical doctors compare it to the dew on the leaves of trees"). Only by passing through metaphor, through poetry, can this *casi sangre* be given new names:

> porque esta sangre que está ya fuera de las venas y va a convertirse en carne es más fina y apurada y tiene más perfición, no está ya bajo del nombre sangre, como lo estaba en las venas, antes se llama "rórida humidad" luego que ha salido de ellas, extendiéndose por debajo de los poros de este nuestro humano cuerpo. Y cuando se espesa más llámase "gluten"; y cuando ya ha de pasar a lo natural de carne, llámase "cambio"; y todas estas tres humidades, una menos y otra más, se llama muy propiamente húmido radical. (264)
>
> because this blood that is already outside of the veins and is going to become flesh is finer and faster/purer and more perfect, and it is no longer called blood, as it was in the veins, but instead, now that it has left them, it is called "dew-like moisture," understood as what is beneath the pores in this our human body; and when it thickens further it is called "gluten," and when finally it has to pass naturally to the flesh, it is called "change"; and these three moistures, one less and the other more, are most appropriately called radical moisture.

Words and concepts created, the reality can be affirmed:

> A nuestro propósito, el sudor de nuestro suavísimo Jesús no fue de sangre de venas, sino de la muy más fina de la rórida humidad; sangre más pura y más viva, la cual en el hombre está desembrada en cualquiera de sus miembros, debajo de cualesquier de sus poros y presta para salir cuando quiera que le sea dado lugar, o con puntura de aguja o de muy sutil espina que no pueda romper vena o por cualquier abrimiento de algún poro. (264)
>
> For our purposes, the sweat of gentlest Jesus was not sweat from his veins, but rather the finest of dew-like damp; a purer and more lively blood, which is sewn in any of his limbs under any of his pores and ready to emerge whenever it is given occasion or with the prick of a needle or a very fine thorn that would not puncture a vein, or through any opening of a pore.

From a logical standpoint, this is a purely circular argument: Christ's "blood" must be of the finest and purest quality; therefore, we invent a sub-cutaneous, non-venous blood that must be the referent in the gospel's description of Christ. The passage can only be understood as not-logic, as a performative example of what meditation on Christ's body in language can do. It is a corporeal parallel to Osuna's detained exploration of the proper word for interior prayer; the fact that Osuna proposes names for an incorporeal process and Laredo for a bodily function is almost incidental. In this second book of the tripartite *Subida*, language is essential in evoking a mystical body.

The second book of the *Subida*, focused on thinking with words about God but still imagining God as man, is an intermediate stage, preparing the mental pathways to take the final jump of experiencing God in words simply as God. The jump from *thinking* to *experiencing* also requires the engagement of affective faculties. The meditations are performative, producing in the reader the simultaneously rational and affective identification that they narrate. For example, when Laredo contemplates the scene of Christ tied to the column (II, 19, 268–72), he begins with the narrative of the punishments inflicted and the sufferings caused. Soon Laredo leaves the specifics of the story as recounted in the Gospels and begins to fill in "novelistic" details, and, equally important, shifts from an omniscient narration to a questioning that interpellates the reader, bringing him in to participate in the creation of the scene. The passage is worth quoting at length, as exemplary of the method of this entire section:

> Y aun el sayón en cuyas manos estaba la soga de la garganta, ¿quién no piensa que tiró cuando se quería mover hacia sí con más crueldad? Y que si otro sayón cruel no se arrimara a Jesús, y para que no cayese sobre el delicado rostro le ayudara con las manos puestas sobre los cabellos, ¿quién duda que no cayera la humanidad fatigada? Mas ¡o ánima mía lastimada! ¿Y no merecieras ir con tu amoroso Jesús desnudo, con ultraje avergonzado, atado e inclinado todo el muy llagado cuerpo? ¿Y no merecieras ir con tu muy llagado Cristo entre gente tan desmedida y profana? ¡O, mi dulcísimo amor, y quién me diera la parte de las salivas, los silbos y bofetadas y el tumultuoso rigor con que pasasteis aquella breve jornada de la columna hasta vuestras vestiduras! ¡Quién os viera quereros vestir temblando y con espantosa furia tornaros a desnudar! ¡Quién os quitara la púrpura de vuestro ultrajable escarnio! ¡Quién os tomara la venda de los delicados ojos! ¡quién os tomara la silla y la caña y los pujeses, las salivas, los golpes y bofetadas! ¡O, si viera las espinas en mi alma penetradas y la sangre que corría por la frente, y por el rostro, por el cabello y garganta! ¡O, mi Dios, quién la cogiera en el pobre lastimado y abrasado corazón! ¡O, quién la viera apuntar a los lacrimables ojos o reventar por los oídos, por

las narices y boca, en lo último atormentada! ¡Y quién subiera con vos al *Ecce homo* de Pilato, a la presencia del pueblo y gente desesperada! (271)

And even the executioner who held the rope around his [Christ's] throat in his hands, who doubts that he pulled it when he wanted to move Christ closer to him with greater cruelty, and if that other cruel executioner had not stepped closer to Jesus, and so that He not fall on his delicate face, had not helped Him by putting his hands on his hair, who doubts that this weary humanity would not have fallen? But, oh, wounded soul of mine! And do you not deserve to go with your loving Jesus, naked, with ashamed affront, your whole wound-riddled body tied up and bent forward? And do you not deserve to go with your wounded Christ among such uncontrolled and profane people? Oh, my sweetest love, and who would give me just a part of the spit, the whistles and blows and the turbulent duress, down to your very garments, with which you spent that brief day on the column. Who does not see you, trembling, try to dress yourself and the terrifying fury with which they undress you again; who would not take the purple of your easily affronted public shame; who would not take the blindfold from your delicate eyes; who would not take the seat, and the cane, and the obscene gestures, the spit, the slaps and blows! Oh, if I could see the thorns penetrating my soul and the blood running down your forehead, and face, and hair and throat! Oh, my God, who would not gather it [the blood] in their poor injured and burning heart! Oh, who does not see it aim for their weeping eyes and burst out from their ears, nose, and mouth, in torment to the very end; and who would not ascend with you to the *Ecce homo* of Pilate, in the presence of the people and desperate crowd!

The affective escalation that accompanies the identification with Christ prepares the reader to exchange thought for feeling, understanding for experience. But this is not the experience of medieval penitents who imitate Christ's passion on their own bodies. The movement from third-person narrative to a rhetorical third person expressed through the subjunctive (¿quién …?) to first person ("oh ánima mía" "Oh mi Dios"), combined with the offers to exchange subject positions with Christ, prepares the reader for the ultimate erasure of selfhood that transcends any clear narrative of imitation, that only occurs in an interior space in the final stages of union.

After the corporeal meditations, Laredo immediately reminds his reader that these are only an intermediate stage, and that "tratando estos misterios, ni quiera el ánima cuerpo, ni huerto, ni monumento, ni cosa que cuerpo tenga" (II, 36, 323) ("in dealing with these mysteries, the soul neither wants a copy, a garden, a monument, nor anything that has a body"). He takes pains, however, to show that the movement from the thinking-through-a-body stage to thinking-without-the-body is not seamless, is not a logical progression that one can follow with guaranteed results. The chapters on the meditation of the Passion end with the ambiguous conclusion that

> Y no sé si hay alguna escritura que tan bien dé a entender esto como escribirlo con sólo un *cetera*, que ni significa cuerpo ni tiempo ni se sabe tasar, y con su sola brevedad tiene muy mayor significado que lo que antes queda escrito; y aun, si bien se considera, no tiene donde acabar, ni hay alguno que lo sepa, sino el que al *cetera* da el ser; así que espíritu de letra y su conformidad puede ayudarnos aquí *et cetera*, y debajo de ella queda muy más de lo que está dicho, y cuando todo se acabe sean grandes gracias a Dios. (325)

> And I don't know if there is any writing that makes this as clear as writing simply *cétera*, which neither means body nor time nor can it be measured, and in its very brevity has a much greater meaning then what is written before, and if you think about it, it even has nowhere to end, nor does anyone know it, beyond He who gives the *cétera* its being; and thus the spirit of the letter and its conformity can help us here *etcétera*, and beneath that there remains much more than has been said, and when all is finished, let there be great thanks to God.

If the "et cetera" is superior to all that "antes queda escrito," it follows that all the previous chapters were unnecessary, that the true mystic treatise would consist of two words: "et cetera." Yet the very Latin phrase contains the paradox: and *so* forth must build upon a *so*; it is as meaningless without a context as a "tú" without a "yo." Furthermore, the "et cetera" that transcends/supercedes writing (*letras*) is in itself made of *letras*, writing. Once again we find the obligatory negation of language for conveying the mystic experience, but here this denial is tied explicitly to the negation of the body. The body, like language, is necessary but ultimately must be transcended.

In the final chapters of book two, Laredo narrates another guided meditation, this time to the City of God. While in many ways the allegorical interpretation he provides of every visual detail is typical of medieval typology, he again foregrounds the power of the imagination to create the images it then interprets, and the power of language to guide the imagination. Laredo speaks directly to the reader, interrupting the description periodically to re-establish the deictic relationship and the journey that author and reader are taking together in a permanent present (the time of the reader, rather than the time of the author). Near the end of the second volume, he reminds the reader of "El cirio pascual que antes vistes, en el capítulo 46, en el gran campo encendido" ("The Easter candle you saw before, in Chapter 46, hidden in the great field") and exhorts him to re-conjure it: "habéisle de ver aquí con el ojo intelectual en el campo como primero se estaba. Considerad en su cera la carne humana de Cristo Jesús suavísimo, y su muy suave pabilo, el ánima racional suya, y en su vivo encendimiento su inmensa divinidad, como allí quedó notado" (II, 49, 367) ("you should see it here, with your intellectual eyes, in the field as it was before; consider the human flesh of Christ, gentlest Jesus, in its wax, and his rational soul in its soft wick, and his immense divinity in its lively ardor, as was noted there [in ch. 46]"). Verbs of visualization and creation are used interchangeably; the reader is told to "ver" and "considerar" the Easter candles, and then to "fabricar" ("create") nine candles of unequal size (367). Finally, the stage set with all nine candles, the author prepares the final conclusion of the allegory and the point where rational exegesis must stop: "Levántese la razón, álcese el entendimiento, quiétese la inteligencia y goce la voluntad" (369) ("Lift your reason, let your understanding rise up, let your intelligence be quiet, and let your will know joy").

In the third book, language will separate from the body entirely, following the tripartite system of mystic prayer that requires eventually leaving the body – even the language of the body – behind. Laredo assigns a prelapsarian role to names throughout the books, but it is only at the beginning of book three that he turns to the name of the practice for which he is providing a guide: contemplative prayer. Etymology is the key to separating two distinct levels of intellectual devotion that he identifies, speculation and contemplation. On this point, etymology (an invented etymology, of course, as he erases the stages of translation and patristic invention in coining these terms) trumps even the Gospels, for Laredo concedes that the two are occasionally used interchangeably in the Bible. Notwithstanding, he cites Richard of St. Victor's *De arca mystica* (bk. 5 ch. 15) to argue that they are distinct:

> más propia y ciertamente se entiende por especulación cuando vemos por espejo, esto es querer darnos a sentir que, cuando meditando en las criaturas, nos despertamos por lo que vemos en ellas al amor del Señor nuestro, entonces diremos que especulamos o miramos en espejo, porque espejo es la criatura cuando en ella miramos a nuestro Criador. (III, 2, 440)

> in the most correct and proper sense speculation denotes seeing through a *speculum*, or mirror, which comes to pass when our meditation on the

> creatures shows us in them that which awakens us to love Our Lord. We say at such a time that we "speculate," or look in the *speculum*, because a creature becomes a mirror when we see our Creator in it. [69]

In contrast, he continues, contemplation is understood "en puro significado" ("in the pure sense") as the lifting of the soul to God "pura y absolutamente, sin algún envolvimiento o nublado u oscuridad o espejo de cualesquiera criaturas ... mas que absoluta, pura y momentáneamente se quiete el alma en Dios por puro y desnudo amor" (440) ("pure and completely, without any covering, or cloud, or darkness, or the use of any kind of creature as a mirror, least of all of any creature ... purely, completely and instantaneously, the soul attains quietness in God through pure and naked love" [69]). The *especulum* introduces a degree of abstraction or problematization of worldly sight – reflections rather than direct sight. The next step removes even the human referent of reflection, and since there can be no linguistic root for the more-than-absolute, eternal/momentary, pure gaze of mystic union, only the etymological act of *taking away* the worldly referent (removing the *especulum* from the term) can convey a higher level.[41]

In fact, Laredo's focus on etymology and nuances of meaning goes beyond that of Osuna. For Laredo, linguistic variation between two known concepts stands in for the difference between the known and the unknown, the "effable" and the ineffable. Even the sections not explicitly dedicated to etymological arguments ultimately depend on etymology. For example, in the midst of an extended metaphorical reading of the soul as traveller and the flesh as a beast of burden, he notes that the saddle, or *silla*, is "para sentar y asentar; y no basta estar sentado, sino estar asentado" (I, 21, 114) ("to sit and to settle; it is not enough to sit, one must also settle"[42]). The distinction between *sentado* and *asentado* seems trivial on the level of signified, but the variation of the signifier leads him in the direction of etymological parallels: "estar posado" is synonymous with *sentado*, and it bears a similar relation on the level of the signifier to *reposado* as *asentado* bears to *sentado*, which is to say, it is one prefix away. By the same process of prefix variation, this leads him to relate *posado* and *reposado* to *desposado* (betrothed), culminating in the choral conjunction of the original verb (*sentar, asentar*) with the three new variations: "En nuestro propósito, es la silla el *reposo* en la oración, y en esta silla *se posa* y *toma reposo* el ánima que es *desposada* con Cristo, su dulce *esposo*, así como *desposada* quietísima v *reposada*, la cual oye de su *esposo* aquella palabra dulce: '*Asiéntate* a la mi diestra' ..." (114, emphases mine) ("For our purpose, the saddle is the repose of prayer, and in this saddle, the soul betrothed [*desposada*] to Christ, the sweet spouse [*esposo*] sits [*se posa*] and takes repose [*reposa*]. There, like a quiet and reposed [*reposada*] betrothed woman [*desposada*], it hears the spouse/husband [*esposo*] say those sweet words: Be seated [*Asiéntate*] at my right hand"). Laredo continues developing the horse symbol – less a concrete symbol than a semantic field in which he can propose new correspondences – both at the level of signified and signifier. Like Osuna, Laredo takes this standard medieval rhetorical procedure and turns it inwards: the points of comparison all connect an external image to an internal process, each chosen symbol is analysed along an axis of interiority. So, after developing the opposition between *posar/reposar* in the saddle, he returns to the saddle itself and finds it to have "dos corazas, que son interior recogimiento y concierto en lo exterior" (I, 22, 118) ("two shells/plates, which are interior recollection and external order"). This brings in another etymological motif, around the root of "lev-": the "interior coraza" is called "por común nombre retoba levadiza" ("in common parlance, a lift-able leather lining"),[43] which echoes the phrase *laeva eius* ("his left hand") from the *Cantares*. Laredo reads the hand resting under the Beloved's head as an allegory for the recollected soul since it lies beneath the head, which represents "la vida ordenada" ("the well-ordered life") in gentle repose (I, 22, 118–19). But *-lev* is also the root for *elevar* (to elevate), and for Laredo, then, "Así que la coraza interior se dice ser *levadiza*, y [la] hace ánima e*lev*ada, y cierto está que esta nuestra *levadiza*, es a saber, la ánima en la oración mental *elevada*, es la cosa que es muy necesaria" (119) ("And thus the interior plate is said to be lift-able [*levadiza*] and it elevates the soul, and it is certain that this lift-able thing of ours, that is to say, the soul elevated in mental prayer, is the most important thing"). This procedure continues, with a new ingredient added around the sound -jin/-gen ("nuestra mística silla dicho está que es *jineta*, porque sigue al uni*génito*; y si *jineta* se dice porque redobla las *genuas*, que quiere decir 'rodillas'" [I, 23, 121]) ("our mystic saddle is said to be *jineta* [a style of riding with shortened stirrups], because it follows the *Unigénito* [Only-Begotten one]: and we say *jineta* because [riding this way] you bend your *genuas*, which means knees") to close with a chorus of the three roots (-pos, -lev-, -jin): "suceda lo que se sigue y que dígase *lévate*, y que lo entienda el espíritu que se ha de *llevar* a Dios de la mano de ese Dios, y que así se ha de *elevar*, y *levadiza* se ha dicho ser la retoba o la coraza interior de aquesta *jineta* silla que es *reposada* oración" (121) ("what occurs is what follows and may you *lévate* (rise), and your spirit understand that it is to *levar* [rise] to God, guided by God, and in this way it shall *elevar* [elevate], and that leather lining or interior shell of that *jineta* saddle [with shortened stirrups] that is prayer *reposada* [in repose] is said to be *levadiza* [lift-able]"). Laredo shifts the level of correspondence from signified to signifier, from prose to poetry.

As we saw in Osuna, in addition to the exploration of etymological variants, mystic writers often explore subtleties of meaning through prepositions and pronouns. The spatial and existential relationship between God and the soul is transformed in mystic union, and the preposition and pronoun, the grammatical elements that denote spatial and existential relationships, are charged with conveying the transformation. A long allegorical meditation on rivers is filled with prepositional/pronominal play: "tampoco digo que los ríos *establecen de sí* el piélago, mas que se establecen *en él*" ("nor do I wish to say that rivers in themselves establish the open sea, but rather that they are established in it [the sea]"); "El río se dice ir *en madre* cuando va por la canal que suele ir; y cuando por su gran llenedumbre toma más de lo que antes ocupaba, quedando llena la madre, se dice salir *de madre*" et al (II, 1, 190–1) ("It is said that the river goes *en madre* [along the riverbed] when it follows the customary channel; and when it is so full that it takes more space than it occupied before, the *madre* being full, it is said to *salir de madre*"[44]). This is all preparation for the final synthesis, where it is shown that the river represents the soul:

> Cuando el río llega *a la mar*, así es recibido *de ella*, que el río se pierde *de sí*, sin le quedar ni aun el nombre, mas *engólfase en la mar*. Y el ánima que por tales pasos camina para su Dios créese que podrá llegar y hallarse en tiempo que, *engolfándose en él*, la trate de tal manera que no se sepa nombrar *a sí misma*, sino que toda esté *en Dios*. (II, 10, 227)

> When the river arrives at the sea, and is thus received in her [the sea], the river loses itself, and it is left without even the name, but instead is engulfed in the sea; and the soul that by such steps journeys toward its God believes that it can arrive and find itself at a time that, engulfing itself in Him, it is treated such that it does not even know its own name, but is instead entirely in God.

Laredo uses the natural world as a "vivo ejemplo" (living example) of the fluidity of identities and borders that characterize the divine union, but a river itself need not be seen in such terms; it requires the very human intervention of language, and of pronouns and prepositions in particular, to make the river and ocean's relationship one of blurred boundaries and identities. Again, language creates the correspondences that it then reveals as truth.

Laredo uses the same preposition play for entirely interior processes. Early in the first book, he establishes three characteristics of mental prayer: "el primero, *entrarse en su corazón* por quieto recogimiento; el segundo, *subirse sobre su corazón*, pidiendo de su ejercicio sola la gloria de Dios, estando con cuidado atento *a* él y *por* él. El tercero es *presentarse a* su Señor" (I, 5, 53) ("the first, to *enter into* your/its [it is not clear if the subject is the person or the soul] heart through quiet recollection. The second, to *rise above* your/its heart, asking from this exercise the glory of God, carefully attentive to Him and through Him. The third is to *present your/itself to* God"). Near the end of the third book, he returns to and expands on this distinction in the chapter titled "Muestra cómo viene el ánima a *entrarse dentro de sí* y a *subir sobre sí misma*, y al fin toca en los arrobamientos" (III, 41, 594) ("Shows how the Soul comes to *withdraw within Itself* and to *soar above Itself*, and at the End touches upon Raptures" [256]). Where the chapters examined above revolve around etymological variations, this chapter is a prepositional/pronominal symphony: "dícese '*sobre sí*' porque excede y pasa los términos naturales que puede poder *por sí*" (594) ("we say 'above itself' because it surpasses and transcends the natural limits which it can set for itself"[45]) [256–7]; "habiéndose recogido y llegándose *a sí* misma, entrarse *dentro de sí* y quietarse con su Dios hasta subirse *sobre sí* misma. Subir el ánima *sobre sí* es sobrepujar y subir *sobre* toda la potencia natural, en tal manera que se encumbra y se sublima *sobre todo* lo que es criado. Y, *saliendo de todo* ello, quiétase *en* solo su Dios" (595) ("having recollected itself and drawn near *to itself*, it will draw *within itself* and be quiet with its God until it soar [*sic*] *above itself*. For the soul to soar *above itself* is for it to transcend and rise *above* every natural faculty, in such a way that it ascends and sublimates itself *above everything* created, and leaving everything *behind*, becomes quiet *in* its God" [257][46]); "Dase en aquesto a entender que, así como es una cosa *llegarse a sí* misma, y otra cosa es *entrarse dentro de sí*, de aquesta misma manera se entienda que puede estar el ánima *sobre sí* misma y *sin salirse de sí*" (595) ("We understand here that, as it is one thing for the soul to *draw near to itself* and another for it to *enter within itself*, so the soul may be *above itself* without *leaving itself*" [258]).

While the drawing of fine grammatical distinctions seems intended to clarify with words a point of unclear doctrine, the final counsel that "los que no entienden esto, pregúntenlo a la experiencia, porque yo he oído decir que en ella se aprende bien" (595) ("Let those who understand not this enquire of experience, for I have heard that by experience it can be learned effectively" [258]) again negates the possibility of using language to prepare for experience. If words cannot convey experience, then they are means to no end, or, as in poetry, ends in themselves. Furthermore, Laredo negates his own experiential authority in the matter of *arrobos* when he admits that, when it comes to this final stage of extasis, "yo confieso en Su presencia que sé que digo verdad, pero torno a confesar que lo sé sin experiencia, ni sin saber qué cosa es experiencia en esta práctica en cosa de alienación o arrobamiento" (599) ("I confess in His presence that I know I am speaking the truth; but I confess further that I know it otherwise than from my own experience, and even without knowing what experience in this matter of alienation or rapture is" [262]). In the end, the lack of a first-person in which to root all the other pronouns undoes the base upon which the entire seventeen-step scale has been constructed. Laredo's denial of his own experience of a method positing the authority of experience over study is a remarkable moment in the birthing pangs of a modern self grounded in experience rather than erudition. It is as if Bartolomé de las Casas were to end his *Brevísima relación* by stating that he had never been to the Americas. The *Subida* posits that the highest, if not the only, path to Christian virtue is through the direct union of the interior self with God, but in the 1530s, only a person who disavowed such an experience himself, and justified his authority through his erudition and institutional position, could transmit such an argument and be heard. The invention of new configurations of pronouns which might, in the context of a poem in the *cancionero*, for example, seem like so much wordplay, is here evidence of a very real conflict between two models of selfhood.

In fact, the entire third volume is prefaced as second-hand (at least) knowledge since, as Laredo states in the first chapter, "por exceder este tercer libro las fuerzas y disposición del autor, va tomado y copilado de los sentimientos y sentencias de los Doctores contemplativos, y vinculado a figuras de la Escritura sagrada" (III, 1, 435) ("And it is to be noted that, as this third book is beyond the author's powers and capabilities, it is taken and compiled from the sentiments and judgments of the contemplative Doctors and explained with the help of figures from Holy Scripture" [63]). Whether or not we take this at face value or assume that the sudden abundance of quotes[47] is a defensive strategy at this most controversial point, the effect on the text is curious. As the text ostensibly moves towards a description or guide to union, the narrative voices and texture become more disjointed, a pastiche of authorities and quotes. The four chapters taken from the *Horologio* are in fact a dialogue between "el ánima que recibe el Sacramento Santísimo" y "la sabiduría" (III, 35–8, 555–65) ("a dialogue between Wisdom and the soul that receives the Most Holy Sacrament" [211]), further displacing the generally consistent voice of the first-person guide (Laredo, speaking directly to his reader) that predominates in the first two volumes.

This is hardly to say that the *Subida* is a failure, since such a designation implies the possibility of success.[48] The ending only confirms the paradoxical premise of any manual of mystic prayer, and at the same time points to the way to a complementary genre which must supply what the manual cannot: the first-person account of mystic experience. The *Abecedarios* and *Subida create* (in conjunction with the institutional spaces and conditions in which such reading occurred) the reader/subject who is then able to fill in the first-person account they lack. We might hypothesize this relation from the spike in nuns' (and later *beatas'*) spiritual autobiographies precisely in the generation after the publication of the manuals of contemplative prayer. But the hypothesis here has concrete proof: Teresa of Ávila's account, in the beginning of her spiritual autobiography, of her own reading of Osuna and Laredo.

Loyola

The post-Trent mystic treatises go in two directions, corresponding to the tendency/tension that coexists in the texts of the earlier generation: on the one hand, as Andrés Martín describes it, "some more theoretical-doctrinal (without leaving behind a basis in experience), and others of a more practical nature; the one with a more logical, static, and systematic orientation, the other more experiential and concrete" (*Historia de la mística de la Edad de Oro en España y América* 378). However, the restrictions imposed by Inquisitorial censorship made the fluidity, ambiguity, and generally affirmative nature of the pre-Trent manuals impossible. Later manuals would seek to fix and clarify the fluidity of an Osuna or Laredo (in fact Osuna and Laredo themselves were forced to limit or re-write their works in the later atmosphere of skepticism), in essence de-mystifying themselves. No text is more exemplary of the systematization of mental prayer than San Ignacio de Loyola's *Spiritual Exercises*,[49] written throughout the 1530s and 1540s but first published in 1548, and a generation later, with the expansion of the Jesuit Order, converted into something of a franchise.[50] Because the Jesuits in the seventeenth century explicitly prohibited certain mystical texts and emphasized superficial and homogenous application of the *Exercises*, the Jesuits have historically rarely been considered as mystics.[51] Yet Loyola's original text should, as Emilio Orozco Díaz and others have argued, be considered as emerging from both the personal mystic experiences of its author and the mystic manuals of contemplative prayer.[52] The tendency towards rigidity and systematization which can be noted from the Franciscans' manuals to the *Exercises* and from the 1548 *Exercises* to their use throughout Jesuit schools and missions in the post-Tridentine era, exemplifies the path that mystic theology took over this period. As mysticism became institutionalized and mystic practice made available to mass audiences of laypeople and the lower classes, *lo místico* became *la mística*, which is to say, not very mystic at all.

It is worth looking in some detail at the *Exercises* since they are at once the product and catalyst of this transition. They have been studied in relation to Ludolph of Saxony's *Vita Christi*,[53] but it is also essential to read them in dialogue with another Ignatian text, one whose almost total disappearance from Jesuit scholarship and practice is striking in contrast to the proliferation of the *Exercises*. This text, a spiritual diary that Loyola kept from February 1544 through February 1545, is a mysterious, anomalous manuscript, one of the very few examples we have of a true spiritual diary, as opposed to the spiritual autobiography or an *autobiografía por obligación* like Teresa's *Vida*. The general purpose of the diary seems to have been to record the effects of the spiritual exercises on their author, a sort of experimental trial on a study group of one.[54] Loyola and his small group of fellows had reached an impasse regarding several details of the order they should form, particularly whether the community should hold certain common assets or take a vow of total poverty, what he refers to in the diary as "no tener nada" ("to have nothing").[55] Rational discussion seeming to have failed, Loyola sets about to use his own method of spiritual decision-making – reflecting on each of the various options and recording the divine response as noted in tears and spiritual movements. Because the text is not intended for any reader but its author, there is no attempt at legibility or coherence. Luis María Mendízabal, editor of the *Diario*, says that "Saint Ignatius, in the *Diary*, writes for himself with the precision of content and the neglect of form characteristic of writing not meant for others," drawing attention to the "imperfect word choice, the impersonal style regarding personal matters, the superabundance of gerunds ... the hybrid words and phrases in Castilian, Latin, and Italian." (175). In addition, Loyola invents words (most importantly, and subject of much theological discussion, *loqüela*[56]), and shorthand, such as a series of dots over letters to denote each of the three daily masses and to register the quantity of tears experienced in each. The earliest entries retain some narrative structure, with Loyola setting the time and place for his meditations. For example, the sixth entry, from 7 February 1544, reads:

> 6.° Jueves – antes de la missa <y en ella>[57], con mucha abundancia de devoción y lágrimas, y todo el día con un calor y devoción notable <hasta

la noche> y siempre más estante y movido a no nada <a lo menos>. Al tiempo de la misa un parecerme acceso notable, y con mucha devoción y moción interior para rogar al Padre, <habiendo interpelado> pareciéndome haber interpelado los dos mediadores[58] y con alguna señal de verlos. (206–7)

6th Thursday before mass <and during>, with great abundance of devotion and tears, and all day with notable warmth and devotion <until night > and each time more settled and moved to nothing at all <at least>. At the time of mass a seemingly notable bout, and with much devotion and interior movement to beg our Father, <having interpellated> the two mediators seeming to have interpellated and with some sign of seeing them.[59]

No entry is longer than a few sentences, but in some Loyola records mystic experiences through the affective, corporeal, and sensory effects they produce. Thus we find in March:

[148] Y con esto comenzaron a ir de mí gradatim las tinieblas, y venirme lágrimas, y éstas yendo en aumento, se me quitó toda voluntad de más misas para este efecto, y veniendo en pensamiento tres misas de la Trinidad para dar gracias, me parecía ser de mal espíritu; y determinando que ninguna, crecía mucho en amor divino, y tantas lágrimas y con tantos sollozos y fuerzas y de rodillas por mucho tiempo y paseando, y otra vez de rodillas <con gozo> con muchos, varios y diversos razonamientos y con tanta satisfacción interior, y aunque esta visitación tanto grande (que sentía notable dolor de ojos) durase por espacio de una hora, poco más o menos, tandem cesando lágrimas y dubitando <si cesaría> si concluiría a la noche con semejante afluencia si hallase, o agora. (267–8)

[148] And with this the shadows began to leave me gradatim, and to come tears, and with these increasing, I lost all will for more masses to this end, and coming into my thoughts three masses of the Trinity to give thanks, they seemed to be from a bad spirit; and deciding on none, the divine love grew greatly, and so many tears and with so many sobs and force and kneeling for a long time and walking, and again kneeling <with joy> with many, diverse and varied arguments and with so much interior satisfaction, and although this visitation so much great (that I felt a notable pain in my eyes) lasted for an hour, more or less, tandem the tears ceasing and doubting if I <would cease> would conclude that night with similar abundance if I so found it, or now.

By April of the same year, however, the entries are strictly notarial, registering only the presence and absence of tears. The language of affect, narrative, and the self disappears entirely: the result could easily be the log of a scientific experiment measuring the production of a protein or enzyme. From 31 August to 2 September, for example, he writes only:

> [331] 102.° .a. 1 d. El domingo. – Lo mismo, continuadas y con mucha abundancia.
> [332] 103.° .a. Lunes. – Antes de la misa con muchas lágrimas, y en ella sin ellas.
> [333] 104.° .a. l. Martes. – <Antes > <Después > Antes de la misa con lágrimas muchas, y en ella con algunas. (294)[60]

> [331] 102.° .a. 1 d. Sunday. – The same, continuously and with great abundance.
> [332] 103.° .a. Monday. – Before mass and with many tears, and during without.
> [333] 104.° .a. l. Tuesday. – <Before> <After> Before mass with tears many, and during with some.

The original manuscript is layered with Loyola's own notations, cross-outs, and additions, evidence that Loyola was assiduous in re-reading and editing the manuscript. Loyola is reading both his text and his body for signs, and it is essential to measure those signs correctly, whether it be through the tears, joy/sorrow, or words.

I have included a brief description of this text in this chapter, as opposed to the chapter on the *autobiografía espiritual*, because of the crucial relationship that this text holds with Loyola's contemplative manual, which eventually became the spiritual touchstone of the Jesuit community. In the *Exercises*, the methods practiced on the self in this private, unknown text are codified and converted into a system for all Jesuits to practice. In the *Diario*, the author and reader are one and the same, and they can only be Ignacio. In the *Exercises*, Loyola splits the role of author and reader and erases the personal markers of his own identity and experience from both. The author becomes an impersonal voice of authority, while the reader can be any Jesuit wishing to purify his/her heart and soul. Likewise, the irregular, open-ended record of personal experiences is re-structured into a weekly system, which, although it is not meant to be followed exactly as written (in the prefatory notes to the spiritual director, Loyola notes that, depending on the individual, "in some cases … the Week needs to be shortened, and in others lengthened") should overall guide the practice of the exercises, which "ought to be completed in thirty days, more or less" (22; point 4).[61] There are also instructions as to the proper duration and time of day for each exercise: for the first week, for example, "The First Exercise will be made at midnight; the Second, immediately on rising in the morning; the Third, before or after Mass, at all events before dinner; the Fourth, about the time of Vespers; the Fifth, an hour before supper" (47; point 72). Again, there are prefatory comments that indicate a certain flexibility for these guidelines, for example, a different order for a penitent who is "uneducated or has a weak constitution" (27; point 18) or a modified version for those "involved in public affairs or pressing occupations" (27; point 19), but the very specification of different systems for different types of penitents suggests more rigidity than we find in Osuna or Laredo. Also, unlike in Osuna or Laredo, the guidelines are specifically directed to a spiritual director and not the penitent him/herself, further separating author and penitent and decreasing the latter's individual agency in charting his own spiritual path. The intimate, irregular dialogue we found in Osuna and Laredo is replaced by a consistent and impersonal address, intended not for a reader whose profile, if not his exact identity, is known, but instead for a wide and diverse audience that will include even non-readers.[62]

The systematized, structured nature of the *Exercises*, in contrast with the *Abecedarios* or the *Subida*, is evident in the very typographical arrangement of the text. Whereas the alphabetic or chronological system of the two Franciscan works is irregular, and only loosely imposed, the *Exercises* are, from start to finish, structured in a series of brief points that sketch out a chronological and internally coherent method, or praxis. Barthes remarks on the "incessant, painstaking, and almost obsessive" systematization of the text, in which "everything is immediately divided, subdivided, classified, numbered off in annotations, meditations, Weeks, points, exercises, mysteries, etc" (52). After setting out in methodical detail the five steps of a preparatory general examination of conscience, culminating in the confession and communion, the work of the exercises begins with "A meditation by using the three powers of the soul about the first, second, and third sins" and further subdivided into "a preparatory prayer and two preludes, three main points and a colloquy" (40; point 45). This same prayer and two preambles are to be applied to each of the successive meditations as well. The first preamble establishes Loyola's distinctive terminology and method of meditation: the "composition made by imagining the place" which, Loyola explains:

> will be to see in imagination the physical place where that which I want to contemplate is taking place. By physical place I mean, for instance, a temple or the mountain where Jesus Christ or our Lady happens to be, in accordance with the topic I desire to contemplate.
>
> When a contemplation or meditation is about something abstract and invisible, as in the present case about the sins, the composition will be to see in imagination and to consider my soul as imprisoned in this corruptible body, and my whole compound self as an exile in this valley [of tears] among brute animals. I mean, my whole self as composed of soul and body. (40; point 47)

This choreography of the faculties becomes even more precise and directed in later exercises, such as in the instructions for the fifth and final exercise of the first week, a meditation on hell:

> (66) *The First Point* will be to see with the eyes of the imagination the huge fires and, so to speak, the souls within the bodies full of fire.
>
> (67) *The Second Point.* In my imagination I will hear the wailing, the shrieking, the cries, and the blasphemies against our Lord and all his saints.
>
> (68) *The Third Point.* By my sense of smell I will perceive the smoke, the sulphur, the filth, and the rotting things.
>
> (69) *The Fourth Point.* By my sense of taste I will experience the bitter flavors of hell: tears, sadness, and the worm of conscience.
>
> (70) *The Fifth Point.* By my sense of touch, I will feel how the flames touch the souls and burn them.
>
> (71) *The Colloquy.* I will carry on a colloquy with Christ our Lord. I will call to mind the souls who are in hell: Some are there because they did not believe in Christ's coming; and others who, although they believed, did not act according to his commandments. I will group these persons into three classes:
>
> First, those lost before Christ came.
>
> Second, those condemned during his lifetime.
>
> Third, those lost after his life in the world.
>
> Thereupon, I will thank Christ because he has not, by ending my life, let me fall into any of these classes. I will also thank him because he has shown me, all through my life up to the present moment, so much pity and mercy. I will close with an Our Father. (46–7; points 65–71)

There are clear overlaps with the Franciscan manuals (as well as with Ludolph of Saxony's *Vita Christi*, as noted), most importantly in the interiorization of *devotio* and *imitatio*, but also the appeal to the senses in a way that both depends on and is incompatible with human sensory faculties, and the insertion of the self into a dialogue with a cosmic narrative. Yet the authorial voice here has total control of its subject matter; he is writing *about* mental prayer without the traces of the mystic process seeping into the text itself. Whether as an actual effect of mystic experiences during the writing process or as a deliberate strategy to evoke that-which-transcends-language, the earlier manuals reproduce the transgression of the *logos* within the text, whereas the *Exercises* reassert the power of the word to coordinate and control the spirit.[63]

The *Exercises* and the *Diario* diverge from the mysticism of the *Abecedarios* and the *Subida*, but in different directions: the *Diario* so completely renounces all claims to legibility, to communication between humans through language, that it has no place in a discursive economy. It has no use because it has, and can have, no reader; it is the bare shell of a text, the traces left by an affective spirituality that was not put into words. It is systematic, insofar as Loyola seems to have had a system in his graphic notations and lachrymal measurements, but only Loyola retained the key to that system. The diary was not meant to circulate except within Loyola's own spirit and process; the only response to the *Diario* was the *Exercises*. The *Exercises* thus are born from mystic experience and may be conducive among certain practitioners to mystic experience, but the register of that experience – the tears, the illegible signs and other markers of *lo místico* – are erased from the text itself, subsumed into *la mística*.

The different fortunes of the two Ignatian texts is evidence of the direct relationship between the "democratization" of mental prayer, as Armando Puig Pegbó has termed it, and its de-mystification. The *Diario* represents an extreme case – a text with a readership of one. But as we have seen, the earliest Spanish vernacular *libros de oración mental*, such as those of Osuna and Laredo, were mostly written with the anticipation that they would be read by fellow Franciscan friars and monks, or perhaps women under the direction of the same, whose formation and basic life experiences were the same as those of the authors. The homogeneity of their circumstances permitted a relatively stable and predictable interpretation, and the institutional setting of the monastery automatically created mechanisms to control and correct any interpretations that might depart from the expected parameters. The Jesuits, in making the *Exercises* a lynchpin of their missionary and educational activities, were sending their doctrine out into a world of women, new Christians, non-Europeans, and the illiterate, and in order to guarantee that, either out of ignorance or malice, this public did not misinterpret the texts and the doctrines being introduced, it was necessary to eliminate the intensely personal, individual, and interior dimension emphasized in the Franciscan manuals. This could be accomplished in two ways, from outside the text – the creation of institutions to guide and control the practice of the exercises (the schools, the missions, the directed retreats) – and from within the text, in all the ways we have seen.[64] The Jesuits quickly and effectively controlled the interpretation of the *Exercises*, and this is why the Jesuit order is rarely included in discussions of mysticism. Yet the Franciscans (and to a lesser extent some of the other orders) were not so immediately wary about the possibilities of the unregulated circulation of their manuals. They seem not to have anticipated the popularity that mental prayer and spiritual autobiography would have found not just among cloistered men but among the laity and among women (not just nuns, but *beatas* and even lay women), and more importantly, the diversity of ways that their texts might be read and experienced among these groups. The Jesuits, it seems, as a new order, were able to create the textual and institutional mechanisms to monitor the interiority of their followers, whereas the older orders were caught somewhat unawares, with the horse already out of the barn door. The reactive attempt to rein in the spirituality that the earlier works had cultivated explains the post-Trent fortunes of these texts and, more importantly, the nature of the next generation of books of *oración mental*.

Recogimiento and the *Index*

All the texts from the first period of *libros de oración mental* were, after Trent and after the *alumbrado* heresy had been "identified," submitted to Inquisitional scrutiny, and many were outright prohibited,[65] while other authors were forced to amend or add to the texts. Terence O'Reilly theorizes the probable censorship or pressure behind Fray Luis de Granada's failure to produce the promised third part of his *Libro de oración*, which, according to Granada's outline of his project as laid out in his introduction, would consist of "diversas oraciones y meditaciones, unas para antes de confesión, otras para antes y después de la comunión, otras para calentar y ejercitar el corazón en el amor de Dios, y así otras semejantes" (648) ("diverse prayers and meditations, some for before confession, others for before and after communion, others to heat up and exercise the heart in the love of God, and so forth"). This third part, which never materialized, would have, in O'Reilly's reading, "made it a handbook for contemplatives, like the *Exercitatorio* of Cisneros but directed to Christians in general." When the volume was published in 1554, without the third part, Granada claimed he ran out of space, but in 1555 he reissued the work with a third part included, "but instead of the prayers he had promised he provided three sermons on mental prayer not lyrical but didactic in tone," leading O'Reilly to conclude that his motives were "more complex" than he let on ("Meditation and Contemplation" 49). While Osuna's *Tercer Abecedario* and Laredo's *Subida* were never placed on the *Índice*, it is likely that Osuna's delays in the publication of the later volumes were tied to the change in the theological climate, and it is impossible not to read the subtext of the controversies around the *alumbrados* in numerous passages of both authors.

Laredo's work, structured as it is according to the three stages of mysticism, ends in the highest and thus most controversial stages of mystic union. Laredo, while emphasizing that he has not himself experienced *arrobos*, stridently defends that they are real and to be desired. After the theological discussion of the *arrobo*, analysed earlier in this chapter, he changes tone completely, leaving behind the poetical-mystical and choreography of scriptural texts, and speaking frankly, in first person, of his "necesidad de satisfacerme de ciertas dudas" (III, 41, 597) ("feeling the need of satisfying myself about certain problems" [259]). The chapter takes on a narrative element, as he seeks out a variety of interlocutors to discuss the matter, ranging from "un aventajado teólogo, muy amigo de virtud y en la lición de sus letras" (597) ("a skilled theologian who was greatly given to virtue and in the duties entailed by his learning" [259–60]), to someone who "lo sabía muy bien" because "me dijo que había bien veinticinco años que no habían pasado entre todos ni diez noches que no estuviese su ánima arrobada" (599) ("someone who knew much about it because for fully five-and-twenty years there had not been as many as ten nights on which his soul had not been enraptured" [262–3]); and even "una mujercita que yo conocía, a la cual muchas veces sé que falta una sardina para comer con el pan" (597) ("a poor woman of my acquaintance who, I know, has often not so much as a sardine to eat with her bread" [260]).[66] All confirm for him, from their diverse perspectives, that scholarly erudition is entirely independent of mystical experience.

The inclusion of the *mujercita* is interesting, given that Laredo lived an ascetic and isolated life in a Franciscan monastery and wrote for his fellow brothers. This *mujercita* was never his intended reader or audience, but by the time the *Subida* was published, the scandal of the *alumbrados* had made it clear that mental prayer had gone far beyond his initial intended audience of fellow Franciscans. It became impossible to defend the doctrine without addressing the possible repercussions in the world of lay practitioners. Thus he must include one representative example to defend against those who would censor the *Subida*, not because of inherently heretical doctrine but for the possibility of its misinterpretation, via chains of unknowable transmission, among those *sin letras*. He provides examples of the behaviours that the skeptics of mental prayer used as proof of heresy – frequent communion, dramatic *arrobos*, even revelations – and in each case defends their legitimacy.[67]

This series of consultations can only be understood as a defense of *oración mental* from all the accusations it faced by the time of Laredo's publication. He chooses for his supposed interlocutors individuals from the most diametrically opposed groups – a distinguished theologian, someone who experiences dramatic corporeal effects of extasis, an uneducated laywoman – to counter each point. They show that the circulation of mystic doctrine broadly throughout society does not represent any threat to the Church, but instead strengthens the faith of the laity and their support for the Church. Instead of a threat to the Catholic hierarchy or a steppingstone toward Protestantism, mystic contemplation becomes a bulwark against the encroachment of Protestantism or *alumbradismo*. Laredo concludes by reminding his sceptics of the scriptural support for "letras interiores": "bien se verifica la autoridad evangélica que muestra que a los pequeñitos revela nuestro Señor lo que a los sabios muy muchas veces se esconde" (598) ("interior learning … is confirm[ed by] that passage in the Gospels which shows how Our Lord oftentimes hides from the wise that which He reveals to babes" [260–1]). And with respect to the violent physicality of some raptures, Laredo reminds his reader that "algunas veces no podían disimular aun los santos que salían en públicos y clamorosos suspiros" (601) ("at times even the saints could not dissemble but heaved sighs and cries in public" [266]). Those who get carried away with "medio arrobamientos" ("semi-raptures") need only be laughed at; it is the sceptic who holds a "falsa opinión" and is thus the heretic (438).

As we have seen, Osuna too takes great pains to separate his proposed spiritual methods from those that, by the time he published his *Abecedarios*, had been condemned. In large measure, he bases the difference between his method (*recogimiento*) and the condemned *dejamiento* in etymology, as if by proposing a new word he could prove that he had created a new practice. His most concentrated response to those who associated all *oración mental* with *alumbradismo* comes in Tratado V of the *Tercer Abecedario*, where he is strident in his defense of the practice, even in the light of its possible abuses. Like Laredo, Osuna creates an exemplary first-person narrative, although his exemplary interlocutors include a skeptic. He recounts that he had come across a book of mental prayer (the artifice of including such a passage *within* a *libro de oración mental* is manifest), "que cierto despert[ó] harto mi tibieza al amor del Señor, y fui a un letrado a se lo alabar por útil y provechoso" ("Once, having read a book about very devout things that undoubtedly roused me from my lukewarmness to love for God, I consulted a learned person, expecting he would praise the book as useful and profitable" [144]) only to find that the *letrado* condemned the book, exclaiming "'¡Oh cuántos ha de llevar ese libro al infierno!'" (V.2.184) ("'O how many souls this book will carry to hell!'" [144]). Osuna, "espantado" ("shocked") asks him to explain, and the *letrado* repeats the critique of the genre's sensuality, its use of sensory faculties to arrive at spiritual ones. Yet "del mismo libro habló otra persona devota a otro letrado, maestro de mucho saber e virtud, y respondió que él había leído aquel libro y había hallado en él todo lo bueno que de contemplación había visto" (V.2.185) ("When someone else spoke about the same book with another learned man, that person, a master of much knowledge and virtue, responded that he had read the book and found that it condensed everything good that had been written down about contemplation in other treatises" [144]). Having laid out the controversy in these two representative opinions, Osuna steps in and offers the reader his judgment to the imagined reader: "En este contrario parecer de estos dos letrados puedes tomar aviso para tu examen, y no creerte de ligero porque uno te diga mal de las cosas devotas. Si en algún libro leyeres que te has de guardar de las personas que tienen arrobamientos, como si tuviesen rabiamientos, tampoco lo creas" (V.2.185) ("Take warning from these opposite opinions of scholars for your own examination and do not be anxious to believe the reasons the one gives for calling devout things evil. If you were to read in some book that you must not associate with people who experience rapture, as if they were raving mad, you would not believe that either" [144–5]). He cannot defend the *alumbrados*, but he clearly wishes to save the holy bathwater. He cites numerous scriptural and hagiographic examples of saints who experienced ecstasy and were judged to be possessed or crazy, and, like Laredo, converts the critique of the ecstatic into a critique of the sceptic, whose doubts arise not from theological rigour but from incomprehension or, he even suggests, jealousy.[68] He acknowledges that it is preferable to limit the external manifestations of interior gifts "si se puede hacer sin perjuicio de la devoción verdadera" ("provided that does not impair true devotion"), but in the end:

> No es en el poder y mando del hombre vedar el espíritu … Cuando alguno tiene en el seno de su corazón a Dios, que se llama fuego gastador de nuestros males, no es maravilla que el ardor del amor que dentro obra se

muestre en la vestidura exterior del ánima, que es el cuerpo, en el cual se causan diversos movimientos. Pues que así es, hermano, toma el consejo de nuestra letra, que te dice haber de tener cargo de examinar bien tus interiores movimientos y obras, para que no temas el examen de los hombres. (V.2.186)

"It is not in the power or province of man to stop the spirit." [Eccles. 8:8] ... When God, who is the fire consuming our evil, is in the breast of the heart, it is not amazing that the heat of love working within is revealed on the exterior garments of the soul; that is, that it cause divine movements in the body. Since this is so, brother, heed the advice of our letter, which admonishes you to bear the burden of examining carefully your inner works and movements so you will not fear being questioned by men. [146]

The reader is assumed to have good intentions and thus can be trusted with his own self-discernment, apart from the nascent "ciencia" of discernment that, Osuna clearly suggests, is misguided and incapable of seeing into the soul of another.

This question of examining, or discerning, the spirits of others,[69] dismissed here by Osuna and only briefly mentioned in the final chapter of Laredo, moves to the forefront of the majority of books of mental prayer written in the post-Tridentine era. The entire genre of discernment manuals which spring up in the post-Tridentine era is clearly a response to the interiority cultivated – created – by the earlier *libros de oración mental*. These discernment manuals are not mystic texts in themselves but a complementary discourse produced to de-mystify the earlier works. Not all the discernment manuals are hostile to mental prayer or interior spirituality; there is a wide range of attitudes towards the practice in theory, but all the manuals shift from the earlier genre's focus on the cultivation of the reader's first-person interiorized spirituality to a diagnosis of a third person's interior space. The discernment manual is never written for *self*-discernment;[70] the reader cannot be trusted to discern his own spirit because the spirit may be demonic or fraudulent – indeed, this seems to be the default assumption of the authors – and thus the person who requires discernment is automatically the person who will not seek it out. The *manual de discernimiento*, often inserted into a manual for confessors, represents the institutional Church's re-appropriation of the interior space, the imposition of an authority and a system (*la mística*) on a space of ambiguity (*lo místico*). Where the mystic manual uses paradox, ambiguity, and the extra-rational possibilities of language and the hidden as a tool for representing and cultivating spirituality, the discernment manual sees paradox, ambiguity, and the non-visible or non-rational as impediments. Even the manuals that recommend confessors encourage mental prayer among their flock pay extensive attention to the possibility of unconscious deception. Osuna and Laredo assume that the individual with good intentions will be able to recognize demonic temptation and that, in the end, the devil cannot do much against a soul dedicated to virtue. In the post-Tridentine era, the assumption is rather the reverse: that even the most sincere penitents can be deceived and damned by the devil.

Besides the shift in perspective in these works that emphasize diagnosis over development, these works also adopt a different tone from the pre-Tridentine guides to mental prayer. The Index established with a certain degree of security the theological lines of what could and could not be promulgated. The persecution of *alumbrados* and the censorship of texts that could be perceived as *alumbradista* put an end to a period of experimentation and pushing of boundaries. Those texts that had been approved were reprinted or repeated in newer texts. Meanwhile, academic theologians set out to rationalize, analyse, and systematize those earlier works that had been deemed orthodox. Thus while still advocating certain practices of interior prayer conducive to mystic union, the later manuals cease to be works that struggle with representation or that seek to produce a mystic language.[71] Yet mysticism hardly disappeared from Spanish literary discourse with the introduction of the Index. On the contrary, most of the authors we think of as the great Spanish mystics wrote in the period of 1560–1600 (the period Melquíades Andrés denotes as the "cima"). What changed was the *genre*. The singular focus of Juan Valdés's Index with *los libros de oración mental* closed off this avenue for an exploration of *lo místico*.[72] The Index supposed a break between the *system* and the *poem*, two components which, as we have seen, coexisted in permanent productive tension in Laredo, Osuna, and their contemporaries. The post-Index mystics would have to reserve their deepest mystic sentiments for lyric poetry, a genre that circulated almost exclusively in manuscript form and even when printed was rarely the focus of censorship.

At the same time, the success and popularity of the books of *devotio moderna*, before their suppression, meant that new subjects – lay people, women, the poor – had assimilated their ideas and were attempting to follow their guidelines. These new subjects represented a threat and a promise to the more orthodox and elite arm of the Church, and in response, Church authorities developed new measures for trying to guide these new would-be mystics. As part of this process, a new genre was born: the spiritual autobiography. These works, unlike Loyola's diary, were in theory compelled texts with a strictly pragmatic purpose: for the confessor authority to judge and guide the interior life of the (almost always female) penitent with interior spiritual gifts. Yet immediately the *autobiografías por mandato* became something else: a rich, complex mystic genre in their own right. The very same impulse that "killed" the *libro de oración mental* was also the catalyst for the new channel of mystic discourse: by seeking to *discern* the spirits of a new class of would-be mystic penitents, the Church compelled them to write, and to write a new form of mysticism.

Chapter Two

Mystic Poetry

Despite being written in prose, the treatises on mental prayer examined in chapter one, as we have seen, rely on linguistic techniques associated with lyric poetry. Indeed, mysticism has long been associated with poetry. As María Jesús Mancho Duque explains, "There exists a general consensus among critics who specialize in mystic literature that the only way to express the ineffable is through poetic language" (132).[1] However, "poetic language" is a broad term, and, as we have seen, poetic language can be inserted into prose. In this chapter, we will examine the poetry of the best-known Spanish mystic poets, but rather than assume mysticism's affinity with poetry, we will step back to consider the relation between poetic *language*, poetic *form*, and mystic discourse. Crucial to our study will be an analysis not just of the poems as works of art or expressions of an authorial vision but as textual objects produced, interpreted, and shared in communities, coexisting alongside (and at times integrated directly into) other textual forms. An analysis of the discursive context in which poetic language about mystic union circulates and sometimes, but not always, coheres into discrete poetic works signed by a single author, challenges assumptions about the essential unity of poetry and mysticism, and helps us understand why the "Big 3" (Santa Teresa, San Juan de la Cruz, Luis de León) mystic poets emerge when and where they do. In sum, it considers how we read them if they are not *a priori* designated as "literature" and elevated (or in the case of my library, lowered) onto a different shelf from manuals of mental prayer or Inquisition cases, and also *why* they came to be differentiated from those other forms in the time and place they did.

Poetry and Mysticism

To show that the expression of mystic experience in poetry is a choice conditioned by socio-historic circumstances, we must first show why mysticsm is not *essentially* poetic, as Mancho Duque and others assume. Emilio Orozco Díaz, whose works are collected in a two-volume anthology called precisely *Poesía y mística*, makes the most forceful case for the confluence of mysticism and poetry, arguing that they represent "two experiences, diverse in nature, but analogous as forms of knowledge" (59). Yet the association between poetry (understood here in the premodern sense of a literary form with a set meter) and mysticism does not, at first glance, hold up to historical scrutiny. Almost none of the medieval Christian mystics were best known for their poetry, and most wrote no poetry at all. The most common form of Christian mystical writing during the medieval period was the scriptural treatise, written in Latin. Women were more likely to write accounts of visions that they composed in various forms: prose narrative, dialogues, sometimes song. Still, the main role of poetry was not in the form of the writing itself but in the centrality of the Song of Songs (*Cantar de los Cantares*), a densely symbolic eroticized poetic dialogue between the Bride and Bridegroom, to mystic prose.[2] Much of the scriptural exegesis of the university-trained mystics takes the form of commentary on the *Cantar*, whereas female mystics tend to appropriate the language of eroticized spiritual devotion to represent their visions.[3]

Part of the problem with critical arguments about the relationship between mysticism and poetry has to do with a historically imprecise definition of "poetry." When Orozco Díaz says that the poet and the mystic overlap in their pursuit of a truth beyond rational inquiry, he is referring only to *lyric* poetry. While today almost all poetry is lyric poetry, we should not forget that in the medieval period, lyric poetic activity represented a small part of the poetic tradition in the Christian West. Certainly, the *romancero* and *mester de clerecía* tradition provide ample evidence of a poetry that favours exposition and clarity over intuition or transcendence. Devotional songs, such as those compiled in the *Cantigas*, are strictly celebratory; the words praise the heavenly figure without exploring the relationship to the singer/author's own human subjective self. It was not until the fifteenth century that the short lyric *canciones* developed into a vital genre and there developed, almost simultaneously, a tradition of spiritualizing these love laments in the genre known as the *contrafactum* (because the poems are "contrahechos a lo divino"). Even so, the majority of the *canciones espirituales* emphasize repetition and basic doctrinal points, rather than exploring mystic union.[4] It is the Petrarchan influence, which does not arrive in Castilian poetry until the 1530s, that shifts emphasis to subjective experience and artistry of the individual, the same impulses behind the movement to an interiorized mysticism. Introspective poetry and introspective spirituality grow from the same humanist impulse; "poetry" itself is no more essentially "mystic" than is theology.

The definition of poetry assumed by Orozco Díaz and others is thus an anachronistic one. Its roots lie in the Petrarchan lyric, but the idea that poetry is by definition concerned with hidden essences is in fact even later, arriving with the Romantics. This is the definition of poetry that Bécquer imagines in his "Rima IV": "Mientras haya un misterio para el hombre,/ ¡Habrá poesía!" (v. 19–20) ("As long as mystery faces man,/ There shall be poetry!" [19][5]). But this equivalence between poetry and the hidden or ineffable did not exist when San Juan et al. were writing; on the contrary, the mystic poets – "rediscovered" and championed by the Romantics – were essential in creating that association. This is the "after" moment in de Certeau's history of mysticism, when, in the eighteenth century, the two fields that the mystics themselves had joined – science and the ineffable – separate again, into experimental science on the one hand and poetry on the other.[6] If Orozco Díaz finds a religious element in secular poetry, it is precisely because Romantic poets adapted and secularized the language of mysticism.

Bécquer's poem, which finds poetry in nature or a kiss rather than in a literary form, points to another problem in the standard understanding of the relation between poetic aims and poetic form. Orozco sees the overlap of poet and mystic in their intentions rather than necessarily in their formal written production. However, he argues that the similarity at the root of the search leads both types of writer to similar linguistic solutions:

> S/he needs a language in which the word and the phrase do not have an exactly precise meaning, that cannot be translated and substituted literally, like that which represents an idea or a concrete object in reality: in sum, s/he needs a literary language, a language in which the phrases – to use a term coined by Matila Ghyka – are endowed with a *lyric charge* … poetic language is a necessity for the mystic's expression. (90–1)

The mystic must speak in a specific sort of poetic language. "In order to convey meaning and make him/herself understood, he/she must recur to all sorts of artifices: simile, antithesis, paradox, hyperbole" (73–4). The motive behind the employment of these poetic devices in the *cancionero* is not necessarily a desire to convey otherness or transcend reality – much of the virtuoso linguistic games in the *amor cortés* (courtly love) tradition respond to an aristocratic impulse to separate a noble, elite poetic style from the popular *romancero* and *cancionero* – but the mystic poet, according to this argument, finds in the poetic devices that invert or disrupt "natural" (strictly communicative) syntax a way to convey the extra-rational mystic encounter. In this way, "a style, like that of the *cancionero*, whose essential structure is its artifice and verbal play, comes to be the expression of the deepest and most transcendent feeling" (76).

Since the mystic experience is ineffable, it cannot be described directly. While some mystic writers emphasize the indescribability of the experience, all, to some extent, must rely on comparisons and imagery to give an approximate idea of what union is *like*, since they cannot say what it *is*. Thus the mystic, like the poet, relies on simile, metaphor, and symbol. Furthermore, the mystic tends to make use of a language of the senses and emotions as an alternative to an appeal to the intellectual, rational faculties. Again, this brings the mystic towards the poet, although again it should be emphasized that these generalizations about poetry do not apply to all early modern verse.[7] The only element of poetic expression that is *definitive* of all poetry in the early modern period is the employment of a relatively fixed rhyme and/or metrical system, with its roots in the musical origins of poetry. The Neoplatonists argued that musical harmonies were a sign of a larger cosmic harmony, and thus "the Pythagoran-Platonic theory ... attributed to music the power to awaken in the soul the memory or recognition of the celestial harmonies it heard before existing in the world, before it had separated from God" (Orozco Díaz 125). Fray Luis includes this claim in his *Oda* to the musician Pedro Salinas, whose music ("son divino") causes "el alma, que en olvido está sumida/ torna a cobrar el tino/ y memoria perdida/ de su origen primera esclarecida" (7–10) ("my soul, submerged in its oblivion,/ recovers sense and long/ forgotten memory in/ its dazzling and primordial origin" [45][8]). In this way, the musical elements of poetry can also be seen as growing from a mystic impulse, but by this definition all early modern music and poetry would be inherently mystical.

While we have seen that poetry is hardly the *necessary* form for mystic expression, it still might seem that lyric poetry is the most *appropriate* form: it is the only form that can convey both visual and auditory harmony; it is historically the genre most open to linguistic innovation and the concentrated use of sensorial imagery and figurative language (symbol and metaphor); and since Aristotle, it has been elevated above the other forms of rhetorical expression for its ability to convey beauty and truth. Yet there are also elements of the poetic form and the role of poetry, as it was conceived in the early modern period, that argue against the lyric expression of mystic experiences. The idea of the mystic-as-poet depends on a Romantic conception of the poet as *individual*, one who experiences the transcendent in solitude and writes it for him or herself, in a natural and spontaneous outpouring of feeling. Ironically, this Romantic concept of the poet is rather more applicable to the medieval mystics than to the early modern ones because more medieval mystics were ascetics, living in isolation, or cloistered religious living in small communities of like-minded individuals.[9] Prior to the invention of the printing press, their ideas did not spread far and thus did not tend to affect religious practices on a large scale. It is the great paradox (although in no way a coincidence) of the early modern period that the modern individual self should be born at the same time as the birth of modern institutions, bureaucracies, and systems of vigilance and control of that individual self. The print revolution meant that theological ideas and expression could circulate much more widely, and this represented a great possibility and a great threat, depending on the particular ideas and interests expressed. The wave of spiritual renovation that sparked such a remarkable number of contemplative treatises, as discussed in chapter one, can be explained by the desire to spread mystical teachings beyond an intimate circle. The early sixteenth-century authors still wrote for a relatively for reduced and relatively homogeneous readership of fellow religious men, but they aspired to share their ideas to brothers across Spain, and thus wished to take advantage of print technology. There existed no tradition of living authors publishing their own poetry because poetry was rooted in music and orality. To access print, they had to conform to the genres deemed acceptable for print works. Thus, instead of publishing collections of mystic poetry, they published prose works but injected them with "un lenguaje poético," preserving their poetic aims (*lo místico*) without adopting poetic form. In the first third of the sixteenth century, printed prose texts could accommodate this linguistic, formal, and theological experimentation.

To understand the role that poetry played for the pre-Trent (pre-Index) mystics, we can turn to Osuna's *Abecedarios*, which, as we have seen, are prose treatises that incorporate many aspects of "lenguaje poético," but the treatises also include several poetic *abecedarios*, a poetic genre of roughly 23 lines, each beginning with a consecutive letter of the alphabet. These poetic works thus repeat, in condensed form, the macro-structure of the treatise. In 2013, Estelle Garbay-Velázquez published her discovery of three verse *abecedarios* in in MSS/74 in the Biblioteca Nacional de España, "an extensive anthology of letters and mystic miscellanea put together by an anonymous compiler in the sixteenth century" ("La circulación manuscrita" 197). While the poems in the manuscript are not signed, they are nearly identical to those Osuna includes, leading her to conclude that they are the ones he used for the *Abecedarios espirituales* and that, in addition, he was most likely the author (197–9). What is striking here is the independent *manuscript* circulation of the poems (never published independently) and their printed insertion into the *Abecedarios*. As Garbay-Velázquez writes, "they thus constitute an unprecedented example of the manuscript circulation of [Osuna's] poetry of a spiritual nature, which to this point has only been known through his published works" (197). Print in this early period was not deemed appropriate for the poetry of living authors, but prior to Trent, prose was more than capable of incorporating poetry, both at the level of form and content.

As is not uncommon with early appropriation of new technologies, the early print works retain many aspects of manuscript tradition.[10] Writers such as Osuna and Laredo sought to publish their works precisely because of the possibilities for a wider circulation than possible in manuscript, but at the same time, as was discussed in chapter one, the authorial voice still seems to expect a homogenous and intimate readership. The realities of a print circulation that would extend beyond monastic communities, whose interpretations could be predicted and guided, inevitably provoked anxiety amongst authorities. These officials did not necessarily seek to suppress all forms of interiorized spirituality, but they wanted to ensure social stability and thus sought to insert mechanisms of interpretative guidance into the new ways that individuals were accessing ideas. The most important mechanism introduced to this end was the Index and the creation of a censorship bureaucracy run by the Spanish Inquisition. To receive the necessary license for printing, book manuscripts would now be screened by censors, whose principal concern was to ensure their doctrinal clarity and orthodoxy. Precisely because contemplative prayer treatises elevated experience over *letras*, and thus always contained a latent threat of justifying unauthorized interpretations (implicitly authorizing each reader to interpret the *letras* of the text in his/her own way), these manuscripts were subjected to particularly strict scrutiny. Censors in many cases denied licenses or required modifications to texts not just on the basis of outright heretical doctrines, but out of concern for *possible* misinterpretation. Opaque, figurative, and ambiguous messages – the hallmarks of poetic language – ran afoul of the censors' demand for clarity. Yet the exclusive focus of the Inquisition on *print* created an interesting "loophole": poetry, which had seemed an inauspicious genre for transmitting mystic contemplative practice precisely because of its orality and manuscript transmission, suddenly became an ideal genre for transmitting mystic ideas precisely because of this same exclusion from print culture. Poems, copied by hand or transmitted orally, could be ambiguous, opaque, and transgressive without being subject to the censors' scrutiny.

Thus a technological change (print) led to an institutional change (the *Índices*) and finally led to a change in the *generic* representation of *lo místico*. Contemplative prayer treatises continued to be published after Trent, but the innovative energy of the earlier generation of manuals moved elsewhere. Returning to de Certeau's terminology, we see the prose treatises moving from *lo místico* to *la mística*. "Lo místico" meanwhile, did not disappear, but was instead transplanted to the great Spanish mystic poets, all of whom wrote *after* the Council of Trent. This shift was neither complete nor without repercussions, and this chapter will trace the changing relationship between poetic language and form, mystic theology, and circles of reception/interpretation from roughly 1550 to 1650.

While I will examine a variety of authors, San Juan de la Cruz will receive particular attention, as he is generally considered the paradigmatic mystic poet: perhaps the only figure of the century whose work has been equally valued for its artistic and its spiritual merits. Furthermore, the fact that he wrote prose commentaries to each of his major poems makes him a particularly suitable figure for studying the way mystic language flowed between and at the same time shaped genres. His poetry has been amply studied by literary scholars, but the anachronistic focus on the poems in Romantic terms – as singular and self-sufficient works of artistic genius – has obscured an understanding of how the poems functioned in a social context, where they were just one of many competing or coexisting forms for the expression of ideas. Furthermore, the obsession with finding the "origins" of one or another symbol used by mystics, which has characterized much work on San Juan de la Cruz's poems, obscures the degree to which the same symbols, embedded in different discourses or circulating within different interpretative communities, can function entirely differently.[11] While conceding that "originality" is an essential element of a symbol's mystical potential, I argue that the very same symbol, and indeed the very same words, can *become* original when placed in a new text or a new context. This chapter thus considers San Juan's poems as objects that make old words do new things by locating them within an unfamiliar discursive landscape. It is thus an interrogation not only of San Juan's poetry, but of the shifting relationship between poetic form and "lenguaje poético," the shifting function of poetry in an economy of words and ideas.

Figurative Language

While it is perhaps impossible to pinpoint a singular defining characteristic of poetic language, the basic element differentiating poetic from prosaic expression is the frequent use of figurative language.[12] Because the mystic experience is *ineffable*, its representation can never be direct, and thus figurative language is inevitable. In general, attempts to represent mystic experience go in two directions: one, an attempt to explain through comparison, the other, an attempt to obscure comparison. (Of course, the act of expression itself implies a certain attempt at communication; a truly negative mystic would renounce writing entirely.) In the analysis of poetic language, these two functions are often conflated, with no distinction made between the essentially clarifying function of the metaphor or simile and the obscuring or anti-representational function of the symbol or the paradox. It is true that the distinction is never clear-cut: there are metaphors that confuse and symbols that clarify. However, when analysing mystic poetry, it is particularly important to consider the opposing forces of representative and anti-representative poetic devices because the tension between affirmation and negation, clarity and darkness, is at the root of all mystic expression and, indeed, mystic theology. While the contradiction between a desire to compare and a desire to reject comparison is inherent in all mystic expression, no one foregrounds this (apparent) contradiction more than San Juan de la Cruz, who makes a sensual, imagery-rich poetry out of a vocabulary of night and darkness. As Orozco Díaz puts it, "his doctrine fundamentally entails the denial and rejection of all that is perceptible … He denies and rejects all things precisely to search for God, but then he chooses these things precisely to represent God. This creates a heightened valuation of all that is perceptible" (78).

The mystic poet who wishes to describe or make comprehensible the mystic journey relies on metaphor and simile because the mystic journey itself cannot be described, only approximated. In this sense, all mystic language, even the most prosaic and didactic, is metaphorical. But there are certain tropes common to lyric poetry that have additional resonance with the mystic experience. Since ancient times, nature and love (often intertwined) are also the predominant metaphoric languages for speaking of mystic union. Thus the language of romantic love and contemplation of nature already developed in a centuries-old tradition of oral poetry lent itself easily to an adaptation *a lo divino*, as Dámaso Alonso and Bruce Wardropper, among others, have shown. The use of natural imagery for supernatural themes has two theological justifications. According to the medieval concept of "the great chain of being," there was a harmony in all of God's creation, and the very contemplation of flora and fauna, God's lesser creatures, could and would lead naturally to the contemplation of the Creator Himself. As Jane Ackerman notes, by the sixteenth century, "faith in a coherent world that reflected God's powers and nature was coming under strain in places but still held firm inside the walls of contemplative monastic communities" (154). By this logic, evocation of the beauty and mystery of nature is not an end in itself, as it might be for the secular poet, but a prompt towards a perception of the beauty and nature of its creator. Yet even the evocation of beauty as an end in itself could be seen as having theological justification; since God is, in Christian doctrine, defined as the absolute source of beauty, the re-creation of beautiful images, sounds, and smells through words was a means for reproducing the experience of union with God in the mind of the reader/listener.

Of course, not every poem celebrating the beauty of nature as evidence of God's creation is a mystic poem. A poet may celebrate the beauty of the natural without connecting this visible beauty to the individual soul or an interior experience. A poem full of clear images, regular meter and rhyme, and/or a refrain, predisposes the reader/singer to repeat the words and accept their surface meaning, and thus is antithetical to any mystical, contemplative interpretation.[13] It is not my goal here to categorize any given author or poem as mystic or not, but to point out how similar natural imagery can, in combination with narrative and formal elements, express the experience of mystical union or serve other goals. We might begin with two poems by Fray Luis de León.[14] "Oda a la vida retirada" is a full of natural imagery and fits squarely in the Horacian tradition of *beautus ille* poems. The poetic voice, who flees from the "mundanal ruido," delights in the multisensory beauty of nature: a running brook, the gentle breeze, flowers, trees, birdsong. The brook winds through the trees,

el suelo de pasada
de verdura vistiendo,
y con diversas flores va esparciendo
El aire el huerto orea,
y ofrece mil olores al sentido,
los árboles menea
con un manso ruïdo,
que del oro y del cetro pone olvido. (53–60)

the ground between the groves/ decked out in green, and weaves/ a multitude of flowers over the leaves./ the wind flows through the fields/ and offers a thousand aromas to the sense;/ it sways the trees and yields/ a gentle sound that bends/ scepter and gold in dreamless somnolence.

The poem is in first person, and the poet ends the poem resting between those trees, "puesto el atento oído/ al son dulce, acordado" (83–4) ("my ear turned to those sweet/ concordant notes") of the music of nature. But this harmony with nature should not be confused with union with Nature's creator, and indeed an earlier line of the poem establishes that the poem's natural beauty hearkens to a pre-Christian worldview. The poet wishes to enjoy the "el bien que debo al cielo/ a solas, sin testigo/ libre de amor, de celo/ de odio, de esperanzas, de recelo" (37–9) ("the good I owe the skies,/ alone, and with no talkative/ friends, and free of lies,/ love, hatred, hopes or fear that might arise"). The foreswearing not just of hatred and rancor but also love and hope – all placing of the self outside the self – is a Stoic ideal, far from the proper Christian attitude of longing and love for the creator. Christian mysticism often overlaps with and aspires to asceticism, but they are not synonymous; the "Oda a la vida retirada" is an ascetic but not a mystical poem. The self-containment of the "Oda" is in marked contrast to the undeniably Christian sentiments of Fray Luis de León's "Noche serena." Here the setting is nocturnal, and the poet begins gazing to the vast heavens rather than celebrating his intimate surroundings.

> Quien mira el gran concierto
> de aquellos resplandores eternales,
> su movimiento cierto,
> sus pasos desiguales,
> y en proporción concorde tan iguales:
> la luna cómo mueve
> la plateada rueda, y va en pos de ella
> la luz do el saber llueve,
> y la graciosa estrella
> de Amor la sigue reluciente y bella; (41–50)

> Whoever sees the great/ concert of this eternal brilliancy,/ its movement straight/ with steps so oddly free/ yet all in a concordant symmetry,/ how the moon moves her silver/ wheel, where the light of comprehending rain,/ turns in pursuit of her/ how the star, gracious plain/ of love, follows dazzling its lovely train.

The image is clearly meant to remind of the unity of God's creation, and the language emphasizes the beauty of the moon ("plateada rueda") and stars ("graciosa … reluciente y bella"). The images are not entirely conventional, and the representation is not a simple question of describing visual sensations; for example, the joining of light, rain, and knowledge is unfamiliar and goes beyond basic visual description. Here a relationship is established between the individual and the divine cosmos, sustained through the gaze, but ultimately the emotion produced is one of distance. The poetic voice concludes that "quien mira" these celestial wonders can only look with disdain on earthly things, and necessarily must "gime y suspire/ por romper lo que encierra el alma" (63–4) ("sigh, moan and hope/ to break what is a band/ around the soul"). There is no union then, only the longing, the hope denied in the self-contained utopia of "Oda a la vida retirada." The choice of stars and moon, rather than plants and flowers, for the natural imagery is crucial; because the earth can only be a site of "bajeza" (lowness) and divine union is impossibly distant, the natural beauty of distant celestial realms is emphasized, and earthly nature is ignored.

If we look at San Juan de la Cruz's "Noche oscura," we see an integration of the beautiful natural imagery of "Oda a la vida retirada" with the transcendent, nocturnal setting of "Noche serena," an integration that parallels the mystic union – the union of earth and heaven – that the poem recounts. As Baruzi notes, this presents a conundrum for the poet: "How can one speak of images, when night represents their rejection? In effect, lyricism facilitates the creation of images whose very emergence constitutes a problem" (319). This is the problem of *all* mystic representation, since the moment of union defies representation, but here the problem is an almost literal question of seeing in the dark. San Juan de la Cruz's solution is to call on an interior light and to appeal to the non-visual senses. Through the repetition of negatives, he evokes the darkness that allies the poem with "Noche serena":

> En la noche dichosa,
> en secreto, que nadie me veía,
> ni yo miraba cosa,
> sin otra luz ni guía
> sino la que en el corazón ardía (v. 11–15)[15]

> On that glad night,/ In secret, for no one saw me,/ Nor did I look at anything,/ With no other light or guide/ Than the one that burned in my heart [295][16]

The last line interrupts the string of negations with an affirmation, the darkness is not complete because this inner light is, as the next verse explains, "más cierta que la luz del mediodía" ("more certain than the light of noon"[17]). From this point forwards, San Juan can use traditional light imagery and visual imagery and at the same time retain the mystic otherness of the experience, as he has established that the mode of seeing is other, it is a light that defies the laws of physical light or human vision. The poem ends in a situation not dissimilar to the final scene of "Oda la vida retirada," with the poet reclining amidst plants.

El aire de la almena,
cuando yo sus cabellos esparcía,
con su mano serena
en mi cuello hería,
y todos mis sentidos suspendía.

Quedéme y olvidéme,
el rostro recliné sobre el amado,
cesó todo, y dejéme,
dejando mi cuidado
entre las azucenas olvidado. (v. 31–40)

When the breeze blew from the turret/ Parting His hair,/ He wounded my neck/ With his gentle hand/ Suspending all my senses.

I abandoned and forgot myself,/ Laying my face on the Beloved;/ All things ceased; I went out from myself,/ Leaving my cares/ Forgotten among the lilies.

He has forgotten his cares, a state that recalls the yearned-for state of self-containment. However, here the poet is not alone but instead is accompanied by and at the same time transformed into the "amado." The presence of the Beloved is stated, while the union with the Beloved is indicated through the fluid use of personal pronouns. Furthermore, the use of verb tense makes it clear that the moment without "cuidados" exists in past and future, exists for eternity outside time, but cannot exist in a human present. I will return to these grammatical elements in the following section, but it is important to note how nearly identical imagery – not just the evocation of the *locus amoenus*, but the specific setting of the individual reclining between trees – can, depending on narrative, grammatical, and, as we will see later, extra-textual factors (the context of production and circulation of the poem) – produce divergent spiritual-philosophical messages.

One way poets emphasize the mystic quality of a beautiful image is by emphasizing the symbolic properties of natural elements, rather than merely evoking comparisons or beauty. In literary usage, metaphor and symbol are cousins, but they differ in the degree of specificity of application between the figure and the thing figured: "the metaphor ties a concrete image," whereas in the symbol, "its application is left open as an unstated suggestion."[18] Thus, when Teresa de Ávila says in the Nativity Poem "Ah, Pastores que veláis" ("Ah, Shepherds who watch")[19] that they must guard the new lamb that has been born, "que el lobo os le ha de llevar, sin que le hayamos gozado" (v. 7–8) ("for the wolf may carry Him away/ before we have enjoyed Him") it is explicitly stated that the "cordero" ("lamb") is "hijo de Dios soberano" ("Lamb"; "Son of God, most Sovereign!"), and by extension, the wolf can only be a symbol of God's enemies. Wolves certainly have other symbolic associations, but within the context of the poem, only their identity as killers-of-lambs is relevant. There is no epistemic surplus, no associations that remain unfulfilled or over-fulfilled within the poem. We can contrast this with the deer in San Juan's "Cántico espiritual," a loose translation of the Song of Songs. In the opening stanzas, the betrothed accuses her beloved: "Como el ciervo huiste/ habiéndome herido" (v. 3–4) ("You fled like the stag/ After wounding me"). The "como el ciervo huiste" would seem to be a simple simile based on the deer's speed in flight, but in the next line the deer becomes a predator, incompatible with the natural properties of a literal deer. Furthermore, later in the poem, the Esposo responds:

> Vuélvete, paloma,
> que el ciervo vulnerado
> por el otero asoma,
> al aire de tu vuelo, y fresco toma (v. 62–5)

> Return, dove,/ The wounded stag/ Is in sight on the hill,/ Cooled by the breeze of your flight.

Now the deer is the wounded party, and the relationship between the Esposo (speaker) and the deer is unclear. Furthermore, the deer/speaker enters in dialogue with a beloved/dove; each animal has its own symbolic registers, but there is no natural, literal correlation to the relationship between them. Unlike the wolf and sheep, whose relationship is empirically defined and long been recognized as a metaphor of predation, a dialogue between deer and dove has no clear antecedent in life or literature. This is the peculiarity of the symbol, what María Jesús Mancho Duque calls its "inexhaustible and peculiar semantic density" (21).

It may be a Romantic anachronism to say that the depth or density of the symbol makes it particularly "poetic," as this relies on a definition of poetry as the preferred medium for suggesting the "the hidden and mysterious relationships between things" (Orozco Díaz 59), but the conventions of reading poetry in the early modern period did allow for density and ambiguity that was not allowed in prose. The reader of the lyric poem does not judge its value based on the clarity of its message; to the contrary, lyric poetry, at least since Petrarch, has been valued for the depth and breadth of the concepts it evokes and the affect it produces. While one reader comes away from "En tanto que de rosa y azucena"[20] with the sense that the poet is sharing an ideal of female beauty and another that he is lamenting the inevitability of change, the debate occurs strictly within the realm of artistic interpretation. The secular lyric poem is judged based on classical criteria of beauty and emotional power, rather than either factual or ideological "truth." Furthermore, the poetic voice was not assumed to be autobiographical, nor was a poem's "worth" measured by its truth value; no one assumed Garcilaso had truly seen nymphs, nor did his admirers care particularly to discern the exact nature and extent of his relationship with the object of his poems of lost love. The secular lyric poem, as long as it does not pretend to transcend that category, was allowed to incorporate pagan gods and rather pre/un-Christian messages, such as the disavowal of hope or the embrace of extra-marital sexuality because, at least in the sixteenth century, the classical precepts for reading and writing poetry still dominated. Sentiments that, had they been expressed in prose would have surely been subject to censorship, could be published in the form of a poem. Censors demanded clarity and orthodoxy of prose but were willing to accept a greater degree of opacity and transgression in poetry.

Not all poetry aspires to opacity or mystery, but all mystic expression does. San Juan de la Cruz defined mystic knowledge as "sabiduría de Dios secreta o escondida, en la cual ... a oscura de todo lo sensitivo y natural, enseña a Dios ocultísima y secretísimamente el alma sin ella saber cómo" (*Comentarios* 39.12.682) ("the secret or hidden knowledge of God. In contemplation God teaches the soul very quietly and secretly, without its knowing how").[21] To convey mystery, it made sense that early modern poets would turn to a form where ambiguity and complexity were not only tolerated but, in the Baroque period, valued. In San Juan in particular natural images are used more as symbols than metaphors; as Orozco Díaz observes, he employs the basic building blocks of the *locus amoenus* not to "avoid realities with an increasing sense of beautification of the real" but instead to "emphasize concrete realities, paradoxically by uniting emotion in the face of the world of nature with a hidden, symbolic, transcendent meaning that also supposes its negation" (Orozco Díaz 198). The symbolic surplus (the elements of the symbol that exceed a simple application of x *stands for* y) of his poems are among the principal elements in the creation of what Colin Thompson, speaking of the "Cántico" in particular, calls "an overwhelming impression of mystery" (*Poet and the Mystic* 84). The dialogue of doves and deer, or the juxtaposition in a single poetic space of mountains, rivers, glens, and forests, "defies any attempt to form a coherent picture" (85). The symbol could almost be defined as a metaphor in motion, taken from its natural context and sent out on journey to form new associative networks, and thus it is particularly appropriate for the description of the mystic process.[22]

There is, of course, a precedent for this deeply symbolic, mysterious poetry: not in classical or Renaissance theory, but in the Song of Songs, upon which the "Cántico espiritual" is based. The symbolic complexity of the *Cantar* explains why, among all the biblical texts, it is the one to which mystic poets return with most frequency (Orozco Díaz 225). Still, the context of sixteenth-century Spain made this symbolic complexity a problem rather than an asset, as Fray Luis discovered when he translated the text.[23] San Juan was able to write the "Cántico" because it enters into a discursive network of poetry, rather than theology. Still, the poem's affinity with a theological discourse, one with its own rules for "legibility" (in the Foucauldian sense), meant that its symbols would have to respond to questions not asked of a Garcilaso sonnet. The result in San Juan's case was the commentary, to which we will return later in this chapter.

Disruption of Rational Processes

Employing sensory language represented one strategy for describing mystic experience, but mystic authors had to develop strategies to differentiate their evocation of sensory perception from ordinary sight, sound, smell, etc. One strategy was to place less emphasis on the sensory input itself and more on the experience of seeing, hearing, and smelling. Frequently, the disavowal of ordinary perception frames a poem, allowing the poet to make use of sensory images within. For example, Cecilia de Nacimiento's "Sin figura en la memoria"[24] begins with this rejection of visual imagery, only to describe the journey of the soul as a "pequeña mariposa" (v. 4) ("little butterfly") who is reborn a "Fénix hermosa" (6) ("lovely Phoenix"), inevitably calling on her own and the readers' memory to supply two visual "figuras," one tied to the natural world, the other to classical myth.

The strategy of negation of ordinary sense perception only frames the poem here, but in many other mystic works the negotiation between negation and affirmation of perception, either through the senses or the higher faculties, is a more fundamental element of the entire work. The movement of San Juan de la Cruz's "Coplas hechas sobre un éxtasis de harta contemplación" ("Stanzas concerning an Ecstasy Experienced in High Contemplation") is a vacillation between these two poles. He affirms that "grandes cosas entendí" (v. 4) ("I understood great things"), but a verse later, that "me quedé no sabiendo" (6) ("I remained in unknowing"). At the outset, he announces "no diré lo que sentí" (5) ("I shall not say what I felt") but by the end he describes mystic union as "un subido sentir/ de la divinal esencia" (52–3) ("the loftiest sense/

of the essence of God"). The mystic contradiction reaches its concentrated essence in the oxymorons that are repeated in these *coplas* and in so much mystic poetry: "no saber sabiendo" (47) ("knowledge in unknowing") "no entender entendiendo" (26, 41) ("the understanding of/while not understanding"), etc.[25] The oxymoron and paradox is inherited from the *cancionero* tradition, which abounds in love poems that mourn a present absence or a living death. Dámaso Alonso was the first to point out the *cancionero* roots of the famous paradox Teresa and others employ *a lo divino* in "Vivo sin vivir en mí."[26] What is important to note here is that the paradox is an acceptable form of poetic expression. A poet is not asked to be coherent or to speak with clarity: the poetic vogue of the day was quite the opposite. Thinking in Foucauldian terms, we can say that, within an established poetic discourse, oxymorons "made sense": rather than disrupting meaning, they conformed to expected patterns of meaning-making. The way to express inner conflict, or unresolved tension, was through the conjoining of two opposites.

Anyone reading the *Cancionero general*, the most important collection of *cancionero* poems in the fifteenth century, will note that the poems begin to blur together in their repetitive use of a limited number of antitheses and oxymorons. Most of the poems seem to be re-workings of the same set of ingredients. The principal obstacle, then, for the mystic poet who appropriates the oxymoron from the *cancionero* is not contradiction or opacity, but cliché. The mystic poem must impress upon its reader the incomparable, strange character of divine union; even as it draws from well-entrenched secular poetic traditions, it must announce its difference from any secular experience. While the "vivo muriendo" or "ausente presente" oxymorons that populate the *cancionero* may originally have produced this effect, by the mid-sixteenth century they had become "dead oxymorons" – the contradiction once produced by the dialectical pairing of opposites having been superseded by a synthesis. "Vivo muriendo" no longer produces an effect of strangeness or mystery, it becomes simply synonymous with anguish.

In many cases, mystic authors revitalize their language not through the invention of new images or symbols but through an interruption of accepted lexical usage or grammatical structures. No poet unsettled the clichés of devotional poetry more than San Juan de la Cruz. María Jesús Mancho Duque has focused on the techniques by which San Juan produces "extrañeza" (strangeness), beginning with his frequent use of the word itself, with ninety-two instances of "extraño" or some derivative in the Carmelite's work, both the poetry and the prose commentaries (76). She details how San Juan maintains the "extrañeza" of the word itself by shifting its semantic associations, its oppositions, and its lexical form. His method at the level of the word is thus the same as at the level of the symbol: a word or image is first employed clearly, and then experiences "a sort of significant progression in which the meanings gradually increase in density without ever losing or corrupting their original semantic nucleus" (142). Mancho Duque divides San Juan's use of "extraño" into three constellations (to use Baruzi's term): "strange/foreign/ withdrawn, separate, remote, solitary/ excellent, extraordinary, unusual, marvelous" until finally "*extraño* thus comes close to 'indescribable', 'mysterious', and ... brushes the threshold of 'ineffable,'" thus becoming a stand-in for the mystic experience itself, both in its meanings and in the instability of those meanings.

Mystic poets also produce strangeness by borrowing. Mancho Duque thus describes how San Juan "borrows words from other langauges, uses archaisms, and invents neologisms: *abisal, aprecio, balbucir, esforzoso, flagrancia, intencional, vibramiento* and many others – especially the abundant mystic technical terms: *coruscaciones, obumbración*"[27] (20). By and large, the words build from a known root, but either by shifting the part of speech or the prefix or suffix, they are de-familiarized, made strange. Mystic poets likewise inject an air of newness and strangeness into their poems though the use of unusual syntax and especially through the unusual use of pronouns. Again, we find a linguistic strategy that, in a sort of convergent evolution, emerges across various schools of poetry but responds to different "environmental" pressures. Whereas the disruption of natural syntax in *culteranos, conceptistas,* and mystics alike stems from a general desire to interrupt passive, unthinking reception, the motive for such interruption, the nature of the desired reception, and the specific syntactic or grammatical elements acted upon differ. In general, the *poeta conceptista* inverts or re-combines structures to provoke a heightened intellectual activity. The reader must use reason, the *ingenio*, to decipher the enigma and appreciate the *agudeza*.[28] As the word "agudeza" implies, the goal is to sharpen intellectual faculties. The mystic, on the other hand, seeks to represent an experience that circumvents rational faculties, using syntactic disruption to aid the reader in dulling his/her own processes of rational thought to access that extra-rational experience. Unlike *conceptos*, mystic contradictions are not intended to be solved or deciphered (although this did not keep church authorities from pushing for transparent, reductive explanations).

Furthermore, the mystic poet interrupts different elements of language than the *poeta culterano*. Góngora and his followers exercise the most extreme disruptions with nouns and adjectives, which both reflects the structure of Latin (particularly the use of declensions) and the strictly aesthetic ends of their poetry. Mystics were not interested in approximating biblical languages but instead sought to approximate the experience to which the Bible testifies: the union with the Holy Spirit. For this reason, they tend to operate on elements of meaning that, in the state of mystic union, are rendered meaningless: time and identity. The creation of an unfamiliar temporal space occurs through the juxtaposition of verbal tenses, suggesting a temporality that only makes sense to the divine. In "Noche oscura" ("The Dark Night" [295–296]) there is a symmetry; of the eight stanzas, the first, fifth, and eighth employ preterite, in Spanish reserved for completed actions in the past, while the rest feature the imperfect tense, reserved for progressive or repeated action. The fourth stanza speaks of the night "que guiaba" ("was guiding"); this same phrase interrupts the soul's journey in stanza five with the apostrophe to the "noche que me guiaste!" ("Oh, night that guided me!"[29]). One reading would be that the climax of union occurs in the centre of the poem and that this climax, no matter how many times the journey is repeated, is always singular, unrepeatable, and thus requires a preterite. The successive stanzas, in this reading, should recount the journey of the soul back to earth. Yet it is at the end of the seventh stanza that the lover's caress, or the wind, "todos mis sentidos suspendía" ("suspending all my senses"). The suspension of the earthly senses is characteristic of the moment of union; were the poet recounting a return to earth, he would experience a restoration of earthly senses, not their suspension. In the poem's last stanza, a total negation – of time, of self – marks the moment of maximum transcendence ("cesó todo, y dejéme" ["All things ceased; I went out from myself"]), but in a further paradox, the poem does not cease with "cesó todo" but instead lingers for two more lines that recall the "cuidados" left behind in earthly flowers. This apparent contradiction reflects the impossibility of writing while in the state of mystic union, which is no more possible than writing one's own death (or birth). There is thus a double chronology operating in and through the poem: the chronology of the poet and the chronology of the poetic voice, and the two can never be in sync. As Baruzi says of the *Subida*, but which applies to all of San Juan's work, "by the time he jots down the first lines … he has already achieved the perfection described in the final stanzas of the poem" (280). Rather than attempt to fuse this double chronology via a literary fiction, San Juan alternates between verb tenses to emphasize the ultimately unresolvable relationship between divine time(lessness) and human time.

In the more complex "Cántico espiritual," San Juan's adaptation of the biblical *Cantar*, the "bewildering variety of tenses and moods"

(Thompson *Poet and the Mystic* 85) is even more pronounced. The dialogic perspective of the poem places it in the present: Bride and Bridegroom speak in the present and exhort each other to actions in the future. However, the speakers refer to various events that occurred in a nebulous past, what Thompson characterizes as "the sixteenth-century equivalent of the modern cinematographic technique: flashbacks introduced without warning." He continues:

> No sequence of events can be followed except through small groups of stanzas, because the thematic progress of the poem is constantly being interrupted by glances into the future or past, and by fragments of conversations and comments. There is no ordered progression in time, place, or argument, except the very basic one that at the beginning the Bride is searching for her Beloved and at the end she is united with him. (86–7)

For Thompson, the temporal confusion in el "Cántico" is inseparable from the indeterminacy of place, speaker, and narrative, all part of the strategy to create the "overwhelming impression of mystery" (91). This confusion "mystifies" the reader and, indeed, this may be its purpose. The *Cantar* itself a strange, diverse poem full of ambiguities, explaining its popularity among mystics. However, San Juan may have felt that the biblical text had, through centuries of study and commentaries, settled into cliché. Certainly, the *beatus ille* setting had become commonplace. San Juan's introduction of a mysterious history between the lovers is one of the most notable departures from the biblical text, which is situated exclusively in the present and future. By moving a familiar setting into an uncertain time and place, where "ninfas de Judea" seem to coexist with Virgilian shepherds, San Juan makes the familiar elements fresh and unsettling. The purpose is not simply to prompt aesthetic appreciation; the de-settling "points beyond the words" (96) to a secret that is beyond words and human notions of time and place. Thus, despite never using the first person or recounting his own experience, the poet manages to provoke the same wonder and awe that characterizes the soul entering mystic union.

As we saw in the treatises examined in chapter one, the personal pronoun and point of view (first, second, third person) is another frequent source of grammatical destabilization in mystic poetry, since precisely what the mystic union erases is the clearly delineated Self. The uniformly first-person poems of Santa Teresa and the depersonalized poetry of San Juan de la Cruz could be seen as attacking the "problem" of the Self from opposite directions.[30] In normal speech, there is a clear relationship between the first-person subject and the first-person object, or between the subject pronoun and the reflexive pronoun. Santa Teresa's most famous poem, "Vivo sin vivir en mí" ("I live without living" [2–5]) takes a common Spanish expression (*estar fuera de sí* – to be out of one's mind, literally to be outside of oneself) and plays with it, restoring the strangeness of the relationship between the self and the self – the "yo" that lives and the "mí" in which that "yo" lives. The self splits into multiple parts – body and soul, self-with-God and self-on-Earth – that coexist in an uncomfortable relationship. In a standard prayer, the "Yo" addresses God as a "Tú"; the mystic union of self and God means that this apostrophe can become a monologue or a polyphony, as occurs at the end of "Vivo sin vivir en mí," as the speaker asks, "Vida, ¿qué puedo yo darle/ a mi Dios que vive en mí,/ si no es el perderte a ti,/ para merecer ganarle?" (v. 53–6) ("Life, what can I give to you,/ to my God, who lives in me,/ if it is not to lose you/ in order to deserve to win you?") Life, which at the outset was a verb, becomes the self's addressee, the "yo" that did not "vivir en mí" has been replaced by Dios, but the self persists in the personal pronoun of *mi* Dios. The poem says that God lives within the self, but grammatically the speaker refers to God as the third person ("le") in a dialogue between "yo" (self) and "tú" (life). In a lesser-known Teresan poem, "Alma, buscarte has en Mí" ("Soul, you must seek yourself in me" [28–31]), the self divides between the poetic voice and the soul. The grammatical strangeness of the opening lines ("Alma, buscarte has en Mí/ y a Mí buscarme has en ti" [v. 1–2] ["Soul, you must seek yourself in Me,/ and you must seek Me in yourself"]), repeated with variations as a refrain throughout the poem, is more pronounced here, and thus the poem does more than tell of a division within the Self; it produces a sense of strangeness and compels the reader to recreate a unified meaning by re-assembling disparate, disjointed pronouns. Unlike a *conceptista* sonnet, there is no one solution, a re-ordering of words that makes everything make sense. The unification of Self and God, body and soul, can only be approximated.

Whereas Teresa's poems announce the problem of the self from the outset, San Juan de la Cruz begins his best-known poems with a stable speaker (or, in the case of the "Cántico," speakers) and progressively blurs the lines delineating that identity. In "Noche oscura," the apparently stable first-person narrative is complicated in the fifth, central stanza, when the poet speaks of "amada en amado transformada" ("The Lover with His beloved,/ Transforming the beloved in her Lover" [296]). This announcement at the level of "plot" (such as it is) is matched by a progressively complex distribution of pronouns through the rest of the poem, culminating in the final stanza: "Quedéme y olvidéme,/ el rostro recliné sobre el amado/ cesó todo, y dejéme" ("I abandoned and forgot myself,/ Laying my face on my Beloved;/ All things ceased; I went out from myself" [296]). In addition to the unusual use of the reflexive with "olvidar" and "dejar," the poet seems to speak from the perspective of "la amada," disturbing the typical assumption of an equivalence between the first-person poetic voice and the poet.[31] Miguel Asín Palacios and Luce López-Baralt have shown that there existed a long tradition among Sufi mystic poets of writing in a feminine voice;[32] San Juan's use of a female poetic voice may stem from that tradition, but for a sixteenth-century Spanish reader/listener, the assumption of a female perspective by a male poet would have been unusual, not only narrating the erasure of human markers of identity, but provoking a sense of strangeness and mystery regarding those markers of identity. In this way, San Juan re-vitalizes the trope of spiritual-as-erotic union, which had become something of a cliché. At the same time, the conventions of poetic expression made it possible to question markers of identity in this way; the assumption of a female poetic voice provoked thought or confusion, but not censure, as it might have had it been expressed in published prose. There existed a tradition – multiple traditions – of feminized poetic expression, or of a questioning of the borders of the self, that made San Juan or Santa Teresa's poetry legible, if not always entirely comprehensible. This would not have been the case had the same ideas been expressed in a juridical or even a theatrical setting: for different reasons, the self cannot melt away before the law or on stage.

Orality and Musicality

Traditionally, poetry was sung. In the case of epic or didactic poetry, this was to facilitate memorization and transmission, but, as has already been stated, music also could be seen as a celestial language, a system of harmonies and beauty closer to God than the arbitrary post-Babel language of spoken words. It is no coincidence that the Song of Songs is a song. Thus, following an ancient tradition, even mystic writers concerned principally with expressing an intimate experience wrote songs. Those who wrote within convents or monasteries also tended to write music, as chant and song formed the backbone of the daily spiritual calendar in the cloister.[33] Santa Teresa believed firmly in the importance and the efficacy of song in bringing the soul closer to God, and music was central to life in the convents of the Discalced Carmelites. Orozco Díaz describes how, in the reformed Carmelite convents, "song invaded everything … [Teresa] composed and improvised *coplas, romances* and *villancicos* for her nuns, not just in the hours of recreation for celebration of festivities, but also in the most varied and unusual of circumstances"

(167–8). Of course, most of these songs were not about mystical union, but in the atmosphere of the convent, where every word and act was imbued with intense spiritual meaning, they might lead to mystical rapture. Teresa's writings, as well as the testimonies gathered in her canonization process, give several examples of songs producing mystic rapture.[34] This could also create a cycle, with the ecstatic nun or monk then composing a song or poem to recreate the ecstatic experience. Fray Diego de Yepes in his 1606 *Vida, virtudes y milagros de la bienaventurada virgen Teresa de Jesús* ("Life, Virtues and Miracles of the Blessed Virgin Teresa de Jesús"), recounts just such a cycle. Teresa, upon hearing the nun Isabel de Jesús sing the verses beginning "Véante mis ojos/ dulce Jesús bueno/ véante mis ojos, muérame yo luego" ("Let my eyes see you/ sweet good Jesus/ let my eyes see you/ and then let me die") "quedó tan sin sentido que la hubieron de llevar como muerta a la celda y acostarla. Y el siguiente día también andaba como fuera de sí" ("was struck so senseless that she had to be taken back to her cell like a dead woman and put to bed. And the following day too she went about as if outside herself [i.e., in a trance]"). The following day, "estando con estos ímpetus" ("under the sway of these impulses"), she wrote the famous 'Vivo sin vivir en mí" (Yepes 208). Furthermore, both expressions, "Véante mis ojos" and "Vivo sin vivir en mí," are to be found in the poetry of Santa Teresa's close collaborator San Juan de la Cruz.[35] While there has been much study of the different poems with the goal of identifying an "original" or of emphasizing differences between the various iterations, what has perhaps been lost is the extent to which the abundance of variations testifies to an extensive circulation of poems and songs, especially in the Carmelite tradition. Orozco Díaz speaks of the existence "around Santa Teresa of lively poetic activity, anonymous in its origins and collective in nature, although it is possible to identify certain names" (170). The groundbreaking work of Electa Arenal and Stacey Schlau went a long way in reclaiming the legacy of those few whose names can be identified,[36] but these are just the tip of the iceberg; for the purpose of this study, it is more important to insist on the size and scope of the anonymous collective, which Orozco Díaz compares to the secular communities that transmitted and transformed the Romancero legacy (178). To be a nun in a reformed Carmelite monastery was to sing and to create poetry *a lo divino*.[37]

The canon of mystic poetry that has come to be valued *as poetry* – mostly limited to the works of San Juan, Santa Teresa, and Fray Luis – represents only a tiny fraction of the total quantity of mystic verse that circulated, interspersed in spiritual autobiographies, saints' lives, letters, and scattered papers that have made their way into convent archives. Almost every spiritual autobiography includes verses; it is often impossible to tell if they are copied from other sources or originals, as originality and authorship were not a concern. The disproportionate weight given to the "Big 3" mystics led to many poems that were probably authored by less-prominent colleagues, including the afore-cited "Véante mis ojos, dulce Jesús mío," being attributed to either Santa Teresa or San Juan.[38] The leaders of religious communities, particularly the founders of convents, consulted each other in person and in writing, sharing and commenting on each other's poetry. For example, Father Domingo de Aspe includes in his continuation of Luisa de la Ascención (also known as la Monja de Carrión)'s spiritual autobiography a poem called "La soledad del alma" (one of thirty-six contained among her writings[39]). One of Luisa's devotees, the abbess María de la Antigua, dedicates three chapters of her own vast spiritual autobiography, *Desengaños de religiosos y de almas que tratan de virtud*, to reproducing and commenting Madre Luisa's poem. The poem is very similar to another, titled "A la soledad y retiro," by one Padre Diego Salablanca, contemporary of both nuns. Luis Vázquez has suggested that the true author was San Juan de la Cruz, basing his claim on the quotations of San Juan's poetry in the *Desengaños* as well as on evidence of direct epistolary correspondence between the two authors.[40] Since none of these works were published during their authors' lifetimes, it is impossible to say for certain who influenced whom. Certainly by the 1620s, it is not infrequent to find references to San Juan de la Cruz's poetry and prose in any number of nuns' writings.[41] Rather than supporting the singular-genius model of creativity, these echoes and parallels point to a circulation that goes far beyond the oral recitation of poems within closed cloister walls.

Letters are another source of evidence of a broad network of reading and collective authorship of mystic poems. In Cecilia de Nacimiento's correspondence with her brother, Fray Antonio, they discuss in great detail their own spiritual experiences, but also her poems and glosses on the Song of Songs, which she is clearly sending to him stanza by stanza. The influence of San Juan de la Cruz on Cecilia de Nacimiento and her poetry is inescapable (in fact, some of her works were misattributed to him) and has been the subject of recent scholarship.[42] But the chains of influence did not stop with Cecilia, nor did poetic influence flow exclusively between distinguished poets or even necessarily in discrete poems. We get glimpses of the constant daily circulation of tropes and snippets of mystic poetry in documents such as a letter that Fray Antonio writes, in which he praises an original poem Cecilia has sent him but suggests an addition to one verse: "Y si me da licencia pondréle aquí lo que añadí al cabo de aquella su divina lira sobre el último verso" (520) ("and with your permission I will put here what I added at the end of your divine *lira*, following the last line").[43] In another letter, he thanks her for sending her glosses on the Song of Songs. "Cuando leo estas Glosas de Vuestra Reverencia, a propósito de cada cosita se me va acordando ya de dichos de San Pablo, ya de David, ya de San Gregorio, ya de San Agustín, ya de otros, va haciendo una música y contrapunto admirable y un deleite del multiforme espíritu de la gracia y la sabiduría de Dios con que es el ánima muy incitada a la oración y suspensión" (526) ("When I read these glosses by Your Reverence, every little thing reminds me of sayings of Saint Paul, David, Saint Gregory, Saint Augustine, and others, and together they create an admirable music and counterpoint and a delight in the multiform spirit of grace and the wisdom of God, all of which incites my soul greatly to prayer and suspension").[44] Cecilia's reading of the mystic song *par excellence* prompts her commentary; his reading of her commentary produces an interior music and leads him into silent prayer and mystic union. He then writes about these mystic experiences to his sister, and the circle continues. From these examples, we see the irony of early modern Christian mysticism, and the point at which it differs most from its medieval predecessor: all these poems about radical solitude were circulating and creating communities.[45] Nuns and monks were copying and creating poems, exchanging them in diverse formats – sometimes alone, often included within texts of diverse genres. This circulation occurred between convents and monasteries, between religious orders, and also extended into the secular world. Because these texts were not printed, they escaped the censorship regimes that limited what could be expressed in prose guides to contemplative prayer.

The invention of the printing press was clearly a decisive factor in permitting the widespread written circulation of devotional poetry. But most of these poems, even in the Baroque period, circulated in manuscript copies. What was new was the *institutionalization* of orders dedicated to interiorized spirituality, and their insertion into urban communities. The infrastructure of Counter-Reformation Spain allowed even cloistered religious men and women to share letters, manuscripts, and confessors. Furthermore, the active involvement of the highest figures in the court hierarchy in the foundation and direction of spiritual communities, not to mention the correspondence of Felipe III and Felipe IV with various visionary nuns,[46] meant that the manuscript and poetic accounts of visionary experience, even when produced within the isolation of the reformed cloister, could circulate around the globe. But this potential for circulation beyond the immediate communities of production and reception presented new conflicts and concerns. Mystic discourse was now occupying a different social role than it had before, and the institutions concerned with the social order, regardless of differences in their concept of the proper form that social order should take, began to ask questions of mystic poetry that had not heretofore been deemed necessary. The very elements we have identified as analogous between mystic and poetic expression – the use of figurative language, difficult grammatical structures – became problematic once mystic poetry spread from its cloistered origins. When an obscure, ambiguous poem circulated among members of a convent, a general homogeneity of interpretation could be confirmed, both because the individuals in a convent generally shared intellectual and spiritual formations and because, in the case of doubts or disagreements, the individuals could communicate directly. But what might illiterate peasants, New Christians, or impressionable young women make of doves speaking to deer, or "quedéme y dejéme," or passionate kisses with the Beloved? Ambiguity, opacity, and hermetic language needed to be explained, to guard against misinterpretation of texts. At the same time, the ambiguity of the "poetic voice" in relation to the writing subject, an ambiguity which, as we have seen, mystic poets in particular cultivated to express the dissociation of the Self during mystic union, would need to be clarified, in order that the institutions controlling subjects and not just ideas could identify and discipline (or promote) the poems' authors.

The mystic poem, which had emerged from the mystic treatise when censorship impeded the expression of *lo místico* in published prose, gradually became subject to similar pressures, furthering a cycle between poetry and prose, *lo místico* ("lenguaje poético") y *la mística* ("sistema científico"). It is truly a circle and not a dialectic because there was not a clear-cut opposition between authorities and mystics. Many authorities looked favourably on the increased devotion that contemplative practice seemed to foster, and many mystics had positions of authority in the Church. The question of the limit between licit and subversive piety was always fraught, and the shift between *lo místico* and *la mística,* or between a prose and poetic expression, was always fluid. If in chapter one we saw prose forms incorporate poetry and elements of poetic discourse and form, here we see prose arising from a need to explain, situate, or contextualize poetry. In Michel de Certeau's analysis, the poem became, for a time, "the substitute for its scientific object" in the sense that the poem, dream, or account of extasis was the space in which the mysticism was codified. But it was, he continues, a "paradoxical alliance," and mystic practices, "to the extent that they separate from the poem, the shadow of which delineated a space for them, drifted away" (77).

Poetic Commentary

San Juan de la Cruz is the Spanish mystic poet *par excellence*, perhaps the only figure equally renowned as a poet and as a Catholic mystic, but while his poetry is widely read and studied, his prose explications of his major poems are largely forgotten or assumed to be theology rather than literature. Yet from the perspective of this study and a comprehension of the circulation of mystic discourse in the period, his movement away from poetry is as paradigmatic as his identity as a poet. There is debate as to when exactly he completed the "Cántico espiritual," but the idea and the outline undoubtedly came to him in 1577 while imprisoned by the anti-reform monks of his own Carmelite order.[47] This fits with the traditional model of mystic production: the individual, in isolation, writing for himself. Sor Magdalena del Espíritu Santo, a nun in the Carmelite convent in Beas for which San Juan served as a spiritual director, states in her *Relación de la vida de San Juan de la Cruz* that the nuns in Beas copied the poem but also that their confusion over the obscure meanings motivated San Juan to write out the much-less-studied prose commentaries. As Thompson concludes, Sor Magdalena's testimony "further suggests that the expositions of the *Cántico* were made over several years, at Beas (1578–9), Baeza (1579–82), and Granada (after 1582), and were started in the first instance at the request of nuns who were moved by the poem but unable – not surprisingly – to grasp its meaning" (26). San Juan would end up writing extensive prose commentaries for all four of his major poems, although the exact motivation for each is unclear: was he solely responding to requests from nuns seeking clarification? Or was he compelled by Church superiors to eliminate ambiguities and demonstrate the orthodoxy of his work? (Certainly, Fray Luis's experience in translating the *Cantar* would support an assumption that some institutional pressure was behind the first *Comentario* to the "Cántico.") Or did San Juan see these prose commentaries as part of the poetic project itself, envisioning a hybrid prose-poem (after all, the *Comentarios* reproduce the poem in its entirety just after the Prologue) as best suited to the expression of his thought and experience? The question becomes even more complicated when we see the same pattern in his spiritual disciples: Cecilia de Nacimiento, for example, also wrote a lyric poem ("Liras de la transformación del alma en Dios" ["Songs of the Union and Transformation of the Soul in God" (178)]) and then, according to the Carmelite historian Fray Manuel de San Jerónimo (1659–1719), "Viendo los confesores y Prelados los tesoros místicos que encerraban estas Canciones y que no era fácil explicarlas otra pluma que la que había sabido componerlas, la mandaron hacer una declaración lo cual ella ejecutó en un doctísimo tratado" (qtd. in Cecilia de Nacimiento *Obras completas* 44) ("Her confessors and prelates having seen the mystic treasures within these Songs, and that it would be difficult for any hand to explain them other the one that had composed them, ordered her to write a declaration, and she complied in an exceedingly scholarly treatise"). There is no textual record of a request from "confesores y prelados" commanding the move from verse to prose, and it seems possible that the production of a prose exegesis had become a generic expectation, following San Juan's example. Whatever the motives, what is essential to note is the effect that the change from the initial locus of San Juan's production (alone, in prison) to the integration into an institutional community in an increasingly urban, mobile cultural landscape, had on the form of mystic writing, pushing it from poetry to prose, literature to theology, *lo místico* to *la mística*.

San Juan's literary renown today is largely due to his "discovery" by a generation of Modernist poets: Dámaso Alonso, Jorge Guillén, Pedro Salinas. It is not surprising that they ignored his prose works or explained them as concessions to external demands. Raquel Asún summarizes the attitude of the Modernist critics to the Commentaries: "while they give us the relation to mystic values – in general entirely unartistic – they add nothing to the poetic and creative dimension that the verses, the freely chosen form of expression, contain" (XVI).[48] Or as Thompson more bluntly puts it, "The commentaries are usually described as methodical treatises, dull to read, which entirely lack the lyrical intensity of the poem" (164).[49]

There can be no argument that the prose commentaries are not primarily works of literature, with an aesthetic *plus* above their doctrinal function. This does not mean that they are entirely without aesthetic innovation or achievement. Thompson identifies "three main strands" in the commentary on the "Cántico": "There is the *lyrical thrust*, where poem and commentary stand closest together; the *interpretative function*, sometimes explaining the images, sometimes interpreting them as part of the spiritual life; and the *systematic approach*, in which the commentary moves furthest away from the poem and could have been written in isolation from it" (118). In other words, the lyric impulse does not disappear completely but is instead interwoven with doctrine and exegesis. The commentaries are both more and less than explanations of the poems; both in terms of theme and form, they exceed the basic task of explaining the stanzas, but at the same time, they do not necessarily clarify many of the poem's ambiguities or obscurities. San Juan says as much in the Prologue to the "Cántico":

> no pienso yo ahora declarar toda la anchura y copia que el espíritu fecundo del amor en ellas [las canciones] lleva; antes sería ignorancia pensar que los dichos de amor en inteligencia mística … con alguna manera de palabras se pueden bien explicar. (Prólogo.1.466)
>
> los dichos de amor es mejor dejarlos en su anchura para que cada uno de ellos se aproveche según so modo y caudal de espíritu, que abreviarlos a un sentido a que no se acomode todo paladar; y así, aunque en alguna manera se declaran, no hay para qué atarse a la declaración, porque la sabiduría mística … no ha menester distintamente entenderse para hacer efecto y afición en el alma, porque es a modo de la fe, en la cual amamos a Dios sin entenderle. (Prólogo.2.467)

> I do not plan to expound these stanzas in all the breadth and fullness that the fruitful spirit of love conveys to them. It would be foolish to think that expressions of love arising from mystical understanding … are fully explainable … It is better to explain the utterances of love in their broadest sense so that each one may derive profit from them according to the mode and capacity of his spirit, rather than narrow them down to a meaning unadaptable to every palate. As a result, though we give some explanation of these stanzas, there is no reason to be bound to this explanation. For mystical wisdom … need not be understood distinctly in order to cause love and affection in the soul, for it is given according to the mode of faith, through which we love God without understanding Him. [408–9]

The prologue to what should be a clarification of the dense symbols and poetic devices ends up rejecting that possibility, as "no pudiendo el Espíritu Santo dar a entender la abundancia de su sentido por términos vulgares y usados, habla misterios en extrañas figuras y semejanzas" (Prólogo.1.467) ("the Holy Spirit, unable to express the fullness of His meaning in ordinary words, utters mysteries in strange figures and likenesses" [408]). Thus, it cannot be said that the *Comentarios* are theology to the "Cántico"'s poetry; as Colin Thompson observes, the author here asserts that "mysterious language therefore has a definite theological function, inside and outside the sacred text" (139).[50] It might be argued that these protestations of insufficiency in the prologue are formulas, to be found in the introduction to any early modern work.

This is true, but it is striking to note here that, in contrast with the general tendency in secular works to admit a lack of skill on the part of the author, here San Juan is protesting the insufficiency of prose, or rational discourse, itself. Language expressing the insufficiency of language is a defining element of mystic discourse. Insofar as the commentaries seek to explain or read the poems allegorically, they are anti-mystical. Insofar as they seek to systematize the process of mystic union, they can be seen as performing the systematization of mysticism, the shift from *lo místico* to *el misticismo*. And insofar as they continue to introduce new "figuras y semejanzas" and decry their own power to decipher them, they return to the mystic register.

The movement between clarification, systematization, and complication is not limited to the prologue, but instead characterizes all the commentaries. There are many examples, but for the sake of this chapter we will select one: the Commentary to Stanza 20 of the "Cántico," one of the most symbolically dense in the entire poem.

A las aves ligeras,
leones, ciervos, gamos saltadores,
montes, valles, riberas,
aguas, aires, ardores
y miedos de las noches veladores (20 y 21.579)[51]

Swift-winged birds,/ Lions, stags, and leaping roes,/ Mountains, lowlands, and river banks,/ Waters, winds and ardors,/ Watching fears of night [489]

The first section of the commentary is strictly allegorical, establishing what Baruzi calls "a parallelism between a system of images and other abstract thoughts" (330). Thus, San Juan tells us that the Bridegroom "Llama *aves ligeras* a las digresiones de la imaginativa, que son ligeras y sutiles en volar a una parte y a otra" (20.5.580) ("He calls the wanderings of the imagination '*swift-winged birds*,' for these digressions are quick and restless in flying from one place to another" [489]); that "Por los *leones* entiende las acrimonias e ímpetus de la potencia irascible, porque esta potencia es osada y atrevida en sus actos, como los leones" (20.6.581) ("By the 'lions' He refers to the acrimony and impetuosity of the irascible power, for in its acts this power is bold and daring like the lion" [490]), and so forth with each symbol. The mystical elements of the poem, those that point to a reality beyond linguistic expression, are systematically eliminated, each symbol replaced, through clear prose language, with a stable earthly referent. Neither the style nor the concepts introduced are new or innovative; both the system of allegorical reading and the tendency towards classification are typical of medieval biblical exegesis. Poetic symbols, as Baruzi points out, always already contain the seeds of their own undoing as mystic symbols, for they inevitably refer to earthly things. "The mystic symbol is practically, at least in its common forms, an allegory," or at least a potential allegory (333). To read of "aves ligeras" in a poem clearly not *about* birds is to ask what spiritual concept they represent and what the point of connection is. To read an oxymoron such as "ojos del alma" or "noche dichosa" is to imagine a point of synthesis that makes what seems like an opposition not one. These activities of the rational brain are latent in the poem and realized in the commentary. In this sense, mysticism always already contains its own de-mystification; if earlier (and later) mystic poets were not compelled to make the process of symbolic identification explicit, it was because they were not spiritual directors, they were not immersed in an institutional system that sought not just to express, but also to spread, the mystic experience.

From a poetic point of view, of course, the *Comentarios* betray the spirit of the poems, but San Juan did not consider himself principally a poet, but first and foremost a Christian and a spiritual director. In a simplistic model in which authority and mysticism are strictly oppositional terms, we would assume an authority commanding the poet to *reduce* his poem to dogma. While, as has been suggested, it seems possible that a superior encouraged the poet to write the *Comentarios*, it does not seem to have been coercive so much as complementary. The textual production of the spiritual director and the mystic poet are at odds, but the mystic poet and the spiritual director were the same person, and the divergent textual products reflect competing, but not mutually exclusive, objectives within a society that sought to promote a particular form of spirituality that inspired devotion but not dissent.

The process of teaching mystical union required the elaboration of a system that could be rationally followed, even if the final product exceeded systems and reason. The *Comentario al* "Cántico espiritual" rarely lay out a system to be followed with the clarity of, say, the *Spiritual Exercises*, but the allegorical exegesis does push the strange, mystic poem back into known theological classifications. The prose commentary to "Noche oscura" is more prescriptive. The shift in focus is announced from the very outset; whereas the Cántico commentary promises only a "Declaración de las canciones," the commentary on "Noche oscura" is to be a "Declaración de las canciones del modo que tiene el alma en el camino espiritual para llegar a la perfecta unión de amor con Dios, cual se puede en esta vida. Dícense también las propiedades que tiene en sí el que ha llegado a la dicha perfección según en las mismas canciones se contiene" (341) ("An explanation of the stanzas describing a soul's conduct along the spiritual road which leads to the perfect union with God through love, insofar as it is attainable in this life. A description also of the characteristics of one who has reached this perfection" [295]).[52] The relative focus on *method* ("modo") over meaning is consistent throughout; the chapters are not titled with verses of the poem itself, as is the case with the commentary to the "Cántico," but with direct statements, such as "De las señales que se conocerá que el espiritual va por el camino de esta noche y purgación sensitiva" (9.363) ("Signs for discerning whether a spiritual person is treading the path of this sensory night and purgation" [313]) or "Del modo con que se han de haber éstos en esta noche oscura" (10.367) ("The conduct required of souls in this dark night" [316]). The *Comentario* of the "Noche oscura" resembles most closely the prose treatises discussed in chapter one, but if Osuna's prose *Abecedarios* represent a *mystification* of a formulaic poetic tradition (the poetic *Abecedarios*), here the prose commentary is a *de-mystification* of the earlier poem. The two, together, are representative of the movement of mystic writing in general in the period under study. But the mystification/demystification is never complete; in truth, each text contains countercurrents and swirls. If we look more closely at the *Comentarios*, we find that the movement towards exegesis and system is often frustrated, and the author returns to the techniques of poetic language discussed in this chapter.

For example, if we look at the Commentary on stanza twenty of the *Cántico* discussed above, we find that San Juan identifies the "aguas, aires, ardores,/ y miedos de las noches veladores" ("waters, winds, and ardors,/ Watching fears of night" [491]) with the four passions and then sets out to explain with machine-like precision the activity of each during mystic union (20.9.582). But the words for the human passions become insufficient to parse the distinctions between spiritual states, and this pushes the author back into metaphor and paradox:

> También las afecciones del gozo, que en el alma solían hacer sentimiento de más o menos, ni en ellas echa de ver mengua ni le hace novedad la abundancia; porque es tanta la que ella ordinariamente goza, que *a manera de la mar, ni mengua por los ríos de que ella salen, ni crece por los que en ella entran*. (20.10.584, emphasis mine)

> Neither do the emotions of joy, which usually caused her [the soul] a feeling of possessing more or less, make her aware of less or added

> abundance, for what she ordinarily enjoys is so great that, like the sea, she neither decreases by the outflowing waters nor increases by the inflowing waters. [492]

Finally, after alternating between systematic and poetic registers, the author concludes that:

> si quisiésemos hablar de la iluminación de gloria que en este ordinario abrazo que tiene dado al alma algunas veces hace en ella … nada se podría decir que declarase algo de ello. Porque a manera del sol cuando de lleno embiste la mar esclarece hasta los profundos senos y cavernas, y parecen las perlas y venas riquísimas de oro y otros minerales preciosos, así este divino sol del Esposo. (20.14.585–586)

> Yet were we to desire to speak of the glorious illumination He sometimes gives to the soul in this habitual embrace, which is a certain spiritual turning toward her … our words would fail to explain anything about it. As the sun shining brightly upon the sea lights up great depths and caverns and reveals pearls and rich veins of gold and other minerals, etc., so the Bridegroom, the divine sun. [493]

Even when nothing can be said, the author continues speaking; the movement is not into silence but into poetry, mystic imagery, "figuras y semejanzas." The paragraph ends with a quote from the *Cantares* (Ct 6:9): "¿quién es ésta que procede como la mañana que se levanta, hermosa como la luna, escogida como el sol, terrible y ordenada como las haces de los ejércitos?" (20.14.586) ("Who is she that comes forth like the morning rising, beautiful as the moon, resplendent as the sun, terrible as the armies set in display?" [494]). The mystic text *par excellence* returns in all its symbolic density. The obscurity of mystic language impels anti-mystical explanation; the insufficiency of anti-mystical explanation impels mystic language.

The cyclic, circulatory nature of mystic language between forms, genres, and even within single works, ultimately tied to the widespread circulation of mystic texts between individuals and institutions, is what makes early modern Spanish mysticism distinct from its medieval precursors. San Juan is hardly the only Spanish mystic who incorporates mystic and de-mystifying elements into his own works. In her insightful study of Cecilia de Nacimiento and María de San Alberto's respective versions of the "Noche oscura," Alison Weber finds that the chief difference is the incorporation of the exegesis into the poems themselves. The difference in strategies between San Juan and his disciples corresponds to the chronological and gender difference between their works. Cecilia and María Alberto were, to use Evelyn Toft's expression, "second-generation mystics of the Carmelite reform,"[53] which means they wrote in a moment of less openness, when the needle had shifted one step further in the transition from *lo místico* to *la mística*. In addition, there was increased scrutiny of any female poet, both regarding her own possible confusion of sinful desire with sacred fervor and, given the precedent that was now clearly established for the extramural circulation of mystic poetry, the fear that a work without a clear interpretative code embedded within it might be misinterpreted. San Juan's ability to divorce his exegesis from the poems themselves saved him as a poet for posterity, for the celebration of his poems "desde esta ladera" ("from this shore"),[54] which, ironically, cemented his reputation as the Spanish mystic poet *par excellence*. However, it is the impulse (whether obeying an order or a friendly request) to provide exegesis, and at the same time the preservation of the poetry within the exegesis, that marks him as the Spanish *mystic* par excellence. The fact of his "discovery" by Romantics and Modernists, who applied their historically particular criteria of the poem as a discrete work of art and focused almost exclusively on four of his poems at the expense of all his other writings and all the writings he influenced, belies the porous, protean, circulatory nature of his actual *oeuvre*. He writes at a moment when the *ladera* was drawn on quicksand.

Chapter Three

Spiritual Autobiography

The two previous chapters trace the appearance and development in early modern Spain of two early modern genres – the treatise of interior prayer and mystic poem – with medieval and classical precedents. Early modern Spanish writers adapted existing traditions and generic forms, although in entirely different socio-historical circumstances, to express a new form of spirituality. This chapter focuses on a genre that can be considered original to the early modern period: the *vida espiritual*, or spiritual autobiography. It is true that Saint Augustine had, with his *Confessions*, established a precedent for a first-person account of spiritual development, and it is undeniable that Teresa de Ávila and other fellow life-writers were influenced by the *Confessions* (in the *Vida* itself, Teresa cites her reading of the *Confessions* as a turning point in her spiritual development[1]), but the Augustinian and Teresan forms of the *Vida* are so different that it is misleading to think of them as belonging to a single genre. Instead, I consider the first person *vida espiritual* as emerging when the mystic treatise and poem entered new circuits of production and reception: when institutions became concerned with codifying the fluid, ambiguous "yo" that emerged to disrupt staid scholastic doctrine and formulaic *canciones*. This chapter will trace the movement of mystic tropes from treatises to poem to *vida* and consider how the early modern *vida*, once it was established as a genre in its own right, with its own canon for imitation, further developed in the ongoing tension between *lo místico* and *la mística*. In chapters one and two, we focused on poetry and figurative/poetic language in the narration of the mystic experience. We may now consider both how poetry enters into the *vida* and how the *vida* pushes language into poetic realms, as we saw in the mystic treatises.[2] Yet we will also see how the extra-textual circumstances compelling the *vidas* pushes poetry into new configurations with narrative and dialogue. The compulsion to narrate an interior process that must be tied to a "yo" who lives and moves in the world ends up creating a literary subject with depth, complexity, agency, and the other hallmarks of the modern self.

The Early Modern *Vida Espiritual*: Precursors and Context

Despite the role Santa Teresa cites for Augustine's *Confessions* in her *spiritual* development, the influence on her *authorial* development, and thus on the development of the *vida espiritual* as a genre, is more tenuous. Augustine's *Confessions* focus on his early life and lead up to his conversion to Catholicism, but no Spaniard after 1492 could technically convert to Catholicism.[3] Some of the Spanish *vidas*, including Teresa's, briefly recount a period of youthful waywardness followed by repentance and commitment to greater devotion, but these occupy at most an introductory chapter or two. While Augustine's story largely focuses on his biographical and intellectual journey, punctuated by two episodes of visionary revelation,[4] the early modern *vidas* are uniformly dedicated to visions, spiritual favours, and interior life. In some of the early modern *vidas*, there is almost no autobiographical framework at all. The text is told in first person, but there is no attempt to narrate a life experienced in the world. Ignacio de Loyola's diary, discussed in chapter one, could be seen as the most extreme example, to the point that it cannot even be read as a narrative. More common were the *libros de mercedes* (books of spiritual gifts) that relate, in narrative form, individual visions or mystic experiences. Most *vidas* exist somewhere on a continuum between the two, mixing exterior and interior, at times chronologically, at times almost with no apparent organizing principle.

A second crucial difference between the Augustinian and early modern *vida* is found in the circumstance of production: when Augustine decided to write the story of his conversion around 397, he was already Bishop of Hippo. His audience, according to biographer Peter Brown, was his circle of fellow "*servi Dei* … a group of highly-sophisticated men, the *spiritales*," who could be expected to read the work as authoritative and exemplary (160). The "confessional" aspect of the title is the author/sinner confessing to God. Every early modern *vida*, on the other hand, is born out of a dialogue – sometimes more collaborative, sometimes more conflictive – with a human confessor (an institution that did not exist in Augustine's day). The compulsory origins of the *vida* have led scholars to term them *autobiografías por obligación*. Fernando López Durán, who, along with Isabelle Poutrin, has done the most exhaustive work on the corpus as a whole, distinguishes between *autobiografías por obligación* and *autobiografías por petición*: the former typical of female visionaries, the latter (a much smaller corpus) written by men and at the instances of a friend or colleague seeking to publicize rather than scrutinize.[5] In fact, the lines between one and the other are blurry, as the exhaustive studies of Teresa's relations with her confessors and censors have shown.[6] In both cases, "there is always an addressee with a first and last name who, in addition, has authority over the writing subject. This authority includes the possibility of altering the text: requiring an expansion, eliminating passages, censuring the author for possible deviations, ordering its destruction, showing the manuscript to others" (Durán López 64). Whatever his stance towards the author, the confessor is present in every sentence of the early modern *vida*. The *vida* is an interpellated text, usually written not *from* a place of authority but in order to achieve authorization.

The crucial difference between the genres considered in the previous chapters and the autobiography is the focus on the self. As we saw in chapter one, even though the treatise authors occasionally insert a first-person perspective, they do not pretend to be writing of their own spiritual experiences. Their system emerges from the synthesis of a study of *letras* and the *experiencias* of others. The majority of mystic poems are also either written in third person or assumed to be about the experience of "the soul" or "a Christian," rather than the subjective individual experience of the poet. Even in the case of a first-person poem such as "Muero porque no muero," which has often been associated with Teresa's own feelings, the strictures of rhyme and meter, coupled with the obvious adaptation of a previously existing poetic motif, impede a reading of the poem as expression of a unique subjectivity. Insofar as it is a sincere expression of the poet's subjective experience, it is a distinctly pre-modern subjectivity, so little individualized that it hardly matters to what extent Teresa created and to what extent she merely adapted the poem. The *vida espiritual* is a particularly curious textual product because, although it still pretends to narrate a universal, timeless experience of the soul (universal in the sense that it could apply to any Christian whom God deemed worthy of such graces), the individual variations *do* permit the emergence of a sense of the author's unique experience.

As a genre, the *vida espiritual* is not born out of any modern desire for self-expression. On the contrary, it is born from the institutional imperative to tie the account of an experience in which the self is erased, to an individual human with a name and history. Thus the motivating force behind the *vida espiritual* and the secular autobiography (a la Rousseau) is quite different. The "auto" in the secular autobiography is the organizing principle, and the author writes to explain how the present, writing self was formed. The very idea of "self" is not, however, questioned, nor does the secular autobiography focus on defining or distinguishing parts of the self; the self is simply assumed. The *vida espiritual* is in fact much more self-centred than the secular autobiography, as the latter almost always includes long passages of description of setting or backstory. In the *vida espiritual* there are long passages of description and sometimes narrative, but these always occur in the interior space of the vision. The objective of the *vida* is to understand those interior experiences: what they mean but, first, where they come from. Yet they are not understood *a priori* as part of the self, but rather as coming from *somewhere else*, the exact nature of where (God? The devil? The imagination?) being precisely what the text itself will help determine. The *vida* is thus inextricably tied to the process of discernment, which in itself created a genre: manuals that guide the scrutiny of individual accounts, written or oral, of spiritual grace. Discernment, unlike textual analysis, is always ultimately a discernment of a single subject. In this way the *vidas* are also far from medieval hagiographies, which serve as *exempla* even when they speak of saints about whom nothing else is known and who may not even have existed. The *vidas* point to a new Renaissance value placed on the individual and the author, but ironically, this idea of a coherent authorial self emerges precisely from a genre dedicated to narrating the dissolution of that self, the transformation of Self into God and vice versa.

The confessor, original audience for the *vida*, is thus reading in a way entirely distinct from how he might read a mystic poem. As we have seen, mystic poetry was subject to little censure or ideological scrutiny, and any demand to "explain" the poems, such as in the case of San Juan de la Cruz, seems to have come from colleagues and subordinates who were interested in comprehending what they assumed to be an authentic account of mystic union, rather than judging the veracity or validity of that account. In general, the questions of veracity and validity were not applied to poetry. Mystic poems recount experiences that, it would seem, cannot be judged from the outside, both because they are experienced as interior and because they are expressed in figurative, poetic language. This does not present a problem as long as *either* the poem does not enter in circuits of interpretation where the truth of the experience matters *or* it is assumed *a priori* that the entire experience being represented is authentic. The first situation describes the situation of most secular lyric poetry – no social interest has a stake in whether Garcilaso was truly mourning a lost lover, much less whether he *truly* found himself with some of her *prendas* in his hands (possible) or at the banks of the river watching a bevy of nymphs (unlikely).[7] This is not to say that the reader of the poem is not interested in the relation between biography and poetry, but readers, even in the age of literary criticism as a discipline, are not in a position to change or censure the poem; nothing is at stake in their theses beyond their own subjective valuation of the poem or, at most, their reputation as critics.

The second situation has generally been assumed for the mystic poem; because we work with a limited corpus of canonical texts, we assume they describe an authentic mystical experience. (Again, we may judge the use of language in one or another to be more effective in conveying the experience, but this already assumes an authentic experience to be conveyed.) Or, seen from another angle, we have such a limited corpus because the only published mystical poems were those associated with a name that had been validated for reasons external to the poetry. Only a saint or doctor of the church had a sufficiently stable reputation that their mystic experiences could be assumed to be true. Before a sixteenth- or seventeenth-century woman, however, could have her mystic poetry authorized, she had to authorize herself, and this form of authorization almost always took the form of a prose account of spiritual experiences submitted to a confessor. The disordered and incomplete *vidas* by and large represent the spiritual experiences of individuals who did not get to be poets, or at least whose poetry (for many of the *vidas* include poems) did not get to be published.

If the point of ordering a nun to write a *vida* is the scrutiny of the visions and other spiritual graces, why, we might ask, need her composition take the form of a *vida* at all? That is to say, if the matter to be analysed occurs in a visionary plane, why must it be framed through the account of the movements and experiences of the human subject? The answer lies in the interest and social position of those ordering the nuns to write. The Counter-Reformation Church – confessors, censors, ecclesiastical tribunals and the Inquisition – acted on *subjects*, hence the importance of certifying the events of individual lives (genealogy, baptism, marriage), the prohibition on anonymous texts, or the compulsion to appear *in person* annually for a confession. Even the censorship arm of the Inquisition, which might appear to be solely concerned with the circulation of *ideas*, revealed though their comments on texts that their principal concern was for interpretation (the subjects' assimilation of the ideas) rather than ideas themselves. This was the logic behind the prohibition of the translation of the Bible, certainly not a heretical or even heterodox text, into the Romance languages, or the comment by the censor D. Baños that Teresa de Ávila's *Vida*, while meritorious in itself, ought not be circulated for fear of misinterpretation.[8] The prohibition of anonymous publication also shows that the Church wished to intervene at the level of the writing subject. Nowhere is the focus on reader and author, rather than on ideas or words, clearer than in the case of Fray Luis de León and particularly his translation of the Song of Songs. While there did exist a generalized prohibition on the translation of the Bible into Castilian, the strictly narrative or genealogical books of the Bible did not lend themselves to misinterpretation and indeed were translated and circulated as parts of hagiographies or devotional books. It was the dense symbolism of the mystic poem and the fear of its misinterpretation among reading communities not properly guided by a church authority that prompted the silencing of this text and the imprisonment of its translator.

This brings us back to our question of why the account of mystic visions is tied to a biographical narrative. The mystic experience, as recounted in poems, annuls the subject and is thus not particular to the person left behind by the soul. The Amado is not San Juan de la Cruz; it is the soul, all souls. There are no proper names in mystic poetry, and we do not tie the mystic poem to the individual biography of the author. However, this poses a problem for discernment: if all accounts of mystic rapture are identical, then they can be faked, and they become useless as evidence for discernment of the spirit informing them. The treatises on discernment of spirits are deeply preoccupied with this, and their "solution" ties the mystic experience back to the subject, the individual self prior to the experience that annuls that selfhood. If, as this linkage suggests, it is the virtuous Christian who will have authentic mystical experiences, then the vision can be authorized from without, by an examination of the subject's virtue as observable in speech and acts. The *vidas* weave together a delicate back and forth between a description of virtuous acts and intentions and the description of an interior life offered up for scrutiny. In this sense, they postulate a self that is balanced between interior reflection and exterior action in a way unique to the period and genre.

The *vidas* as have they come down to us were written over widely different time spans and under widely different circumstances; some are, like Teresa's, coherent single works written over a short period. Some more closely resemble diaries, while others seem to be pastiches of recollections, letters, and personal reflections, arranged with little chronological or thematic organization. These are functional works, and any editing or literary standards were secondary, generally only applied once the initial stages of discernment and approval had been achieved and it was understood that the texts might provide a useful example for others. In their introductory essay to the volume *Letras en la celda*, the editors draw attention to the functional nature of conventual writing and the consequential apparent disorder of their textual output, often combined in "miscellaneous" manuscripts in which "writings of very diverse origin, authorship, content and intention" coexist in "happy confusion" (14–15). While the individual circumstances bringing a collection of manuscripts together may be arbitrary, the very fact of the disorder is important in what it tells us about the circulation of these works in the nuns' own lifetimes: namely, that these nuns were mostly writing either for a single reader (as in a letter or written response to a confessor) or for fellow members of their convent. In the case of nuns who, following Teresa, wrote of their spiritual gifts, this produced a paradox: they were imitating a nun whose example and writing had been copied, printed, and, in modern terminology, had gone viral, and in many cases, their words reveal that they too held a similar goal. But this could only be a very long-term goal, attainable in posterity; in the short term, they wrote for a readership of one or perhaps a few, and in manuscript copies they could not reasonably expect ever to be reproduced by hand or in print. It is important to insist on this because modern textual reading habits, ironically further ingrained through the efforts of scholarly series that, in the process of making these women visible, condense and edit a dispersed and diverse textual legacy into single works, have entirely obscured the anarchy of the original context of production and reception.

The case of María Astorch provides a useful example of the diversity of materials that a nun might produce, some (but not all) of which eventually coalesce into a single manuscript.[9] Lázaro Iriarte, the work's modern editor, drawing on Astorch's own account of her writing, notes that "María Ángela was accustomed, from childhood, to communicate, in writing, her spiritual experiences with her confessor." However, none of these accounts remain, as "having informed him – she says – she would immediately tear up or burn the papers" (81). Later, when she had gained certain renown and ascended to a position of authority in a new convent, she continued to destroy the *relaciones* "once they had served their purpose," but some of her readers (her confessor but also other spiritual directors) began to save her accounts, and as Astorch herself records, she also "fue conservando una buena parte, si bien sin orden, en borradores escritos, en blancos de cartas y de modo que yo sola me entendiera'" (quoted in Astorch 81) ("began saving the better part, although without any order, written in drafts, on the blank space of letters, and in such a way that only I could understand"). It was only once she was elected abbess, in 1626, that her confessor, Father Arbués, asked her to save all her accounts, to put them in order, and to retroactively fill in the missing years. Father Arbués, along with *his* confessor, to whom he had turned over many of the letters and notes, worked to create order out of the diverse material, but, according to Iriarte, he lamented that he could only match the fragments to the liturgical season, not the calendar year. From 1626 to 1642, the entries are periodic but identified chronologically. Finally, in 1642, the future Inquisitor Alejo de Boxadós decided that "it was worth the trouble" to make the entire history of her spiritual journey into a "legible presentation." Between 1642 and 1651, they worked to assemble the diverse accounts into in a single manuscript, to which she continued to add updates until 1656 (82). Thus, the *Camino interior* is a *Vida* produced over the entirety of Astorch's adult *vida* but not conceived of as a single coherent work until relatively late in the author's life.[10]

As this example of one nun's voluminous production indicates, the most remarkable aspect of early modern spiritual autobiography is the sheer *quantity* of material produced. The scholarly focus on Teresa's *Vida* obscures the fact that hers is merely one of hundreds, probably thousands. (Indeed, it has even obscured Teresa's other accounts of visionary experiences, similar in substance but not incorporated into the canonical *vida* text.[11]) It is impossible to venture a number, as the majority of efforts were incomplete, unpublished, and either lost or destroyed. Letters between nuns and confessors and testimonies to the Inquisition often read as catalogues of "papeles" that have been lost, burnt, or buried.[12] Even so, López Durán includes 161 women and 20 men in his bibliography of authors of religious autobiography in the sixteenth and seventeenth centuries, and more fragments can be found interspersed in other texts or documents.[13] It seems that every literate nun in Spain had scribbled out at least a fragmentary "relación de mercedes,"[14] and Teresa's *Vida* provides one of the few moments in this study where we can definitely point to a specific, linear chain of influence; her life and her *Vida* were the spark for the generations of subsequent life-writing nuns. One need not read between the lines to trace this influence; in what was undoubtedly both a sincere and strategic allusion to an authorized model, all the later *vida*-writing nuns (which is to say, all the *vida*-writing nuns) cite Teresa's life and works explicitly in their texts. Not only do the nuns model their texts after her *Vida*, they also follow her spiritual system, they praise her in hymns, and she appears to them in visions.[15] Confessors and censors use Teresa's writings as a benchmark of authenticity for judging her imitators; in a remarkably short period, the *Vida* went from being a text to be scrutinized against the authority of Scripture and Church fathers, to being *the* authoritative text – joining Scripture and overshadowing Augustine or Aquinas – against which other *vidas* would be measured.[16] However, the mass female appropriation of this generic form meant that future writers did not necessarily have the stature, education, or temperament to create a polished, coherent, sophisticated work of literature. The legions of life-writing nuns who spring up from the 1580s onwards are able to imitate their foremother with varying degrees of success. While the majority of these works (unpublished, unedited) can make no pretense to the status of literature, they are important windows into early modern subjectivity, not of a few remarkable individuals but across a surprisingly broad swathe of the early modern Spanish population.

Poetry and the *Vida Espiritual*

Scholars of the early modern have long decried the dearth of accounts of reader responses. Not only do we have few accounts of how texts were read, we are often in the dark about what texts were read and by whom, since print runs and sales figures, even where they exist, cannot account for the transmission of texts orally or in manuscript copies. This blind spot particularly affects poetry since, even in the print era, poetry tended to be shared orally and/or copied by hand. Those who study the periods before literary criticism emerged as a discipline must be creative in seeking out accounts of reception and transmission of texts, and particularly of poems. One place to which we can look is the *vidas*, which attest to the widespread practice of conventual reading and recitation, particularly of mystic poetry. Poetry finds its way into the *vidas* through diverse paths. Sometimes the poems are clearly set off from the prose accounts; for instance, the published version of María de la Antigua's *Desengaño de religiosos y de almas que tratan de virtud* (*For the Disillusion of Religious Men and Souls Who Attend to Virtue*), opens with the poem "Socorredme, alma mía" ("Succor me, my soul"). Yet it seems misleading to view this as the sort of commendatory verse prefacing so many early modern books, if only because Sor María never imagined the *Desengaño* as a "book"; her papers were edited and published in 1678, sixty-one years after Sor María's death. If we look at the thousands of folios of notebooks she filled throughout her life and from which the *Desengaño* is drawn,[17] we find a much more copious and chaotic insertion of poetry, almost always without authorship. One exception is the inclusion of the "Romance de la soledad del alma" ("*Romance* of the Soul's Solitude"), attributed to Sor Luisa de la Ascensión.[18] Sor Luisa herself wrote that, although she was not a poet, she "compuso algunos romances que por ser suyos se divulgaron entre personas religiosas" ("composed a few *romances* which, because they were hers, were shared by certain religious [could be nuns or clergy]") and that the "Romance de la soledad" came to her "estando arrobada en oración, estando presente nro sr cristo, a quien se le cantó juntamente como le iba componiendo, y quedósele tan impreso en la memoria que nunca se olvidó. Después lo escribió para su consuelo en un librillo, de cuyo original se sacó" (qtd. in García Barriuso 223) ("while she was in ecstasy during prayer, in the presence of Christ our lord, to whom she was singing at the same time she was composing it, and it remained so stamped in her memory that she never forgot it, and, for her own consolation, later she wrote it down in a little book, from which it was taken").[19] Sor Luisa was a mentor to Sor María, and Sor María writes in the prologue to a manuscript copy of the first seven books of the *Desengaños* "este libro es una de las mercedes que yo he hecho al mundo y es obra mía y no mía, porque mi querida Luisa de la Ascensión me lo ha pedido" ("this book is one of the gifts that I have made to the world, and it is mine and it is not mine, because my dear Luisa de la Ascensión asked it of me"). The early notebooks of the *Desengaño* are fairly straightforward, recounting life experiences or providing clear allegorical exegesis of visions. The third notebook begins with a collection of poems, some prefaced with the notation that they were composed "en rapto" ("in extasy"). A note at the end of one poem is evidence of the circulation and scrutiny of the poems outside their inclusion in the notebooks. "Mandóla Vuestra Merced que este romance sobredicho se diese al padre Fr. Juan de San Ramón del convento de S. Joseph de la villa de Lora" ("Your Grace ordered that the aforementioned *romance* be given to Father Juan de San Ramón in the convent of St. Joseph in the town of Lora").[20]

At the same time that the *Desengaño* points to the circulation of poems within and between convents, it also testifies to the nuns' appropriation of mystic poetry for their own interior lives. In the entry for one day, María reports that "Fuime a la cama, y en ella estuve algo despierta entre estos regalos …" (113) ("I went to bed, and lay there half-awake amongst these gifts"). Lying awake, she asks God, "¿por qué echáis las perlas de vuestros favores en lugar tan asqueroso y sucio?" ("why do you place the pearls of your favours in such a vile and dirty place?"), and God replies:

> Yo quiero que hoy se cumpla la palabra que tienes de mi esposa la iglesia dada tantos años ha. Entendí luego, que se me decía esto por un verso, que yo tengo escrito, que dice:
>
> De flores, y esmeraldas
> en las frescas mañanas escogidas,
> en tu amor florecidas, haremos las guirnaldas,
> y en un cabello mío entretejidas

> Así que le oí decir esto, y lo entendí, dejéme caer en el triste abismo de mis pecados. (114)
>
> It is my desire that today you fulfill the promise that you made to my Bride the Church so many years ago. I understood then that he said this to me because of a verse that I have written that says, "With flowers and emeralds,/ Chosen on cool mornings/ We shall weave garlands,/ Flowering in Your love,/ And bound with one hair of mine."
>
> And once I heard him say that, and understood it, I let myself fall deep in the sad chasm of my sins.[21]

In the notebooks, there is no further attribution of the poem; the Spanish "que yo tengo escrito" ("that I have written") leaves it unclear as to whether María is the author, a copier, or the owner of a written copy. (In the printed version, the editor clarifies, "Observación: De flores y esmeraldas/ en las frescas mañanas escogidas. Esta es la Canción 22, que se halla en las obras del Bendito Padre Fray Juan de la Cruz" [114] ["Observation: Of emeralds, and of flowers/ In the early morning gathered. This is Verse 22 of the *Song*, to be found in the works of the Blessed Father Juan de la Cruz"], who in turn took many of the images from the Song of Songs.) Sor María does not use the poem here as an authority or an allusion to an external text; on the contrary, she has so fully assimilated the verses that she can insert them into a circular mystic narrative. In her own mystic practice, which she represents in the form of dialogue, she receives a reply from God that she can only comprehend by thinking of San Juan's mystic poem, also represented as a dialogue with God. While Sor María's understanding of the poem's meaning may come from her exposure to commentaries, it is important to note that she finds an explanation for her vision not in recalling an exegesis of the Song of Songs or the "Cántico" but in the dense, figuratively rich poem itself. There is no *theological* exegesis, only a personal understanding of the poem that she then applies to her own life. Indeed, the relation between God's words to her, this particular stanza of the poem, and her conclusion is not automatically clear to the reader. The stanza seems to function mnemonically, as representing the entire allegory of the bride of Christ, and the prompt to consider her sins might be seen as a strategy to minimize (and at the same time legitimate) the self-aggrandizement implicit in the act of inserting herself into a divine narrative. However, these are only speculations; it is impossible to say for sure. What is essential to note is the multiple levels of her personalization of the poem. The sentence from God takes the narrative of the Song of Songs about an unnamed bride and makes it about María; the mental recollection of the poem that she has either copied or saved ("que yo tengo escrito"), also about an unnamed bride, at least in her interpretation of it, confirms the interpretation.

In this episode from María de la Antigua, the cited fragment of the "Cántico," while recalled through memory and applied to understand a mystical audition, is still specified as a physical object, written on a piece of paper. This is but one way that the *Cantar* finds its way into the autobiographical narratives, above and beyond any other scriptural passage. In other visions, as we will see, it enters as in more abstract form: as a template for understanding experience and even a shorthand for the ineffable, as in the autobiography of Ana de San Bartolomé, where she records, after an experience in which she saw and felt Christ reach out and take her head into his arms, "Lo que el alma sentía en este rato no se puede decir ni creer, si Dios no alzara la fuerza de aquel amor que encendía mi espíritu. Era en aquella gracia lo que dice la Esposa en los *Cantares*: 'Entrado se ha la Esposa en el vergel …'" (84) ("What my soul felt during this cannot be told nor believed, nor could it be endured if God had not increased the strength of love that inflamed my spirit. It was in that grace that the Bride says in the Song of Songs, 'The Bride has entered the garden, she rests in the arms and pleasure of her Beloved, her neck reclining over the sweet arms of the Beloved" [65]).[22] Here the movement is not from experience to figurative language in an attempt to push rational comprehension; instead, the figurative, poetic language becomes both the template for understanding the experience and representing it comprehensibly. In many of the other accounts, the words of the *Cantar* are experienced internally. For example, Teresa de Jesús María writes that "me parecía que interiormente me decian estas palabras de los Cantares *surge propera amica*" (64) ("It seemed that in my interior I head these words from the *Cantares: Surge propera amica*").[23] María Astorch – who claimed that her ability to understand Latin was a mystic gift – wrote that "Me fui al comulgador a recogerme y, haciéndome su Majestad merced por su bondad infinita, me cogió el interior con unas palabras de los Cantares, que dicen: *Ego flos campi et lilium convallium*" (357) ("I went to take communion and to withdraw in prayer and, His Majesty in His infinite kindness granting me mercy, He seized me in my interior with the words of the *Cantares*: I am the rose of Sharon, and the lily of the valleys").[24] Again, the particular passage seems irrelevant: it is the interiorization of the poem itself and, by extension, the spousal relation with God that matters. At times, the *Cantar* is heard in Castilian. Ana de San Bartolomé is passing through a period of spiritual desolation when:

> como por una resquicia entra un rayo de luz en un aposento oscuro, así entró en mi alma una migajita de luz, y entendí que me decían: 'El esposo te quiere bien y es contento de verte padecer.' Con esta pequeña luz, el espíritu se levantó, y salía diciendo este verso que dice la Esposa en los Cantares algo disfrazada: "Oh cristalina fuente/ Si en esos tus semblantes plateados/ Formases de repente/ Los ojos deseados/ Que tengo en mis entrañas dibujados!" Esto satisfizo y dio hartura a mi corazón. (187)

> Just as a ray of light enters a dark room through a crack, so a little sliver of light entered my soul, and I understood that they were telling me, "The Beloved loves you well and is not content at seeing you suffer." With this little light my spirit rose up and I came out saying this verse that the bride, somewhat disguised, says in the Song of Songs: O crystalline fountain!/ If only you could form/ Suddenly on your silver surface/ The beloved eyes I carry inscribed within me!" This satisfied and gave fullness to my heart. [113]

The "disfraz" is actually the poetic intervention of San Juan; she says her spirit sings the song of the bride of the *Cantar*, but the words are those of San Juan de la Cruz. The intertextuality is possible because the words of the *Cantar* are the words of God, and these exist in a space prior to and beyond any given text. The specific expression is merely a "disfraz." This internalization and then textual reproduction of the internalized *Cantar* is all the more remarkable in light of the controversy surrounding the book. While Fray Luis was censured for his attempts to publish a vernacular translation for widespread circulation, within a controlled space of a convent and the private text that is the *vida*, there was no censorship of interior, personal, and at times idiosyncratic identification with the Beloved.

It is not coincidental that Astorch's mystic audition of the *Cantar* occurs during communion, as both the mystic wedding and the sacrament of communion were frequently taught as allegories for the physical-spiritual union between the Christian and Christ. Many nuns wrote of communion in terms of interiorization: the spiritual assimilation (via corporeal ingestion) of the body of Christ.[25] In the spiritual diaries of María Vela y Cueto, she records that, while waiting to receive communion:

> comenzóse a ablandar el corazón y a sentir el olor de aquel pan divino, con que crecía el deseo. Y parecíame que este cuerpo santísimo de Cristo Nuestro Señor era como la flor del campo ... Y que mientras más le

quisieron hollar y deshacer [al Señor], más olor dió con que lo trajo todo a sí, conforme a aquellas palabras: *Cum exaltatus fuero a terra, omnia traham ad me ipsum.*[26] Y que tocada de este olor la esposa, le dice: *Trae me, post te curremus in odorem unguentorum tuorum.*[27] (116)

My heart began to soften and I began to note the smell of that divine bread, causing its desire to grow. And it seemed to me that this holiest body of Christ Our Lord was like the flower of the field ... And the more they tried to offend and tear Him down, the more fragrance He gave, with which He drew all to him, according to those words: "And I, if I be lifted up from the earth, will draw all men unto me." And the bride, touched by this smell, says to Him: "Pleasing is the fragrance of your perfumes; your name is like perfume poured out."

Unlike in Astorch, here neither quotation is identified as coming from a biblical text; the only marker is the shift from Castilian to Latin. The *Cantar* is so fully assimilated that María experiences *both* the Bride and the Bridegroom's words in/as her own voice. In fact, the two sentences are from different books, even different Testaments. As discussed in previous chapters, the focus on bodily senses permits a departure from discursive reason. The entire passage is a linking of literal and metaphoric interpretation, bodily and spiritual experience. The ritual of communion is the natural point of departure for this experience, as it is the moment in which a physical object becomes a spiritual one, and also because the *reality* of the transformation, as insisted on in Catholic doctrine, defies rational explanation. The implicit metaphor of the sacrament (even if it is a metaphor that doctrine denies as a metaphor) seems to impel a series of metaphoric associations: the bread is the body of Christ; the smell of the body of Christ is like the smell of a flower; the smell of a flower is like the smell of perfumes discussed in the Song of Songs. As we have seen, Laredo and Osuna perform similar textual tapestries, linking diverse texts through etymology or metaphorical resonances, but in María's vision, in contrast, it is her own experience that confirms the unity of the Scriptures. In her account we do not find, as we might in a sermon connecting Old and New Testament passages, an explanation of the connection. The connection between the two evoked phrases is the author's own experience of smelling and desiring the communion wafer. Instead of explaining either passage, she creates a text that is as densely symbolic and sensorial as a mystic poem but entirely personalized, not only because it is recounted in first person and the voices speak directly to her but because it is inserted into a daily record of spiritual experience.

Interiority and the Baroque Fold

Contemplation and the cultivation of divine union occurs within the contemplative's interior, but the *vida* authors often, in true Baroque fashion, recount, within their visions, interiors within interiors. To see the way this folding of interiority is recounted, we can examine another passage from Vela y Cueto's diary, in which she recounts a miraculous exchange of hearts with Christ. The episode recalls a similar miracle attributed to Catherine of Siena, and on the surface it might seem to show nothing more than Vela y Cueto's familiarity with the Italian saint and aspiration to follow her example. However, the differences in the textual accounts – who writes, how the authors use language and construct their authority – are, for our purposes, more important than the obvious filiation. The contrast is, I argue, exemplary of the distinction between the mystic account as narrated within a *vida* and earlier hagiographic or visionary narratives. Let us consider first Raymond of Capua's account of the famous scene of Catherine of Siena's heart exchange with Christ. Raymond was Catherine's confessor but also her strongest advocate, having assumed the role already convinced of her sanctity. By the time he wrote the *Legenda maior*, he was campaigning for her canonization. The work, in Latin and published after Catherine's death, is thus directed at a public of Church officials in a position to promote this cause. He begins a description of Catherine entering into "the kind of excess that is known as ecstasy" (II.2.112)[28] by clearly differentiating between his third-person perspective and the interior experience that he cannot access: "This [her ecstasy] I experienced personally time and time again, and so did others, who saw and touched, as I did, her arms and hands, which remained so numb while she was in a state of contemplation that it would have been easier to break them than to get them to move. Her eyes remained tightly shut, her ears could not hear the loudest noise, and none of her bodily senses performed its accustomed functions" (II.6.164). But immediately and without marking the transition, he enters the interior narrative – "The Lord began to appear to His bride not only privately, as He had done at first, but in public too, in fact before everyone's eyes and quite familiarly, both when she was walking about and when she was standing still, and He set such a fire blazing within her heart" – before ending in a retreat back to the external, third-person narrative position: "He set such a fire blazing within her heart *that she herself told her confessor* that she could not find words to express the divine experiences she had" (164, emphasis mine). Crucially, the third-person relativization of the experience is only applied to the protestation of ineffability. The thing-that-she-cannot-express has already been expressed within the omniscient affirmation: it is God who appears to her and produces the fire of love in her heart, rather than a mysterious sensation subject to discernment. The protestation of ineffability, having been made, is quickly abandoned, and the language with which Raymond relates the narrative, while marked off as "it appeared to her," is clear, unproblematized, and indeed she doubles down on her certainty when her confessor (not Raymond, but one of the earlier, more sceptical ones) expresses doubt.

> It appeared to her that her Heavenly Bridegroom came to her as usual, opened her left side, took out her heart, and then went away. This vision was so effective and agreed so well with what she felt inside herself that in confession she told her confessor that she no longer had a heart in her breast. He shook his head a little at this way of putting it, and in a joking way reproved her; but she repeated it and insisted that she meant what she said. "Truly, father," she said, "in so far as I feel anything at all, it seems to me that my heart has been taken away altogether. The Lord did indeed appear to me, opened my left side, took my heart out and went away." Her confessor than [sic] pointed out that it is impossible to live without a heart, but the virgin replied that nothing is impossible to God, and that she was convinced that she no longer had a heart. (165)

Lest the reader side with the skeptical confessor, a second account confirms Catherine's narrative, now completely abandoning any mark of subjectivity ("it appeared" "it seemed") or distance between narrator and the events narrated.

> One day she was in the church of the Preaching Friars, which the Sisters of Penance of St. Dominic in Siena used to attend. The others had gone out, but she went on praying. Finally she came out of her ecstasy and got up to go home. All at once a light from heaven encircled her, and in the light appeared the Lord, holding in His holy hands a human heart, bright red and shining. At the appearance of the Author of Light she had fallen to the ground, trembling all over, but He came up to her, opened her left side once again and put the heart He was holding in His hands inside her, saying "Dearest daughter, as I took your heart away from you the other day, now, you see, I am giving you mine, so that you can go on living with it forever." (165)

This is the account that is translated into Spanish under the auspices of Cardinal Cisneros's reform, and as Gillian Ahlgren shows, directly influenced the Carmelite reformers.[29] The heart-exchange miracle in particular becomes nearly metonymic to Catherine's life, akin to Teresa's moment of transverberation in her own legend. Yet unlike Teresa's transverberation, the story has been, in Heather Watt's words, "entirely transformed" from the original autobiographical account (814). Watt's analysis is important and convincing, but it is crucial to note that the transformation, which involves downplaying Catherine's active intercessory role to conform to a more accepted model of passive feminine spirituality, does not affect the clarity and confidence of the account narrated.[30] In Catherine's letter 371 to Raymond,[31] she enters into a dialogue with God, who speaks in clear doctrine, unproblematized as speech (359–61). The words attributed to God not only authorize Catherine as God's interlocutor but provide an exegesis of the Song of Songs, the sort of theological discourse that a woman could not express in her own voice. After "channeling" this sermon, she, just as her hagiographer Raymond did, makes a nod to the insufficiency of words "to describe such mysteries, or what my understanding and affection conceived" (361) and then proceeds with a clear exposition.

> Then, I got up, and God set me in his presence. True, I'm always present to him because he holds all within himself, but this was in a new way, as if my memory and understanding and will had nothing to do with my body ... Then the devils let out an enormous screeching over me, trying with their terror to hinder and slacken my free and blazing desire. They struck against the husk of my body, but my desire blazed up, and I called out, "Oh eternal God, accept the sacrifice of my life within this mystic body, holy Church! I have nothing to give except what you have given me. Take my heart and squeeze it out over the face of this bride!"
>
> Then God Eternal, turning the eyes of his mercy [on me], tore my heart out by the roots and squeezed it out over holy Church. He had drawn it to himself with such force that if he hadn't encircled the vessel of my body with his strength (not wanting it to be broken), the life would have gone out of it. (362)

While the account is not identical to that provided by Raymond, the first person and third person share clear exposition, confident and clear narration that, despite occurring within an interior space, is narrated as if it were an external experience. The raw mystic experience has already been processed into language, with a clear separation between devils and divine, the Lord and Catherine. The moment in which the boundaries between Self and God are blurred – the exchange of hearts – is narrated against a backdrop of a clearly delineated Self and God.

We may compare these two accounts with a heart-transfer episode narrated in María Vela y Cueto's *Libro de las Mercedes*.[32] She begins recalling her desire for a more literal relationship with God. Rather than seek to understand Him through abstractions or metaphors, she asks that He show her His face, praying "Señor mío, revélaos como hacíades con vuestros amigos" ("My Lord, reveal yourself as you did to your friends"). Immediately, however, she criticizes herself for presumption and asks His pardon. In that instant:

> ofrecióseme luego que de la misma manera entraba la esposa, diciendo: *Osculetur me osculo oris suis*, y que luego se lo habían concedido, pues dice: *Meliora sunt ubera tua vino*. Y parecíame que lo mismo hacía el Señor conmigo, que me mantenía no sólo con la leche de sus pechos, sino con sus mismas entrañas y corazón ... Con esto torné a recoger y acordándome de mi joya, presentéla al Señor, diciendo: *fiat mihi secundum verbum tuum*. Representóseme aquí cómo el Señor preciaba tanto esta piedra preciosa, y la traía siempre sobre su corazón: *Et legam tuam in medio cordis mei*. (162–3)[33]

> then it came to me that the Bride had entered in the same way, saying: Let Him kiss me with the kiss of His mouth, and that it had been granted to her, since she says: for thy love is better than wine. And it seemed to me that our Lord did the same with me, that He sustained me not only with the milk from His breast, but with His very bowels and heart ... With this I gathered myself again and remembering my jewel, I presented it to our Lord, saying: Let it be, according to your word. And it was represented to me how much our Lord esteemed this precious stone and carried it always above His heart: And your law is the law of my heart.

Here there is a repeated blurring between María and the Lord: between languages, between bodies, and between texts. The physical contact begins on a "realistic" plane, with a kiss between mouths, passes through the ingestion of what can only be a spiritual milk (given the address to a "Señor"[34]), and finally becomes the entry into the "entrañas y corazón." There is an inverse movement between what is happening in the diary entry – God entering the mind/heart of María – and what is happening within this vision – María entering into the interior of God. Likewise, if the spiritual grace itself is, in the context the diary, evidence of God giving spiritual gifts to María, within the vision it is María who gives a precious gift – her "joya" (the symbol is a frequent one within the Song) – to God. God, in showing his appreciation, places the gift over His heart, adding another layer of interiorization within an interiorization. Estefanía de la Encarnación has a similar vision, wherein she sees, with her "ojos interiores" a vision of Christ reclining, and, as she gazes into his "pecho Santissimo, que traía descubierto" ("Most Holy breast, which was uncovered"), she hears (with her "oídos interiores") him say, "díjome, mírate, parecióme veía en su pecho un espejo, según estaba de trasparente, y dentro del mismo pecho me vi echada como si fuerta muerta ... mi rostro era el mismo" (86r) ("he said to me, look at yourself, and I seemed to see in his breast a mirror, it was so transparent, and within that same breast I saw myself laid out as if I were dead ... my face was the same"). In Christ's interior within her interior, she sees her own exterior face. María de Cristo sees "por una visión intelectual como su majestad me trocó mi corazón en el suyo y al instante empecé a abrasarme en su amor ... sentí que mi querido esposo se había puesto sobre mi corazón sacramentado y me decía, 'ahora estoy en mi centro'" (20) ("in an intellectual vision that His Majesty exchanged my heart for His and in that instant I began to burn with His love ... I felt that my beloved bridegroom had settled above my sacramentally purified heart and was saying to me, 'now I am in my centre'").[35]

In each of these examples, there is an obsessive, literally impossible proliferation of interiorities. In contrast to the verticality of medieval visionary works – think of Dante's *Paradiso* or Hildegard's *Scivias* – as an index of spiritual value, in these authors inner depth is the sign and proof of a spiritual encounter. Even in a late medieval visionary like Catherine, we saw that the interior space framed the account but did not affect the narrative, at least not beyond the single moment of the miraculous exchange. In the seventeenth-century writers, interiorization and its contradictions/complexities are not the frame: it is the object to be narrated. It is useful here to think of Deleuze's definition of the Baroque, not as a temporal period but as an operation that produces continuous folding and unfolding, "all the way to infinity." In fact, he continues, these folds go to two parallel infinities: "the pleats of matter, and the folds in the soul" (3). Deleuze's examples centre on architecture, and the question of the soul is left unexamined. Instead of interiority of the soul, he contrasts the Baroque façade with the crypt, the interior of the building. Yet had he ventured one step further inwards, he would have found, within these Baroque churches, nuns writing of their interior lives, translating the linguistic obsession with inwardness that we saw in the mystic treatises into lived experience, mapped not just onto but into their own bodies.

The *vida* authors rely on some of the same strategies we have identified in these other genres in their attempt to represent interior, ineffable experience: alternation between precise ekphrastic detail, vivid sensorial imagery, and disavowal of the power of language or sensory imagery to adequately describe the visions; figurative language; paradox. Yet the diagnostic purpose that compels the *vida* means that often the emphasis shifts. For instance, we find similar evocations of sensory detail in both mystic poems and *vidas*, but in the latter there tends to be an emphasis on the subjective experience of perception rather than the sight, smell, or sound itself. María Astorch writes of "olores suavísimos" ("the sweetest of smells"), but instead of describing them through comparison or adjectives, she focuses on her own thoughts and senses: "verdaderamente se me llevan el sentido interior, y son tales estos olores que no se pueden distinguir sus particularidades. Algunas veces he querido reparar si conociera algo de él, y, al instante, secar dichos olores sin poder apercibir cosa; otras veces de pronto apercibo algo" (125–6) ("truly they transport me in my inner senses, and these smells are such that their particular elements cannot be distinguished. Sometimes I have tried to pause and see if I can know recognize something in them, but in that instant, the smells dry up and I cannot detect a thing; at other times, suddenly I detect something"). This is subtly distinct from the formulaic disavowal of language that we find in all genres of mystic language: instead of a simple, concise expression of the ineffable paradox, here the author is recreating a process of self-discernment, enacting the first steps in the task for which the account has been ordered to begin with. Because female virtue was so closely linked to humility, she cannot complete the discernment process, arriving at any definitive interpretation or judgment of her vision. The focus on her subjectivity, but always in terms of her subjective limitations, reveals a willingness/desire for self-scrutiny but also a willingness to let the confessor's superior judgment fill in the gaps or "particularidades." This emphasis on subjective perceptions and the degree to which they escape representations is what differentiates these mystic visions from first-person medieval vision texts, such as Hildegard's or even Catherine of Siena's, which tend to be narrative and prophetic.[36] The *vida* writers' success (approbation from the confessor, permission to continue her contemplative practice) depends, at least in the early stages of her spiritual career, on appearing to relinquish the role of interpretation to her confessor. Where she does assign meaning to the elements of her own vision, it tends to be one of unimpeachable orthodoxy, as in an anonymous nun's visionary revelation of the paradox of God's incarnation.[37] The nun entered into:

> oración de unión muy sensible, sintiéndome anegar en una profundidad sin suelo y ser llevada y presa en un abrazo. Otras veces estaba como

tragada y de otras maneras la imaginación con el entendimiento y memoria estaban ocupados en grandezas de Dios. El entendimiento se quedaba luego suspenso, viendo mejor que con los ojos corporales lo que entonces entendía, y la memoria e imaginación en los ejercicios de él o en diversas cosas se ocupaban. Entendía en esta oración que he dicho cómo Dios cabía en la pequeñez del hombre porque veía yo dentro de mí un lugar infinito, espacio profundo, y luego se ofrecía a la imaginación imaginar aquello que veía tan claro como he dicho.

a very delicate contemplative prayer, feeling myself drown in a bottomless depth and be transported and overcome in an embrace and other times it was as if I were swallowed up and in other ways, the imagination, with the understanding and memory, were occupied in God's glories. The understanding was then left in suspension, seeing better than with the bodily eyes what it then understood, and my memory and imagination were occupied with its exercises or various things. I understood from this prayer that I have said how God fits within the tiny space of man because I could see within myself an infinite deep space and then it was offered to my imagination to imagine that which I saw so clearly, as I have said.

Although there is an interpretation of the vision here, the focus of the narrative is neither on the image seen nor the interpretation drawn but is instead on the author's process of perception and comprehension. Not atypically, the vision is one of depth, another example of the Baroque inward fold towards infinity. This is an entirely closed system: God speaks (in images) to the nun to help her understand His own ineffable Word, she writes words to gain permission to continue this communication. The outside world drops away; the visions compel no action in the external world, no construction of a statue as in the rural Castilian visions analysed by William Christian, no advice for the King or the Pope, as in Catherine's letters or the "visions" of a Lucrecia de León or María de Ágreda. Instead, they focus on the interior space and on the most comprehensive representation in language of the interior experience. The inward Baroque fold stems not from a "horror al vacío" or a fascination with complexity for its own sake, but instead the need to reconfigure space to represent a spiritual encounter that can be offered to but also protected from vigilant authorities.

Linguistic Innovation

Those *vidas* that were not edited into single, coherent narratives sometimes allow us a glimpse into how the transactional nature of the *vida*'s production shaped choices in metaphor or vocabulary, how a certain metaphor might be chosen through the dialogue between penitent and confessor. María Astorch writes in a letter included in the *Camino*:

> Lo que V[uestra] S[eñorí]a dice en este mismo número que declare unas palabras que dicen: "Me recibe su Majestad con atracción, como suele," respondo, Señor, aunque [sic] así como la piedra imán atrae para sí por su virtud propia a una pajuela y las cuentas llamadas lambres hacen lo [sic], así se digna su Majestad eterna hacerlo, cuando es servido, con mi espíritu: es un instante y con suma brevedad y sutileza, como un rayo y con más brevedad, si decirse puede, me siento llamada con una sutileza extraña. (293)

> With respect to what Your Grace says in this same point, that I expand on the words that say: "His Majesty receives me with attraction, as is his custom," I respond, sir, that as the lodestone attracts a little straw to itself by its own power and the beads called *lambres* do, so deigns his eternal Majesty, when it suits him, with my spirit: in an instant and with maximal quickness and subtlety, like a ray and even quicker, if such a thing can be said, I feel myself called with a strange subtlety.

An editor's note clarifies that *lambres* "probablemente se trata de las *cuentas de leche*, que las madres se colgaban en la creencia de que atraían la leche" ("this probably refers to milk beads that mothers wore around their necks in the belief that they drew out milk"). We see that Astorch had originally described her interior experience as a process of attraction, and then, asked by her confessor for further clarification, she shifted to metaphoric comparison: it is *like this* (beads), but it is also *like this* (a ray), and at the same time it is not exactly like either or both ("si decirse puede," "una sutileza extraña"). While in the *libros de oración* we saw the authors using similar language of comparison/difference to simultaneously describe mystic union and show the impossibility of its description, here we arrive at the strategy through different means. Instead of a poetic strategy to represent the unrepresentable, it is the dialogic nature of the *vida*, particularly one assembled *ex post facto*, that produces a negotiation of terminology and a plurality of poetically rich approximations.

Unlike the mystic poets, where such protestations are countered by the achievement of a precise rhythmic and metrical scheme, here description often *does* fail, or it succeeds in representing the failure of representation. We might compare two similar sentiments expressed in a poem and a *vida*. María Astorch speaks of a "herida en el corazón y desmayo" ("wound in her heart and fainting spell") that results in a "cautividad interior [que] es tan profunda como si viera en lo profundo, y en las comuniones es cosa asentada, si no es que esté actualmente en oscuridades, cuales tengo ya tocadas y dicho algo de ellas" (123–4) ("interior captivity that is as deep as if I were seeing in depth, and during communion these are a given, unless I am in a period of darkness, which I have already touched upon and said some things about"). Teresa de Ávila, in her poem "Vivo sin vivir en mí,"[38] describes the "divina prisión/ del amor con que yo vivo/ ha hecho a Dios mi cautivo,/ y libre mi corazón" (2–3) ("divine prison/ of love with which I live/ Has made my God my captive/ And set my heart free"). In poetry, the paradox is symmetrical, precise, whereas in prose, it is insufficient and only pushes the author to attempt further approximation of the sensation: *como si, si no es*, and recursive reference to previous attempts.

Frequently, the most linguistically innovative passages emerge from a frame that pretends to present a methodical description of prayer practice. Astorch, after describing a particular prayer experience, often presents, in list form, the resulting "penas" ("sufferings") and "efectos" ("effects"). Yet far from being a coherent or unified series of measurable effects, they blossom into a mix of sensory and poetic images. We saw a similar dissolution into poetry of the scientific system in Osuna and Laredo, but there the division between the systematic and poetic portions of the text is more marked. Laredo set out a week-long program of reflections that became poetic and unsystematic in the prose exposition, but the majority of *vida* writers do not separate out a third-person account of the rules and principles of contemplative practice before narrating their own experiences; the unpublished *vida* is solely concerned with the author's experience, and thus the paradox of a systematic mystic practice permeates the narrative. Astorch, after she concludes a series of excruciating physical-spiritual tribulations relates that:

> De modo, Señor, que, a lo que yo entiendo, las penas distintas por continuación pasaron y he quedado con la fuerza de sus efectos, porque tengo continuamente en el corazón un ardor que se me abrasa, un fuego que me gasta las fuerzas y casi me voy desmayando; … un leer en mis mismos papeles algunas misericordias recibidas; y cosas mucho menores: un mirar el cielo, soledad o arboleda, un oler un suave olor, un sentir tocas las campanas para los divinos oficios, un ver llover con serenidad, un día cubierto, un sentir truenos, ver un puesto lleno de nieve, qué sé yo, Señor mío, mil niñerías que es imposible decirlas todas …

> Such that, Sir, from what I understand, the different tribulations then passed by and I was left with the force of their effects, because I have an ongoing burning in my heart that inflames me, a fire that exhausts my strength and I go along almost fainting; ... a reading within my own papers of certain mercies I have received; and much smaller things: a gazing at the heavens, solitude or grove, a smelling of a gentle smell, a hearing of the bells chime for the holy offices, a watching it rain with serenity, a cloudy day, a hearing thunder, seeing a spot covered in snow, what do I know, my Lord, a thousand trifles, it is impossible to say them all.

It would not be hard to pass off the second half of this passage as a modernist poem.

In the anonymous nun's account discussed earlier,[39] the author sets out to write a methodical account of her prayer habits. She begins "Mi exercicio ordinario ha sido desde el principio" ("My regular exercises have been, from the start"), seeming to promise a systematic account, but again, the system quickly gives way to the sensory. She does not manage to list the "exercicio" because "un afecto penoso – se adelantaba al exercicio" ("an arduous feeling interrupted the exercise before it started"). And then, seeming to return to a methodical structure, she announces that "este afecto penoso causa diversos efectos en mi espíritu" ("this arduous feeling caused diverse effects in my spirit"), but the description of the effects is all poetry:

> Sentía encenderse interiormente un fuego que crecía hasta que con deleite el alma se abrasaba en él. A veces a este fuego soplaba un aire delgado y fresco mansamente que amortiguándose con él quedaba mas encendida y a veces muerta y algo apagada aquella ansia por entonces, mas después y mas crecida. Llenábame otras veces todo de este aire y me parecía que estaba como hinchada, otras veces sentía que mi espíritu era llevado por una soledad y niebla obscura y en ella se quedaba el alma como sin fuerzas y ahogada sin que Dios obrase nada en ella y las potencias de la misma manera; y con un resuello que a deshora venía a mi espíritu era como sacada de una pesadumbre y entraba en cada resuello un grado mas en mas obscura mi niebla cuanto era mas oscura daba mayor satisfacción al alma. (334r)

> I felt a fire light in my interior, it grew until the soul was ablaze with delight. Sometimes a thin, fresh breeze blew gently into this fire and tempered by this, that yearning was left even more inflamed, and sometimes dead and somewhat diminished at that time but later and greater [*sic*]. At other times I was all filled up with this breeze and it seemed I was swollen,

> and other times I felt that my spirit was transported by a solitude and dark cloud in which the soul was as if without energy and drowning, and God could do nothing in it [the soul] and the faculties likewise, and with a breath that comes to me unexpectedly I am as if taken from a nightmare and with each breath my fog entered a greater degree of darkness, the darker it was the greater satisfaction given to my soul.[40]

The attempt at a method is belied by the diversity of the effects but also the disorder of their representation. She does not invent a poetic language but instead represents the unsystematic, unsystematizable experience of union in a whirlwind of inherited metaphors: a "lenguaje poético" that stands out precisely for its escape from any stricture of poetic form.

In general, no *vida* author "invents" a metaphor; a common language of fire, water, flowers, birds/flying insects, and castles/palaces runs from text to text. It is not the language of the visions that is new but the way the visions are integrated into the non-visionary life. On the one hand, there is a constant attempt to match the interior experience with scientific or objective measurements: the time of day, the position of the body, the liturgical season. In essence, the authors are performing similar measurements to those Ignacio de Loyola made in his *Diario*, as discussed in chapter one, but because, unlike Ignacio, they write for someone else, they cannot assume their reader will share any common code or experience. The interior life must be narrated alongside the record of externalities. For example, María Vela y Cueto narrates:

> A la noche me sentí muy descaecida y casi no pude cenar. Acabadas Completas me fui a la celda a las 8 y me encerré hasta dadas las 11. Al principio estuve tan floja y remisa que estuve sentada hasta las 9. Lo demás llevé de rodillas y en pie, con harta sequedad y durmiéndome. Estando así sentí ruido en la celda y hube un poco de temor, mas pasóseme luego considerando que naide me podía hacer daño sin la voluntad del Señor … Sirvióme el miedo de despertarme, y cayóme en gracia la ganancia que sacó del demonio. Después tomé la disciplina y me fui a la cama. Y me senté como la había propuesto y así me dormí dadas las doce. Y desperté a las 3 y media. La oración que pude tener fue una hora. Y ésta llevé haciéndome fuerza a no dormirme. Y medio soñando volvía con ansias de la comunión. Tañeron a Tercia y fuime, y en ella y la misa hube de estar con un cuidado del Oficio, y acabada [134] comenzó el Señor a dar toques al corazón para recogerme. Y parecíame que no era con tanta fuerza como solían, que bien podía disimular en esta pelea. Estuve toda la Sexta y como vi que iba adelante el impulso me fui a la celda y postrada en la presencia

del Señor me ofrecía lo que su Majestad quisiese hacer de mí. Sentíame herida, mas no sabía la causa de aquel dolor, que me hacía gemir y suspirar de lo íntimo del alma. (133–4)

At night I felt very weak and I could barely eat supper. Once *completes* were finished I went to my cell, at 8pm and stayed there until 11. At the beginning I was so weak and remiss that I was seated until 9. The rest I spent kneeling and standing, with dryness and nodding off. While I was seated I heard a noise in the cell and I felt a little fear, but it passed quickly when I considered that no one could hurt me if it were not God's will … The fear served to wake me up, and I was grateful for the advantage He took from the devil. Later I disciplined myself and went to bed. I sat down as I had had planned and fell asleep around twelve. I woke up at 3:30. I was able to manage an hour of prayer. And this was by using all my energies not to fall asleep. Half asleep I came back with a longing for communion. The bells for morning prayers rang and during them and the mass I had a responsibility to fulfill, and once that was done our Lord began to tap my heart to draw myself inward. And it seemed to me that it was not with as much strength as usual, and that I could conceal this struggle. I was there for all of noon prayers and as I saw that the impulse was growing I went to my cell and prostrated myself in the presence of the Lord and I offered myself for whatever His Majesty wished to do with me. I felt wounded, but I did not know the cause of that pain, that made me moan and breathe from deep within my soul.

The details of the discipline in the cell, as well as the struggle to dissimulate the interior impulses in public, speak to another narrative that runs through many of these autobiographies: the conflict between dedication to contemplation and the life in the community, and the scepticism or opposition of fellow members of that community. The *vida* author writes for her confessor's validation, and this validation will have very real effects on her status and treatment in her convent or religious community. Yet she must prove within her text that she is not *principally* seeking validation or special privileges. The text becoming a strategic tool in privileging the mystic's truth over those of her sceptics because it allows her to reveal what is hidden from sceptic's eyes, either because it occurs alone in her cell or because it occurs hidden within her interior. "Estando en Tercia me sentí recoger y como no podía irme, tomé por remedio callar y dejarme llevar. Y así lo hice hasta que hube de salir a cantar un fabordón y decíanme dentro. Déjate abrasar" (38–9) ("During midmorning prayer, I felt myself gathering inward and as I could not leave, my solution was to remain silent and allow myself to be carried away. And that's what I did until I had to sing a faux bordon [a liturgical song] and they said to me in my interior: Let yourself burn").

Darkness and Secrets

The *vida* allows, and in fact compels, the author to express and communicate what San Juan de la Cruz counseled should not be expressed. (From his *Avisos y sentencias*: "Calle lo que Dios le diere. Y acuérdese de aquel dicho de la Escritura: Mi secreto para mí" [Aviso 292] ["Be silent concerning what God may have given you and recall that saying of the bride: *My secret for myself.* (Is. 24:16)" (Maxim 74, 679)]). The spiritual diary becomes the authorized space of the secret. Yet the author, through her writing, is requesting permission to make her interior life not secret, to be allowed to give in to her *recogimientos* and *mercedes* during or instead of participating in the external tasks of a community. And should her confessor deem it appropriate, she is further asking that the interior content of her visions become public through the circulation of the *vida* itself.

The *vidas* do not focus on elements of communal life that are entirely external to their practice of mysticism, but, as suggested above, they conceive much more broadly than mystic poetry or theology of the elements of life that are relevant to mystic practice. Mystic poetry is the highlight reel of goals scored; the *diario* includes not only the whole game, with all its missed shots and shots not taken, but also the training regimen and post-game rituals. Even the mystic treatise emphasizes the systematic ascent; while it is expected that the reader will not be able to follow each step without backslides and frustrations, the prose itself does not narrate these struggles. For instance, Bernabé de Palma indicates in the opening to the *Via spiritus*, that "Un aviso es necesario en los principiantes para que no se engañen, y es que sepan que cualquier autor no escribe sus primeros principios, esto es, la frialdad, sequedad, tentaciones y cosas semejantes por que ellos pensando esto no yerren, comenzando por cosas altas su edificio sin haber pasado por las menudencias de los principios" (7) ("A caution is necessary for beginners so they not be deceived, and that is they know that no author writes of his first beginnings, that is, coldness, dryness, temptations and things of this nature. This [his warning] is so they do not err by starting to build lofty things without having gone through the minutiae of the beginning"). In contrast, the struggle of *sequedad* is a constant theme in the *vidas*. María Vela y Cueto writes that "El domingo estuve como una hora después de haber comulgado, sin poderme entender con el Señor.

Como si no le tuviera conmigo, sino que estuviera allá en las Indias" (84) ("On Sunday I spent an hour after communion without being able to communicate with Our Lord. It was as if he were not with me, as if he were in a faraway land"). While in this passage there is a dryness of style that matches the *sequedad* described, at other times her spiritual failures are detailed in the same sort of emotive language as the periods of mystic vision: "el haberme quitado a mí la oración, que por lágrimas que derramé ni por más tiempo que perseveré pidiendo y partiéndose el corazón de dolor, no hay más parecer que somos oídas que si fuese el cielo de bronce" (183) ("my ability to pray having been taken from me, for all the tears I shed and all the time I persevered, pleading and my heart breaking in pain, there was no better chance of being heard than if the sky were made of bronze"). The obsessive interiorization is applied even to an absence of interior prayer, which she repeatedly refers to as a "desamparo interior" (135, 202) ("interior desolation").

In the more complete *vidas*, written after their authors achieved a certain degree of recognition and subject to rounds of editing before being published, there is progress from *sequedad* to grace. The progressive ease and fruitfulness of mystic prayer is a sign that the method is legitimate and the subject worthy. But the reverse is not necessarily the case, and most *vida* authors also speak at length about their own trials and tribulations in getting even to the first rung on the ladder of mystic union. Yet while the *vida* can admit extended considerations of doubt and despair, it does seem to require a modicum of transcendence. The limits of the *vida* can be sensed through a fascinating passage in the anonymous and incomplete manuscript discussed previously in this chapter.[41] While the nun does experience visions and other spiritual graces, at one point while she is still a novice, she writes of a period of struggle which, unusual for this genre, encompasses much more than her spiritual practice. She fears that "mis padres hermanos y parientes y amigos todos tenían un olvido de mi como de muerta y sabía hacían burla de mí" ("my parents, brothers and relatives and friends had all forgotten me, as if I were dead, and I knew they were making fun of me") and laments that "no había suceso en mi favor" (337v–338r) ("nothing went in my favour"). Even when she is not talking about prayer, however, she frames her experience in the language of interiority and interior faculties (*potencias*, *espíritu*, etc.). She is in a state of "profunda tristeza … tan amortiguada que el uso de los sentidos me daba pena y no quisiera hablar palabra, no podía exteriormente encubrir una melancolía de esto muy grande" (338r) ("deep sadness … so depleted that the very use of my senses made me sad and I did not wish to speak a word, I could not on the outside hide this great melancholy"). At this point, she repeatedly attempts to return her thoughts to a spiritual framework, but each time the narration digresses:

> no quitaba el insaciable deseo que me daba de dios, antes crecía. Estos trabajos fueron creciendo desde el principio y cuanto es mayor el sentimiento de ellos es mayor el provecho que siento, aunque los que ahora tengo no sé si estaré para decirlos ni son algunas cosas para escritas. (338r)

> it did not take away the unquenchable desire I have for God, but on the contrary these trials grew, and they kept on growing from the beginning and the more I feel them the more I benefit I feel, although, as for the ones I have now I don't know if I can manage to say them nor are they things meant to be written.

In a similar passage, María de Cristo writes that "estaba mi Señor tan retirado y oculto de mi alma que me quitó la memoria de pensar que había Dios. Fue tanto lo que padecí de oscuridades y desamparos de mi criador que no tengo capacidad para explicarme ni en esto ni en lo que padecí" (22r) ("My Lord was so withdrawn and hidden from my soul that I had no memory of thinking that there was a God. I suffered so much from the darkness and desolation of my creator that I am incapable of explaining myself about this or about what I suffered"). The trope of the insufficiency of language to express the ineffable is, in both cases (and many others), used to express the inability to feel God's presence in the first place. It is not clear whether the anguish cannot be written because it is impossible to express in words or because it is out of place in a narrative of spiritual graces. The anonymous nun eventually turns for guidance to mystic literature and to her spiritual authorities, but neither is successful in drawing her spirit or her text out of its darkness. The passage is worth citing at length.

> Lo que ahora más siento es la oscuridad con que dios se me comunica y ausencia de dios careciendo de todo alivio espiritual ni de otra manera no hallar ningún ejercicio de oración sino una pena y ansia y si hallo algún ejercicio no puedo detenerme en cosa más de en la pena o afecto que he dicho … los temores que traigo de estar en desgracia de dios y escrúpulos y sobre todo no tener con quién comunicar esto ni quién me aconseje porque cuando estoy más necesitada está nuestra madre priora más ocupada … ni creo que nadadie [*sic*] bastaría a aliviarme, leía la Noche oscura del Santo Fray Juan de la Cruz primera y segunda y así como muchas cosas de las que leía[42] estaba padeciendo no ha querido el Señor que me consuele con pensar voy yo por aquel camino sino que se me ha pegado y

> es imaginación o antojo. Solo pienso que pago o que lo causa mis pecados y que estoy en desgracia de Dios, aunque por otra parte … veo claro es lo que Vuestra Reverencia y Nuestra Madre Priora me han asegurado y que el Señor se sirve de mi padecer. Deseo con afecto que el Señor (no por que se acaben mis trabajos mas por estar toda unida con Él) … abreviase ya el tiempo y esclareciese mi mente para que le conozca, que las potencias verdaderamente están sin algún conocimiento aunque el alma no hay en cosa que halle tanta satisfacción como en la comunicación que se le comunica mas dejando esto porque no estoy para alargarlo tornaré a proseguir lo que dejé comenzado. (338r–9r)
>
> What I lament most now is the darkness with which God communicates with me and the absence of God, lacking all spiritual relief and in no way can I have any prayer exercise but instead only pain and anxiety and if I do manage any exercise I can't focus on anything beyond the pain or affections I have mentioned … the fears I bear with me of being out of God's grace, and the scruples, and above all, not having anyone with whom I can speak about this or who can counsel me because when I am in greatest need our prioress is at her busiest, nor do I believe that anyone would be able to alleviate this, I read 'The Dark Night' by San Juan de la Cruz, first and second [?], and so like many of the things that I read [when] I was suffering, Our Father has not wished that I find consolation thinking that I am traveling that same path. Instead, I cannot shake the thought that it is my imagination or a whim. I can only think that I am paying for or that the cause is my sins and that I am out of God's grace, although on the other hand … I can clearly see that Your Reverence and our mother prioress have assured me and that Our Father has a use for my suffering. I desire with great feeling that Our Father (and not so that my troubles might end but in order to be completely one with Him) unload on me as many as He wishes and shorten the time already [of suffering] and clear my mind so I may know Him, because my faculties are truly without any knowledge [of Him] although there is nothing that satisfies the soul more than in the messages He communicates but I am leaving this became I am in no condition to extend it, I will go back and continue with what I left unfinished.

She simply stops the narrative here and picks it up in another moment, one in which she has recovered her connection with God. In later folios, she again experiences "sequedad" but is always able to channel into a moment of spiritual redemption (e.g., "saliendo de una sequedad me pareció se difundía por toda el alma un licor tan confortativo que me parecía me llenaba de fortaleza" [340r] ["emerging from a period of dryness it seemed that a sweet liquor spread through all my soul, so comforting that it seemed to fill me with strength"]). Throughout her *relación*, our author continually turns to Scripture or hagiography to understand her own visions. However, in the above-cited passage, she turns to a near-contemporary mystic poem, not to understand a vision but to understand a lack of visions. She is relating to the "night" of the title in a very personal way; she seeks personal guidance from a poem that tells of a universal journey of the Christian soul. We see here, as in many other sources, the use of mystic poetry not as a reflection of the experience of the author but as a prompt to enable the reader to understand her own spiritual journey. This nun uses the poem as her guide, but perhaps precisely because what she is experiencing is *depression*, and not self-annihilation, it is useless in guiding her out of her darkness. In fact, as Denys Turner has convincingly argued, the poem is not speaking about "depression" at all: the "dark night" of St. John's theology is not the absence of grace but an essential part of mystic union: the emptying out of the self, the complete openness to God.[43] The anonymous nun cannot find in the speaker of the "Noche oscura" "con quién comunicarme" because the poetic voice has already left behind the trappings of a Self, whereas the "yo" of the *vida* is not the soul but the suffering human ego, trapped in a house that is not yet *sosegada*. The formal dissolution of her prose echoes the disorder and mis/non-direction of the spiritual struggle (just as the poetic form, with its symmetry and rhythm, echoes the successful journey of the poetic voice of the soul in San Juan de la Cruz). Whereas Teresa's *Vida*, written retrospectively and after the author had overcome her early years of difficulty and *sequedad*, can be organized into chapters and structured along a narrative of spiritual progress, this author can only announce the author's own inability to "alargar" her situation and resolve to begin anew, somewhere else. The self that feels itself to be entirely without God cannot be integrated into a narrative of spiritual grace. Just as the spiritual autobiography cannot be a secular story of friendships and community ties, it cannot be a story of unbroken spiritual desolation.

Doubt and Discernment

However, the narrative of spiritual mercy does admit – in fact, it seems to demand – a great deal of doubt about the true nature of spiritual mercies, in a way that no spiritual poem does. Mystic poetry begins with an assumption of the experience as true: not only are there are no mystic poems that relate a vision that turns out to be false, I know of no mystic poems in which the poetic voice expresses doubt about the truth of the mystic experience. In the spiritual treatises, as we have seen, when the theologian needs to supplement his *letras* with first-person *experiencia,* he elects (or invents) someone whose experience he has already validated. The whole point of citing, as Laredo does, a "mujercita que yo conocía" ("a poor woman of my acquaintance") who can confirm that "a mí me ha acontecido" (III, 41, 597) ("it has happened to me" [260]) is to assuage any doubt within the reader caused by the treatise writer's own lack of experience.[44] Thus any insinuation of doubts as to the truth of this "a mí me ha acontecido" would be counter-productive. Laredo's authority as a theologian gives the necessary stamp of truth to the anecdote and hence the woman's experience. However, as we noted in chapter one, the *mujercita* is almost certainly a rhetorical strategy; he was not writing for *mujercitas* or imagining the repercussions of a widespread assumption of mystic practice among "little" (poor, lower-class, less-educated) women. Yet this is precisely what occurred. Viewed from this angle, the *vida* can be read as the text that the *mujercita* was compelled to produce to prove to her confessor and superiors (her "Laredos") that "a mí me ha acontecido."

Doubt is absent from mystic poetry and is the motivating force behind all spiritual autobiography: penitents were asked to write their experiences either because their spiritual directors doubted the divine origin of their experiences, or to assuage doubts, their own or others'. It is through writing, editing, and scrutinizing the text of the *vidas* themselves that the decision about that truth is made. The exact position of doubt – within the author, within the spiritual director to whom the text is directed, within an unspecified third-person censor – varies from text to text. However, even where the author may be understood to be affirming against sceptics the reality of her experience, she must perform doubt to demonstrate her humility and thus her conformity with the Christian virtues that, in turn, authorize the visionary.

Alison Weber and others have argued that much of that struggle, that representation of doubt, may be a rhetorical strategy meant to convince the confessor rather than a sincere representation of self-interrogation.[45] The Catch-22 of mystic experience, particularly for women, was that the more forcefully an individual defended her spiritual gifts, the more these gifts were suspected to be false. Thus, it was imperative for women to feel, or at least to express, doubt about their revelations and visions. Unlike other virtues, such as charity and chastity, humility is largely an act of representation, of language. The *vidas* offer an opportunity not just for a Self to write a few disclaimers but for an individual to *write a humble Self.* The expressions of humility are woven into every level of the text, from the usual self-deprecations we find across all literature of the period, to the construction of dialogues that thematize doubt and reassurance, to the constant invitation to be censored. It is undeniable that in some instances this exaggeration of doubt is more strategic than sincere.[46] However, I believe we must take at face value the desire of the writers of *vidas* to be spiritually virtuous Catholics, and that included a general belief in the virtues of humility and the wisdom of authorities. This did not imply the submission to authorities in every particular instance, but in general, we can take the pervasive doubt expressed in the *vidas* as more than a rhetorical strategy. And even if the doubt is in some instances a pose, the fact that such a pose becomes obligatory in the author-subject of the *vida espiritual,* while it is mostly absent in the pose of the mystic poet or the author of the contemplative prayer treatise, indicates the different discursive landscape to which the *vida* belongs. It is not just a different genre in formal terms, but it is subjected to different criteria of truth, and its author is required to answer for the narrative voice in ways foreign to the mystic poet or the contemplative theologian.

The principal source of doubt the nuns describe is to the origin of their extra-rational experiences: divine, demonic, or natural. Many of these accounts, and in particular the published or more complete ones, are structured so that an initial doubt is ultimately resolved. Teresa's *Vida,* certainly the best-known model in her lifetime and our own, is written from the point of view of someone who has already scaled all the levels of prayer; thus, while in the early chapters she can recall her confusion as to a vision of Christ she has, remembering that:

> Hízome mucho daño no saber yo que era posible ver nada, si no era con los ojos del cuerpo, y el demonio que me ayudó a que lo creyese ansí, y hacerme entender que era imposible, y que se me había antojado, y que podía ser el demonio, y otras cosas desta suerte, puesto que siempre me quedaba un parecerme era Dios y que o era antojo. (VII.7.146)

> I was much harmed at that time by not knowing that one can see things with other eyes than those of the body. It was the devil who encouraged me in my ignorance, and made me think any other form of sight impossible. He made me believe I had imagined it, that it might be his own work, and other things of that sort. The thought remained with me, nevertheless, that it was of God and not of the imagination. [53]

The experience is recounted entirely in the past and Teresa-author, in language that unambiguously affirms the vision's truth, says that she saw it with the "ojos del alma." As the text transitions from first-person recollection to manual for mental prayer, references to her own experience are inserted into asides in such a way that they reinforce the certainty of advice offered to the person who might be subject to doubts, someone who is passing through stages she has overcome. For instance, when she warns against excessive mortification, she bases her authority on her own experience:

> He pasado por esto, y por eso lo sé; y no sé yo que mejor vista, ni salud podemos desear, que perderla por tal causa. Como soy tan enferma, hasta que me determiné en no hacer caso del cuerpo, ni de la salud, siempre estuve atada, sin valer nada; y ahora hago bien poco. Mas como quiso Dios entendiese este ardid del demonio, y como me ponía delante el perder la salud, decía yo: poco va en que me muera: sí, el descanso: no he ya menester descanso, sino cruz. Ansí otras cosas. Vi claro, que en muy muchas, aunque yo de hecho soy harto enferma, que era tentación del demonio, o flojedad mía; que después que no estoy tan mirada, y regalada, tengo mucha más salud. Ansí que va mucho a los principios de comenzar oración, a no amilanar los pensamientos: y créanme esto, porque lo tengo por experiencia. (XIII.7.205)

> I have been through all this, and so I know it. I know too that we can desire no better kind of sight or health than to lose both in such a cause. As my own health was so bad, I was always hampered and useless until I decided to take no notice of my body or of my state of health; and now I bother very little about either. It pleased God to let me see this trick of the devil's. Then, whenever he suggested that I was making myself ill, I would answer "It doesn't matter if I die!" and "Rest! I don't need rest but the Cross," and so on. I clearly saw now that although I am sickly, in most cases my illnesses were temptations of Satan, or arose from my weakness. Since I have given up caring so much for my ease and comfort, my health has been very much better. It is very important at the beginning, when we embark on prayer, not to be frightened by our own thoughts. You may take my word for this; I know it by experience. [90]

The doubt is resolved by what "quiso Dios entendiese" and "vi claro," and there is no subjection of these "entendimientos" to scrutiny or discernment. For the nuns who imitate Santa Teresa in their own spiritual practice, this is a clear lesson about the dangers of excessive penitential practice, but it provides little guidance in *how* to distinguish virtuous desires from demonic temptation.

We see nuns struggling with this uncertainty in various works, particularly those written in diary form and without retrospective editing. María Vela y Cueto's diary returns again and again to questioning of the origins of her visions, spiritual graces, and impulses to practice extreme mortification. She writes with respect to this latter point that:

> Paréceme que la penitencia que se va añadiendo de cada día con parecer que Dios lo manda, ha de venir a quitarme las fuerzas y si no me las quitare, porque el demonio también me parece que puede ponerlas: a lo menos en sabiéndose me han de notar por singular y tengo de escandalizar a todas, si voy adelante. Y teniéndolo por voluntad de Dios, no se puede dejar de hacer sin mucho escrúpulo … Todo este combate duró hasta el domingo y no me atreví a comulgar por no saber la voluntad de Dios. (140–1)

> It seems that my penitence grows and grows every day, seemingly because God so wishes, and it will eventually take away my strength entirely if it is not the case that I take it from myself, because the devil, it seems to me, can also add them [the mortifications]: at least knowing that I will stand out as singular and scandalize everyone if I go forward. And holding it to be God's will, I can't cease from performing them without great scruples … All this struggle lasted through Sunday and I did not take communion because I did not know God's will.

While the possibility of identifying evidence for the truth of the interior in exterior acts and events is what prompts the spiritual *vida* or *diario*, here the relationship between external act and invisible cause is reversed, or hopelessly tangled. The acts of mortification, which would in traditional or medieval guides to spirituality or hagiographies be a clear sign of virtue, are (as Teresa warned) just as likely to be impostures from a demon who appeals to her pride, her desire to be seen as "singular." Both acts of virtue and vice can stem from a demonic source, and temptation by the devil can be both a sign of vice and a sign of virtue. The act of linking the internal vision to external acts is circular and thus paradoxical. This paradox was highlighted in Osuna and Laredo, but presented as a philosophical puzzle, not an existential crisis. In the *vidas*, the contradictions of mystic interiority and exteriority are lived in first person, and because the writing subject does not have access to the future (in the sense that an author who writes a retrospective account of her life does) or an omniscient authority (her access to the divine perspective being precisely the matter that is to be discerned through her writing), the paradox becomes a source of anguish and doubt, rather than a mere theological puzzle.

In general, the nuns have two sources of authority to consult regarding their experiences: church authorities (usually the confessor, sometimes a female superior) and God. However, the former's judgment may be mistaken, and while the latter's judgment is always true, it is subject to the very obstacles of access that make the confessor necessary. Narratives such as Teresa's *Vida* (but also the biblical examples of revelations to uneducated women) provide a model for questioning the judgments of sceptical authorities. However, the reliance on the divine response traps one in a paradox since the divine reaction can only be accessed through visions and voices: the very experiences whose truth or origin is to be determined. The spiritual diaries and *vidas* without exception narrate a triangulation of consultations, as the author demonstrates her virtue by submitting her experiences to the wisdom of these two higher powers. Teresa's *Vida* is paradigmatic in this respect, with her constant alternating between the addressees: Vuesa Merced (her confessor/human interlocutor) and Vuestra Majestad (God). This double audience reflects the reality of her position, but it is also a sophisticated rhetorical strategy.[47] If we look at several lesser-known narratives, we see a variety of approaches to the same end.

One common way the authors write, and through writing resolve, doubt is by narrating the consultations of authorities prior to the writing of the narrative we read and at times including in the text the responses from these authorities. For example, Cecilia de Nacimiento's first-person narration in her *Relación de mercedes*[48] ends abruptly and she proposes instead "Referiré algunos párrafos de cartas de mi santo hermano y Padre, Fr. Antonio Sobrino, a quien le comuniqué por las mías, y me hizo grande instancia en que le mostrase los papeles que escribí, conque en extremo se consoló e hizo estima de ellos" (309) ("I will relate a few paragraphs from letters from my holy brother Father Antonio Sobrino, with whom I communicated in my letters, and he urged me with much insistence that I show him the papers I wrote, as they consoled him greatly and he valued them highly"). What follows are, precisely, a series of excerpts from his correspondence to her, many of which assuage doubts about her visions, doubts we do not read directly but intuit from their denial in the voice of the male authority figure. In a letter from 1605, Fray Antonio writes:

> Y una de las muy admirables [obras y labores] suyas es aquella duda que Vuestra Reverencia me dice le queda al alma, en medio de tantas misericordias y mercedes, de no saber si agrada; que son las pigüelas por donde la divina mano tiene presa esta ave tan voladora; *Timor ipse* (dice Agustino) *omni securitate appetendus.*[49] Es un raro primor que, en medio de una tan firme confianza, resignación y seguridad, brote de lo más íntimo aquel

recelo. Que unas veces dice: No sé si agrado a este Señor; otras: Aún vivo en vida que podría perderle. (518)

And one of the most admirable of your [works and labors] is that doubt that Your Reverence tells me remains in your soul, in the midst of so many mercies and gifts, of not knowing whether you please Him; and these are the jesses with which the divine hand keeps captive such a high-flying bird; *Fear* (Augustine says) *for the security of the soul is to be desired.* It is rare delicacy, in the midst of such firm confidence, resolution and security, and springs from the most intimate of scruples. That sometimes says: I don't know if I am pleasing to the Lord, and others: As long as I am alive, I could still lose Him.

The first-person narrative has given way to a voice of authority, and this voice gives way to a voice of even greater authority, Saint Augustine. Doubt is not something to be denied but instead is a sign of authenticity. Each authority *encourages* the visionary to feel doubt. Doubt, paradoxically, is a sign that certainty is warranted, and a narrative that wishes to achieve or demonstrate certainty must narrate the experience of doubt.

In other accounts, this can be represented as an almost stream-of-consciousness voicing of the authors' extra-rational experiences and then their own rational efforts to discern the truth of those experiences. Vela y Cueto, speaking of the voices she hears, wonders if "estas hablas, que me parecía por ser tantas si algunas de ellas me las hablaba yo" (70) ("these inner voices, of which there are so many that it seemed to me that some of them might be my own") and goes on to narrate her own attempts over a period of years to resolve such questions through submission to human and divine authorities:

ayer tarde, mientras cenaban, me fui a la cerca, y abrazada con una cruz grande que allí estaba supliqué al Señor, como Vuestra Merced me lo manda, que me diese a conocer cuánto eran estas hablas suya o cuándo del propio espíritu. Y díjome que siempre que quedase con humildad y resignación, creyese que era Su Majestad el que hablaba. (192)

yesterday afternoon, while [the others] ate supper, I went to the wall and, embracing a large cross that was there I begged God, as Your Grace ordered me, to let me understand which of these were his voices and which were from my own spirit. And He said that as long as I retained humility and resignation, I should believe that it was His Majesty who was speaking.

Like Madre Cecilia's *Vida*, Astorch's self-narrative includes her consultation of recognized authorities. Rather than cite Juan de Ávila directly, she writes the process of relating her own experience to what she has read in his works:

> Estando pensando cómo decía el Maestro Ávila y otros que cuando estas hablas interiores eran de Dios, eran raras veces y en casos de mucha necesidad, y que ser tantas y a cada cosa las hacía sospechosas, se ofreció que en general era verdad, pero que cuando tomaba cargo de un alma para regirla por sí mismo en todo, y el medio por donde quería declararla su voluntad era éste, ¿cómo podía dejar de ser muy continuo el hablarla habiendo de poner reglas en beber y en comer, en hablar y en callar … en la composición interior y exterior y esto a cada paso … Cuadróme mucho esta razón, y parece que convence. (180–1)

> While I was thinking how Master Avila and others said that it was rare for these inner voices to be from God, and only in cases of great necessity, and if there were a great many and with respect to every little thing it made them suspicious, it occurred to me that in general this was true, but when He took charge of a soul to guide in in every way, and this was the way through which He communicated His will to her [the soul], then how could his speech to her be anything but continuous, needing to lay down rules for drinking and eating, speaking and remaining silent … in her interior and exterior composition and all this at every step. This reasoning clicked for me, and it seems convincing.

Again, the initial move is not to affirm the validity of her experience by citing the authority but instead the exact opposite: to use the authority to put her own experience in doubt ("que ser tantas y a cada cosa las hacía sospechosas"). Only once the discrepancy is acknowledged can it be addressed and tentatively resolved.

The doubt need not be resolved at all; a frequent strategy is for the author to cede authority to the reader/confessor. Teresa's *Vida* frequently employs this strategy (i.e., "No sé si digo desatinos; si lo son, vuesa merced lo rompa; y si no lo son, le suplico ayude a mi simpleza, con añadir aquí mucho" [VII.22.156–57] ["I do not know if what I write is foolish. If it is, your Reverence must strike it out. But if it is not, I entreat you to help me in my simplicity and add a great deal to this" (59)]). Other authors interpolate the confessor/reader in a variety of ways. María Astorch narrates within her *Vida* an *Examen* ("Examination") of her own spiritual experiences by Father Bartolomé de Jesús María. This examination was, as described earlier in the chapter, key to authorizing her production and editing of the *Camino* itself. The section begins with Astorch's desire to consult with Father Bartolomé "algunas dudas y tentaciones y llamamientos interiores" ("certain doubts and temptations and inner callings") but, unlike the texts we have seen addressed to a prospective, future confessor/reader, Astorch narrates the examination in a past-tense dialogue, which allows her to introduce multiple layers of authorities and voices:

> Y así le dije: – Padre, llevo una tentación grande en persuadirme soy molesta y enfadosa a mis confesores; y sí lo soy. Mis temores me los ocasionan por parecerme debo decirles todo lo que pasa en mi interior y, en particular, los llamamientos e inspiraciones …
>
> Respondióme dicho padre: – El demonio, carísima madre, no pretende tanto impedirle el cumplimiento de las inspiraciones cuanto el desbaratarle el interior con esa inquietud y perturbación … Y advierta que de dos maneras habla Dios a las almas: la una, dándoseles a conocer, y es con un conocimiento muy claro, que no hay que poner duda en ello, porque se conoce con el murmurio de las aguas y avenidas que trae consigo de gracias … el otro modo, madre, es dándose a conocer al alma a sí mismo, y es un conocimiento quieto, sosegado, tranquilo y amoroso, que suavemente la desase, humilla y aniquila, con tanta certeza y claridad, que no lo puede ignorar la misma alma. (93)

> And so I said to him, "Father, I bear a great temptation to persuade myself that I am bothersome and annoying to my confessors; and yes, I am. My fears spring from the situation of feeling that I should tell them everything that occurs in my interior, and particularly the calls and inspirations …"
>
> The Father replied, "The devil, dearest Mother, does not so much try to interrupt the compliance with those inspirations as he tries to throw your interior into disarray with this unease and disturbance … And note that there are two ways that God speaks to souls: one, making Himself known, and with the clearest knowledge, such that there can be no doubt about it, because it can be known through the murmur of the waters and floods of thanks that it brings forth … The other way, Mother, is by allowing the soul to know by itself, and it is a quiet, calm, peaceful and loving knowledge, that gently undoes, subjects, and obliterates her [the soul], with such certainty and clarity that the soul itself cannot ignore it."

As with the previous examples, the author projects reassurance about her doubts on to a voice of authority. As in Cecilia de Nacimiento's *Vida*, the need for external confirmation causes the authorial subject to recede from her own autobiography, in this case giving way to the voice of the interlocutor and closing a paradoxical circle. The confessor/addressee of the *Vida* ends up reading his own words. At other times, the paradox runs in the opposite direction, with the author writing to her confessor about her temptation or resolution *not* to reveal to her confessor the very experiences she is writing. María de Cristo provides the most tangled examples in this regard:

> Acuérdome que días pasados me pidió mi confesor estos papeles. Yo quedé pare entonces muy contenta juzgando que ya no había de escribir mas pero aguóseme el gusto con una tentación que tuve muchos tiempos de estar considerando y creyendo que mi confesor me los había pedido para vengarse de mí, como no me podía ver, y que los había llevado al santo tribunal de la inquisición para que me castigasen y verse libre de mí. Con esta pena estuve muchos meses sin poderle decir lo que me estaba pasando. Cometíanme grandes desesperaciones que dejara este camino porque iba por él muy errada, que presto me vería castigada con estas i otras cosas que por no acordarme bien no las digo. Andaba harto afligida sin tener átomo de consuelo porque él que podía yo tomar era el decir a mi confesor lo que me estaba pasando. Esto no pude hacer porque así lo dispuso mi Señor para que yo padeciese. Después entré algo en razón considerando mi mala vida, mas que por malicia no había callado ni dicha cosa contra mi Dios. Apretábame mucho la tentación de dejar a mi confesor, que ésta la he tenido infinidad de veces. Queríale mucho y esto fue causa para que no determinase tal disparate como el demonio procuró que hiciera para mi perdición. Al final, después de muchos tiempos, me volvió los papeles, mandándome de nuevo que escribiese. No puedo significar el sentimiento tan grande que tuve y siempre tengo, con la rienda del temor de que vivo engañada y que todo esto es ilusión diabólica, y aseguro que padezco en este punto muchos trabajos. (74)

> I remember that some days ago my confessor asked for these papers. I was quite content then, judging that I would not have to write any more, but the pleasure was tempered by a temptation I often felt, and that was to consider and believe that my confessor had asked for them in order to take revenge on me since he could not see me, and that he had taken them [her writings] to the Holy Tribunal of the Inquisition so they would punish me and he would be freed of me. I had this pain for many months without being able to tell him what was going on, I was assaulted by great desperation to leave this road because I was far off track and I would soon find myself punished, with these and other things that, because I don't remember them well, I will not say. I went around in a state of great affliction, without an atom of consolation because that [consolation] I could have

found would have been by telling my confessor what was happening with me, but I could not do that because my Lord ordered that I suffer thus. Later I came to reason, considering my sinful life, but that I had never said nor abstained from saying anything against God out of malice, I was sorely tempted to leave my confessor and I have felt this an infinite number of times, I loved him a lot and that was the reason I did not decide on such a crazy act, as the devil was trying to make me do, for my damnation. Finally after a long time he returned my papers to me, ordering me once more to write, and I cannot convey the great emotion I felt and always have, reined in by the fear that I am deceived and that all this is a diabolical illusion and I promise that on this point I suffer great trials.

The *vida espiritual* takes on the aspect of a stream-of-consciousness narrative in which the topic for contemplation is not Christ but writing itself. In this way, the *vidas* transcend medieval vision narratives and become psychological narratives, focusing on thinking about visions rather than the visions themselves. María de la Antigua's juxtaposition of consultation with her confessor and her own internal narrative is paradigmatic:

Las hablas interiores que conocidamente las tenía entre mis desventuras; y conocí por un libro que cosa eran, no las quería creer; por parecer que esto era imaginaciones vanas. Cuando en esto me vei [sic] tan perdida, acudía (y no como era razón) a mi Señor, sino con una flojedad como mía y pensaba en mí, visto esto … ¿son tan grandes las mercedes, que me haze? ¿Esto podía yo hacerlo? ¿Es esta sombra, o puedo yo hacer lo que no sé, ni entiendo? Pasaba esta consideración tan de corrida, y tan en el aire, que tasadamente había llegado … y yo me volvía a quedar en mis tinieblas, y desabrimientos … Eran mis penas, si me engañaba en las hablas interiores, si eran pensamientos y no cosas de Dios; y como V.M. me dijo, que son las hablas de los sueños distintas, y claras en sí, es verdad; y tanto lo son, que algunas dellas me parece a mí que el cuerpo también las oía, y era engaño … (697–8)[50]

The inner voices that I was known to hold among my misfortunes, and I learned from a book just what they were, and I did not want to believe it because it seemed to me that these were vain imaginations. When I found myself so lost in this, I turned (and not as I ought) to my Lord, but with a weakness all my own and seeing this, I thought to myself … the mercies He grants me are so great: Could I do this? Is this a shadow, or could I do something I do not know or understand? This consideration passed so

> rapidly, so much in the air, as lightly as it had come ... and I was left in my darkness and despair ... My pains lay in thinking if I was deceived in my inner voices, if they might be thoughts and not from God; and as your grace told me that the voices in dreams are distinct and clear in themselves, and they are so [clear] that it seems to me that my body heard some of them, and it was a trick.

The nuns, in their own ways, imitate Velazquez's gesture in *Las meninas*, their act of representing taking centre-stage in their own representations.

The form of the *Vida* – a prose narrative produced over time and in dialogue with a confessor – is inextricable from this effect. The text produced in dialogue with the confessor is almost always composed over a long period; even when the author seems to feel certainty in one section, the reappearance of doubts and the circularity of the experiences produces an overall tone of doubt and uncertainty that we never find in poems or in the texts published in the period. The confessor–confessant relation does not have a fixed starting and ending point but is instead an open-ended *process*. The confessor may make definitive judgments in one moment, but the confessant is still free to revisit these issues with him, or within her writing. In this way, the aspect of the Counter-Reformation most closely associated with conservative orthodoxy, the "confessionalization" of private experience, paradoxically pushes open the realm of discourse towards the sort of fluid narrative and self-reflective narrator we associate with modernity.

The dialogic, temporally extended confessor–confessant relationship creates the very aspects of the *vida* that make many of them almost unreadable: the repetition, circularity, and sheer verborrea. The *vidas* expand where poetry condenses. Rather than synthesizing the vision into its essential, universal form, as occurs in the mystic poems, they offer again and again similar visions occurring over an extended period, framing them with their temporal and spatial particularities (the date or event and the location when each vision occurred). Indeed, it is the push and pull between the spiritual vision – inherently poetic for all the reasons discussed in chapter two – and the prosaic, quotidian, human, and corporeal, that is distinctive of the spiritual autobiography. These two aspects of the spiritual life and the spiritual autobiography work together, or against each other, to push both poetry and prose in a new direction. The influx of a poetic language, replete with metaphor, symbol, and other imagery, pushes the prose beyond the very spare, factual accounts we find in life stories produced for secular audiences (a *relación de méritos*, for example).

Conclusion

The particular circumstances of Counter-Reformation Catholicism (not limited to Spain, but most strictly enforced there) produce this unique genre of mystic discourse: the spiritual autobiography. The need to tie an experience that erases identity to a single biography, to prove its authenticity or to best cultivate its development, results in new hybrid genre, the *libro de mercedes* or *vida espiritual*. The tropes of mystic poetry persist, but they must be inserted into a prosaic, corporeal, narrative, implicated in very real and very specific networks of power. Whereas the poetic voice need not be tied to the author's own experience, the spiritual autobiography must be tied to a name because its primary function is to determine a response to the author. Thus where Teresa writes, in the midst of her *Vida*, addressing her confessor-reader directly, that "ni quiero, si a alguien lo mostraren, digan quien es por quien pasó, ni quien lo escribió, que por esto no me nombro, ni a nadie, sino escribirlo he todo lo mejor que pueda por no ser conocida, y ansí lo pido por amor de Dios" (X.7.179) ("If the rest is shown to anyone I do not wish him to be told whose experience it describes, or who wrote it. That is why I mention neither myself nor anyone else by name and have done my best to write in such a way as not to be recognized. I beg your Reverence, for the love of God, to preserve my secrecy" [74]), it is an entirely impossible request. A spiritual autobiography depends on a name, both in its initial circumstances of production and after its approval: unlike a hagiography, it has value only insofar as the first-person narrative links to a real being in the world.

I have focused on incomplete and unpublished *vidas* because the expansion of the corpus beyond a few canonized, edited texts gives a fuller picture of the way the language of mysticism shaped and was shaped by early modern religious women's experience. It is worth speculating as to whether there is some element of the texts themselves that can explain why certain *vidas* were selected as models (both the texts and their authors) while others were relegated to forgotten archives or destroyed. As I have suggested, the answer is somewhat circular: those *vidas* that failed to order themselves in an overarching narrative of spiritual progress were the ones not selected for editing, a process that itself entails the organization of primary materials into an overarching narrative of spiritual progress. Confessors needed to see some basic substrate of potential for *exemplarity*, understood as a conformity to pre-existing authorized models, to promote the conversion of their confessants' lives into exemplary *vidas*. The authors whose spiritual experiences seemed to march in place rather than ascend a ladder were not published, but their writing was not necessarily censored or prohibited.

There exists a separate corpus of first-person visionary narratives that "fail" (fail to be promoted as *vidas*) for an entirely different reason. These accounts end up in archives, but those of the Inquisition rather than convents. The visions in these narratives are almost uniformly non-mystical, having nothing to do with ecstatic union, but rather visions that transmit prophetic messages, usually with threatening implications for contemporary society. These visions in fact follow much more closely the visions in the Bible, which were principally a form of revealing information to God's chosen ones. Francisca de los Apóstoles had visions that clearly supported the cause of Bartolomé Carranza, and Lucrecia de León's apocalyptic visions directly implicated Felipe II; both of these women initially received considerable support from church officials, and both were punished by the Inquisition. After Lucrecia de León's arrest and condemnation, the Inquisition took a more active role in delegitimizing politically tinged prophecies from their first manifestations. Thus, it could be argued that the mystic vision, with its emphasis on the subjective experience of the visionary, rather than any prophetic content, was a sort of compromise: a form of visionary spirituality the Church could permit because ultimately the visions did not threaten political structures. The Counter-Reformation's "compromise" with affective, direct interiorized spirituality was to permit only such visions with no potential for provoking change in the world or the Church. Mysticism then plays a role almost the reverse of that imagined by de Certeau and that we identified in its earlier iterations; rather than the destabilizing, transgressive force it represented for the medieval church, once re-inscribed in convent walls and a text with a built-in editing system (be it collaborative or censorial), it became a conservative, stabilizing force, one that gave individual women a space to realize their spiritual and literary potential without disturbing the institutions of a patriarchal church.

Chapter Four

Mysticism before the Inquisition

In the conclusion to chapter three, we suggested a division between mystic *vidas* that ended up being preserved, either in print or convent archives, and prophetic visionary narratives, which ended up in Inquisition archives. This dichotomy assumes a clear-cut separation between the two types of vision that did not, in fact, exist. Dyan Elliott has shown how, in the late Middle Ages, "inquisitional procedure" was essential in defining and applying the categories of visionary "saint" *and* "heretic" (*Proving Woman* 3). As in the period she studies (roughly 1200–1400), many early modern visionaries experienced a wide range of visions, with verbal and corporeal manifestations, and part of the task of discernment exercised by confessors and at times by the Inquisition, was to ensure that visionaries were not *using* mystic discourse as a means towards gaining authority, either for personal enrichment or, more dangerously, to offer heretical or politically themed prophecies. The task of discernment was a fraught one, filling chapters of confessors' manuals and entire treatises. However, a confessor was at least accustomed to dealing with interiorities and the language of contemplative prayer.[1] While confessor and mystic might differ in their interpretation of the mystic's visions and their source, they occupied the same discursive landscape. This was not necessarily, or even usually, the case with the Inquisitors called on in post-Trent Spain to judge between heretical and orthodox visionaries. The shift from a theological to a juridical institutional sphere was also a hermeneutic shift, and one with profound implications not just for mystic practice and discourse but for the Inquisition itself. We tend to think that the decline of the Inquisition came from the efforts of secular liberal reformers.[2] However, a closer look at Inquisition trial proceedings suggests that the Inquisition succumbed to internal contradictions; the incompatibility of legal discourse and a post-Reformation language of mystic spirituality forced a separation of

God and Law, the withdrawal of God to private spaces, and the consequent atrophying of an institution created to treat religious practice as a matter for public control.

To understand the source and repercussions of the conflict between judicial and mystic language, it is important to reflect briefly on the origins of the Spanish Inquisition. In the period between its founding and the Council of Trent, the Inquisition's principal task had been to seek out and punish covert Judaizers. The post-Trent decision to use the institution to defend against the incursion of Protestantism via the prosecution of Catholic heterodoxies meant more than a simple switch of targets. The constructions of proof required to convict a person of Judaism (or Islam) were entirely different than those required to prove someone guilty of *alumbradismo* (as these heterodox interior spiritual practices would come to be termed). The inquisitional judicial procedure, first formulated in the twelfth century and officially instituted in Church practice by the Fourth Lateran Council in 1215, is partially defined in terms of the types of proofs deemed admissable. As John Langbein explains, "Historians today attribute to the Inquisitionsprozess two cardinal and interconnected features ... The one, called *Offizialmaxime* ... is the officialization of all the important phases *except* initation," that is, the responsibility of *inquiry* – investigation and prosecution – which passes from private inviduals to an established institution. But the other part, called *Instruktionsmaxime* "is primarily concerned with the nature of judicial proof. In contradistinction to the nonrational proofs of ancient Germanic law, it represents the view that the object of criminal procedure is to permit a judgment to be made about the authorship of criminal acts, based upon a rational inquiry into the facts and circumstances" (131).[3] There are important parallels here with the fifteenth-century establishment of the Spanish Inquisition; again, a centralization of power, in this case that of the Spanish monarchs, and the perception of an increased threat of heresy, in this case that of Judaism, led to the institutionalization of a legal process with the goal of eliminating heresy through trials based on rational proofs. It is undeniable that in the early period of the Spanish Inquisition proofs were often fabricated or ignored. Because almost all the documentation from that early period has been lost, it is difficult to make definitive judgments about the degree to which the Inquisition's own established standards of proof were respected. However, what is essential to note here is that there were established and undisputed acts or facts that could be understood as proof of Judaism. The Inquisition was called a tribunal of the faith, but Judaism, like medieval Catholicism, did not distinguish between *faith* and *praxis*. Prior to the Reformation, religious belief was always conceived of as manifested through speech and ritual acts, both of which could be verified through the same mechanisms as any secular criminal act.

Ironically, the elimination of the openly Jewish community in Spain and thus the possibility for Jews to consult religious officials or sacred texts, meant that among believers as well as persecutors religious practice was increasingly identified with rituals.[4] The practice of Judaism, and the proof of practice of Judaism, amounted to a few basic rituals: not eating pork, observing the Sabbath on Saturday, or simply declaring that "la ley de Moisén" was superior. The Inquisition, like any modern secular court, took depositions from witnesses and judged them according to their internal coherence: their confirmation or contradiction by other testimonies. They also considered a factor that would not be admitted by a modern court: ethnic identity, or blood. This last criterion brought in a body of evidence which, like "faith," has experienced a resignification in modern times from something exterior to something interior. For fifteenth-century Inquisitors, "blood" was not a substance coursing through the hidden recesses of the human body, but the verifiable chain of ancestry that linked individuals to their forefathers. Jewish or *converso* ancestry, along with the practice of Judaic rituals, were the main forms of evidence used to convict Judaizers. Two eyewitnesses and a suspect genealogy was sufficient for conviction, making investigation of a defendant's thoughts and feelings largely unnecessary. There was some room for ambiguity regarding intentions, as defendants often claimed they had engaged in seemingly Judaic rituals by accident or coincidence. For example, Pedro Villegas, accused of Judaizing in 1483, admitted that he might have rested on occasional Saturdays but claimed it was out of necessity rather than principle: "my job of cloth making wasn't flourishing; there happened to be a month or two during which I did not work at all."[5] Even here, however, the claim could be verified by outside sources, such as testimony by individuals who had seen him idle during the week or documents confirming the termination of contracts or payments. In the ultimate instance, if additional proofs were obtained but the accused still refused to concede any Jewish practice, torture could be used to extract a confession.

Proof after Trent

The Reformation, and the new threat of Lutheran heresy, made this model of prosecution untenable. External acts became insufficient as evidence, since there were no clearly reliable external signs that pointed towards Lutheran heresies or to the Catholic heterodoxies that, after Trent, made up the bulk of the Inquisitors' docket. In fact, many of the same practices – an intense spiritual relationship with God, supernatural or prophetic visions and miracles, extreme self-mortification and piety – could be indicative of Protestant heresy (a crime of faith), demonic possession (not a crime, unless it could be shown that an explicit pact had been made), illness, or true holiness. Thus, the responses of many visionaries to their interrogations feature an unprecedented dynamic: the accused's *affirmation* of each of the individual charges ("capítulos"), despite a plea of innocence to the main charge of *alumbradismo* or complicity in a demonic pact. For example, one can contrast the responses of Pedro Villegas, cited above,[6] with that of María Pizarro, accused as "ilusa e iludente" in 1635–9.[7] Both Villegas and Pizarro adamantly denied the charge of heresy, but the relation between the general plea and the response to individual charges was quite different. Whereas Villegas could point to his enforced resting during the week to explain away the fact of his resting on Saturday, no such verifiable defense was possible for María Pizarro against the charges of false sanctity. She claimed that "no ha hecho ni cometido ningunos embustes de los contenidos en dicho capítulo ni tiene pacto con el demonio ni sabe qué es pacto" ("she has neither done nor committed any of the frauds contained in the given chapter nor does she have a pact with the devil nor does she know what a pact is"), but in the very same sentence she affirmed having been possessed, explaining that "el demonio la maltrata muchas veces desde de edad de nueve años" ("the devil has frequently mistreated her since she was nine years old") and adding details of her first demonic vision. The responses to the eighty-six charges follow this pattern: to the charges of creating public scandal with her public episodes of *arrobamiento* and possession, she replied that "es verdad" ("it is true"), but where the Inquisitors characterized such episodes as fraudulent, she amended that "lo hacía sin poder más, con el fervor que la daba de amor de Dios" ("she did it without the power [to stop], with the fervor her love of God gave her"). In such cases, the evidence that could be verified using the traditional procedures of gathering and comparing witness testimony and personal accounts was irrelevant, since guilt or innocence hinged on invisible, supernatural, and extrarational forces (not just God or the devil but all the subtle gradations of possible assent to demonic visions) behind these external signs. The emergence of the treatise of discernment of spirits is more evidence of the newly pressing problem of ascertaining subtle gradations of interior states than it is of a solution. As can be seen in the transcriptions of *audiencias* with defendants accused of interior crimes, the criteria and process of discernment were more suited to a theological than a judicial setting. The legal system assumed a rational subject using language to represent facts; the language of discernment, like that of mysticism, allowed for the absence of the rational subject and/or for a non-transparent use of language. The Inquisition was in a bind. As a religious tribunal, its task was to diagnose subjects using such discourses, but as a legal body it was unable to do so.

The great scholar of *alumbradismo*, Álvaro Huerga, proposed three chronological stages of *alumbradismo* in Spain: *alumbradismo radical, sensual,* and *teatral,*[8] highlighting the diversity of the different spiritual tendencies grouped under this invented term. Among the differences were the criteria for prosecution and the language of those prosecutions. To see how the cracks appeared between the language of the accused and that of the accusers, it is useful to contrast the Inquisition procedure when dealing with a representative case from the early "radical" period with its handling of later cases. The early "radical" stage developed alongside the appearance of the contemplative prayer manuals discussed in chapter one. The first group, led by Pedro Ruiz de Alcaraz and María de Cazalla, were familiar with Osuna, Laredo, Ávila, and others, as well as translations of Erasmus, some medieval mystic texts, and the Gospels. Ruiz de Alcaraz and Cazalla were not the intended audience for the manuals in that they were laypersons, but they were not far off: literate urban men and women with close ties to Franciscan learned circles (María de Cazalla belonged to a family of clergymen and theologians). The group gathered in the members' homes to discuss theology and practice contemplative prayer. The majority of the members of the group were *conversos*, and it is undoubtedly this fact that caused the Inquisition to view their enthusiastic embrace of the *devotio moderna* with suspicion. More worrying was the apparent overlap with Protestantism, which was just taking root in Europe. The interrogations provide clear evidence that the Inquisitors at this stage were less concerned with policing visions or mystic experience than with detecting Protestant heresy. Furthermore, the questions show that at this point they still viewed Protestantism according to the model of previous heresies, as being codifiable in a series of acts and statements. Thus, the Inquisitors repeatedly ask Cazalla if she approved of Luther and if were true that she had said Erasmus deserved to be canonized.[9] The Inquisitors also asked incessantly about her stance on other known Lutheran heresies. She was asked if "ha dicho a alg[un]as personas que el rezar y ayunar y disciplinas e ir a los templos y hacer reverencia a las imágenes y otras cosas semejantes que era cosa de imperfección y no lo tenía en nada porque Dios quería ser adorado en espíritu y no en templos hecho[s] por mano y arte" (109) ("if she had told certain people that praying, fasting, penitences, visiting temples, and showing reverence to images and other similar things was a sign of imperfection and she considered it worthless, because God wanted to be adored in spirit and not in temples made by hands and artifice")[10] or if she had criticized sacramental communion ("Preguntada si dijo esta declar[ant]e que cuando se había de comulgar mas Dios sentía recogiéndose en sí misma que no yéndose al sacerdote, que cuando de allí, se levantaba mas indevota y sin Dios [107]) ("Asked if this declarant had said that when she had to take communion she felt God more by withdrawing into herself and not by going up to the priest, that when she got up from there [the altar, where the priest gave communion] she felt less devotion and without God"), particularly focusing on her supposed rejection of oral prayer and "actos exteriores de la oración" (112) ("exterior acts of prayer" [i.e., vocal prayer]). The *fiscal*'s accusation repeatedly uses *alumbrada* and *luterana* as synonyms, accusing Cazalla of being a "hereje luterana y alumbrada" (128 et al). Cazalla, clearly well aware of the Protestant heresies to avoid, repeatedly denied any incontrovertible Protestant acts or speech: she had never read or praised Luther; she had never condemned "actos exteriores de la oración"; "preguntada si ha enseñado o dotrinado esta declar[ant]e a algunas personas que la oracion vocal no es necesaria, dijo que no lo ha enseñado ni dotrinado" ("asked if this declarant had taught as doctrine or instructed certain people that oral prayer was not necessary, she said that no, she had neither instructed nor taught thus").

Yet to many of the charges her response is *not* a denial of an attributed statement, but rather a denial of the interpretation given that statement by the *fiscal*. The defense rests on semantics.[11] At times the disagreement is over the context or tone in which a statement was made, such as her response to the accusation of having said she could feel God more "recogiéndose en sí misma que no yéndose al sacerdote" ("drawing herself inward instead of going to a priest"), on its face a clear rejection of sacramental communion and a proof of Protestantism. She responded that she might have said this a few times, but "esto, echándome la culpa, quejándome de mi poca devoción; que en los sacramentos, ya lo tengo dicho, nunca dije que por las gentes dejaba de confesar" (135) ("but, blaming myself, complaining of my lack of devotion; for, with respect to the sacraments, as I have already said, I never said that people should not confess"). Her "culpa" here is moral but not judicial, it is the guilt of every Christian who experiences a distance from God, but it is neither a heresy nor a crime. Her response to the charge, cited above, of declaring worship in temples or acts of penitence to be an "imperfect" means of reaching God, is similar. She explains that "decía esta declar[ant]e que hacer las cosas de penitencia y lo demás que dice la preg[unt]a sin la intención recta de buscar por ellas a Dios era imperfección" ("this declarant said that doing acts of penitence and the rest of what is contained the question without the correct intention, that of seeking God through these acts, is imperfect"). The Inquisitor's rejoinder and her response show the impossiblity of digging into the intentions behind words: "Fuele dicho que la información no dice que decía lo susodicho con la limitación que ahora dice, sino que lo decía de la manera que le está preguntado y por tanto que diga la verdad. Dijo que ella no lo dijo de la manera que la pregunta dice sino como lo tiene dicho" ("She was told that the the information [the denunciation] does not say that she said the above with the limitations that she now states, but rather that she said it in the way that is in the question and thus she should tell the truth. She said that she did not say it in the way that the question says but instead as she has stated").

If in these points there is still a small difference in word order or phrasing between Cazalla's account and that of the accusation, at other points in the trial the difference rests entirely on choosing between two possible meanings of the same word. This is the case with the accusation of having declared "no le satisfacía la comunión ni le contentaba la confesión" ("communion did not satisfy her nor did confession make her content"), apparently a clear alignment with Protestantism. María affirmed the statement but gave it entirely different meaning: that the lack of "satisfacción … era de su parte, porque no estaba tan bien dispuesta coma esta declar[ant]e quería" ("satisfaction … was on her part, because she wasn't as prepared/disposed as she would have liked"). Both the words "la comunión" and "satsifacción" have different meanings in the accusation and the defense. The Inquisitors understand "la comunión" to mean the ritual of communion in itself and "satisfacción" to refer to the fulfillment of a penitential obligation; María resemanticizes the statement to refer to a lack of emotional satisfaction from a single act of taking communion, a personal failure rather than a flaw with the ritual itself. Again, the Inquisitors and Cazalla go in circles, not as to what she said but as to "la manera que lo dijo" (105) ("the way she said it"). The difference between general and specific referents is again at the heart of a disagreement over what Cazalla meant when she said that "el confesor es como una piedra" ("the confessor is like a stone"). The *fiscal* sees a rejection of confession to a priest itself, whereas Cazalla claims her critique was of one confessor in particular "que estaba alli como una piedra e no le daba un buen consejo ni cosas desta calidad" (107–8) ("who stood there like a rock and did not give good counsels or other things of that sort"). Witnesses are useless to clarify this point, as the disagreement rests in the "interior" of the words, not the facts of what was said or heard.

In the absence of external markers that could prove one interpretation over another, the Inquisitors recur to the only option that bypasses language entirely: torture.[12] Torture, although regularly practiced in secular and Inquisitorial trials in the period, was in many ways a legacy from the pre-Inquisitorial system of the ordeal in its dependence on a pre-/extra-rational production of truth. In this case, Cazalla maintained her innocence throughout the torture and as a result was absolved, with a warning to stay away from "aquellas personas de quien tiene dicho que eran alumbrados" (472) ("those persons who she has said were *alumbrados*").

As we have seen, the interrogation of this first group of *alumbrados* rested squarely on the relative merits of interior versus external devotional practices, but there is a striking absence of any discussion of visions. It is entirely possible that Cazalla and her circle experienced visions, but because they did not write them down, and because the Inquisition in that period was focused principally on extirpating Protestantism, none of the charges concerned the content or representation of visionary experience. Remarkably, there is also almost no mention of the devil in the trial; while Protestant heresies were certainly considered evil by the Inquisitors, they conceived of these heresies as a rational, intentional, and codifiable heresy, transmitted through books and texts. Thus, while we see a linguistic impasse in the discussion of intentions behind words that we do not generally find in trials of alleged crypto-Jews or Muslims, we do not find a conflict between a mystic and a judicial discourse. It was only with the second "wave" of *alumbrados* – or through the decision to apply this term to a later group of would-be visionary mystics – that poetic, mystic discourse enters into the Inquisitorial *proceso*.

Alonso de la Fuente and *Alumbradismo*

As Huerga has shown, the impulse behind the second wave of persecution of *alumbrados*, in the 1570s, came from one Alonso de la Fuente.[13] De la Fuente wrote a series of *memoriales* to the Inquisition emphasizing the threat of this group of would-be mystics and codifying their supposedly deviant behaviours.[14] It seems clear that the root of de la Fuente's objection to the devotional practices he is observing rests less on *what* than on *who* is experiencing them. Whereas Osuna and Laredo both cited the spiritual gifts of *mujercillas* as proof of the truth of contemplative prayer, for de la Fuente it is precisely the practice of such prayer among uneducated, non-cloistered women, and the threat that such a mass devotional practice could pose to the established social structure, that provokes his suspicion. It is, he clarifies, "cosa admirable y que viene bien a cualquier espíritu … meditar a paso y a menudo las cosas divinas para despertarse al amor de Dios y para tomar aliento para saber obrar y ejercitarse" ("an admirable thing that is suitable for any spirit … to meditate, steadily and often, on divine things, to awaken the love of God and to get inspiration to know how to act and conduct oneself"). But this should be a time-out from active life, from which good Catholics "luego vuelven de proposito a la vida activa … que es el camino general del cielo" (397) ("then return purposefully to the active life … which is the main road to heaven"). But the *beatas* and other *alumbrados*, despite being "almas ruines o imperfectas" ("imperfect or contemptible souls"), instead choose to "arrojarse a la contemplación divina, haciendo estado de contemplación y dejando los exercicios de la vida activa … Esto es lo que hacen las maestros desta doctrina, que sacan la ramera del lugar público y luego le mandan meditar y contemplar dos horas, dándole a un alma desgarrada en pecado el ejercicio de los santos" (397–8). ("throw themselves into divine contemplation, declaring themselves contemplatives and leaving aside the exercises of the active life … This is what the teachers of this doctrine do, they pull the prostitute out of the public square and order her to meditate and contemplate for two hours, giving a soul that is torn apart by sin the exercises of the saints"). Later he repeats that "esta oración y contemplación enseñan a todo género de gentes, buenos y malos, grandes y pequeños, tanto que si una ramera entra en su discipulato o un ladrón o soldado, luego le dan por ejercicio la dicha contemplación de dos horas" (398) ("they teach this prayer and contemplation to all sorts of people, good and bad, large and small, to the point that even if a prostitute enters their discipleship, or a thief or a soldier, they assign them two hours of contemplation as an exercise"). His objection is to the *democratization* of interior prayer, a universality proposed as a virtue, but only a hypothetical one, in the original contemplative manuals, but in the subsequent years realized beyond what Osuna or Laredo could have imagined. The *alumbrados* were imitating the manuals' original audience of friars and monks, not only in their spiritual practices but also in declarations of chastity and obedience to their confessors, but they did not belong to the social or educational strata of that first audience. This threat of a mass mysticism had obvious consequences to the social order if spread across society, as de la Fuente warned, because its practicants "pervierten el orden que Dios puso en ella de que obedeciesen las hijos a las padres, las mujeres a sus maridos" ("pervert the order that God made, that children should obey their parents, wives their husbands") and "hac[en] carnicería en sus personas y bienes" (410) ("make a bloodbath of their persons and estates").[15]

The fear of a mass spiritual movement that might overthrow established social orders was not new; similar phenomena shook medieval Europe (the Beguines and the Beghards, the Brethren of the Free Spirit), and undoubtedly de la Fuente had these heresies in mind when he thought of the *alumbrados*. However, his codification of the *alumbrado* threat is unique in the way it locates hereresy *within* language: not in heretical statements but in the hidden transmission of heretical beliefs embedded somehow within expressions of orthodox doctrine. The heretical propositions de la Fuente attributes to the *alumbrados* are also superficially identical to statements of doctrine, with the difference lying exclusively in the intentions or emphasis behind and within words. The introduction to the *memoriales* lays out seven identical phrases identified as "lenguaje espiritual" ("spiritual language") ("sentimiento divino" ["divine feeling"], "celo de Dios" ["zeal for God"], etc.), promising to show the difference between "el sentido católico" ("the Catholic sense") and "cómo entienden este lenguaje los herejes de este tiempo" (380) ("how the heretics of these days understand this language"). The systematic structure that characterizes the entire document might be seen as a structural response to the disorder and generic fluidity of the mystic texts analysed in previous chapters. The language itself is the same; in fact, the next point in the introduction is that "esta herejía se siente y no se dice" (380) ("this heresy is felt and not said"). De la Fuente warns:

> Hase de advertir que esta herejía comienza por el sentido; y así estos maestros no dicen las herejías ni enseñan herejías al entendimiento, antes huyen de ello cuanto es posible; sino todo su intento es enseñar a sentir la herejía y practicarla y que, si fuera posible, no la sepa el entendimiento, porque si la supiese luego la diría. De aquí nace que estos maestros, siendo preguntados por los discípulos en caso que los obligaban a decir la herejía, huyen el golpe y responden por parábolas.
>
> Be advised that this heresy begins through the senses; and in this way its teachers do not say the heresies nor do they teach them to the understanding – on the contrary, they avoid this as much as possible – but instead their entire intention is to teach how to feel this heresy and practice it, without (if possible) the understanding knowing, because if it knew, then it would say something. From this stems the fact that these teachers, when they are

asked by their disciples in a way that forces them to state the heresy, avoid the blow and respond with parables.

In de la Fuente's view, then, the figurative language of the mystics is not a strategy for representing the ineffable but instead a strategy for masking heresy, and the parable, used by Jesus to clarify, becomes a technique of obfuscation. The move away from the literal, in de la Fuente's allegations, masks a move *towards* the corporeal. The hidden *sentido* (sense) is always a sensible and, by extension, sensual one. Fully aware of the double meaning, he warns that "este error camina por el sentido" (394). A parallel chart contrasts the correct Catholic doctrine with the *alumbrados'* sensual-sensory misinterpretation.

1) Viene Dios al alma y vase sensiblemente y con mutación corporal
2) Inspira Dios al alma y alúmbrala con revelaciones sensibles.
3) Todas sus inspiraciones son revelaciones sensibles
4) La contrición del alma es con dolor sensible y a veces es tan fuerte que mata
5) Las consolaciones del alma son tan sensibles que matan a veces el paciente
6) Los conocimientos vivos del alma son con ilustración sensible
7) Sienten en sí la imagen de Cristo sensiblemente
8) La sacra comunión causa gusto sensible
9) Muchas formas causan mayor gusto
10) Siéntense llenos de amor con efecto sensible
11) Ven, huelen y palpan al mismo Dios sensiblemente
12) Los actos interiores de las virtudes son conocimiento sensible
13) Los actos interiores de los vicios son con inmutación sensible
14) Finalmente, todo el gobierno del alma es sensible (394)

1) God enters the soul and He goes out sensibly and with corporeal mutation
2) God inspires the soul and illuminates it with sensory revelations
3) All His inspirations are sensory revelations
4) The contrition of the soul comes with a sensory pain so strong that at times it kills
5) The consolations of the patient soul are so sensorial that at times they kill the patient
6) The living knowledge of the soul comes with sensory enlightenment
7) They feel within the image of Christ through the senses
8) Holy communion causes sensory pleasure

9) Many hosts cause more pleasure
10) They feel themselves full of love with sensory effects
11) The see, smell, and taste God himself sensibly
12) Interior acts of the virtues are sensory knowledge
13) Interior acts of the vices come with sensory disturbance
14) Finally, all government of the soul is sensorial.

The problem with classifying such *sensibilidad* as heretical is, of course, that the Bible is full of the language of the senses, and thus it is essential to re-associate the senses with the lower bodily faculties, to deny the use of the "spiritual senses." He asserts that the *alumbrados* see God "con los ojos corporales, como ellos lo testifican" (405) ("with the eyes of the body, as they testify"), but he also places the emphasis on the "lower" of the five senses, enumerating, as part of a list of errors, "24. Este Dios [de los *alumbrados*] se huele con el sentido del olfato, causando grandísima suavidad de olor sensible. 25. Este Dios se gusta, según la doctrina de los dichos maestros. 26. Este Dios se palpa y siente con el sentido general del tacto y en todas las partes del cuerpo, como se colige de los sentimientos" In summary, wherever "el católico pone *sentimiento espiritual*; ... el Alumbrado [pone] *corporal*" (405) ("This God [of the *alumbrados*] can be smelled with the olfactory sense, causing the most gentle of sensible smells. 25. This God can be tasted, according to the doctrine of said teachers. 26. This God can be touched and felt with the general sense of touch in all the parts of the body, as can be inferred by the senses"). The difference becomes one of means and ends: where Osuna argued in favour of using the body to reach the spirit, de la Fuente accused the the *alumbrados* of using a language of spirituality and interiority to achieve bodily pleasure and worldly fame. However, as he describes the difference between the orthodox and heterodox interpretation of each of the phrases cited above, it becomes clear that only an omniscient narrator could distinguish between the correct and inverted intentions of one and the other group, as the actual external manifestations in speech and act would be identical. For example, according to de la Fuente, "el *sentimiento* divino llaman aquellos [los Alumbrados] movimientos *sensibles* que son calores y desmayos. Y si ellos, por ventura, ponen otro *sentimiento interior* que es raíz de estos *sentimientos corporales.*" ("they [the Alumbrados] call the *sensory/sensible* movements such as fevers and faints divine sensation. And if they, by chance, use another *interior sensation*, it is at root one of these *bodily sensations*").[16] The relative weight of body and spirit are coded in the sceptical verbs that de la Fuente uses (*llaman, ponen*), but no outside observer could distinguish a faint that came from an interior "sentimiento divino" from a fake or purely physical faint, at least not without some other form of external evidence. De la Fuente seems to allege that such evidence would be found in speech, in the *alumbrados'* claim that "estos *sentimientos corporales* son indicios ciertos e infalibles de la gracia" ("those *bodily sensations* are certain and infallible indications of grace"), but he immediately concedes that the *alumbrados* do not in fact make this claim since "esto fuera jugar al descubierto" (430) ("this would mean showing their hand"). Again, it is only his omniscience that seems capable of discerning between the intention "cubierto" and the speech or act "descubierto." His admission that "son errores callados y enterrados en lo interior del sentido" (432) ("they are errors kept silent, hidden within the interior of their meaning") ironically echoes Osuna; they disgree on what is hidden within "el sentido" but agree that the new practices are invisible and interior to sense and the senses.

The key to de la Fuente's interpretation lies in an alternate interpretation, not just of the invisible and interior but of invisibility/interiority itself. For the mystics, the heart of mysticism lies in the positive connotations of interiority and mystery. De la Fuente returns the hidden to the realm of sin and evil, citing the gospel: "Cristo nuestro Señor dice que lo que de Él oímos lo prediquemos en la plaza. Satanás es amigo de secreto, *et omnis qui male agit, odit lucem, et non venit ad lucem ut non manifestentur opera eius*" (384) ("Christ our Lord says that what we hear about Him should be spoken in the public square. Satan is a friend of secrecy: Everyone who does evil hates the light and will not come into the light for fear that their deeds will be exposed").[17] The devil is behind every act in de la Fuente's reading of the *alumbrado* spirituality, completely replacing Martin Luther or other organized sectarian heresies. In sharp contrast to the charges against the first *alumbrados*, the word "Protestant" does not appear in de la Fuente's warnings. Instead, the *alumbrados* are accused of being *hechiceros* ("sorcerers") and of making pacts with the devil. The pacts are crucial because, as we have seen in the autobiographies, being influenced or even possessed by the devil was not necessarily a crime and could even be seen as a sign of virtue since the devil was most envious of the purest souls. De la Fuente was thus at pains to show that the *alumbrados'* collusion with the devil was voluntary. However, lacking any evidence of such a deliberate pact in the writings of the *alumbrados*, he is forced to imagine with novelistic omniscience the scene of an originary demonic pact. He imagines a reunion in which "Los autores de esta maldad y el demonio consultaron sembrar un herejia sin que se hablase, y dieron una traza maravillosa: tomaron el demonio por instrumento para que diese esta herejía por escrito, porque sus maestros ahorrasen el decirla, por el peligro que hay en ello" (395) ("The authors of this evil and the devil met and consulted on how to sew a heresy without having to say it, and they came up with a marvelous scheme: they used the devil as their instrument to put this heresy into writing, so their teachers could be spared from having to say it, for the danger it presents"). The evidence of this pact is, thus, the absence of hard evidence. Only the omniscient narrator, with access to the devil's acts and intentions, can recount that "Viene el demonio, aceptó el oficio. Y comenzó a escribir y dibujar esta herejía en los sentimientos, va y viene a la gente y hínchalos de amor y vacíalos, dales regalos sensibles, contrición sensible, gustos sensibles … muéstrales por ilusión la Santísima Trinidad, mortifícalos, inspírales, alúmbralos de mil sutilezas …" (396) ("The devil comes, he has accepted the job. And he began to write and trace this heresy in the senses, he goes away and the people come and he fills them with love and then empties them out, he gives them sensory gifts, sensory contrition, sensory pleasures … he shows them with illusions the Holy Trinity, he mortifies them, inspires them, illuminates them with a thousand subtleties"). In other words, the devil imitates to perfection the actions of the Holy Spirit; only someone with insight, not just into the interior of individual souls' but also into a past secret pact, can identify the imposture. This makes the identification of heretical *alumbradismo* even more difficult than witchcraft, for if the theory of witchcraft depends on similar pacts and secrecy, witches at least use their power to do or say evil or heretical things (according to said theory). As mentioned, even the visible manifestation of demonic possession could lead to opposite conclusions since both saints and demoniacs could suffer possession and temptation. By placing the pact in a remote past, however, de la Fuente must confront the problem as to whether individual followers in the present are also culpable of such a pact or if they are merely misguided. He recognizes that the moral status of individuals in the present "es dificultoso de entender, particularmente a las que i(g)noran el camino y misterios de esta secta. Pero entendidos los fundamentos de ella, queda llano este negocio que parece muy obscuro" (420) ("is difficult to understand, particularly for those who are ignorant of the way and mysteries of this sect. But once the fundamentals are understood, this business that seems so obscure becomes plain"). Again, the only solution to the obscurity of the problem is to review a "fundamento" only accessible from an omniscient perspective. From this perspective, de la Fuente identifies a demonic bait and switch: at first, "los discípulos de esta secta reciben en sus sentimientos al demonio por Dios y, entendiendo que aquellos sentimientos son divinos y obra de Dios, perseveran en aquellos ritos supersticiosos" (420) ("the disciples of this sect receive the devil in place of God through their sensations, and, understanding that those sensations are divine and the work of God, they persist in those superstitious rites"), but given entry, the devil slowly proceeds to gain their will. Presented with evidence of their error (of course, a circular argument, as to this point there is no external evidence of error that could not equally be external evidence of virtue), "ellos no se quieren desengañar, sino seguir el movimiento de aquel espíritu ... ni se les puede persuadir que aquel espíritu que las gobierna es malo, antes tienen por engañados a los que así lo condenan. De aquí se colige claramente que el demonio a los principios entra condicionalmente y asi se recibe y sustenta sin condición alguna" ("they don't wish to be disillusioned, but instead to follow the movement of that spirit ... nor can they be persuaded that the spirit that governs them is bad, and instead they consider those who thus condemn them to be deceived. From this one clearly concludes that the devil enters conditionally at first and and then is received and supported completely unconditionally"). The original passive error becomes a voluntary pact at this point, "en virtud de los actos precedentes, todo lo consecuente es voluntario, y coma voluntario se debe castigar" ("in light of the preceding actions, everything that follows is voluntary, and as voluntary should be punished"). Yet the identification of the point of transition from passive to voluntary is, even if we were to concede its existence, again an invisible, interior one, presenting grave problems, as we will see, for a tribunal obligated to maintain certain standards of proof.

From Theory to Practice: Mystic Language on Trial

Alonso de la Fuente was not an Inquisitor, nor did his *memoriales* necesarily convince the Inquisitors that all affective piety was a demonic imposture. His line of thought, however, did represent the opinion of a significant portion of the Church, one with influence on Inquisitors but also on the Inquisition functionaries – *comisarios, calificadores, fiscales* – who participated in the Inquisitorial process. We know this because these functionaries' opinions are all included, in the form of *memoriales*, letters, formal charges, and transcribed interrogations, in the final Inquisition *procesos*. This polyphony of the *proceso* is precisely what makes it such an exceptional historical source. Unlike the spiritual autobiography, in which the "other" voices of the dialogue must be imagined from their traces in the voice of the author, the *proceso* file actually contains documents written by various hands and the transcription of multiple voices (albeit mediated by the interventions, often unknowable, of the *escribano*). The complete Inquisition *proceso* is like a novel in the sense that it does not have its own discourse but is, rather, the sum of all the discourses that it admits as evidence, as well as the texts that opine about that evidence. This is true of all *procesos*, but what I wish to emphasize in the remainder of this chapter is the way that the *procesos* reveal a collision of language in the case of the post-Trent would-be mystics. By the seventeenth century, a language of Teresan mysticism, a language of discernment, and the anti-*alumbradismo* discourse we find in de la Fuente, were all fairly codified. Thus *calificadores*, *fiscales*, and would-be mystics already had an idea of the proper language with which to represent their respective ideas of interior experience of God; the *proceso* represents what happens when these seemingly incompatible discourses meet. The transcripts of an Inquisition *audiencia* are not, of course, records of a "pure" linguistic encounter between accuser and accused; the available documents are still products of a single quill and a written culture. Yet to lament the lost voice of the accused, to posit its subsumption into the voice of power, is to ignore the complexity and superposition of multiple power structures in early modern Spain, as well as the circular flow of languages at all levels of discourse. We have already been reading *vidas* and letters as archaeological objects which contain evidence of their own discursive movement; the interrogation transcription and the *proceso* of which it forms part are, in this sense, far more explicit. They are like striated rocks, embedded with fossils and mineral deposits. To shift from a geological to a medical metaphor, if *vidas*, *memoriales*, or letters provide an X-ray of a (social) body, the complete *proceso* is something closer to an fMRI, the functional imaging of discourse as it circulates within the social body.

Precisely because of the problems posed by the discernment of interiority, the trials of mystics always include an attempt to locate evidence on the body, principally through the identification of sexual transgressions and, if the accused claimed to subsist on communion wafers or was renowned for rigorous fasting, the analysis of ingestion and excretion.[18] These were the old categories of physical evidence and proof with which the Inquisitors were comfortable. Yet in a substantial number of cases, the accused conformed to external norms completely, and the trial rested solely on events occurring in an interior space accessible only through language. I will focus on a representative few for which we have relatively complete transcriptions and which provide the clearest example of the negotiation of legal and mystic discourse. Mateo Rodríguez, the leader of a group of mystics in Madrid in the 1630s, led an external life seemingly beyond reproach.[19] He rose at four, practiced self-mortification, attended mass, confessed and took communion daily, and worked a full day at his trade.[20] The "problem" lay in the six hours he spent daily *recogido* in mental prayer. The use of the term *recogido* is in itself direct evidence of the spread of contemplative prayer practices beyond monasteries or circles of learned laity, and Rodríguez confirmed that he had come to spiritual prayer through authorized channels, initiated by a priest and then through study of approved devotional books such as the *Flos sanctorum* and the works of Santa Teresa. His enthusiasm had led him to extend his experiences beyond the space of the confessional or the privacy of his home, leading his own prayer groups and circulating his raptures and visions in a spiritual autobiography, closely modeled on Teresa's. The Inquisitorial investigation thus depended, not on his reading or theological statements, as we saw with Cazalla, but instead on the nature and source of his visions. The Inquisitors attempted to apply the categories of spiritual discernment, originating with Augustine but codified in the discernment manuals that proliferated in the later sixteenth century, and the *fiscal* argued for a pervasive demonic influence, but both of these models depended on access to interior processes, which, because they are interior, would have to be expressed in unequivocal language. A confessor might work with paradox and ambiguity, but a jurist only had jurisdiction over reality. The mystic language with which Mateo Rodríguez and others responded was, on the contrary, principally concerned with transmitting the sheer unreality, or at least the lack of correspondence with any earthly reality, of the divine vision.

The interrogations of would-be mystics represent a prolonged attempt to dissociate mystic experience from mystic language, to get the accused to represent mystic visions in the language of evidence and proof. In *Vanities of the Eye*, Stuart Clark writes that the relation between vision and knowledge was "particularly unsettled" in late Renaissance Europe (2), and the status of apparitions "became vastly more complex and precarious during the sixteenth and seventeenth centuries than ever before" (205). In earlier centuries, he argues, spirits presented a theological quandary, but by the sixteenth century, they "had also turned into visual puzzles" (209). Clark's study hints at, but fails to note, the degree to which they also became linguistic puzzles. Indeed, the linguistic impasse is present in the charge itself, the investigation of *visions*. The Inquisitors understood vision according to contemporary theories of sight, memory, and understanding; they wanted "seeing" to be a synonym for "witnessing." The mystics understood visions as experiences that transcend reason; they make do with earthly linguistic and scientific categories only as concessions of failure.[21] This difference regarding the properties of "vision" extends to every aspect of the interrogation of the visions. By Inquisitorial logic, the things seen should obey the properties of things; in mystic logic, the essences perceived may be recognized by their similarities with things, but they fundamentally do not belong to that order. For example, when Mateo Rodríguez claimed that he had "seen" a celestial choir, the Inquisitors pushed for details: "Cuando dice ... que vio a Nuestra Señora, San Joseph, el niño Jesús, y los ángeles, y danzaron, ¿qué es lo que danzaron y de qué era[n] los instrumentos?" ("When he says ... that he saw Our Lady, Saint Joseph, the baby Jesus, and the angels and they danced, what dance did they do and what were the instruments?"). By their logic, when one sees a choir, one necessarily sees the instruments being played. But Rodríguez's "vision" has been a revelation, as he explains using the language of contemplative prayer: "Dijo que lo que se le ha preguntado le sucedió interiormente y no sabe ni pudo distinguir cómo eran los ángeles, nuestra señora, y niño Jesús y los instrumentos" ("He said that what they have asked him about occurred in his interior and he does not know nor could he distinguish what the angels, Our Lady, the baby Jesus, or the instruments looked like"). Interrogating two separate visions Rodríguez claimed to have had of Christ, the Inquisitors fixated on his inability to say what Christ was wearing. They were not satisfied when he was able to specify that in one vision experienced while *recogido* that Christ "tenía unas rosas blancas por ligas compuestas de oro muy ricas" ("had white roses for garters, made of gold and very luxurious"). The Inquisitors wanted imaginary matter to obey the laws of material matter. Noting that in his autobiography Rodríguez had said Jesus wore a *long* tunic, they ask "si tenía una túnica larga puesta como dice en el libro, ¿cómo vio las ligas? si levantó Cristo la túnica para que las viese" ("if he was wearing a long tunic as it says in the book, how could he see his garters: did Christ lift his tunic so he could see them?"). A similar exchange can be found in the questioning of the wayward monk Juan de Yegros, who recounted seeing Saint Gregory surrounded by angels and presiding over an altar with "las formas ... en un vaso de oro muy hermoso" ("the hosts ... within a very beautiful gold cup").[22] How, the Inquisitors interrupted, could he know that there were hosts inside: "supuesto que dice que las formas estaban en un vaso de oro parece que no las pudo ver, supuesto que el oro no es transparente" ("given that he says that the hosts were in a golden cup, it would seem he should not have been able to see them, given that gold is not transparent")? Stephen Haliczer quotes the case of Francisca de los Apóstoles, in which the Inquisitor poses an almost identical objection, in this case to a vision in which Francisca "said that she had seen Christ holding a folded paper in his hand containing the 'divine justice' that would be apportioned to mankind." How, he countered, could she have seen what was written within a folded piece of paper "as she said" (139)?[23] In each case, the accused responded by appealing to a different kind of vision. Yegros, for example, responded that "todo lo vio interiormente y así no quedó nada de la visión que éste no lo viera" ("he saw everything in his interior and thus nothing remained in the vision that he did not see").

A related point of divergence between the mystic and the juridical concept of vision concerns the vision's relation to knowledge. According to early modern theories of sight, there was a necessary step between the perception of images and their identification and analysis. Although usually instantaneous and unconscious, the process can be recovered and represented in language. "I saw X" can, if necessary, be elaborated to "I saw components X_1, X_2, and X_3, which, based on my previous encounters or education about X, led me to propose that what I had seen was, indeed, X." The Inquisitors, as jurists, did not accept a logic of sense-based knowledge that could not be broken down into these steps. Hence, their insistence on what the people in visions were wearing, on the external signs by which María Pizarro recognized individual souls in purgatory ("¿en qué se diferenciaban las ánimas de los hombres a las de las mujeres?" ["how were the souls of men different from those of women?"]), on how María de la Encarnación[24] came to know someone was dying in sin ("si fue viendo cosa corpórea, como verbigracia ver [a] un hombre que caminaba éste que estuviese enfermo, o de qué suerte se le representó para que tuviese noticia – por el oído o por alguno de los sentidos – de suerte que lo pueda explicar la dicha noticia" ["was it by seeing something corporeal, for example if she saw a man walking and she could see he was sick, or in what way was it represented to her so that she received the news – through hearing or through one of the senses – in such a way that she can explain the said notification"]), how Isabel Briñas[25] identified a particular guardian angel ("si tiene diferentes señas el un ángel del otro" ["if one angel has different markings than another"]) or soul in purgatory ("si estaba vestido o desnudo o de qué suerte y si traía alguna seña de que estaba en el purgatorio o en otra parte" ["if it was clothed or naked or in what way and if it bore some sign that it was a soul in purgatory or in some other place"]). The replies read like a catalog of attempts to convey, via metaphor, negation, and neologism, a different relationship between seeing and knowing. María Pizarro said that her knowledge "no fue sino que en su pensamiento se le ofreció sin saber cómo … despierta y cerrados los ojos y le parece tiene allá dentro otros ojos con que ve todo lo que se le representa como si fuera con los ojos corporales pero no la habla con palabras ni lo oye" ("was only in her thoughts and it came to her without her knowing how … [she was] awake and with her eyes closed and it seems to her that she has on the inside other eyes with which she sees everything that is represented to her as if it were with her corporeal eyes but it [the soul in purgatory] does not speak to her with words nor does she hear it"). The subjunctive abounds in these declarations: "como si fuera" ("as if it were"); "sin que ella viese ni entendiese por algún sentido corporal cosa" ("without her hearing or understanding anything through her bodily senses").[26] Language turns in circles, as when María de la Encarnación stammered that "solo que le dieron a entender lo que ha dicho y esta inteligencia no fue con diferente modo del que tiene dicho en sus confesiones de que la daban a entender lo demás que tiene dicho y dichas inteligencias eran de suerte que ésta no puede decir cómo son ni las puede explicar mas de la suerte que ha dicho" ("it's just that she was made to understand what she has said and this intelligence was not in a different way from the one she has said in her confessions, in which she was made to understand all the rest of what she has said and said intelligence was in such a way that she cannot say what they are like nor can she explain except in the way she has said"). Ultimately, communication is frustrated, and the accused can only explain that "le vino una certeza de que aquello fue así … interiormente la dan a conocer con señas muy claras que es el ángel de la persona necesitada de tal modo que con palabras no lo puede explicar" ("a certainty that it is like that came to her … in her interior she is made to know with clear signs that it is the angel of the person in need, in such a way that she cannot explain it in words").[27]

The questioning can read like a cat-and-mouse game, with the mystics searching for vocabulary that might convey a new relationship between seeing and knowing, signifiers and signifieds, and the Inquisitors attempting to pin words down in old frameworks. Ribera, the *comisario* in María Pizarro's case, asked María to elaborate on a vision she had of the entire cosmos. "Me dijo que así como en un espejo que tenemos de cama se ve todo cuanto hay en él, y si pasa delante, va colando por él, así en Dios como en un espejo purísimo se ve todo cuanto hay delante de él, y va colando por él (este vocablo usa por pasar) … y repreguntándola qué era aquello de colar me respondió que no colaban, sino que se estaba todo allá por la noticia" ("She told me that, just like in a mirror that you have by the bed you can see in it everything that is there, and if something passes in front of it, it goes *colando* by it, similarly you see in God, as in the purest mirror, everything that goes before, and it goes *colando* by [she uses this word for *passing*] … and asking her again what this *colar* was she answered that *no colaban* but rather that everything was there in the notification"). We see the linguistic struggle in this confusion over the meaning of "colar."[28] Pizarro introduces the word in this new context to express the otherness of her vision, and then rejects it when her interrogator attempts to pin it down to a certain meaning. Ribera returns his questioning to the body, asking "si veía a Dios en el espejo con ojos y manos y partes corporales" ("if she saw God with eyes and hands and body parts in the mirror") but she replies with the spirit: "que no, sino como a espíritu purísimo … y preguntándola que me declare más esto del espíritu puro, y espejo, y siempre me ha respondido que no tiene más que decir ni sabe cómo declararlo más y que no la pregunte más" ("no, like the purest spirit … and asking her to tell me more about this pure spirit and mirror business, she always responded that she doesn't have anything more to say and that I shouldn't ask her any more"). This evocation of the ineffable, which forms the backbone of so much mystic poetry or theology, was, in the courtroom, seen as evasion. For theology and poetry, there is a truth that is beyond expression, while the law could only conceive of withheld information as evasion and falsehood.

By the seventeenth century, the concept of "ojos interiores" had, through the circulation of Teresan discourse, become frequent and widespread. It was a cliché, no longer suggesting a contradiction or destabilizing a discourse, and thus part of what de Certeau would call mysticism-as-noun. Yet the struggle over this phrase in seventeenth-century interrogations shows that such words, if perhaps they lost their radical potential within theology or poetry, retained the power to disrupt in other contexts. The ocular metaphor seems to have been the source of particular contention within the Inquisitional records, more so than other mystic commonplaces, because of its ambiguous relationship to the body. The Inquisition, as has been noted, operated essentially on and through the body: they sought evidence of blood and circumcision, eyewitness (and "ear witness") testimony, and when it was absent, they exacted truth through the torture of the body. Thus, they wanted *ojos interiores* to be a precise description of eyes in every way, like *ojos corporales* except for their location. However, for the mystics, *ojos interiores* and *visión interior* exist only in metaphorical relationship with earthly concepts of sight, and indeed the terms are meant to be oxymorons as much as descriptors. After all, eyes are fundamentally external; their form is even more essential to their identity than their function. Blind people still have eyes. The mystic phrase *ojos interiores* is both a metaphor (like eyes, but interior) and an oxymoron; like a metaphor, it proposes a point of identification (the perception of visual input), and like an oxymoron, it negates the possibility of identification. Furthermore, unlike a typical oxymoron, it can suggest a space where the limitations that make the relationship oxymoronic no longer exist. Before God, internal and external, body and spirit, are all meaningless dichotomies. The proper weight of literal, metaphoric, apophagic, and transcendent interpretations is determined by context, by the expectations of speaker and auditors. When speakers and auditors have different codes of interpretation, they might as well be speaking different languages.

Precisely because the Teresian lexicon had, by the seventeenth century, been given the stamp of orthodoxy, the Inquisition found itself pulled in two directions when dealing with Teresa's spiritual descendants. Theological orthodoxy became incompatible with legal efficacy. The Inquisitors certainly suspected that defendants' use of mystic language was an evasion tactic. After the *beata* María Bautista replied to hours of questions with the same response that she had seen her visions "in spirit," the Inquisitors frustratedly replied that "que es acudir a una respuesta muy fácil el decir que todo lo vio en espíritu" ("it's very easy to respond that she saw everything in spirit") and that it was clear she "ha tomado esa escapatoria" ("had taken this way out") to evade an honest response.[29] Yet they could not completely condemn such discourse because powerful theologians advocated precisely this "escapatoria" – not from the truth, but to the truth, out from the limitations of earthly concepts. The *calificador* of María Pizarro's beatific vision seen "como en espejo" could not impeach its content, as he himself noted that it was the very image used by Saint Augustine. Yet the doctrinality of the image, rather than confirming the truth of the vision or the miracle of its appearance to an illiterate woman, prompted the *calificador* to suppose an entirely rational explanation: that María had stolen the words ("no sé de dónde tomó el ejemplo del espejo, que es [el] que San Agustín usó" ["I don't know where she got the mirror example, the same one that Saint Augustine used"]). He noted his frustration that when he pressed her to describe the mirror vision further, "se cerraba con decir que se recogía a lo interior y al espejo y no hay más razón" ("she shut down by saying she withdrew to her interior and to the mirror and there is no other reason"). The use of *razón* here is intriguing; the absence of *razón* – logical discourse, rational explanation – must inevitably frustrate the investigation into an experience defined by its extra-rationality, its transcendence of logical discourse.[30] It is both tempting and ultimately impossible to determine how the defendants understood mystic phrases or their intentions in using them before the Inquisition. What is clear is the degree to which identical discourses, when employed in different institutional settings, serve distinct purposes and have different effects.

The problem was not that in answering with figurative, poetic language the would-be mystics were answering the wrong way. The problem was that in these cases, the wrong answer *was* the right answer (and vice versa). For example, although the Inquisitors saw the inability to cite details of visions as proof that they were invented, the guides to the discernment of spirits specified that true mystic experience would transcend materiality and added that their failure to do so was a sure sign that the visions were human or demonic counterfeits. When Mateo Rodríguez gave a precise account of a vision, complete with details of adornment and affect, the prosecutor challenged that "si tan embebido [estaba] en los favores que Cristo le hacía, ¿por qué reparaba tan menudamente en los colores de los ángeles, toallas, y guarniciones?" ("if he [was] so absorbed in the favours that Christ was granting him, why did he pay such close attention to the colors of the angels, towels, and decorations?"). When the Inquisitors asked Maria Pizarro if she had been sleeping or awake when she was abused by the devil and she responded "que le parece que estaba durmiendo porque ... se quedó dormida, aunque cuando la llevaron iba despierta" ("it seemed to her that she was sleeping because ... she fell asleep, although when they [the devils] took her she was awake"), they seized on this as evidence that the vision had been a meaningless dream rather than a true possession: "Fuéle dicho que pues fue sueño, ¿para qué lo contó como cosa verdadera? ... en esto se conoce que todo lo que ha dicho ha sido sueños y ficciones" ("She was told that since it was a dream, why did she relate it as if it had been real? ... in this it can be seen that everything she has said has been dreams and fictions"). Juan de Yegros's affirmation that during his periods of *arrebatamiento* he heard "hablas [que] le dictan sin que sea en su mano" ("voices [that] dictate to him without it being under his control") with his "oídos corporales" prompted a similar response: "Fuéle dicho que pues dice que oye, es señal que no está privado de sus sentidos y así que lo que responde cuando le preguntan algo es voluntariamente y sabe lo que responde" ("He was told that since he says he heard them, it is a sign that he was not deprived of his senses and thus that what he replies when they ask him something it is voluntary and he knows what he replies"). The Inquisitors return again and again to the question of "which" eyes or ears perceived a vision/audition. In many cases the accused's response of "ojos interiores" or "corporales" in an original deposition or interrogation is underlined or the word copied again in the margin, direct evidence of the Inquisitors applying, or attempting to apply, clear-cut guidelines to the vague and unclear space of the mystic. The problem was that the doctrinally correct answers to these questions – that the visions occurred in a space that was neither waking or sleep but "suspended" or "withdrawn" and that the visions were seen with the *ojos interiores* – were also the answers that rendered all further interrogation and discernment impossible.

On the one hand, the subjective, ambiguous, mystic language used by visionaries *was* (whether intentionally or not) a successful "escapatoria"; it took the Inquisitors out of the realm of language in which they were capable of making legal distinctions of guilt or innocence, heterodoxy or orthodoxy. On the other hand, the "failure" of the Inquisition in these cases represented a larger "victory" for the conservative sectors of the Church and society. Unlike earlier visionaries who prophesied great disasters or issued warnings about specific monarchical policies or powerful individuals, these seventeenth-century visionaries presented visions that, in the end, represented no threat to any established institutions. As Stephen Haliczer concludes, "Faced with the combined influence of the monarchy, the church, and the Holy Office, the 'holy woman' who wished to survive with her reputation intact would have to support not only the faith but also the entire structure of power as it then existed" (91). In the trials of suspected *alumbrados*, an immediate separation was made between individuals whose behavior or speech was explicitly scandalous (usually this meant a sexual relationship with a confessor) or those who refused to accept Church doctrine and authority ("the entire structure of power as it then existed"). In the first case, judgment could be rendered quickly; in the second, trials might last longer due to attempts to procure repentance, but if the accused remained firm, sentences were severe. For those like Mateo Rodríguez and María de la Encarnación, however, trials went on and on, as *fiscales* who thought like de la Fuente struggled with defendants who spoke like Francisco de Osuna. In the end, sentences tended to be relatively mild and inconclusive.[31] As long as the visionary´s mystic experience had no political implications or told the most powerful what they wanted to hear, the only possible threat she offered was in the possible credence that might accrue to her person. The creation of a cult, even around a doctrinally orthodox cult figure, had the potential to disrupt the proper social hierarchy. Because of the class and gender prejudices that girded such a hierarchy, the threat was greatest when the visionary was poor or not a confined nun, as in the cases of María Bautista and María de la Encarnación.[32] Even in these cases, however, the Inquisition needed only to re-establish its own authority over such subjects, and to do so it was not necessary to brand them as heretics. It was enough to terrify them through interrogations and confinement and then mark them as insignificant or misguided. They could espouse whatever they chose as long as no one took them seriously. The fact that there was no seventeenth-century Lucrecia de León – no popular prophet whose calls of political doom gained the support of powerful social figures – represents the triumph of hegemony, of censorship and self-censorship at the level of the convent, confessor, or community.

Mysticism in the Courtroom

There are hundreds of cases with similar exchanges that illustrate the linguistic impasse created by interrogation of the past mystic experience. Much less common are records of a mystic experience in the courtroom. Were God or the devil for some reason reluctant to make themselves present during an Inquisition trial? In the spiritual autobiography and first-person accounts, the impossibility of writing the actual experience of extasis is an epistemological one: the experience of the ineffable cannot be written, only recalled in writing. Authors may attempt to recreate the irruption of the ineffable in their texts by trailing off mid-sentence or writing a string of exclamations, or this may in fact reflect an ecstatic moment experienced during the writing process. However, there is no external perspective according to which we can relate the time of experience to the time of writing or the external and internal presentation of the rapture. The Inquisition transcription, a document taken down as events and speech unfold, should, if an ecstatic experience were to occur during an *audiencia*, allow us the diachronic narrative from an exterior perspective – the *escribano* or the Inquisitors commenting on the physical or verbal manifestations of the *arrobo* – and then the accused, once the experience has ceased, recounting his/her memory of the ecstatic moment. There are a few scant moments where such an event and double perspective can be glimpsed within the extant *procesos*, and that give us an idea of why they are so rare.

It is not, perhaps, surprising, that no defendant should experience an ecstatic vision during an *audiencia*. As the manuals for mental prayer make clear, mystic union requires mental preparation, a period of silence and meditation to clear the mind of the worldly cares. The *sala* of the Inquisition was hardly the sort of space imagined by Osuna or Laredo in their guides to achieving the most elevated states of prayer. However, as the practice of contemplation spread from a select group of educated or cloistered men, and as theorists and contemplatives alike emphasized the role of the devil in tempting the mystic, we increasingly find accusations of uncontrollable fits, ambiguously demonic or divine, in public places and at inopportune moments. Most of the accusations recount such fits/raptures occurring during mass, but there were exceptions. For instance, María de la Encarnación said she had experienced a state in which "estaba de manera que parece que reventaba y de tal que los circumstantes lo echaban bien de ver y esto le duró por espacio de dos años en todas las misas" ("she was in a state that it felt like she was bursting and such that everyone present could see it, and this lasted for a period of two years during every mass") but also "que cuando estuvo presa en Madrid le dio tres veces" ("it happened three times while she was imprisoned in Madrid"). She added that when she was thus struck, "daba siempre cabeceando ansí en la iglesia como en la calle y en casa" ("she was always nodding off, be it in church, the street, or at home"). When a priest reproached her, asking "que para qué hacía aquello y alborotaba la iglesia, que era mal espíritu y obra del demonio y esta l[e] respondió que no podía mas, que en cualquier parte que le daba hacía lo mismo sin poderlo remediar" ("why did she do that, it disturbed the church and it was an evil spirit and the work of the devil, and this declarant responded that she could not help it, that wherever she was, when it came to her she did the same, without being able to help it"). Thus, it would seem that the later *alumbrados* could experience *arrobos* and *raptos* in unlikely settings, and while the discernment manuals agreed that such public or corporeally extreme fits were evidence of a diabolic rather than divine origin,[33] a diabolically inspired fit did not necessarily connote a pact or malicious intent on the part of the sufferer. A fit in the Inquisition *sala*, even if it appeared more demonic than divine, would still require further judicial discernment to determine not just the source but also the degree of complicity of the accused.

The Inquisitors certainly took seriously the possibility of demonic possession, voluntary and involuntary. They interviewed exorcists as expert witnesses, charged individuals with making Satanic pacts, and suggested to self-proclaimed visionaries that their experiences were delusions imposed by the devil. Yet while in theory they admitted the possibility of the sudden and involuntary substitution of a subject with a demonic or divine presence, records of possessions during the proceedings show that in practice they were not willing to allow for the possibility that defendants' spirits could leave the courtroom while their bodies remained present. A note in María Bautista's case[34] reports that after months of interrogations the accused:

> comenzó a dar voces muy tremendas y se puso en cruz, los ojos cerrados y temblando la cabeza … y habiéndola dado voces el dicho Señor Inquisidor y dicho que todo aquello era invención, que tratase de decir verdad y descargar su conciencia, turnó en sí, al parecer con mucho juicio, y le fue

dicho que ¿para qué hacía aquellos embustes? que no pensase engañar al Tribunal, que ya estaban conocidos sus embelecos.

began to give tremendous yells and she put her body in the form of the cross with her eyes closed and her head trembling ... and the Inquisitor, having yelled at her and told her that this was all an invention and that she should try to speak the truth and discharge her conscience, she returned to her senses apparently in perfect sanity and she was asked why she used these tricks, and told that she should not seek to trick the tribunal, that they already knew about her tricks.

The Inquisitors accepted possession and rapture in theory, but their judicial procedure could not accommodate it in practice: they could only act on rational subjects and think in terms of intentional acts. Thus, an episode of possession or demonic temptation *in person*, as opposed to merely the textual account of a prior episode, could only be understood as deliberate fiction, an "embuste" or "invención." Ironically, María Bautista's sentence – she was gravely reprimanded in the courtroom and advised of the "los engaños que ha tenido de sus revelaciones" ("deceptions she has been under regarding her revelations") allows for the possibility of demonic intervention that the Inquisitors denied during the proceedings. They admitted in theory – in theology – what they could not prove, and therefore could not accept, in practice.

Hilaire Kallendorf has shown that the exorcist's role, as scripted in the manuals of exorcism, has formal similarities with that of the prosecuting attorney in a classical trial.[35] She argues that the exorcism "thus becomes a trial, a *tribunal domini nostri*," but María Bautista's case shows that by the seventeenth century, the Inquisition, despite being a "tribunal of faith," was procedurally restricted to "homines nostri." The Inquisitors were not exorcists, not only because they did not have the formal training or title, but because their categories for understanding the subject, and his/her relation to language, were vastly different. The juridical process depended on the ability to compel testimony from a rational subject, one whose faculties of memory, will, and speech all coincided and were consistent over time. The speech of the demoniac, both as catalogued in guides to exorcisms and in the accounts of exorcisms so richly studied by de Certeau, is not admissible as testimony, and we find nothing like it in the *procesos*.[36] Or rather, we find it in the *procesos*, but only as second-hand evidence, in the narratives of exorcisms or possessions in the past. They interviewed exorcists and men and women who claimed to have been possessed, but, just as we saw with the examination of those who claimed past divine raptures, they were still applying rational criteria to these testimonies: looking for contradictions, confirmation from external sources, or conformity with published guides. When such rational methods could not discern truth, they were at a dead end. For this same reason, they could or would not interview a spirit during an *arrobo* or a possession. They could only deal in the courtroom with the rational subject, able to access past moments of unreason via memory and able to relate them via speech. The Inquisitors could not interrogate a subject who was not there, and, unlike exorcists, they were not invested with the authority to interrogate supernatural beings.

Nowhere is the distinction between exorcists and jurists more starkly illustrated than in the rather late case of Agustina Salgado, a *beata* and practitioner of mental prayer who was accused in 1712 of being "ilusa e iludente."[37] The Inquisitors interrogated dozens of witnesses to Salgado's raptures and fits: medical doctors, exorcists, neighbours, priests. The questions posed to Agustina in the interrogations show that the Inquisitors were contemplating the possibility of demonic imposture. They asked her if "todas las demás revelaciones, raptos, inteligencias, hablas interiores, visiones, y otros favores que tiene confesados en todas las Audiencias que hasta aquí se han tenido con ella, ha dado o da asenso de suerte que en su alma no lo hayan dejado la menor duda de ser dios" ("all of her other revelations, raptures, intelligence, inner voices, visions, and other favours that she has confessed in all her *audiencias* that thus far they have had with her, she assents or has assented to them in such a way that in her soul she has been left without the slightest doubt that they are from God"), and when she replied in the affirmative, they reminded her that "debiera tener presente que transfigurándose muchas veces el demonio en ángel de luz, contrahace y remeda los espirituales y verdaderos consuelos y gozos" ("she should keep in mind that the devil, transfiguring himself into an Angel of light, counterfeits and mimics true spiritual consolations and joy"). The *proceso* dragged on with sporadic *audiencias*, in which Agustina answered rationally and affirmed that her visions came from God, until, ten months in, the dynamic changed. In the midst of an interrogation, her hand began to tremble. When the Inquisitor asked her what was causing this:

> respondió riéndose que nada … reconociendo dicho Señor Inquisidor la falta de palabras de la declarante y que iba demudándosela de rostro, llamó al alcalde y habiéndole mandado la tuviese (por parecer sería accidente que la turbase los sentidos respecto de su corta salud), al ir a tenerla con excesiva violencia arrojó la muleta; se levantó del asiento, y se tiró al dicho alcalde dándole puñadas y a un mismo tiempo, poniendo el rostro tan horroroso especialmente de ojos y boca, teniendo ésta

sumamente negra por la parte de adentro, que causaba notable pavor … y sin embargo de hallarse tullida, y de ser algunas las fuerzas del dicho alcalde, portero y secretario que la tenían, no podían sujetarla, y echó al suelo al dicho alcalde, con lo cual, dicho Señor Inquisidor empezó a ponerla preceptos invocando la Santísima Trinidad, y diciendo algunas palabras concernientes (por creer eran efectos del demonio) y aunque tuvo resistencia para obedecer, sacó dicho Señor Inquisidor un rosario, y volviendo a repetir los preceptos e invocaciones, se le echó al cuello, e inmediatamente se serenó, cesando en ejecutar los expresados extremos, y volviendo como quien ha tenido cualquier otro accidente, sollozando y mirando a los circunstantes, exclamó diciendo "¿qué es esto?" repitiendo el nombre de Jesús.

she responded, laughing, nothing … nevertheless, after various instances, the Inquisitor, recognizing her lack of words and that her face began to change, called the warden and ordered him to hold her down (because it seemed that some accident had clouded her senses related to her poor health), but when he went to hold her, she threw down her cane, rose from her seat, and threw herself at the warden, punching him and at the same time, her face becoming so horrible, especially her eyes and mouth, this latter all black on the inside, causing the Inquisitors, secretary, and warden notable fear … and despite the fact that she was lame, the forces of the warden, secretary, and doorman were insufficient to restrain her … the Inquisitor began to invoke the precept of the Holy Trinity … believing that these were effects of the devil … and although she resisted obeying, the Inquisitor took out a rosary and, repeating the invocations and precepts, she calmed down … and returning like someone who has had any other accident, sobbing and looking at those gathered, she exclaimed, "what is this?" repeating Jesus's name.

The Inquisitors began the next *audiencia* as if nothing unusual had occurred; since the devil could not be incorporated into the human judicial process, the only way to deal with his possible entrance was to deny it entirely. They had to pretend it had not happened because it was not until the verdict that it could be decided whether it had truly happened. And yet it happened again: the scribe recorded the breakdown of the *sala* into absolute chaos, with Agustina responding to the Inquisitor's calls for obedience to the rosary by shouting that she would obey no one, throwing off the warden attempting to restrain her and tearing the rosary out of the Inquisitor's hand. Unlike in María Bautista's case, the Inquisitor here clearly fully believed in the possession; his response was not that of the rationalist lawyer but that of the exorcist.

Yet the final sentence from the Suprema shows that in 1715 these two roles and spaces could not coexist. Agustina was reprimanded, sentenced to abjure *de levi* and to seclusion and instruction in a hospital for two years, but the Inquisitors on the case were "gravemente reprendidos por haber procedido judicialmente contra el diablo que se dijo tenía Agustina" ("gravely reprimanded for having proceeded judicially against the devil that Agustina was said to have"). The Suprema's sentence re-establishes Agustina as the only legitimate subject, grammatically and judicially. The devil is reduced to a status of object and then further relegated to judicial irrelevance by the use of impersonal indirect discourse ("se dijo [que] tenía"). Even the Inquisition did not accept as evidence hearsay with no identified sayer. Furthermore, the Suprema ordered "quémense los autos que se hicieron en razón de compeler al diablo ... como los que hayan quedado en el tribunal para que no quede memoria de tal procedimiento" ("burn the [records of] the acts that were held to compel the devil, so that no memory remains of these proceedings").

It is historians' good fortune that in this instance not only was the act of destruction not fulfilled but the order itself was preserved. One wonders how many similar cases there were in which such an order was carried out. The Suprema's concern for the impact of possible divulgation of the complicity of the Tribunal in a non-rational discourse gives us a clue to the real impact of the encounter between the rational and the supernatural as it played out in early modern Spain. The lengthy trials and relatively light sentences given to those accused of interior crimes – light sentences that, as has been shown, resulted less from an agreed-upon narrative of limited guilt than from a surrender in the face of a process incapable of providing any definitive conclusion – revealed the Holy Office to be anachronistic, not because its methods were too brutal but because its methodology was too rational to meet its stated aim of "protecting the faith" when that faith had moved beyond the realm of judicial proof. A docket of suspended cases and behind-closed-doors reprimands could not sustain the pedagogy of fear that had been the Inquisition's strongest weapon.

It is undeniable that a generation of Liberal reformers mounted the final campaign that ended the Inquisition, but historians may have simplified the relationship of cause and effect in this narrative. The rationalism that the Liberal reformers espoused and that they used to argue against a Holy Tribunal could well be said to have come from that tribunal itself, or at least from the breach that opened between the Tribunal of Faith and the faith that, from the later sixteenth century onward, was on trial before the tribunal.

Chapter Five

Mysticism on Stage

As noted in the previous chapter, Álvaro Huerga proposed three stages of *alumbradismo* in Spain: radical, sensual, and theatrical.[1] The first two phases correspond to the shift we have seen in mystic theory and practice; an earlier period of intensely intellectual and abstract focus on interiorized spirituality (the *tratados de contemplación*) gave way to a generation of mystics who, while still emphasizing the interiority of the mystic experience, locate it on/in the body (Santa Teresa and her imitators). However, it is more difficult to integrate the third development with mysticism, given its focus on interiority, if we understand the adjective *teatral* (as Huerga seems to) as defining an activity performed primarily for an audience. Huerga does not in fact define what he means by *teatralidad* when he says that "the peculiar aspect of the Seville *alumbradismo* was its theatricality"; instead, he gives synonyms, including "spectacular," "sensational," and "showy" (71). Based on these adjectives, we can assume the association with theatre is the desire to be seen, to experience *arrobos*, extasis, and demonic temptation/possession *in public*. The Inquisition in its prosecution of *alumbrados* assumed a second connection of *alumbradismo* with theatre: inauthenticity, the "playing of a role" that did not correspond with actual belief. However, there is no reason to take an Inquisitorial perspective, and we may assume that many of the men and women who are recorded as *being seen* experiencing extreme bodily symptoms, were not consciously playing a part. They may have been *performing*, in the sense that the word has assumed in performance studies (*performing* gender, etc.) but they were not *acting*. There is another fundamental difference between *alumbradismo teatral* and theatre *strictu sensu*, and that is the absence of a text in the former. Almost all the manifestations of *alumbradismo* that Huerga cites in this category are corporeal; they are neither based on textual interpretation, nor do they manifest themselves in discourse (aside from denunciations and responses to interrogations). To what extent, then, can they be considered *mystical* in the sense proposed by de Certeau, as a transgression in language? And without a language to attempt to connect these exterior manifestations to some interior experience, to what extent can it be considered an interiorized spirituality? Huerga concludes that, with the Sevillan *alumbrados*, the movement "lost its essence" (71). Whether we define the "essence" of mysticism as the interiority of the experience (Huerga) or as a form of representation (de Certeau), we can agree that a purely exteriorized, non-verbalized *alumbradismo* is not mysticism.

The question this presents, then, is how mysticism gets to the point of not being mysticism. As noted, de Certeau repeatedly refers to the dissolution of mysticism at the end of the seventeenth century but gives little attention to the specific mechanisms through which this occurs. He seems to see the (d)evolution of mysticism as, on the one hand, inevitable, a result of mysticism's pursuit of an impossible object, and on the other, as the result of the appropriation of mysticism's transgressive-inventive discourse by the sciences (83–5). We have seen in previous chapters the tension between transgression and system in mystic language, and the confrontation of mystic language with rationalist judicial discourse. This chapter picks up on the adjective "teatral" to think of how *theatrical* language affects mystic discourse and also to consider how the medium and institutions of the theatre *strictu sensu* (represented by actors, with scripts, in *corrales* or on *carrozas*) might have influenced this *teatralización* of spirituality. Our study thus comes at the problem of the relation between mysticism and theatre from two directions: considering first the representation of mystics and mysticism in theatrical works themselves, then considering how these words and works might have been perceived by seventeenth-century audiences, the same urban publics from which the "theatrical" *alumbrados* – many of them *beatas* and thus able to attend secular theatre – emerge.

In *Shakespearean Negotiations*, Stephen Greenblatt addresses the question of what is "made negotiable, traded" in the appropriation (or transference) of sacred practices and objects to the theatre (112). We may ask the same question of the transference of the mystic experience to the Spanish stage, although the parallels with Greenblatt's study end here, since the relationship between city, temple, and stage differed so greatly between England and Spain.[2] In England, theatre was a more marginal activity and religious theatre strictly prohibited; while there were certainly a minority of Catholic moralists in Spain who attacked theatre as desacralizing,[3] they had only limited success in separating stage and religion. As José Maravall argued in *The Culture of the Baroque,* the conservative interests in Spain recognized the "incomparable force" of simulating "direct presence – or at least the presence of symbolic representations" for "igniting movements of affection, adherence, and surrender" to the structures of power (253). No artistic form had a greater potential for recreating that "direct presence" than the theatre, combining as it does the affective power of the visual image and the spoken word. And indeed, the theatres in Spain, unlike the English stages, were literally and figuratively at the heart of the Hapsburg city.[4] The great Spanish Golden Age playwrights all wrote for the palace and for religious festivals (principally *autos sacramentales*). Lope de Vega, Tirso de Molina, and Calderón de la Barca were all ordained priests (although Lope's religious vocation came after his period of greatest dramatic production). If, in London, the transference of a religious practice, like exorcism, to the theatre meant sending it "from the center to the periphery … where stringent urban regulation had already driven the public playhouses" (Greenblatt 113–14), in Madrid the journey from church to theatre was a journey within the centre.

However, this did not necessarily mean, as Maravall would have it, that ideas and ideologies were running in place. The problem with Maravall's model of Spanish Baroque culture is that it presupposes a unified "structure of power" and a stable concept of exactly what should be "directly represented," "adhered," and "surrendered to." The debates surrounding the reality of mystic experiences and practices reveal that within the highest levels of the Church there was disagreement about how popular affect and enthusiasm should best be manifested. The divisions over mysticism are particularly interesting for a study of theatre – more so than other splits in the power structure such as those between Church and Crown, or royalty and aristocracy – because it is precisely the question of "direct presence" that lies at the heart of both. We would imagine that, in the theatre, questions of how to represent the divine and the human experience of the divine could find their most complete, complex exploration since it was in the theatre that the visual, verbal, and emotional elements of this debate could all be explored simultaneously.

On the other hand, it might be supposed that theatre is, by definition, incompatible with a profound exploration of mysticism: that theatre, because it cannot have a first-person narrator, because it is spectacle, cannot represent mystic discourse. However, the theatre of the period made full use of the dramatic monologue for representing interior states, and the scenic technology of the period could well have been used to represent mystic visions, voices, and states in ways that disrupted rational categories. In theory, theatre could be a medium for a rich exploration of mystic experience, as much so as the poem or the autobiography. It would seem logical that the theatre, a cultural form that steps to the forefront of Spanish cultural life precisely in the same period as the movements of popular interiorized spirituality, would be fascinated by the negotiations of the status of the mystic in early modern Spanish society. The tools of the theatre would seem ideal for an exploration of the essence of mystic experience, and at the same time, we must assume that early modern Spaniards' ideas about piety were influenced by their exposure to religious theatre.

The first section of this chapter will examine how the language of mysticism that had begun to condense into a recognized discourse by the mid- to late sixteenth century is changed when it enters into the nascent Spanish theatre. I am focusing here on the theatre of the *corrales*, rather than the older paratheatrical tradition with roots going back to medieval times. This is not in any way to deny the influence of paratheatre in Baroque Spain – indeed, Baroque Spain expanded and multiplied the processions, festivities, and liturgical spectacles that constitute this liminal genre.[5] Undoubtedly, from the point of the view of the spectator, the distinction between paratheatre and theatre *strictu sensu* was a porous one. From the point of the view of the scholar, however, there is a marked difference between processional or paratheatrical spectacle on the one hand and the *entremés*, *comedia*, or *auto* on the other, and that is the presence of *texts*. We may get an idea – although, I would argue, a fairly inexact one, given the propagandistic intents and rhetorical conventions of the *relaciones de fiestas* – of what was seen in the visual spectacles elaborated for religious or civic celebrations, but we have very little notion of how these visual experiences (if at all) were translated into language. The purely visual encounter with images of the sacred undoubtedly influenced the way that would-be mystics envisioned their own encounters with the divine – experiences that, in various institutional and generic spaces, they later sought to translate into language. But since my interest in this book is the languages of mysticism, my focus here will be on the genres which include a linguistic component accessible to the modern scholar. My interest in this chapter is precisely the intersection of image and word, visual and linguistic representation, found in early modern theatre.[6] The second half of my analysis shifts away from the texts themselves to consider the circulation of this new theatrical-mystical language among the theatre audience. To what extent can we see echoes of theatre (*strictu sensu*) in the *theatricalization* of *alumbradismo* that has been identified? The purpose here is, once again, not to identify a strict logic of cause and effect, but to propose a feedback loop that gradually, and in broad temporal strokes, changes from the Renaissance to the Baroque.

Mystic Language and the *Auto Sacramental*

We should begin with the question of where and with what frequency the question of mystic experience entered into the early modern theatre. There are two main genres of religious theatre in the period: *comedias* with a religious subject (particularly *comedias de santos*), and the *autos sacramentales,* the allegories of the Eucharist written explicitly for the Corpus celebrations. Let us begin with the *autos,* as these plays are explicitly framed as instruments of religious education, and thus where we would most expect to find resonance with the theological issues of the day. Indeed, the central subject of the *auto* – the transubstantiation – engages many of the paradoxes (body vs. spirit, literal vs. metaphor, interior vs. exterior) that structure mystic discourse, and many of the mystics experienced union during communion. Another area of overlap is the predominance of the Song of Songs and its allegorical interpretation as the marriage of the soul to Christ in both mystic texts and *autos.* For example, the *loa* to Lope's *La maya* introduces the theme, invoking "aquel Cupido/ de amor vendado, y por amor vendido/ Esposo de los Cantares" (22) ("that Cupid/ blindfolded by love, and sold for love/ Groom of the Canticle")[7] and immediately following, the actor delivering the prologue makes explicit that the Eucharist is a foretaste of this mystical marriage in heaven:

> Esperad, pues, Alma, vos,
> y gozaréisle en el cielo,
> que aunque es Dios en cielo y suelo,
> aquí veis pan, y allá Dios.
> Del cielo somos aldeas,
> pues hoy, Alma venturosa,
> que Dios con vos se desposa,
> da por colación obleas. (23)

> Wait, then, Soul, and you will know joy in the heavens. For although it is God in the heavens and on the ground, here you see bread, and there you will see God. We are like heaven's villages, and this is why, fortunate Soul, when he weds you, he serves wafers as the repast.

The main characters of this *auto* are "Cuerpo" (Body) and "Entendimiento" (Intellect/Understanding), and most of the play consists of a discussion of the relationship between the two and in particular, on the proper role of the body in salvation. A dualist view (mind good, body bad) prevails but does not go unchallenged: at the outset, Cuerpo concedes:

> Ya sé que soy sin nobleza,
> grueso, tosco y material,
> y del Alma la riqueza,
> que es su tela y mi sayal
> distinta naturaleza.
> Pero es tal nuestra amistad,
> Que no hay miembro en mí vacío
> de su virtud. (24)

> I know I am without nobility, thick, coarse, and material, and all the riches belong to the Soul, for her [the soul's] fine cloth and my rough wool are of a different nature. But such is our friendship that not one of my members is empty of her virtue.

This body's participation in the experience of the divinity is, of course, the central question debated by mystic theologians and expressed in spiritual autobiography. The treatment of the issue in the *auto* is, despite the verse and multi-sensory appeal, more closely aligned with scholastic theological treatises than the lyric poem or autobiography. The final wedding/fiesta of the Maya (the soul) is full of music and, we can imagine, rich visual imagery, but all of the play leading to this point consists of intellectual discussion. At times, the dialogue includes a more affective language, such as when "entendimiento" tells "cuerpo" that "Sus ojos quiero que hoy vean/ A Cristo hermoso galán" ("I want your eyes to see today, Christ as a handsome young man") and Cuerpo replies that "De amor se abrasa" (25) ("They burn with love"), but these are fleeting. The early scenes involve different vices tempting "cuerpo," but the temptations are described in purely intellectual terms: love and pleasure are spoken of and contemplated as conscious choices but not experienced on stage.

It is the "entendimiento" who introduces the mystical union to "el alma vestida de maya" ("the soul dressed as the *maya*"),[8] and this narrative reliance on the character of "entendimiento" also characterizes the overall tone of the treatment of mystical union. The "músicos" first establish the allegory of maya-alma and the mystical wedding: "Esta Maya tan hermosa/ tan compuesta y tan graciosa,/ viene a ser de Cristo esposa" ("This beautiful spring maiden, so modest and lovely, has come to be Christ's bride"), and then Entendimiento speaks to her.

Alma gallarda y hermosa,
pues siendo pobre mujer
te busca para su esposa
Cristo, mira que has de ser
santa, honesta y virtuosa.
En su mística y divina
compañía gozarás
sus riquezas, e imagina
que todas las perderás
si al vicio el Cuerpo te inclina …
Pues está en tu castidad
tu gloria y tu perdición. (29)

Beautiful and elegant soul, since, you being a poor woman, Christ seeks you out for his bride, take care that you must be holy, honest and virtuous. You will enjoy his riches in his mystical and divine company, and imagine that you will lose them all if you turn to the vices of the body … Your glory or downfall rests on your chastity.

The Maya (alma) responds in a similarly intellectual, affect-less vein:

Grandes excelencias tengo
pues en la parte inmortal
con los ángeles convengo,
y a mi patria celestial
es el centro donde vengo.
De Dios, que todo lo excede,
soy a su imagen formada:
cuando pueda ser que quede
de otras cosas ocupada,
solo Dios henchirme puede.
Y ojalá el esposo mío
Maya y gallarda me viera. (30)

I have superior qualities, since in the immortal part of me I gather with the angels, and my celestial fatherland is the centre from whence I come. I am made in the image of God, He who exceeds all: While I may become occupied with other things, only God can fill me. And I hope that my spouse finds me to be spring-like and attractive.

The *auto*'s use of abstract allegorical concepts instead of individual humans means that there can be no subjectivity. Thus the exposition of the mystic marriage is presented as doctrine rather than an active struggle with language and experience. The theatrical setting – the mass public and the expectations of visual and narrative stimulus – impede any real theological exploration. Instead, the playwright employs the "mystic marriage" with the certainty that it would evoke a predictable image and understanding. The abstract poetic celebration of the marriage of Christ and his bride had solidified in the discursive landscape.

This tendency towards abstraction and the erasure of subjectivity is even more pronounced in Calderon's *autos*. The concepts of the mystic wedding have become so well-known that Calderón can use them as a building block, a given, upon which to experiment with the limits of allegory.[9] In typical Baroque fashion, the area of innovation and experimentation has shifted entirely to the formal, external level; without denying the sincerity of Calderón's religious faith, when it comes to the trope of the mystic wedding, he seems more interested in the mechanisms of allegory than the experience allegorized.[10] If, in Lope, at least the abstraction of "cuerpo," "entendimiento," and "alma" still pointed towards a *person*, in Calderón, we are more likely to find the allegory translated to an entirely de-humanized setting.[11] In *La hidalga del valle*, it is "placer" (pleasure) who hears celestial music even though she sees nothing ("mis ojos no ven/ quién es quien canta, ni a quién/ es la mósica tampoco" [678–80][12] ["my eyes do not see who is singing, nor who is the musician"]) and cries out "¡Válgame el Cielo! ¿Qué voces/ me están hablando al oído,/ llevándome suspendido/ de sus acentos veloces?" (673–6) ("Heaven help me! What voices speak into my ear, leaving me suspended by these swift strains?"). But instead of representing the subjective experience of that "suspensión," Calderón has *Placer* recall that "que en los cantares habrá/ que he escochado de una esposa," (683–4) ("I have heard that in the Canticle, there is a Bride"), and from here she concludes that the object of the song is the same as "aquella a quien predice/ la canción misterio tanto" (697–8) ("the one for whom the mysterious Canticle foretells so much"). For theological reasons, Pleasure cannot be the *Esposa*, the one who experiences mystic union. Thus, when she goes on to recite a clearly *Cantar* (and "Cántico")-inspired poem about the harmony of the mystical song, it is a third-person description, not a first-person experience.[13] Furthermore, Pleasure (somewhat incongruously) goes on to recite a long monologue of Old Testament history and its accompanying moral interpretation, hardly compatible with a representation on stage of ecstasy or struggle with language.

The increasingly Baroque and meta-theatrical nature of Calderón's allegories reaches the point of complete erasure of the subject in *La humildad coronada*.[14] Moral, Cedro, Laurel, Almendro, and Espino[15] come across "el Árbol de la Ciencia" (the tree of knowledge), who seems to be asleep, but Moral clarifies that "no es sueño" ("it is not sleep") but instead:

> ... Suspensión,
> por quien allá Salomón
> en sus cantares dirá,
> que aunque está durmiendo está
> velando su corazón. (827–31)

> Suspension, about which Solomon in the Canticle says, that although you are sleeping, your heart is awake.

Espino replies that:

> Pues ya que en la alegoría
> de los árboles parece
> que el misterio deste día
> las pasiones nos ofrece
> como humanas, no querría
> despertarle, hasta saber
> qué árbol éste pudo ser. (832–7)

> since already in the allegory of the trees, it seems that the mystery of this day offers to us the human-like passions, I would rather not awaken her until we know what Tree this could be.

An allegorical conversation between varieties of trees and abstract concepts, about an abstract tree, that not only passes immediately into allegory but declares its own allegorical nature, could hardly be expected to provoke a response of *identification* among the audience.

While Calderon's "late-stage Baroque" *autos* bring the literal dehumanization of the *auto* to extremes, in some sense the *auto* is, by definition, incompatible with a representation of the mystic experience. As Aurora Egido writes, "While the *autos* are the sum of diverse elements that intertwine, creating a plural text, it must be said that allegory is what gives them unity and meaning, by integrating each of the parts and synthesizing them into a reading that – from imagery to affect – allows them to convey that which in itself is ineffable" (118). Mystic literature is also a writing of the ineffable, but the *auto*'s strategy of allegory represents a different and incompatible pathway, one that takes an intimate, human experience-in-time and makes it universal and abstract. Although generally allegory is thought of in terms of personification, the *persons* that are created, because they represent abstract concepts, do not have interiority. The *auto* version of the mystical sacrament is more "personified" than it might be in pseudo-Dionysius, but in comparison to the deeply individualized representation of mystic union that predominates in the sixteenth century, it represents a de-personification. While the actors in the *auto* are bodies on stage in the present, their speech and their choreography erase their identity as bodies and subjects and substitutes for it a timeless allegoric identity.

Interiority in the Comedia de Santos: *El Divino Africano*

To find theatrical representations of individuals with some degree of interiority, we must therefore look to the *comedia*, and for representations of the individual experience of God that is at the core of mysticism, we would logically look to the *comedia de santos*. The prohibition on the representation of the adult Christ in the *corrales* meant that almost all biblical re-enactments were taken from the Old Testament, which gave little opportunity for mystical interludes.[16] The New Testament *comedias* tend to focus on early Christian martyrs, whose exemplarity rests not in their spiritual practice but on their willingness to die.[17] As with the Old Testament plays, we find little retroactive projection of interior spirituality, and even among the plays about medieval saints, dramatists tend to choose as their subjects those saints whose lives are defined by extreme acts of penitence, suffering, or reversal (the sinner-to-saint narrative) and not the medieval saints known for their innovative spiritual practice. The canonization of Santa Teresa in 1622 finally prompted a unique occasion for a theatrical representation of the life of a mystic, one whose mystic writings might well be familiar to the audience at a *corral*. A close examination of the treatment of mysticism in Lope de Vega's hagiographical play about the saint[18] provides insight into the mechanisms that led to the transition identified by Huerga: the simultaneous *teatralización* and demystification of the *alumbrados*.

Before we turn to Lope's Teresa play(s), it is useful to study another work: *El divino africano*, also by Lope, which stages the life of Saint Augustine and in fact provides the most complex integration of mystic language and interiority on a Spanish stage. It is not surprising, perhaps, that among all the early saints brought to the early modern stage, Saint Augustine would provide the opportunity for a complex treatment of visions. In the sixteenth- and seventeenth-century debates about mysticism, Augustine is cited both by mystics and by those sceptical of mystic experience. Augustine doubted men could distinguish between divine visions and demonic illusion and thus counseled against giving them too much credence or cultivating them as an essential part of Christian life.[19] Yet the *Confessions* provided mystics a model and language for the narration of an interiorized spiritual life, and at a narrative level, Augustine seemed to contradict his expressed disavowal of visionary experience through the account of his mother and her unlettered, revelatory Christianity. Lope focuses on the early years of the saint's life – the Augustine of the *Confessions* and not Augustine, bishop and martyr. In particular, the play's action centres on books 4–8 and thus skips the seemingly more "theatrical" early scenes of sin and spectacle, choosing instead to engage Augustine's intellectual and spiritual struggle between Manicheism and Christianity. Indeed, Lope stages his protagonist in the process of writing his *Confessions*, the only early modern staging of a spiritual autobiography of which I am aware.[20] The triumphal Augustine is foreshadowed twice, and the final scenes of the play find Augustine at the height of his power and in his martyrdom at the hands of the Vandals. However, in comparison with other hagiographies (as we shall see with Lope's treatment of Teresa), this play is unusually focused on internal struggles, rather than external confirmations of faith. *El divino africano* is unusual in Lope's output for two reasons. First, it is one of the few Lope plays that we know to have fallen afoul of the Inquisition. In 1922, Américo Castro published his discovery of a 1608 note by Lope protesting the censure and requesting that his play be returned to him with guidelines as to how he might amend it. It is unclear what changes were made between this original version and the *comedia* by the same name that figures in the *Obras completes* (1623). Castro speculates that the censors might have found fault with the eloquency with which Augustine expresses his doubts about Christianity, prior to his conversion, but it is impossible to know. The second anomaly of *El divino africano* is that, unlike almost all of Lope's religious plays, *El divino africano* was not commissioned to commemorate a religious festival. Lope's motives for dramatizing the *Confessions* are unknown, but it is reasonable, given the lack of evidence of any commission, to suppose that the play's subject and focus was his own choice and thus reflective of his own artistic and spiritual interests.[21]

Early in the first Act, Augustine, a famous professor of rhetoric and an avowed Manichean, has a dialogue with his mother in which she proposes to tell him of a dream she had of his eventual conversion. He cautions her against believing in dreams, although using the argument of the religion he himself has not come to believe in: "En la religión/ cristiana, a superstición/ los condena cada día" ("In the Christian religion, they [dreams] are every day condemned as superstition"). Monica replies with a defense that would be familiar to Teresa and the *alumbrados*:

Los sueños que el cielo envía,
que, en fin, son revelaciones,
verdades son, no ilusiones;
mira a Josef, que interpreta
la hambre a Egipto sujeta;
mira otros claros varones;
mira el ángel, que aparece
al esposo de María
en sueños. (398–405; act I) [22]

The dreams that the heavens send, which are, after all, revelations, are true, not illusions. Look at Joseph, who interpreted the famine Egypt was subject to. Look at the other upstanding men, look at the Angel, who appeared to Mary's husband in a dream.

And, of course, her dream proves true, as the play's audience already knows. Yet it is important here to distinguish between the dream or revelation and mystic discourse. Although they often overlap, there is nothing inherently mystical about prophetic revelation, and indeed the revelations that Monica cites from the Bible are not recounted there with any sort of mystic language. As we have noted, both in historical documents and literature, the prophetic vision exists independently of mystic union. The difference lies in the emphasis: narrative or affective. Almost all Baroque dramatists use the dream or vision as a plot device and, in religious plays, as a way of revealing supernatural truth. The "symbolic staging" (to use the term proposed by Teresa Kirschner), of such scenes has been amply studied.[23] For our purposes, however, it is sufficient to note that Monica's vision (in this instance not staged but only narrated) is recounted without any of the hallmarks of the mystic vision; it is not experienced during a period of suspension/contemplation, neither its interpretation nor its expression in language is problematized, and there is no emphasis on the affective experience of the dreamer. Furthermore, given the audience's certain familiarity with the play's subject, its truth is never placed in doubt. It is a plot point that foreshadows an already-known future.

In almost all early modern *comedias de santos*, the dream/vision functions in this pre-modern[24] and non-mystical way (we shall see further examples shortly). Yet in *El divino africano*, it is not his mother's dream alone, or any divine apparition, that prompts Augustine's conversion. Or rather, it *is* a divine intervention, but the perception and interpretation of this intervention is represented from "este lado" and not immediately given as truth to either Augustine or the audience. The scene is the famous *tolle et lege* episode in the garden. Augustine, alone on stage, begins speaking to himself/the audience. He has begun his journey to Christianity but cannot overcome his doubts. He expounds on this despair, asking:

> ¿Hasta cuándo, gran Señor,
> te has de olvidar de San Agustín,
> y cuándo veré yo el fin
> deste mi confuso error?
> ¿Hasta cuándo este rigor
> de mi dureza tirana,
> dirá: "mañana, mañana"?
> ¿Y cuándo querrás que un día
> llegue la miseria mía
> a tu piedad soberana?
> ¿Hasta cuándo diré: "Voy,
> espérame, buen Jesú"?
> ¿Y cuándo me dirás tú:
> "Ven Agustín, que aquí estoy"? (491–504; act II)

> For how long, great Lord, will you forget Augustine, and when will I see the end of this my confusing error? For how long will this rigor of my tyrannical stubbornness say, tomorrow, tomorrow? And, when will you desire that one day my misery arrive at your supreme mercy? For how long will I say, I'm coming, wait for me, sweet Jesus? And when will you say to me: come Augustine, I am here?

Lope undermines the true representation of doubt by having Augustine contradictorily affirm that he already recognizes that his doubts are mistaken (a "confuso error") and thus that the faith he does not yet have is also the correct one. Yet this separation of intellectual knowledge from affective faith makes the monologue a psychological explanation instead of a narrative exposition. His prayer from this position of "oscuridad" begins to mix in language and imagery from the *Cantar*: he asks God to approach him with "la flecha de su amor" (515) ("the arrow of his love") so he may be "herido … tiernamente" (514) ("tenderly wounded). It becomes clear that he is speaking, not to God as an abstract omnipotent being, but to a mental image of the crucified Christ: "que aunque cinco fuentes veo/ la del costado deseo,/ porque es amorosa fuente" (518) ("for although I see five wounds, the one I want is the wound in the side, for it is a wound of love").[25]

At this point, the stage instructions alert that an angel enters, and the next line is the angel's voice instructing, "Agustin, toma y lee" ("Augustine, take up and read"). The appearance of the angel would seem to shift a focus on the character's internal struggle to an exteriorized confirmation of divine favour. However, Augustine does not see the angel but merely hears a voice. Moreover, rather than seize on the voice as confirmation, he continues with a series of stream-of-consciousness questions and emotional outpourings, which has the effect of emphasizing his subjective process over the angel's doctrinal truths. It is also worth noting that the angel's entrance is, at least as written into the stage directions, unaccompanied by sound or light effects or iconographic "props," as tends to be the case when supernatural figures descend onto Lope's stage (as we will see shortly). The scene is enacted from the human point of view, and the emphasis is, as in mystic writing, on the interiorization (intellectual, affective) of the divine, rather than an exteriorization of thought. Augustine's monologue has something of a catechistic tone; he asks questions ("Mas ¿cómo se ha de medir/ Cristo conmigo? ¡El tan bueno y yo tan malo y ajeno/ de podérmele vestir" ["But, how can I measure myself with Christ? He is so good and I am so wicked and far from being worthy of assuming Him"]) and promptly answers them ("pero atrévome a decir/ que, como en la Cruz le he visto,/ me podré medir con Cristo,/ que clavado y con mi nombre,/ no ha de extenderse a mas que hombre,/ aunque Dios y hombre me visto [I, 575] ["But I am so bold as to say that, as I saw him on the cross, I can measure myself with Christ, since nailed and with my name, he does not extend beyond a man, although I wear the cloak of God and man."][26]). Lope's Augustine struggles to understand the command to "vesti[rse] a Iesu Christo," and develops an extended *concepto* between clothing and identity: the act of putting on a bodily garment and that of assuming Christ's spiritual legacy. There is no experimentation with grammar or poetic form, but the first-person direct dialogue with Christ, the erotic/emotive language (Augustine speaks of Christ's garment as a "raso blanco aprensado/ del hierro ardiente de amor" [585–6] ["white satin pressed with the burning iron of love"]) and the juxtaposition of corporeal and spiritual language, all recall the mystic poem. Most importantly, the relative absence of external spectacle places the audience in a space of intimacy and private reflection such as that counseled in the manuals for contemplative prayer.

We might contrast this vision with two scenes that foresee Augustine's role as a Church Father. In the final scene of the first act, Augustine's student Simpliciano, already a Christian, hears a voice (identified only as "Voz" in the stage directions) calling his name. He responds, and the stage directions indicate, "*Descúbrase una Iglesia en hombros de Ambrosio y Jerónimo, y los otros dos lugares vacíos*" ("Revealed: A Church on the shoulders of Ambrosio and Jerónimo, with the other two corners empty"). The voice immediately explains the stage tableaux, revealing that the empty spots will be filled:

Este Agustino,
aunque tienen en mí su fundamento,
será de sustentar su parte dino,
y un Gregorio después. (1139–43; act I)
...
Buenaventura, con Tomas de Aquino,
le darán resplandor divino y claro,
y yo haré que los veas algún día,
más que el mármol y pórfido de Paro,
firmes diamantes en la Iglesia mía. (1144–8; act I)

Although they have their foundations in me, this Augustine will be worthy of sustaining his part, and Gregory after him ... Bonaventure, with Thomas Aquinas, will give it a divine, clear brilliance, and I will let you see them some day: firm diamonds in my Church, more than marble and porphyry from the isle of Paros.

When the vision disappears, Simpliciano contemplates that it might have been a result of his desire, rather than reality, but he quickly decides that "no puede engañarme luz tan pura,/ despierto estoy, conozco, siento, y veo" (1153–4) ("a light so pure cannot deceive me, I am awake, I know, feel, and see"). The language here responds to the criteria established for discernment of spirits, but the vision and its clear interpretation have no mystic quality; Simpliciano was not in a state of contemplation, the vision precisely identifies future events and human identities, and there is no affective result or spiritual transformation. Furthermore, as Natalia Fernández argues in "Imagenería sacra y espacios pictóricos en las comedias de santos de Lope de Vega," the tableaux of the temple being sustained by Church Fathers was an iconographic tradition that would have been familiar to the audience, and they would already know who would fill in the empty spaces (636). Lope does not allow the audience any ambiguity as to how to complete the tableaux, for in the final act, when Simpliciano again is called by the "Voz," the gaps are explicitly filled in.

VOZ: Mira en el templo militante mio
de qué columna ocupo aquel vacío.

Aqui se ve a la Iglesia en hombros de Ambrosio, Gregorio, Jerónimo y Agustino.

SIM: Ahora sí, Señor de cielo y tierra,
que habéis dado firmeza, al edificio,
con que siendo vos piedra, tanta encierra,

que es de su duración eterno indicio;
pero parece que a la dura guerra
que tienen los contrarios por oficio,
habéis dado en ingenio tan profundo
nueva defensa y nueva luz del mundo.
Ya me dejó de la visión divina
la nube celestial bañada en oro;
santo doctor, tu celestial doctrina
será de nuestra fe rico tesoro. (579–94; act III)

VOICE: Look at the militant temple of mine, see with what pillar have I filled that void.

Here we see the Church on the shoulders of Ambrose, Gregory, Jerome, and Augustine.

SIMPLICIANO: Now, yes, Lord of heaven and earth, you have given solidity to that structure, that with you as its rock, contains so much, it is a sign that it will last forever. It seems that, for the fierce war that your enemies wage as a matter of course, you have come up with a new defense, an intellect so deep and a new light for the world. Already the divine vision has left me, the heavenly cloud bathed in gold, holy Doctor your heavenly doctrine will be a rich treasure for our Faith.

Again, the triumphal language, clear image, and clear doctrine all align. The audience's perspective is that of witness to a divine truth, not seen through a glass darkly but in the light, clearly. And this is the nature of almost all the supernatural visions presented in *comedias de santos*. What is unusual in *El divino africano* is that the protagonist's own spiritual experience is not, by and large, treated with such clarity. In fact, Lope rearranges the historical chronology to extend Augustine's own period of spiritual struggle beyond the writing of the *Confessions*. The reader of the *Confessions* may assume that, by the end of Chapter X, Augustine's spiritual transformation is complete; his later writings are all in the voice of the Church, not the sinner. Yet Lope has Augustine on stage in Act III writing his *Confessions* and, even after he has been baptized, still struggling intellectually with his faith.

The scene of Augustine writing his *Confessions* again places the audience in the space of private contemplation. While many dramatic monologues occur with an actor alone onstage, it is unusual for such a setting to be verisimilar; in general, the dramatic monologue of the period is a theatrical convention that allows for plot or character development. Yet when Augustine contemplates the written page, his monologue offers a plausible representation of an internal thought process, his language repeating the paradoxical *balbuceo* of thought as it struggles with the infinite. Contemplating the page, he asks:

> ¿Qué puedo, Señor, decir
> de vuestro inmenso poder,
> si de materia carece
> vuestra esencia santa en fin?
> ¿Qué dirá della Agustín,
> aunque en ella resplandece
> aquella forma informada,
> formada de formas, forma
> hermosa? (139–48; act III)

> What can I say, Lord, about your immense power, if in the end your sacred essence is immaterial? What can Augustine say about it, although within it there shines that in-formed form, formed of forms, a beautiful form?[27]

Augustine is not alone on stage for long, as the Devil immediately appears to tempt and torment him. This is not the first time the Devil (in addition to the allegorical figure of Heresy) has appeared in the play. The supernatural characters are seen by multiple characters and thus the audience is guided to interpret them as a literal, exterior reality. There is no difficulty of discernment, no sense that, as Augustine himself counseled and so many mystic writers struggled with in their own spiritual lives: what seem to be divine favours could actually be demonic impostures.

Lope is not drawing on anything in Augustine's own writings when he has the Devil appear next to the writing Augustine.[28] The play overall dramatizes two different genres of sources (the *Confessions* and hagiographical legend), but this scene in particular also stages two modes of writing: the mystic/spiritual and the demonic. As Michel de Certeau analysed in *Possession in Loudon*, demonic speech is full of proper names.[29] In this scene, the Devil has his own book literally placed side-by-side with Augustine's manuscript, and rather than narrative or poetry, it is simply a list: sinners' names and their sins. As the Devil himself explains, first commenting favourably on Augustine's own mystic prose and then on his own:

> … Que bien conforma
> esta letra mal formada
> y aquella forma de letra,
> que con tal velocidad,

volando a la Trinidad,
hasta su trono penetra.
Él escribe la excelencia
de la esencia soberana,
y yo la malicia humana
contra la divina esencia. (148–57; act III)

how well these poorly formed letters conform with the form of that letter, that flying so swiftly to the Trinity penetrates even His throne. He writes the excellence of the supreme essence, and I write of human malice against the divine essence.

The contrast is between a writing of human names and one of divine abstractions. There is also a contrast between the ease of the Devil's speech and the difficulty of mystic language; the Devil boasts of his brimming book while Augustine addresses the blank page. When, in a subsequent scene (the Devil now gone) he again attempts to write, he gets lost in apparent contradictions and grammatical impasses, such as the contradiction between God's "communicability" ("Padre, sois comunicable,/ que a vuestro Hijo engendrastes/ 'ab aeterno,' y lo igualastes/ a vuestro ser inmutable" [407–16; act. III] ["Father, you are communicable, for you engendered your Son *ab aeterno*, and you made Him equal to your immutable being"]) and his inability to communicate this, even to himself. But in the midst of his aporia, the stage directions note that "Detiénese" ("He pauses"). No supernatural figure appears or speaks to him. But something – invisible to both audience and character – has intervened. The reflexive verb form in the stage directions is crucial; nothing explicit detains him; instead, he is detained from within. "El alma turbada siente!" (422) ("I feel my soul aflutter!"), he exclaims, before returning to his struggle to understand the relationship between the three beings of the Trinity. "Como son correlativos/ Padre e Hijo, está muy claro/ que [el Hijo] es eterno. ¡Oh sumo, raro" (427–9) ("As Father and Son are correlative, it's very clear, that [the Son] is eternal. Oh what a supremely strange"), and again he is interrupted by an invisible force that "detains" him. The pause is both written into the stage instructions and reflected in the monologue.

… misterio! ¡Oh pasos altivos!
De mi corto entendimiento,
donde está Dios penetráis,
adonde intrépido vais
siguiendo mi atrevimiento. (430–4)

> ... mystery! Oh lofty steps! With my limited understanding, you penetrate to where God lies, where, following my boldness, you, intrepidly, go.

Lope writes the transition from speaking about the divine to experiencing the divine, that fine line between intellectual and spiritual that is, as we have seen, a fundamental element in mystical writing. After a third "Detiénese aquí," and just when Augustine despairs of understanding "este misterio divino/ de cómo es Dios uno y trino" (439) ("this divine mystery of how God is one and three") there appears a *Niño* (Child), visible first to the audience but not to Augustine.

At this point the scene becomes a more familiar theatrical treatment of divine apparition and inspiration. Still, it is worth noting that the Niño's speech is not a clear prophetic or doctrinal announcement as much as an additional layer of mystic paradox. The Niño does not initially appear to respond directly to Augustine, instead playing with a shell and expressing a desire to pour the entire sea into a conch shell. Augustine continues his monologue; this time, when "detiénese" it is to note the presence of the child and to ask him "Muchacho, ¿qué haces ahí?" (474) ("Little boy, what are you doing there?"). When the child repeats his parable, Augustine reprimands him that he is labouring in vain, as it would be impossible to enclose the sea in a shell. He concludes with a brusque "Vete a tu casa, a tu madre,/ trata cosas de tu edad" (483–5) ("Go home to your mother and deal with things appropriate for your age").

At this point the Niño reveals the meaning of his parable.

> Ese consejo, en verdad,
> que es bueno para vos, padre;
> porque como no es posible
> poder yo todo este mar
> adonde veis encerrar,
> es a vos, padre, imposible
> querer el grande Oceano
> de Dios, inmenso, uno y trino,
> reducir por tal camino
> al entendimiento humano. (486–95)

> That advice, in truth, is appropriate for you, father; as it is not possible for me to capture this whole sea in here, it is impossible for you, father, to hope to reduce the great Ocean of God, immense, one and three, to human understanding.

He then immediately disappears, leaving Augustine to recognize the fundamental incompatibility of human reason and divine essence.

While the scene does end with a visible, non-problematized apparition of the divine, it is still an apparition whose contribution to the scene is to re-enact the fundamental paradox of mystic discourse; it is a scene of metaphors and precise language that teaches the impossibility of representing the divine through metaphor or language.

The penultimate scene in the play inverts the dynamic seen thus far of figures/voices appearing *to* Augustine. At the end of the play, with the impending invasion of the Goths, Augustine's disciple Alipio has a vision *of* Augustine. This scene has all the trappings of a Baroque representation of a vision: it is marked as occurring in a dream, the stage directions indicate the pulling-back of a curtain[30] ("Duerme, y descúbrese una cortina, y allí Agustín entre dos imágenes de Cristo y nuestra Señora de rodillas" ["He falls asleep, and a curtain is drawn, and there is revealed Augustine between two images of Christ and Our Lady, kneeling"]), and when the "imagen" of Augustine (in fact, the character Augustine himself) begins to speak, the Mobius strip of *pictura* and *poesis* folds in true Baroque fashion: the audience sees an image praying to/between two images of images. Augustine's long monologue (within the vision) is, however, unusual among visionary scenes. Instead of a static visual tableaux, we get another contemplative moment, a stream-of-consciousness meditation on the relationship between Christ and Mary; instead of a contemplative vision, the vision of contemplation. In Lope's version, Augustine, even at the height of his authority in the Church, is still working through the mysteries of the Christian faith, in direct and intimate dialogue with the two most commonly addressed figures of mystical devotion. Augustine concludes his monologue by citing Dionysius the Areopagite, the first-century biblical figure who in the early modern period was also thought to be the mystic author, and playing with pronouns (vos, Dios) in a way that is familiar from mystic poetry.

Pues digo ..., ¡válgame Dios!
¿Qué es lo que voy a decir?
¿Quién puede, mi Dios, sentir
que no sois lo mejor vos?
Pero, María, si os viera
sola, sin Dios, que ignorara,
como a Dios os adorara
y por mi Dios os tuviera.
Dionisio lo dijo así,
que en carne mortal os vio:
eso mismo digo yo,
después que a Dios conocí.

Miro a Dios, míroos a vos,
porque vos con Dios estáis,
y Él con vos, y así quedáis
vistos de Agustín los dos. (785–99)

So, I say … Good God! What was I going to say? Who could, my God, think that you are not the greatest? But Mary, if I were to see you alone, without God, who I did not know, I would worship you as God and I would hold you to be a God. Dionysius, who saw you in the flesh said it thus, and I say the same, now that I know God. I look at God, I look at you, because you are with God, and He is with you, and thus both of you are seen by Augustine.

The scene is striking and seems out of place, given that the impending Goth invasion has already been announced and the audience knows Augustine's end is near, on top of the expectation of a triumphal vision that is triggered by the tableaux mechanism. Lope counters this in the final image of the play, a vision which structurally echoes the one just analysed but is externalized and epic rather than internalized and mystic. Augustine has died and the Goths have invaded. Just when the hordes are preparing to sack the city of Hippo, their leader asks to see the body of the deceased bishop. The stage notes inform us that "Descúbrase san Agustín vestido de Obispo con su cayado, y la Iglesia en la mano, como le pintan, la Heregía a los pies con algunos libros" ("Saint Augustine is there revealed, dressed as a Bishop with his staff, and the Church in his hand, as he is painted, Heresy at his feet, with some books").[31]

Augustine's disciple Alipio closes the play explaining symbol by symbol the iconography of the vision to the Goth Vladimiro. The scene is clearly seen by all and thus does not lend itself to interpretation as a subjective or interiorized experience made visible for the purpose of theatre.

ALIPIO: Vele aquí: ya el alma adorna
el cielo, como su pluma
la Iglesia que ilustra y dora;
que el rayo que della sale
la baña de lumbre, toda;
la Herejía está pisando
con la planta poderosa.
VLADMIRO: Y porque es justa razón,
perdono, amigos, a Hipona. (991–9; act III)

ALIPIO: Look at him here: already his soul adorns the sky, as his pen illustrated and glorified the Church, as the ray that she [the Church] emits bathes her entirely in light; he crushes Heresy with his powerful foot.
VLADIMIRO: And because it is a fair reason, friends, I pardon Hippo.

The play thus closes with the supernatural perspective, emphasizing power and miracles and, as Thomas Case has argued, the ultimate triumph of the City of God, or divine history, over the City of Man, or human history.[32] This sort of apotheosis is typical in Golden Age religious plays; what is unusual in *El divino africano* is the degree to which Lope allows the *other* Augustine, Augustine the contemplative, to coexist alongside the triumphal bishop. This representation is all the more striking given that Augustine himself was primarily known for his role as a Church Father, *not* as a contemplative or a mystic (and, indeed, as we have seen, he was often appropriated as an opponent of mystic experiences), and we may conclude that Lope was seeking, within the strictures of dramatic and doctrinal expectations, to preserve that other Augustine. Indeed, if we believe that the exploration of Augustine's doubts was what incurred the Inquisitorial censure, then we can see him exceeding those strictures.

Interiority (Not) on Stage: *Santa Teresa de Jesús*

In Lope's *comedia* based on the life of Santa Teresa, a figure whose life and written work were undeniably mystic, it is remarkable to find that the very acts of contemplation Lope invents and prolongs in Augustine's life, even where there is no textual-historical evidence to support them, are erased. The first act of Lope's *Santa Teresa de Jesús* is an invented *comedia* plot of rival lovers, with no basis in historical documentation beyond the few elliptical mentions in the *Vida* of an early proclivity for "vanidades." Already Lope is inverting his treatment of Augustine, whose detailed description of youthful sins Lope leaves out of his *comedia. Santa Teresa* shifts genres at the end of the first act, when Teresa, seeking refuge from both of her wooers, runs to a convent and asks "¿Con cuál marido iré?" ("With which husband should I go?") and a voice responds, "Con Cristo se puede ir" (818; act I) ("You can go with Christ").[33] The audience can see that it is the sacristan speaking, although Teresa, not seeing the sacristan, takes the reply for divine guidance: "es el cielo quien me habló" (825; act I) ("the heavens have spoken to me"). From this point, the narrative picks up the historically documented aspects of Teresa's life, but Lope seems to rely exclusively on the hagiographic, third-person accounts gathered in the process of Teresa's canonization and not on her own writings.[34]

The scene immediately following Teresa's entrance into the convent (the first scene of the second act) is the scene of the transverberation. If we look only at the poetry of the scene, we can identify many elements of Teresa's and others' mystic poetry. Teresa cries for the angel to:

> Herid, herid con golpes más continos;
> dejadme el pecho, si gustáis, rasgado,
> y una ventaja os llevaré en el suelo,
> pues a vos, dulce Esposo, os dio Longinos
> la lanzada con que os rompió el costado,
> y a mí me abrasa un serafín del cielo:
> heridme sin recelo,
> seré herida cierva, y vos la fuente,
> a mi sed suficiente,
> que otra agua no apetezca;
> la fuente salutífera merezca,
> en cuyas aguas vivas dé a mi fragua
> el dardo el fuego, y vuestra fuente el agua. (963–74; act II)

> Wound, wound me, with more continuous blows, leave my breast torn, if you like, and I will have an advantage over you on the earth, since Longinus gave you, sweet Bridegroom, the lance wound that tore your side, and it is an angel from heaven that sets me aflame. Wound me without misgivings, I will be the wounded deer, and you the fountain that quenches my thirst, for which no other water tempts. Let me deserve the healing fountain, in whose living waters let the dart give the fire to my forge, and your fountain the water.

The affective language, the reference to the *Cantares*, and the paradoxical combination of sensory opposites, are all standards of mystic poetry. Yet here the theatrical apparatus works against *lo místico*. The techniques of theatre are all enlisted in the elimination of doubt and the shift of the perspective from the human first person (Teresa's perspective) to a divine third person. Teresa's verses are not part of a monologue, but instead she maintains a dialogue with the angel itself, whose appearance on stage is announced in the stage directions that open the act: "Sale un ángel con una lanza y Teresa de Jesús" ("Enter an angel with a lance and Teresa de Jesús"). In the play, the transverberation is not the result of years of contemplation, doubt, and spiritual work, but an immediate miracle that legitimizes all the terrestrial work to come. Lope's *Teresa* does not need to perform spiritual work; when she enters the convent, the angel is already waiting with his lance, and he speaks first.

Si el corazón de Dios habéis herido
con vuestras oraciones amorosas,
recibid estos golpes que os envía,
rásguese vuestro pecho enternecido,
y causen las heridas rigurosas
pena, dolor, contento y alegría.
Y si es ferviente fría,
la punta de este dardo fuego tiene,
fuego de amor, que enciende y nunca abrasa;
no os quemara su brasa,
porque templado con el hierro viene;
sufrid agora, y luego
podréis tocar con el amor a fuego,
que es lo que más le agrada,
veros arder y veros ahumada. (948–62; act II)

If your loving prayers have already wounded God's heart, receive these blows that he sends, rend your tender breast, and let the rigorous wounds cause you pain and sadness, happiness and joy. And if it is a burning cold, the point of this dart bears fire, the fire of love, that lights and never burns; its embers will not burn you because they come tempered by iron; suffer now, and later, you will be able to touch the fire with love, which is what most pleases Him, to see you burn and to see you burnt/Ahumada.[35]

The bulk of the *Vida*, then, which details the arduous process, full of doubt and difficulties, of achieving that mystic union, is reduced to an allusion to "vuestras oraciones amorosas." Furthermore, since it is the angel who introduces the metaphors and oxymorons of mystic discourse, these can no longer be understood as the individuals' partial solution to represent the ineffable. The very purpose of mystic language is compromised, then; instead of marking the absence imposed by language and the ultimately insuperable gap between divine and human (even as it describes the instant in which the gap is subsumed), it becomes the language of presence, shared by divine and human in a single cosmic space. Rather than mystic language being appropriated by human authorities, here it is appropriated by divinity itself. The effect of both appropriations is to reduce the mystic, transgressive potential of that language, which is rooted in the human struggle to perceive and represent the divine. Lope uses theatre's tendency to erase the role of the playwright, the illusion that makes theatre "seem" real even when it presents a scene beyond any human reality, to change the nature and impact of mystic language. When Teresa narrates her transverberation, it is inseparable from her own first-person experience as a nun who must recall and represent that experience through writing. In Lope's representation, the scene occurs in the present, and no medium of memory or re-creation appears to have been necessary. (Of course, Lope is writing the scene, but theatre allows the playwright to disappear in ways that the prose author never can, and particularly the author of a *Vida* whose original purpose is precisely to produce a verdict, not on the vision but on the person.) When the audience sees the transverberation from the divine perspective, the emphasis and interpretation of the scene is changed entirely. Because representation is not problematized and the transcendent elements are exteriorized, it can no longer be said to be mystic, despite the repetition of mystic language.

Almost the entirety of the second and third acts of the play take place in what William Egginton has termed the "crypt," in opposition to the modern stage. Unlike the stage, which is a "flat space" where all representations are appearances, the crypt is a remnant of the medieval "full space" theatre and still contains "pockets of presence" (105), spaces of truth that are deemed to transcend screens of projection and appearances. To use Augustinian terms, we might say that it is the Stage of God, not the Stage of Man. Thus, Lope's intervention is again the exact opposite of the one he exercised in *El divino africano*: there, he extended the period of doubt and struggle within the biography, here he erases it. In her *Vida*, the bookends of her spiritual journey are her near-fatal physical illness as a young woman and her final achievement of the ultimate *grado de oración* in the transverberation. Lope inverts Teresa's mystic timeline; he places the final stage of ecstasy at the very beginning, even before her near-fatal illness. When, in the following scene, he represents her illness – which in Teresa's *Vida* is experienced as a suffering of the flesh, and only the point of departure for her long spiritual journey – her body is erased from the narrative, and the stage space is occupied exclusively by supernatural figures, announced with the visual and auditory iconography that assures their proper and unambiguous interpretation. "Suena una trompa en lo alto; aparecen la Justicia, San Miguel, con un peso, y en lo bajo un ángel y un demonio" ("A trumpet sounds on high: Justice and Saint Michael, with a scale, appear, and below, an angel and a devil"). The scene that follows is, as Saint Michael declares, "el pleito, Señor, que se litiga entre el Ángel de Guarda y el Demonio, sobre un alma que sale ya del cuerpo de una doña Teresa de Ahumada" (1109–12;

act II) ("the lawsuit, Sir, that is litigated between the Guardian Angel and the Devil, over a soul that is now departing from the body of Doña Teresa de Ahumada"). The Devil displays the "silla de fuego" ("seat in flames") that he has prepared for Teresa, but when "Justicia" finds against him ("Justicia: Ha de vivir y ser gran sierva mía" [1149; act II] ["Justice: she shall live and be my devoted servant"]), he concedes that this was merely a trick and that Teresa's soul was never in doubt. The stage notes mention at one point in the scene that "Teresa tiembla en la cama" ("Teresa trembles in her bed"),[36] but her role in her own salvation here is entirely erased: it is a battle waged and decided on a higher (and lower) plane. Once Teresa's life is spared and her salvation confirmed by both saints and demons, they "corren la cortina" ("draw the curtain")[37] (the curtain that, in Egginton's terms, marks the space between "crypt" and "screen"), and the supernatural figures depart ("Éntrase el ángel por una puerta y el demonio por otra; sale la abadesa y vuelve en sí Teresa" ["The angel exits through one door and the devil through another; the abbess enters and Teresa comes to"]). At this point, the Abbess, echoing the stage directions, remarks that Teresa is coming to (1171; act II), and Teresa attempts to recount the previous scene, which only now – after it has been shown as an unambiguous reality – is re-cast as a human vision. Teresa has difficulty in expressing what she has seen; at first she can only repeat "!Ay de mí!" and "Ay, mi Cristo!" and then her sentences fade off into mystic aporia ("Vi que el Angel …" "Vi que el Demonio …" "Vi la silla, y vi …" [1172–9; act II] ["I saw that the Angel …" "I saw that the Devil …" "I saw the seat, and I saw …"]), but the audience has already seen what fills in these ellipses, so they do not share the mystic's perspective. The typical mystic protestation of linguistic insufficiency seems more a theatrical convention to avoid repeating what has already been shown than an actual engagement with the limits of language or human knowledge of the beyond.

The third act finds Teresa further along in her "earthly" biography (she is an abbess, founding convents), but there is nowhere to go spiritually. Her extended ecstatic dialogue with "Amor" (Christ allegorized as Love) just before her death returns her to the state of mystic union she has (always) already experienced. However, Lope shows a progression in Teresa's degree of spiritual union by having the Amor figure remain on stage throughout her dialogue. In the transverberation scene, the angel spoke first and left Teresa to respond to the air, emphasizing the imaginative quality of the vision *for Teresa* (without ever placing it in doubt for the audience). In contrast, the scene at the end of the play is an extended dialogue between Teresa and "Amor Divino." As in the transverberation, the staged vision is not the result of contemplation; Amor

Divino, like the angel, comes unbidden. The sacred-erotic is amplified in the final scene of Teresa's death, with the marital bed transformed to a scene of sacred union: "Corren la cortina; está Teresa en una cama con un Cristo, y algunas monjas alrededor" ("They draw the curtain: Teresa is in bed with a Christ figure, with nuns gathered around").[38] Lope draws on all the multisensory resources available to the theatre: the image is accompanied by music, impossible imagery of flight and transformation, and when Teresa dies, a sweet smell.

MARIANO: Murió nuestra madre amada,
la virgen santa expiró;
una paloma salió
con la primer boqueada.
El alma se va sellando
con el gran dueño que ha visto,
y con el esposo Cristo
a su esfera va volando.
MÚSICA: "Romped el aire gozosa,
mi blanca paloma hermosa."
MARIANO: ¿Veis algo?
VALLE: Yo sí.
DIEGO: Yo no.
MARIANO: Sólo Dios ha permitido
que el milagro sucedido
lo viésemos vos y yo.
DIEGO: ¡Jesús, qué olor tan suave!
¿Sentísle?
MARIANO: Y, ¡cómo que siento! (2666–80; act III)

MARIANO: Our beloved mother has died, the holy virgin passed away, a dove flew out with her last breath. Her soul is being sealed with the great master she has seen, and with Christ her bridegroom she goes flying to his realm.
MUSIC: "Cut through the joyous air, my beautiful white dove"
MARIANO: Do you see anything?
VALLE: I do.
DIEGO: I don't.
MARIANO: God has only allowed you and I to see the miracle that has happened.
DIEGO: Jesus, what a sweet smell! Do you smell it?
MARIANO: And how!

Despite the use of so many elements of mystic imagery, the inversion of perspective reverses the mystic impulse. The audience is not seeing a vision or hearing an audition; what in the spiritual autobiography is expressed in first person is here affirmed in the third-person omniscient as *being true*. Furthermore, by employing mystic imagery specifically into and past the moment of death, the one moment the spiritual autobiography and the mystic narrative can never recount, Lope converts mysticism into hagiography. Teresa's most famous mystic poem "Muero porque no muero" epitomizes the intrinsic impossibility of mystic impulse and the narration of death. Once the mystic can die and realize permanent union, there is no need for mysticism.

Theatre against *alumbradismo*: Agustín Moreto's *Santa Rosa del Perú*

A third saint's play provides a perfect example of the mechanisms by which theatre could be used to promote the legends of ecstatic, visionary saints and at the same time discourage the pretensions to ecstasy or visions among the audience. Rosa de Perú (1586–1617) was known for her extreme penitence and ecstatic, visionary spirituality, but unlike Santa Teresa, the Peruvian nun was not a mystic writer (or a writer at all).[39] The hagiographical accounts of Rosa's life emphasized her mystical marriage to Christ, despite her father's decades-long attempts to marry her to a rich suitor, as well as her role in the defense of Lima against the Dutch. In Agustín Moreto's hagiographical play of her life, *Santa Rosa del Perú*, the first *jornada* focuses on the struggle to escape marriage to Don Juan, the second on her spiritual devotion, and the third enters into the epic-heroic, combining the defense of Lima with all manner of supernatural battles.[40] If we focus on the representation of her spirituality and its integration into the heroic-epic narrative, we can see a playwright threading a delicate line, engaging the theatrical potential of the ecstatic vision and at the same time discouraging would-be ecstatic mystics among a diverse audience.

The scene that ends the second *jornada* and begins the third is a long dream that Rosa has, an oneiric struggle between virtue and vice. The repeated emphasis on the battle as a *dream* technically disqualifies it as a mystic experience, although in preceding scenes it has been established that Rosa spends days and nights in divine contemplation and experiences raptures. Indeed, a conversation between Rosa's father and a priest directly addresses and resolves the status of Rosa's mystic practice before her spiritual experience is presented directly to the audience.

Her father expresses concern because, he says, the opinion of Rosa's extreme penitence and mystical gifts is mixed:

> Unos dicen, que es ilusa,
> que su devoción es falsa;
> otros, que hace su flaqueza
> visiones imaginarias:
> otros, que estoy en peligro
> de que la lleven mañana
> a la Inquisición, y quede
> sin honra toda mi casa. (242–9; act II)

> Some say that she is possessed, that her devotion is false; others, that her weakness causes imaginative visions: others, that I run the risk that the Inquisition will take her tomorrow and my entire home will be dishonored.

The playwright here acknowledges the proper scepticism towards popular, self-professed saints, according to the teachings of the more conservative church sectors, but also precludes the application of such a critique to Rosa, first by having Don Gaspar affirm that all of Rosa's confessors, as well as:

> El Doctor Juan del Castillo,
> y el Maestro Lorenzana,
> que del glorioso Domingo
> son las Antorchas mas claras,
> y toda su Religión
> aprueba, admira, y ensalza
> su vocación por segura;
> y para mas confianza,
> también de la Compañía
> de Jesus a examinarla
> han venido los Maestros
> de mas letras, y mas fama,
> y todos están conformes. (270–82; act II)

> Doctor Juan del Castillo and Master Lorenzana, who are the brightest torches [lighting the way] of Saint Dominic, and all their Order approve, admire, and applaud her [Rosa's] vocation as firm; and for more certainty, members of the Company of Jesus have come to examine her, their most learned and renowned masters have come, and all agree.

This level of unanimity is an entirely fictional creation; as we have seen, no historical mystic received such unanimous approval during her lifetime. The process of discernment through speech and writing was fraught, as we have seen in chapters three and four, and must be erased – placed in the past and represented only through a unanimous *ex post facto* conclusion, historically never achieved during a mystic's lifetime – for the play to move forward with a representation of a mystic experience. The conclusion precedes the evidence so that the audience who sees the scene of a contemporary and low-status woman having a mystic vision knows beforehand that they cannot identify directly with her, as they have not received similar verdicts of unanimous approval.

As noted, the stage directions and dialogue repeatedly insist that the vision Rosa has is a dream rather than a contemplative vision, but Rosa's language and description of her spiritual practice is that of the mystic. In the scene immediately preceding the vision, she defends her extreme penitential practice to Don Gonzalo, who has taken the Teresan line and advised her to mitigate her self-mortification, arguing that "hay medidas proporcionadas/ a lo que alcanza de esfuerzo/ la naturaleza flaca" ("there are measures proportionate to the effort expended by a weak nature") and cautioning against allowing her penitence to become "indiscreta," and a vice in itself (494–8; act II). Rosa one-ups him in Teresan doctrine, citing the different stages of contemplation. What Gonzalo says is true for the beginner, she concedes:

Mas cuando un alma está ya
de sus pasiones purgada,
el Espíritu divino
la mueve, y entonces anda
al paso que Dios la mueve.
No ay allí prudencia humana,
porque es el don de Consejo,
que a la prudencia aventaja,
quien la guía, y la dirige,
y la mueve a empresas arduas.
No padece duda alguna,
porque da una luz tan clara,
que de todo lo asegura,
y en este estado se alcanza
aquella gran muchedumbre
de dulzura extraordinaria,
que para los que le temen,
escondió Dios en su gracia (515–32; act II)

> But when a soul is already purged of its passions, the Holy Spirit moves it, and then it goes at the pace that God moves it. There is no place for human prudence there, because it is the gift of Counsel, which takes precedence over prudence because of who guides and directs it, and moves it to undertake difficult enterprises. The soul does not suffer from the slightest doubt, because it gives off such a clear light, that it guarantees everything, and in this state one achieves that great multitude of extraordinary sweetness, which, for those who fear Him, God hid within His grace.

Although this is framed as a defense of extreme mortification, the language is that of the doctrine of contemplation, and indeed, one scene later, Rosa is alone on stage before a Christ icon, asking:

> Dulcísimo Esposo mío,
> recíbeme este dolor,
> no ha de perderte hoy mi amor,
> que yo del tuyo lo fio. (703–7; act II)

> My sweetest spouse, take this pain from me, my love shall not lose you today, since I have faith in yours.

The stage instructions specify that, in response, "va subiendo la Rosa en elevación, y en llegando a proporción, baja Cristo a juntarse con ella" ("Rosa gradually elevates and Christ descends proportionately to join her"). On the one hand, by making visible the "other side" of the mystic union, Moreto, like Lope in his *Teresa* plays, exteriorizes and de-mystifies the experience. But here, the image does not speak; instead, the response comes in the form of a song sung from offstage, rendering the "dialogue" more ambiguous in its subjectivity. Furthermore, after warning her of upcoming struggles, the image disappears ("cúbrese la apariencia"), and Rosa speaks to the now-absent Christ: "O Esposo dulce, y eterno!/ si tú en él me has de valer,/ ¿qué riesgo puedo temer?" ("Oh, sweet and eternal spouse! If you are to make use of it [pain] for me, what risk can I fear?") (728–30; act II). The explicit representation of a dialogue into empty space – to the absence of an absence (since the Christ figure was already only an icon) is a staging of the paradox at the heart of mystic discourse, and I have not found other examples in the *comedias de santos*. During and immediately after the dream, in which Rosa is tempted by the devil in a variety of clearly visible and non-mystic forms, Rosa expresses anguish at the apparent absence of her Esposo. Within the dream, she asks, "¿dónde estás Esposo mío?" (936; act II) ("where are you, my spouse?"), and after it is specified that she has awakened, she asks "¿Qué fuego es este, que estaba/ dentro del alma escondido,/ dulce Esposo?" (957–9) ("What fire is this, hidden within my soul, sweet spouse?"), although there is no divine figure on stage visible to the audience. For a moment, then, the audience thus sees the scene strictly from the human, doubting perspective. However, this doubt is immediately erased since when, a few lines later, Rosa invokes Jesus (969), the stage instructions specify that "Al decir Jesús, se hunden los vicios, y baja el Ángel con espada en la apariencia que mejor pareciere, y echa al Demonio, y el Niño Jesús se aparece en una apariencia" ("Upon saying Jesus, the vices sink, and the Angel descends in the form that seems best, and removes the Devil, and the Baby Jesus appears in an apparition"). Any mystic ambiguity is erased. The scene returns to a more traditional "symbolic staging" and the offstage voices serve as preludes to the "real" encounter of the saint with "el mundo más allá," a not infrequent technique.[41] Now Rosa can repeat her previous lament of absence but to a visible presence ("¿cómo tan cruel conmigo,/ que me habéis desamparado,/ pues sin mí, ni vos me he visto?" [991–4] ["how can you be so cruel as to have abandoned me, since I saw myself without myself and without you?"]) and hear his response, that he has always been with her ("porque yo en tu corazón me quedo, aunque me retiro" [1007–8] ["because I remain in your heart, even when I withdraw"]). Moreto is not breaking with the genre in his representation of the world beyond/within, but he does focus more on the human side of the experience than do Lope or Calderón.

The emphasis on the human sense of absence and loss, even after the direct and exteriorized representation of presence and plenitude, is repeated during the first scene of Act III. The demonic temptation has been overcome, and now Rosa's dream/vision is of the mystic marriage. María and a group of singing virgins, all present on stage, sing to the sleeping Rosa. When María, exhorting her to awake, leaves the stage, Rosa cries out: "¡Ay de mi! Señora, espera,/ o ¡qué visita he perdido!" (37–8; act III) ("Alas! My Lady, wait ... Oh, what a visitation I have lost") and laments that "me deja inflamado/ el corazón fervoroso/ aquel rostro tan hermoso,/ que vi de luces bañado!" (40–3) ("Ay, that beautiful face that I saw bathed in light, leaves my eager heart all inflamed! Alas!").

In a long dialogue with her servant, the *gracioso* Bodigo, she returns to the mystical paradox of the joy of a union that can only be spoken upon the pain of its loss. Bodigo asks her "¿Quién anda allá?" ("Who goes there?"), and she replies that "Quien ya no vive consigo/ quien está ardiendo/ ¡ay Bodigo, qué regalo!" (45–8) ("One who no longer lives with herself, one who is burning, ay, Bodigo, what a gift!"), introducing the destabilization of the subject common to mystic poetry. She also employs the common mystic technique of describing the indescribable through oxymoron: pleasure and pain ("un dolor que no puede ser mayor, y no le quiero perder/ ay, que en el pecho amoroso/ me revienta el corazón! [249–53] ["a pain that could not be greater and I do not want to lose. Ay, my heart is bursting within my loving breast"]); sweetness and bitterness, presence and loss ("Aquí ha estado, y su dulzura trocó el ausencia en acíbar" [73–4] ["she has been here, and her sweetness transformed her absence into bitterness"]). Bodigo's contributions to this dialogue, comic and literal, mitigate the mystical tone, but at the same time they highlight the metaphoric and non-literal use of the imagery. For example, when Rosa recalls the sweetness of her vision, Bodigo asks if it "¿vino en seco/o en almíbar?" (75) ("did she come dry/ all of a sudden, or in syrup?").[42] Rosa counters his literality with synesthesia, responding that "vino en la misma hermosura" (76) ("she came in beauty itself") and later, when he suggests they follow the sweet smell to the bakery to find "cosa de boca" (79–80, 84) ("something for the mouth"), she replaces his idea of sweetness in the mouth with "dulces del alma" (85) ("sweets for the soul").

In a near repetition of the scene that closes Act II, Rosa again laments her sense of the vision's absence. "Divino Amor, que de mí/ te retiras tan esquivo,/ mira que sin ti no vivo/ ¿dónde estás?" (99–103; act III) ("Divine Love, who withdraws from me so elusively, look at how without you I am not alive. Where are you?"). Again, Moreto has the Niño Jesús appear to reassure her, but this time Bodigo is still on stage and repeatedly affirms that he does not see the Christ figure. Given Bodigo's vulgarity and sinful nature, the audience is not tempted to give credence to his perceptions, but once again, we can note a tendency in this play to emphasize the human point of view.

However, this emphasis does not last. For the remainder of Act III, Moreto forgoes *lo místico* for *lo épico*. Rosa is never again alone on stage; she is always accompanied (and more or less replaced) by a cast of angels, saints, and defeated demons. Spectacular effects dominate; angels descend singing around three sprigs of rosemary arranged in the form of a cross; Rosa, on her deathbed, calls out to Christ, the Virgin, and Santa Catalina, and miraculously "Bajan en tres apariencias el niño que hace a Christo, la Virgen que haze una niña, y Santa Catalina; el niño se queda sobre la Santa elevado en el aire, y la niña sobre el romero de la mano derecha, y en el de la mano izquierda S. Catalina" ("There descend, in three apparitions, the boy who represents Christ, the girl who represents the Virgin, and Saint Catalina; the boy remains elevated in the air above the Saint [Rosa], the girl above the rosemary in her right hand and over her left hand S. Catalina").[43] A few moments later, she dies, and, accompanied by singing angels, "se suben a lo alto los tres romeros como están, y el niño siempre sobre la Santa, y el Angel Custodio arrimado a la Santa de rodillas" ("the three sprigs of rosemary ascend as they are, and the boy always above the Saint, and the Guardian Angel clinging to the kneeling saint").[44] The human emphasis that prevailed in the second and early part of the third *jornada* is not only substituted here by the divine viewpoint, but the audience must also retroactively re-interpret the middle scenes since any doubt or ambiguity about Rosa's mystic practice is settled with this final confirmation. It would seem that this spectacular, humanly impossible confirmation, along with the historically inverisimilar pre-confirmation that precedes the expression of doubt, was the necessary condition for an exposition of mysticism on stage.

The plays I have analysed thus far are important to our study but not because they go against the mystic impulse by exteriorizing the relationship between the human and the divine. Almost all the religious theatre of the period does so, just as we would expect. The innovation of early modern Spanish mysticism was to interiorize what had, throughout medieval Christianity, been represented as exteriorized: extreme acts of heroism and penitence, physical encounters with demons and saints, divine favour shown through physical miracles and divine displeasure through plagues and calamities. What is striking in Lope's *Teresa* and Moreto's *Santa Rosa* is that the playwright *does* engage with the mystic tradition and does employ mystic imagery and language, and yet by reworking chronologies and perspectives, de-mystifies it.

Inner Demons on Stage

In the discussion of the two Lope plays thus far, I have alluded to scenes with the Devil but have postponed a specific discussion of the representation of the demonic. Yet certainly in Teresa's own writing and, as we have seen, in spiritual autobiography in general, the demonic is inextricable from the divine, due to the difficulty of distinguishing, *desde este lado*, between the two. A central theme of Teresa's chapters dedicated to her early years of mental prayer is the possible confusion of a divine presence for a demonic imposture; again and again she warns, and is warned, that "podrá transfigurarse el demonio en ángel de luz: y si no es alma muy ejercitada, no lo entenderá" (*Vida* 219; ch. XIV sec. 8) ("the devil can at times transform himself into an angel of light, and if the soul is not very experienced, it will not realize this" [101]). Indeed, the difficulty of discerning between the divine and the demonic is, as we have seen, an overwhelming preoccupation in all the spiritual autobiographies, and the proliferation of manuals of discernment as well as general confessors' manuals and the Inquisition trials of would-be mystics all testify to the difficulty that the separation of the divine and the demonic presented both from within and without. In *Santa Teresa*, Lope has the Devil – clearly visible and identifiable to the audience, although not to the characters on stage – appear to Teresa's confessor and tell him that Teresa's visions have been "alguna ilusión." As he whispers into Mariano's ear, Mariano repeats to Teresa the words being fed to him by Satan.

MARIANO: El demonio fue, sin duda,
pues tantas formas tomó.
DEMONIO: Discretamente la informas.
MARIANO: Esto que os he dicho creo:
que no es Cristo el dios Proteo
para tomar tantas formas.
DEMONIO: Dile que huya esas visiones.
TERESA: No hay duda que me poner.
MARIANO: Pues yo soy de parecer
que huyas esas tentaciones. (1301–10; act II)

MARIANO: Without a doubt it was the devil, since it took on so many forms.
DEVIL: You advise her most discreetly.
MARIANO: I have told you what I believe: Christ is not the god Proteus who takes on so many forms.
DEVIL: Tell her to flee from these visions.
TERESA: I don't feel the slightest doubt.
MARIANO: Well I am of the opinion that you should flee from these temptations.

When Teresa asks what to do if the visions persist, he counsels that she make the sign of the fig ("dar higas"), an ancient sign believed to ward off demons. Teresa is, as in her own narrative account, left in doubt, forced to choose between following what she believes to be God's will and what her confessor has ordered. In the *Vida* she writes:

> Dábame este dar higas grandísima pena, cuando veía esta visión del Señor; porque cuando yo le veía presente, si me hicieran pedazos, no pudiera yo creer que era demonio, y ansí era un género de penitencia grande para mí; y por no andar tanto santiguándome, tomaba una cruz en la mano. Esto hacía casi siempre, las higas no tan contino, porque

sentía mucho ... suplicábale me perdonase, pues yo lo hacía por obedecer al que tenía en su lugar, y que no me culpase, pues eran los ministros que él tenía puestos en su Iglesia. Decíame, que no se me diese nada, que bien hacía en obedecer, mas que él haría que se entendiese la verdad ... Dábame causas para que entendiese que no era demonio, alguna diré después. (378; ch. 29 sec. 6)

The duty of snapping my fingers[45] when I had this vision of the Lord deeply distressed me. For when I saw Him before me, I would willingly have been hacked to death rather than believe that this was of the devil. It was a heavy kind of penance for me, and so that I need not be so continually crossing myself, I used to go about with a crucifix in my hand. I carried it almost continually, but I did not snap my fingers very often, because that hurt me too much ... I begged Him to pardon me, since I was only acting out of obedience to one who was in His place, and not to blame me, seeing that he was one of the ministers whom He had Himself placed in His Church. He told me not to worry, since I was quite right to obey, and that He would Himself show them the truth ... He showed me ways of making sure that these visions were not of the devil, and I will give some of them later. [207]

Teresa here is confident in her vision, but she cannot point to an external source that will verify it. The visions can only authorize themselves, and if the visions are subject to illusion, so is their internal authorization. Her emphasis throughout these chapters is on her own process of anguish and recurring doubt, for despite her confidence here, she returns again and again to the question of the source of her visions.[46]

In Lope's version of the scene, however, there is no space for doubt or anguish. The moment Mariano and the Devil leave the stage, the baby Jesus appears. Teresa attempts to flee, following her confessor's advice, but the stage directions indicate an immediate and incontrovertible divine intervention: "Va a huir y detiénela San Pablo" ("She is about to flee and Saint Paul detains her").[47] This "miracle" is repeated with Saint Peter, as he intervenes in the material, corporeal world by stopping her attempt to flee. As with the divine apparitions of Amor Divino and the angel discussed above, divine favour here is shown externally as miracle rather than internally as grace or union. The audience sees the clear opposition between the divine and demonic in the two characters' opposing appearances on stage; every element of the heavenly figures' characterizations (their physical presence, their words) opposes that of the *Demonio*, deliberately separating for the audience what was so muddled for Teresa's confessors and contemporaries and, at times, for Teresa herself.

I cannot point to a single *comedia* where the audience is ever in any doubt as to the identity of el *demonio*, nor to any example of a staged vision where a hero or heroine is incorrect in perceiving an angelic source behind a demonic vision or vice versa. The majority of the devils in the *comedia* are represented just as every other character, in the sense that they take human form and interact with other humans through language and gesture. There is nothing mystic in their representation, either from a theological or linguistic perspective. However, many *comedias de santos* also feature possession, an *interiorized* experience of the demonic, which would seem to bring us back into the sphere of mystic discourse. And yet, as we will see in a brief look at scenes of possession in the plays already analysed, this literary discourse of possession and exorcism has almost no overlap with mystic language. Remarkably, since spiritual autobiography treats divine and demonic possession as overlapping and not easily separable categories, when presented on stage, they belong to entirely separate discourses. It will be important to consider the reasons behind such a radical difference in the representation of the relationship between these two categories in diverse genres, and also to consider what the public, exposed to such diverse representations, might make of the contrast.

The possessed/exorcised figure appears in many *comedias de santos* but almost always as a side plot or with the *santo* as the exorcist, rather than the person (possibly) possessed. Lope's *El divino africano* provides an example of such a scene when Augustine exorcises an "endemoniada." Lope thus completely separates the question of demonic temptation (the Devil, who appears as an exteriorized figure to tempt Augustine) and demonic possession, as represented in Augustine's exorcism of *la endemoniada*. Also crucial is the ease with which we can speak of *la endemoniada*; she enters on stage as "la mujer endemoniada" and is never given another name. The *fact* of her demonic possession is established before/outside the play and never placed in doubt; discernment is unnecessary. In a world where *endemoniadas* present as this one does – her identity, actions, and the response to an exorcism so unequivocally adhering to the stable discourse of demonic possession as laid out in the *Ritual Romanum*[48] – discernment as a category is absurd. What is there to discern?

The *mujer endemoniada*'s first words in the play – "¿Dónde perros me lleváis?" ("Dogs, where are you taking me?") – could be spoken by a woman, but what follows reveals that it is not the woman but the devil within who speaks:

Las manos me atáis
¿sabéis que a Dios me atreví?
Pues como quien tuvo manos,
que a Dios se atrevió con ellas,
borrando tantas estrellas
de sus cielos soberanos:
¿Las ha de tener atadas? (600–6; act III)

You tie my hands. Do you know that I dared to go challenge God? You think you can tie the hands that dared to challenge God, erasing so many stars from his heavens supreme?

The *manos* belong to the *mujer*, but the character is not a *mujer endemoniada* so much as a *demonio "enmujerada."* There is no struggle between the women's soul or psyche and the occupying demon; the woman's "I" has been completely silenced. The devil speaks, as we would expect, in heresies and blasphemies – the counter-discourse to orthodoxy – but it is worth noting that the true opposite of such easy, confident blasphemy is not the easy, confident doctrine of the saint but the the *balbuceo* of mystic speech.

The representation of the conflict between the "host" and possessing spirit is most often represented in the *comedia* as a comedy. Tirso de Molina's *Santa Juana* trilogy stages the life of the fifteenth-century Castilian saint Juana de la Cruz, who could with verisimilitude be represented as having a contemplative spiritual practice, and indeed, Juana is several times described as "arrobada."[49] Nonetheless, the play never stages her contemplative practice, nor do we find any incorporation of mystic language or spirituality. In Tirso's trilogy, Juana's interaction with the divine is purely exteriorized, manifest through miracles and a huge cast of divine/demonic characters whose objective status is never problematized. In the first play of the trilogy,[50] she is accused by a jealous Mother Superior of being "endemoniada" or "hechizada," but the constant authorization of Madre Juana by divine figures, and the evil intentions of the Mother Superior, mean that the audience never has any doubt as to Juana's motivations. The Mother Superior is a villainous character whose demonic temptation seems to come purely from within; just before she accuses Madre Juana of being a "hechichera," she admits that "las telas del corazón/ alguna sierpe me come" (683; act III scene XIII verses 760–1) ("some serpent eats away the fabric of my heart"), but this demonic influence is not treated as possession, but instead as an inherent character defect. The *Maestra* has from her first encounter with Juana expressed her jealousy, pettiness, and desire for revenge, so her accusations can only be read as strategies to discredit Juana rather than true theological doubts.[51]

As with *El divino africano*, the possession scene in *La Santa Juana* shows the saint not as possessed but as the exorcist. This time, it is a *niña* who is possessed. Like the "mujer endemoniada" in the Lope play, Tirso's *niña*'s only role in the play is to be possessed and exorcised, although he does give her an identity that is independent of her possession. She is Marica, the daughter of Gil, one of the *labradores rústicos* who serve as the play's comic relief (the *graciosos*). Gil brings her to Juana having already been "diagnosed" by the local priest ("tien la chica/espiritos, según dize nueso Cura" [679; act III scene IX verses 549–50] ["the girl has evil spirits, according to our priest"]). Once again, the process of discernment is rendered doubly unnecessary; first because the character arrives having already been discerned, second because her actions on stage admit no ambiguity. This *niña* begins in a similar vein to the *mujer endemoniada*, speaking unambiguously in the voice of Satan, lamenting that Juana "las ánimas me saca de las uñas" (575) ("is tearing the souls out from my clutches"). Tirso places more explicit emphasis on a transformation of the girl's body as well as her mind/soul; this *endemoniada* must be dragged to Juana by two two able-bodied *labradores*, and after she threatens to set the house on fire, she bites both of them. However, the violence is treated comically, with the first *labrador* exclaiming, "Medio brazo me lleva de un bocado./ ¿Qué, también come el diabro carne, Crespo?" (She tore off half my arm wid' one bite, duz the devil eat meat too, Crespo?") and the second replying that "Come huevos y leche y no tien bula,/ ¿y deso os espantáis?" (680; verses 584–5) ("He eats eggs and milk an he don' have no Bull, and dis shocks you?"). The exchange proceeds in a comic vein, with the *niña* exposing the *labrador* for various picaresque sins in his past, until they are finally able to quiet her by throwing a cord of St. Francis around her neck. They drag her to Juana, and at this point the devil's confident and violent speech changes, and he cries out in pain that "me quemas" ("you are burning me") and "esto me abrasa" (681; verse 622) ("this sets me on fire!"). As a last gasp, the *niña/demonio* begins to speak in Latin, as the manuals of exorcism and accounts of possessions predict. However, unlike the possessions examined by de Certeau in Loudon, this threat is never serious. The *labradores* interject comic responses to each demonic utterance, and the devil's Latin quickly devolves into a pidgin Italian, clearly a comic literary device used by the playwright to amuse the audience and not an attempt to represent demonic speech. The scene continues in comedic banter until Juana invokes the Holy Spirit and "Cae la niña en tierra, desmayada" ("the girl falls to the ground in a faint"). Juana orders her father to take her away, "que ya el Angel condenado/ dexó a la niña libre" (658–9) ("for the condemned Angel has left the girl free"), and the scene ends. As in *El divino africano*, there is no representation of a linguistic or epistemic struggle between selves; we never hear Marica, only her possessor.

These two scenes described are typical of representations of possession on the Spanish stage.[52] It seems logical to ask why the theatrical representations of the devil are so dissimilar to the accounts of temptation and possession in mystic autobiography, why the theatre goes to such lengths to render discernment unnecessary when the theological, juridical, and spiritual literature of the period focuses obsessively on its importance and complexity. Hillaire Kallendorf alludes to this disparity in a curious epilogue to *Exoricsm and its Tests*, her analysis of exorcism in literature, in which she points out that the clarity of the category of demonic possession she has assumed throughout the book does not, in fact, hold: "demonic possession was not always the stable category we have assumed it to be for the purposes of this study" (205). She maintains that "the model developed in this study makes it clear that there is a difference between demonic possession and melancholy, demonic possession and ecstasy ... but the boundaries between these phenomena could become blurred" (205), finally concluding that "the recognition of this complexity is no excuse for not trying to analyse literature about demonic possession as literature with all it of its 'marvellous' genres and theologemes" (206). The distinction between *literature* and historical documentation is implicit here, but she does not draw it out. In literary texts (understood as texts written primarily for entertainment), there is a single, coherent representation of demonic possession. In historical documents, this distinction falls apart. Limiting ourselves to theatre, it seems that the clarity of the demonic phenomenon – its total separation from ecstasy, melancholy, and madness – is a deliberate choice made to *counter* the confusion so evident in the spiritual autobiography, treatise on discernment, Inquisition *proceso*, etc. We need not imagine a back-room strategy in which cardinals and councilors decided to counter the "plague" of *beatas* justifying their public displays of disorder with claims of sanctity (or harassing their confessors with obsessive scruples) by projecting for them a world in which the devil is always external and easily distinguished as a force for evil. More likely is that Church officials who authorized *comedias de santos* and the playwrights who wrote them shared a scepticism of popular *alumbrado*-type displays and this, combined with genres' tendencies to reproduce themselves, led to a preference for a staged representation of possession that seems entirely at odds with the same topic in other areas.

Discouraging Identification: Miracles on Stage

The clarity of the representations of the devil, and the codification of two forms of representing his actions in the world – Satan as villainous external foe or possession as comic relief – has its parallel in the representation of the divine. Although, as we have seen, there is a somewhat more complex treatment of the internal workings of grace and prayer in the *comedia*, by and large the direct interaction with the celestial is also mostly exteriorized, shown either through engagement with heavenly figures as real, external entities, or through miracle. Like the clarity of the demonic intervention, miracles are never represented as ambiguous; either because the supernatural agent appears on stage to demonstrate the intervention or because the miraculous effect has no possible natural explanation, there is never a need to discern between natural, preternatural, and supernatural.[53] Again, we see theatre imposing clarity where the historical documents show confusion. And while many of the *comedias de santos* present miracles as true signs of God's grace, the comic subplots also tend to include a comedic treatment of miracles, parallel to the comedic treatment of possession in *La Santa Juana*. Juan Pérez de Montalbán's (1602–38) *La gitana de Menfis, Santa María Egipcíaca* is exemplary in this regard, although there are many others.[54] The *graciosos* repeatedly fake miracles or misunderstand the category of the miraculous to comic effect. In the third act, Ventura decides to become (as indicated in the stage directions) a "ermitaño a lo gracioso" (22; act III) ("a hermit-fool"), and his companion asks that he "haz un milagro aquí" ("perform a miracle right here") in proof of his new status.[55] Ventura claims that he has already managed three miracles "que mucha opinión me han dado" ("that have brought me great fame"), but the "milagros" he cites are burlesque; for example, he "cures" a man from lameness in "un pie" by injuring the other one as well. A few moments later, Ventura reveals that his intentions in professing virtue have been false and earthly:

> … bien he fingido
> lo santo; y pues que ya he dado
> en fingirlo, he de salir
> con ello ya, y prevenir
> un artificio extremado,
> con que estando de rodillas,
> puesta la vista en el Cielo,
> me alce una vara del suelo,
> que con estas maravillas
> vendrán locos los Pastores,
> y me traerán mil regalos. (23; act III)

> … I have feigned sanctity well, and since I've decided to fake it, I will keep going, and prepare an outrageous trick, one where while kneeling, my eyes looking toward the Heavens, I elevate a yard from the ground, and with these marvels the shepherds will go crazy and bring me a thousand gifts.

The reference to the levitation makes this a clear parody of the *alumbrados* and would-be mystics; Pérez de Montalbán here shares the point of view of the *fiscal* (and generally the Inquisitors as well) in so many *procesos*. The would-be saint is motivated purely by a desire for "fama" and "mil regalos." Later in the play, Ventura attempts to *arrobarse* again, this time using a rope.

> Famosa está la invención:
> gallardamente me elevo;
> hoy tengo de ver si llegó
> alguna manducación.
> No hiciera tal artificio
> el mismo diablo. (27; act III)

> This is a famous invention: I raise myself gallantly; today I will see if someone brought some grub. The very devil could not come up with such a trick.

Ventura's miracles are all parodies of biblical ones – he "miraculously" produces bread and wine in the desert (in reality he has been given the rations in the previous scene), revives a dead man (who was not really dead), and in his final attempt to be taken as a saint, he proposes to cross a river by walking across a sheet. In each case, he clearly states his devious intentions to the audience and the mechanism of his deceit, and in each case the proposed miracle is either exposed or fails. His river crossing ends in him being fished out from certain drowning, and when his rescuer asks if "En fin, ¿que tu desvarío da todavía en ser Santo?" ("In short, you are sticking with this madness of being a Saint?"), he replies that, since he seems to be "santo ahogadizo … Ya no mas de aquí adelante" (29; act III) ("a saint prone to drowning … No more, from here on"). The lesson Ventura learns is not to embrace sanctity but to renounce it, or at least to renounce a sanctity that demands proof and recognition on earth.

As with the parallel representation of the devil as terrible foe and comic foil, the burlesque miracle can coexist with "legitimate" miracles. For every burlesque miracle of Ventura's, the play's heroine effects a legitimate one. Yet just as Ventura always shows the audience the mechanism of his deceit, the play always reveals the divine cause of the true miracles. María Egipcíaca is never the agent of resuscitations or miraculous conversions, but only the intermediary, the woman whose virtuous life and prayers call down from heaven Christ, Mary, and other supernatural figures who can make miracles happen. The playwright's attitude seems to be akin to that of the Inquisitor: celebration of the miracle, or the demonic possession in theory (a reality in the past, a moral lesson in the present) but scepticism as to the occurrence of such events in everyday life or among everyday people.

The View from the Audience

And yet, I think it is possible to imagine how the erasure of mystic practice from the stage could have had the opposite of the intended effect: encouraging and shaping the popular *alumbradismo teatral* mentioned at the outset of this chapter, rather than uniformly instilling scepticism. The Inquisitors responded to displays of possession or what they deemed "irrational" behaviour by silencing it – not just in the sentences, which so often entailed the reclusion of the "disruptive" (ecstatic, *ilusa*, etc.) in a convent or hospital and an order to refrain from further "publication" of visions – but in the *procesos* themselves. It is impossible to know how much is left out of the transcriptions, but the fortunate lapse that preserves the order to go back and destroy the account of Agustina Salgado's possession, as well as the not infrequent scribe's interjection that a defendant's statements were not written because "no se pudieron entender ni reducir a escrito" ("they could not be reduced to writing")[56] suggests how much the Inquisitors had to leave out in order to create a rational discourse, legible to the law. The secrecy of the Inquisition proceedings, of course, and the isolation of the Inquisition prisons, meant that an arrest and trial removed the would-be mystic from the public sphere, his/her discourse from circulation. When the individual re-emerged, it was as a silent penitent who only listened as the Inquisitors read aloud *their* narrative, which in the case of the later *alumbrados* was one of an ethical lapse into fraud and greed.[57] The Inquisition in the seventeenth century acted on bodies, but in a larger sense it acted on discourse, removing and correcting the disordered/disorderly *sign* – the *arrobo*, the *alboroto* – from circulation and replacing it with a clear, rational narrative. Mystic practice in itself was acceptable in private and within a closed community, as long as it only reproduced and confirmed doctrinal truths. The fabric of public discourse, however, could not admit the transgression implied by *lo místico*.

The plays we have examined erase mystic practice from discourse, but unlike the Inquisition narrative, they do not replace it with silence or rational argument. Instead, they fill the void of lived, first-person contemplative practice with a world of spectacular, exteriorized apparitions. On the one hand, they seem to set the bar for "proof" of divine intervention or miracle so high as to preclude any identification between audience members and the visionary characters; since angels and Christ children did not descend from the sky and speak unambiguously to multiple witnesses, it should be clear to the audience that the world of the *comedia de santos* was not *their* world. But as scholars of the *comedia* in performance remind us, the audience of the *comedia* was diverse, and different audiences responded to different messages.[58] The visual effects of the *comedia de santos* – the spectacle, the exterior descent and ascent via hidden *tramoya* of all manner of angelic, saintly, demonic, and divine beings, as well as the miraculous resuscitations and reversals, and the most extreme physical gestures – would be the most broadly visible elements of the play, whereas the dialogue and doctrine could be lost in the noise of the *corral* or the difficulty of the language. The *comedia de santos* created a new visual vocabulary, one that took the pictorial imaginary of visions that the Christian faithful had been accustomed to seeing in churches and chapels for centuries, and made it come alive. Indeed, as we have seen, the plays frequently imitate the iconography of paintings and sculptures in revealed tableaux. However, the *comedias* also staged other visions as dramatic action, and even when "lo visto" was staged as a static tableaux, the actors experiencing the visions and possessions were on stage, and the necessities of theatre required they exaggerate the corporeal signs associated with visionary experience to make them visible to the audience. Thus, they performed an exaggerated embodied spirituality, often aided by staging effects, of *levantamientos*, fits, swoons, etc. I think it possible then to imagine a public that missed the niceties of the dialogue and doctrine and instead saw the moving, emoting bodies – both of the visionaries and of the visions.

The influence of this theatrical imaginary would help to explain the increased theatricality of the mystic movement in the late sixteenth and seventeenth centuries, and particularly among *beatas* and *beatos*, in contrast to the abstract and intellectually complex interiority of the early *alumbrados* and contemplatives. The *beatas* and *beatos*, unlike *religiosos*, were free to go to the theatre, and it does not seem coincidental that the major "focos" of *alumbradismo* and *santidad fingidad* occur in Sevilla and Madrid, centres of theatrical activity. In Seville, according to a relación:

> Lucía de la Ossa, doncella … se delató de muchas revelaciones que había tenido, en que veía demonios en diferentes formas y otras veces a Cristo, nuestro Redemptor y Nuestra Señora, y le hablaban … y que había sido llevada a la iglesia de Burgos y estando presentes Cristo, nuestro Redemptor, Nuestra Señora y San Juan Evangelista y otros santos, Cristo se había vestido de pontificial y dicho misa, y luego se desposó con ella – la cual tenía una vela blanca encendida en las manos, siendo madrina Nuestra Señora; y que el desposorio se escribió, y a ella le pusieron por nombre Teresa de Jesús, y que diciéndole a Cristo que no era digno de tal nombre, le respondió su Majestad: *calla, que más gracias tienes tú que ella*. Y diciéndole Cristo que firmase aquel desposorio, y respondiendo ella que no sabía, lo firmó San Juan Evangelista. Tiene cuatro testigos de vista contestes; y uno añade que dijo la dicha que tenía escrito el nombre de Santa Teresa en el corazón con letras de oro.[59]

> Lucía de la Ossa, maiden … was denounced for many revelations she had had, in which she saw devils in different forms and at other times Christ our Redeemer and Our Lady, and they spoke to her … and that she had been transported to the church in Burgos and in the presence of Christ our Redeemer, Our Lady, and Saint John the Evangelist and other saints, Christ was dressed as the Pope and said mass, and then He wedded her – she held a lit, white candle in her hands, and Our Lady was her godmother; and the wedding vows were written down, and she was called Teresa de Jesús, and when she told Christ she was not worthy of such a name, His Majesty replied: be quiet, you have more graces than she does. And when Christ told her to sign the wedding vows, and she replied that she did not know how, Saint John the Evangelist signed them. There are four witness that corroborate this and one who adds that the aforementioned said the name Saint Teresa was written on her heart with gold letters.

This is not a static vision but instead a dramatic spectacle that mixes divine entities and human figures who lived centuries apart, with description of setting, costume, and dialogue. In the same document, María de Cristo, "beata mercedaria descalza" ("*beata* of the discalced Mercederians"), is accused of celebrating the profession of a new *beata* and claiming that the *beatas*, "estando tañendo en una guitarra y bailando, vieron baxar al Niño Jesús envuelto en un pañal blanco, y empezó a bailar con una de ellas visiblemente, y cuantas vueltas ella daba, tantas daba el Niño, descubriendo la piernecita" ("while playing the guitar and dancing, they saw the Baby Jesus descend, wrapped in a white cloth, and He danced visibly with them, and for every time she spun around, the Child spun as well, revealing his little leg").[60] Both the "human" activity and the vision are drawn from a vocabulary of theatre. And the extreme bodily displays that the anti-*alumbrados* denounce also could have been influenced by the particular way of experiencing divine grace that the *comedias de santos* performed for the public. Whether or not the *arrobos* and fits of the later *alumbradas* were feigned or sincere, whether these were *santas fingidas* or *legítimas* is beside the point: somehow, sanctity was displayed and recognized in a way that would have been unrecognizable to a late medieval Christian, accustomed to the iconography of pious, head-bowed saints. There existed a medieval narrative and visual tradition of *performing* demonic possession, but we do not find any comparable information about how to experience divine grace. There are certainly no fifteenth-century accounts of saints holding for twenty-four hours the position "en pie en el canto de la cama, firmando con solos los dedos de los pies, y caído el cuerpo hacia adelante en el aire, los brazos y manos abiertos, y también los ojos abiertos más de lo ordinario" ("one foot on the edge of the bed, holding on with only her toes, and her body falling forward and upward in the air, arms and hands open, and also her eyes open beyond what is customary"), as is reported of the *alumbrada* María Romera (Huerga *Historia de los alumbrados v.* 4 569). Does it not seem possible that this *beata* had learned or assimilated the representations of so many *arrobadas* and *postradas* on the stage of the *comedia de santos*, even when the text of those plays advised against identification or imitation of the rapturous saint? It does not even seem far-fetched to imagine that individuals watching scenes of romantic love on stage assimilated the exaggerated performance of "turbación," "suspensión," etc. that Agustín de la Granja amply catalogues and, following the movement *a lo divino* that so many allusions to the mystical marriage and the Bride of Christ seem to invite, embodied that "suspensión" in their own performance of piety.[61]

María Romera was reported to have been seen by many people:

> arrobada en la cama y se levantó muy recia con grande ligereza y se puso de rodillas sin tocar ni firmar con las piernas ni pies, puesta en cruz, como pintan a san Francisco, los ojos vidriados; y, mirando ansí a un rincón, se levantó como en el aire y anduvo corriendo como buscando algo que se le iba, diciendo: ¡Por aquí, por aquí!
>
> transported in ecstasy in her bed and she got up with great strength and with great lightness and knelt, without touching the ground with either

> her legs nor her feet, her body in the form of a cross, as Saint Francis is painted, her eyes glassy; and in this state, gazing at a corner, she rose as if in the air and went running as if in search of something that was getting away from her, saying: Over here, over here!

Here, the movement from a *visual* imitation (*como pintan*) to a narrative, dramatic one is clearly marked, just as in the moving tableaux that we find in the spectacular scenes of the *comedias de santos*. María Romera may not be consciously playing a part, but she has a public and she is *performing*, using body and voice to embody an appearance of sanctity that belongs to the *comedia de santos*. Is it not hard to imagine María in the audience of a representation of Tirso's Segunda Parte de *Santa Juana*, watching the kneeling Juana say:

> ¡Ay, Seráfico Francisco,
> quién con las insignias santas
> os viera que el Serafín
> os dio por joyas preciadas!
> Vos, que imitación de Cristo
> sois, vos en quien se retrata,
> vos en quien su pasión pinta,
> vos en quien puso sus llagas,
> venidme a ver, y lloremos
> los dos el ver cual maltratan
> los lobos nuestro Cordero. (729; act III scene XVI verses 696–706)
>
> Ay, Seraphic Francis, who might see you with the holy insignia that the Seraphim gave you as precious jewels?! You, who are the imitation of Christ, you in whom He portrayed himself, you upon whom He painted his Passion, you upon whom He placed his wounds, come to see me, and let us cry together at how the wolves mistreated our Lamb.

and watching in response, San Francisco appear "en cruz con el Serafin como se pinta" ("on the cross with the Seraphim, as it is painted") to reassure Juana, "Contigo estoy hija cara" (729; act III scene XVI verse 707) ("I am with you, dear daughter").

I do not mean to suggest that theatre is the only influence on this development, nor do I wish to trace the source for any particular vision to a theatrical *tableaux*. The spectacularity and dramatic intensity of the Baroque was manifest in many aspects of cultural life, and surely processions, liturgy, and the other non-text-based performances also shaped the way individuals imagined devotion. However, despite the recognition of the theatricality of late-stage *alumbradismo*, the role of the theatre in the development of mysticism/*alumbradismo* into the seventeenth century has not to my knowledge been highlighted. The theatre's assimilation of a language (corporeal and verbal) of mysticism without interiority had a paradoxical effect: it had, by presenting the *externally recognizable* performance of mysticism to a mass audience, given those in the audience inclined to visionary spirituality a model for how to play the part of a recognizable, believable receiver of spiritual gifts and, at the same time, gave life to these men and women's visions. Instead of forestalling identification with mystics, the plays seem to encourage identification with a corporeal, dramatic, *exteriorized interiorized* spirituality. The fainting, screaming, trembling *alumbrados teatrales* were less "mystic," by our definition, than Santa Teresa, but they remained unsettling, disturbing, and transgressive, if not of Catholicism itself, than certainly of social stability and tranquility.

Chapter Six

The Missionary Impulse

I stated in the introduction to this work that even a study focused on circularity would have to – perhaps arbitrarily – establish a starting and ending point. I chose my starting point of the first decades of the sixteenth century, following the chronology traced by Melquíades Andrés Martín, for all the reasons adduced in the introduction and chapter one. Of course, in addition to the translation and composition of treatises of mental prayer that was gaining momentum in that period, there was another process taking place in exactly that time span that would have much greater repercussions for every aspect of Spanish society. I refer of course to the "discovery," exploration, colonization and conquest of the New World. Was there any relation between these two simultaneous processes? Certainly, the traditional study of the development of Spanish mysticism has not found one, nor seemingly found it expedient to look for one. There have been studies of the *traslatio* of certain mystic authors or practices to the Americas, but to my knowledge it has never been suggested that the *traslatio* could also have worked in reverse: that the experience of colonization could have shaped currents of European mystic spirituality. Dana Bultman comes the closest; in a provocative 2017 article comparing Franciscan and Nahua concepts of interior life forces, she proposes to "turn the tables of comparison" between native Mexican and European categories and goes as far to point out "suggestive correspondences" between "Native and Franciscan metaphysics" (296), but she stops short of suggesting any sort of causality behind the correspondence. Yet recent scholarship in early modern and colonial studies, beyond the field of religious studies, has progressively emphasized the degree to which the "discovery" of the Americas changed European ways of thinking: about culture, about law, about history. In this chapter, I wish to extend this shift to consider the ways the experience of the first missionaries in Mexico, and their task of inventing a language for indigenous Christianity, might have contributed to the renovation of language that we have identified as the fundamental impulse behind "lo místico." After all, if we return to a phrase quoted by Michel de Certeau to describe the birth of a new mystic discourse – Lorenzo Valla's call for a "new word for a new reality" – it seems impossible not to see parallels with the very new reality that was encountered, named, and narrated in the New World. Thus, in a work that has emphasized circularity, we end our study by returning to the beginning. Or more accurately, a beginning.

First, it is worthwhile to consider why this proposed relationship seems counterintuitive. To do so, it will be necessary to lay out an extremely reductive and overgeneralized account of the period of early colonization. My purpose here is not to confirm this narrative – in fact, I will return to it precisely to poke holes – but to show how a certain narrative that held through the majority of twentieth century would *seem* to preclude the possibility of a causal relationship between New World missionary activity and Old World mysticism. According to this simplified narrative, the majority of European discourse about the New World inhabitants during the first decades after the "discovery" was focused on their very humanity. While the missionary orders were, from the start, ardent defenders of the natives' full humanity and potential to become Christians, they argued this point by emphasizing indigenous innocence and simplicity. This paternalist attitude precluded any attempt to instruct natives in theologically complex practices like mystic prayer. While some missionaries did recognize and even admire the sophistication and variety of indigenous American societies, they drew a clear line between laudable native *cultural* practices and their religious beliefs, which could only be conceived of as idolatries to be fully extirpated.[1] Furthermore, the sheer enormity of the task of missionary evangelization in the New World, both in terms of the number of natives to be converted and the obstacles mounted by *conquistadores*, *encomenderos*, and others with no interest in native spirituality, meant that, in practice, New World religious instruction was limited to the most basic and superficial doctrinal points. The missionaries were aware from early on of the power of the printed word and image in mass evangelization, but they were producing basic catechisms, prayers, and *doctrinas*. They were not mass-producing tomes of Augustine or pseudo-Dionysius or translating Richard of St. Victor or Catherine of Siena into indigenous languages. The goal was quantity, not quality. Since there was no evidence of European Spaniards attempting to instruct natives in mystical theology, there would seem to be no evidence tying the two phenomena, despite their approximate simultaneity.

No one denies that Spanish missionaries had an impact on native spirituality, although the scope and nature of that impact has been the source of much debate in the last century.[2] There has been much work on syncretism in American religious practices but always *in the Americas*, and usually among indigenous peoples, people of African descent, or *mestizos*. The idea that Spanish missionaries' contact with the New World could have influenced religious expression *in Spain* would require that Europeans came to the New World with minds open enough to recognize and admit otherness and that channels existed through which that new, transformed knowledge was brought back across the Atlantic.[3] There is significant evidence against both halves of this supposition. As Michael Ryan observes, "the bewildering variety of peoples and diversity of cultures did not bowl over a Europe which had cause to appreciate that variety was a fact of life" (519). Humanism's rediscovery of classic texts gave European missionaries a category with which to interpret variety, difference and otherness, which they projected without hesitation onto the new continent. The American native "simply provided more grist for mills that were already operating" (520). This insistence on finding sameness or historical repetition in the face of novelty is evident even in the texts of missionaries who most stridently defended indigenous communities and chronicled their cultures. "Bartolome de las Casas scolded his contemporaries for seeing the Indians as new, utterly foreign creatures and not realizing similarities they shared with heathen antiquity; he then went on in his Apologetica Historia Sumaria to catalogue those comparisons exhaustively … Even the meticulous Bernardino Sahagun … paused now and again to point out the presence of an ancient Greek god here and there in Mexico" (527–8). John Elliott observes that, despite the vast accumulation of descriptions, objects, and data from the New World:

> even by the mid-seventeenth century the explosive potentialities already glimpsed in the early sixteenth had scarcely begun to be realized. In spite of the problems raised by the growing knowledge of America, no sustained attack had yet been mounted on the historical and chronological accuracy of the Biblical story of the creation of man and his dispersion following the flood. European political and social philosophy was still almost untouched by the results of ethnographical observation and inquiry. (29)

Contrary to an older narrative according to which textual authority was immediately replaced by empiricism, European intellectuals were unwilling or unable to see their American experiences through anything but a European lens. Columbus's increased insistence throughout his writing that he was in *India* becomes emblematic and prophetic of centuries of European encounters in the Americas that, in Anthony Grafton's words, "did not shake but confirmed European prejudices" (5).[4]

Furthermore, even if we concede that some of the Spanish missionaries in the Americas were at least partially open to the difference they encountered, this does not mean that this recognition passed back to Europe. The majority of the volumes cataloguing native practices remained unpublished for centuries after their authors' deaths. Sometimes, as in the case of Sahagún's *Historia general,* this was due to censorship. But in large part it seems to have been the result of a lack of interest in Europe. John Elliott, observing the dearth of titles from or about the Americas printed in Europe and/or held in European libraries during the sixteenth century, concludes that "all too often, Europe remained in ignorance of the pioneering methods and the novel findings of those who worked among the native peoples of America. It is not therefore surprising if the evidence for a direct influence on Europe of pioneering techniques developed in America turns out to be scanty." He concedes that influence "is also, by its nature, difficult to interpret. Apparent cases of direct influence tend to be ambiguous. The original impetus behind some new departure is as likely as not to be European" (35).

However, Elliott's criteria for "evidence of direct influence" – printed matter explicitly mentioning the Americas – is a limited and limiting one.[5] For as Elliott and Ryan both note, the initial effect of the New World "discovery" on Europe seems to have been that "it forced Europeans to come face to face with ideas and problems which were already to be found within their own cultural traditions" (Elliott 47). The fact that universities and presses of the 1500s were obsessed with ancient knowledge and literature was neither independent of nor a reaction against the influx of modernity. Europeans were not ready to shed their classical framework entirely and adopt a new paradigm, but they did recognize that to fit the New World into a story of biblical messianism or classical otherness, they needed to understand in much more detail the facts and texts of these older periods. The growth of literature on paganism "to epidemic proportions in the sixteenth and seventeenth centuries" (Ryan 525) *was* a "direct" result of the discovery of the Americas. Europeans were reading about Greeks' contacts with pagan others to understand how to understand and deal with the American natives. They processed "novelty" by returning to antiquity, not as retreat but because ancient texts – classical and biblical – were the available guides for understanding (naming, categorizing, legislating) *otherness.*

What we see then is a "direct" reaction to novelty that, at least superficially, looks like a reaction against novelty but in fact should be understood as a reworking of past models to incorporate new evidence (even when that meant ultimately denying or erasing its novelty). If this characterizes European intellectual reactions to new evidence about geography, human societies, and natural science, then it makes sense that we might see a similar indirect-but-direct response to the encounter with New World spiritual practices, not just the questions of natives' place in biblical genealogies but also the ways to understand a "natural" spirituality of peoples who, as Columbus famously put it, "no conocían ninguna secta ni idolatría" ("they knew no sect, nor idolatry"). The belief that the indigenous Americans were pagans and idolaters soon appeared alongside this opposite conception of a peoples *without* religion, but the "blank slate" concept was the dominant one in the earliest year of missionary activity, gradually giving way to a more cynical *desengaño* as the colonial "experiment" became an institution. If the indigenous Americans were "pure" souls untouched by Christianity but also by idolatry, their evangelization necessarily compelled a reconceptualization of the relationship between *letras* and *experiencia* in the acquisition of faith. And just as the conceptual framework for the question of encountering new lands and new peoples came from the Greeks, the conceptual framework available to Christian missionaries for thinking through a faith through experience rather than intellect was mysticism. Thus, it would seem logical and fit in with the responses to the *conquista* in other intellectual fields that the direct response to the evangelization of the natives would take the form of a renewed interest in a prior mystical tradition. This would explain why Spanish theologians turned to this topic in the first decades of the sixteenth century, exactly when the New World evangelization project began.

Because, as John Elliott noted, there is no *direct* influence, and "the original impetus behind some new departure is as likely as not to be European" (36) we must have some additional evidence to show that a direct influence is *probable.* An absence of direct influence cannot *a priori* be taken as proof of indirect influence. Beyond the larger pattern I have identified of European responses to American discoveries, is there specific evidence connecting the early evangelists with the authors of mystic treatises? Columbus and other *conquistadores* writing to Spain might have characterized the natives as "natural" Christians, but this characterization, like similar ones in letters from Brazil or Mexico, were always deeply embedded in rhetorical constructions whose larger purpose was to unlock funds for further exploration and conquest, not to shape the missionary project itself. They wrote for an audience of royals and Court functionaries, not theologians. Is there evidence that the missionaries in the Americas saw the natives in ways that could make them re-think the "natural" acquisition of faith by experience? If the missionary textual production consisted of basic statements of doctrine and ritual, what is the evidence that New World evangelists were in any way connected to a theological movement that went beyond and even eschewed rote recitation of doctrine or empty external compliance with sacraments?

Franciscan Missionaries and Mysticism

In the rest of the chapter, I will argue that there is evidence for a connection, although it is evidence and not proof. To see a colonial evangelism that aspired to transcend rote inculcation of doctrine, we must return to the very beginnings of European–American contact, to a moment of utopian messianism that would later be obscured by the realities of imperialism. The first evangelizers to Mexico belonged to the Franciscan orders, the order most closely tied to medieval mysticism and, as we saw in chapter one, to the flourishing of mental prayer in sixteenth-century Spain.[6] In his seminal study *The Millennial Kingdom of the Franciscans in the New World*, John Phelan makes the case that the early Franciscan missionaries saw the discovery of the New World as a sign of the impending Last Judgment predicted in the book of Revelations, and the conversion of the natives as the essential final step to usher in the End Times.[7] The first mission to Mexico, consisting of twelve rigorously selected friars sent in imitation of the twelve Apostles, was a deliberate echo of the "First" Coming.[8] Millennialism and mysticism are not synonymous but have often gone hand in hand. At the very least, a utopian faith in the promise of the Mexican Church to bring in the Second Coming would be propitious for promoting missionaries to think of their spiritual practices in new ways, to go beyond the letter and interrogate deeply the spirit of the natives' and their own spiritual practices.

One way to get a sense of the first missionaries' spiritual inclinations is through their biographies and libraries, and while the documentary evidence is hardly complete, all of it points to a nucleus of early Franciscan missionaries whose lives were steeped in Scripture and contemplation. Francisco Morales has made the most forceful case for a Franciscan mystical practice cultivated by the Franciscans and enhanced by their encounters with native Mexican spirituality. As he summarizes: they came from reformed friaries "characterized by their fondness for contemplative life" (74). He quotes from the Minister General's mandate to the missionaries as they set out, which alluded to their previous dedication to study and contemplation in its call to "bajad hora apriesa a la vida activa" ("hurry and descend to the active life"). And while this direction might seem to indicate that the friars were being asked to relinquish that contemplative focus, in the next sentence the mandate enjoinders the friars to integrate "la vida activa, juntamente con la contemplativa" (75) ("both the active and the contemplative life").[9] In general, Morales's definition of "mysticism" includes ascetism and prophecy and is thus much broader than the one employed in this study; there is ample evidence of the extreme poverty and penitential practices of the first Franciscans, but much less of the cultivation of union or interior spirituality. The exception here is Fray Martín de Valencia, leader of the Twelve and subject of several hagiobiographies by fellow Franciscans, all of which emphasize not just his extreme self-discipline and piety but also his practice of contemplative, mystical prayer. Fray Martín's confessor, Francisco de Jiménez, related in his "Vida de Martín de Valencia" a noteworthy conversation when Fray Martín, still a young novice, rhetorically asked a group of monks whether it was more important for a preacher to "ser letrado, y no spiritual o ser spiritual, y no letrado" ("be university-educated but not spiritual, or to be spiritual but not university-educated") and then expounded "en pocas palabras, *ex abundantia cordis*" ("in few words, but with an abundance of heart") on the vanity of *letras* in the absence of "devoción, oratoria y contemplación" ("devotion, prayer and contemplation").[10] Jiménez also notes Valencia's devotion to the Psalms, which, along with the *Cantar*, is the Bible text most frequently subject to mystical interpretation, and tells of a mass in New Spain in which Valencia, during the Psalms, "vio en espíritu" ("saw in spirit") a mass conversion of "infieles" ("heretics") and "fue tanto el gozo y alegría que su espíritu sintió interiormente que no pudo sino echarlo afuera, y como loco fuera de sí" (233) ("such was the joy and happiness that his spirit felt inside that he could not but let it burst out, like a crazy man, out of his mind"). Jiménez also notes that Valencia was "notorio" for his devotion to the Passion, and during his meditations "Dios le daba sentimientos exteriores en su cuerpo de sus dolores sacratísimos y tormentos, no digo exteriores y visibles sino sensibles en su cuerpo, allende de lo que interiormente sentía en su alma" ("God gave him external sensations in his body of his holiest of pains and torments, I don´t mean exterior and visible but rather felt in his body, in addition to those he felt in the interior of his soul"). Jiménez quotes Valencia himself, explaining his physical ailments during Holy Week: "siente tanto mi espíritu siente interiormente que no lo puedo sufrir sin que exteriormente el cuerpo lo sienta y demuestre" ("my spirit feels so much internally that I can't take it without my body showing and demonstrating it externally"). Most importantly, Jiménez, writing in 1536 when the valence of *alumbradismo* had begun to change and the Inquisition to warn against *false* mystics, specifically addresses this point, and the recent trend of confusing rapture with holiness. Jiménez abstains from such a blanket assumption, acknowledging "que ya podría uno arrobarse y no estar en gracia" ("that one may go into rapture without being in a state of grace") and going on a digression about the three forms of "arrobamiento" with the terminology and neologism ("exceso" vs. "sobrepujamiento de espíritu de Dios" "transportación sin gracia"[11]) characteristic of the treatises of mental prayer we examined in chapter one. Just as in those treatises, the subject matter compels a change in authorial style and a digression from the hagiographic template, as Jiménez not only enters into theological distinctions but also illustrates them with examples of mystics of the time. When he returns to his subject, it is to specify that "no fue de arrobamientos desa manera que otros ha habido de nuestros tiempos como la Beata del Barco"[12] ("these were not raptures of the sort that others in our times have had, like the *Beata del Barco*"), but instead, "su exercicio" consisted of "continuar la oración" ("continuing to pray") and "canta[r] un canto muy suave, que parecía voz de ángel" ("singing a very gentle song, with a voice like an angel"), although "lo que en aquel canto decía, él y Dios los sabían, que no había quien lo pudiese entender" ("what he said in that song, only he and God knew, as there was no one who could understand it"). Despite this disavowal, Jiménez confirms that, at times, Fray Martín "fue visto en exceso y arrobado" ("was seen *in exceso*[13] and rapture/extasis") and recounts two examples, one of which ends with Fray Martín coming to and remarking "con un suspiro de las entrañas 'O que cosa es estar siempre con Dios!'" (240) ("with a sigh from deep within his interior, 'Oh, how great it is to be always with God!'"). There is no denying the mystic emphasis of this version of Fray Martín's life; rather than a narrative focused exclusively on extreme acts of external devotion and service, Jiménez insists on the unitive, contemplative, ineffable aspect of the missionary's spirituality. After proceeding with a linear account of Fray Martín's selection for the mission and work in the Americas, he returns at the end to the question of Martín's visions. Again, this particular subject produces disruption to the smoothly ordered text, as Jiménez interjects that "aunque no creo en sueños y visiones, adelante diré lo que acerca desto he leído, y que quiero ahora decir algunas cosas que se me representan y acuerdo haber oído al siervo de Dios [Valencia] que vio en espíritu" (247) ("although I do not believe in dreams or visions, further on I will say what I have read about this, and now I wish to say a few things that were reported to me or I recall having heard that this servant of God [Valencia] saw spiritually"). The visions and revelations he goes on to recount are of the biblical or hagiographic model – emblematic images or parables that are both clear in their narration and interpretation – in keeping with their presentation in a third-person hagiographic account. Still, when combined with the earlier description of contemplative practice, they give us incontrovertible evidence of mystic tendencies in the leader of the first Franciscans.

Another connection, although more circumstantial, lies in the biography of Francisco de Osuna, whose *Abecedarios* were studied in chapter one. Around 1529, Osuna was named Commissary General for the Indies, and although he ended up withdrawing from the post and did not travel across the ocean, this suggests that he was in contact with missionaries, presumably both those yet to make the trip and those already abroad. His books certainly did find their way to Mexico, although we cannot know exactly when or how they arrived. Lino Gómez Canedo has studied the earliest colonial libraries and concludes that, although "the inventory of books that the first Franciscans who arrived in 1523 or 1524 brought with them is unknown ... it is difficult to believe they did not bring some, as books were never missing from a missionary's bags" (409). Gerónimo Mendieta, historian of the Franciscans missionary work in sixteenth-century Mexico (in which he too participated), also remarks on the importance of books among "preachers and confessors." Mendieta's additional mention of a concession to all the friars of "a book of devotion for their particular consolation" indicates that their reading material went beyond catechisms or other strictly programmatic texts.[14] The first bishop of Mexico, Juan de Zumárraga, was openly sympathetic to Erasmus and his emphasis on inner spirituality; Zumárraga occupied the post in 1527, before the Church had condemned Erasmus as dangerously close to Protestantism. Zumárraga was responsible not only for the first printing press in the Americas but also wrote the first catechisms and *doctrinas* for use in the evangelization project; Mark Christensen hypothesizes that the reason Zumárraga's successor, Alonso de Montúfar, replaced Zumárraga's *doctrina* was that it "clearly showed Erasmian sympathies" (65). Zumárraga also was the driving force behind the creation of the Colegio de Santa Cruz at Tlatelolco in 1536, the cornerstone in the Franciscan project of creating an indigenous priesthood with an education equivalent to that received at any European seminary. Although the goals and fortunes of the Colegio were in decline by the 1540s, it did come to possess the largest library in Mexico.[15]

Library catalogues and printers' catalogues provide additional evidence of early colonial interest in mysticism; Martin Nesvig relates the imprisonment and torture of Pedro Ocharte, a sixteenth-century Mexican printer whose shop published religious texts in Nahuatl as well as European languages, for allegedly praising a book with the *alumbrado* heresy that mental prayer alone was sufficient for salvation (161). It is not clear whether the text in question was in Nahuatl or Spanish. Fernández del Castillo cites evidence that by the 1570s, Franciscan friar Francisco de Ribera, formerly Commissary General of the order in Mexico, owned Osuna's *Abecedarios*, and a 1573 Inquisition document confirms numerous copies of books by Osuna in individual collections and Franciscan convent libraries (471–95).[16] By the seventeenth century, we have concrete evidence of mystic works in the library of the Colegio de Buenaventura, opened in 1667 on the site of the shuttered Colegio de Santa Cruz. It is unknown which of the titles in the library, if any, were also part of the former Colegio, but Gómez Canedo finds in the mid-seventeenth-century catalogue "works by Santa Teresa, fray Alonso de Orozco, fray Luis de León (*Los nombres de Cristo*), fray Francisco de Osuna (*Abecedario espiritual*), *beato* Juan de Ávila (*Obras*), Ludolfo de Sajonia (*Vita Christi*), Gersón, Dionisio Cartujano (5 volumes) and others" (411). But this is a large temporal jump and, since are all European authors, shows only the influence of European mysticism on/in Mexican Franciscans. Why might it make sense to see a missing link crossing the Atlantic *the other way*?

The key, I will suggest, has less to do with the first friars' private contemplative practices and everything to do with a task that at first might have seemed purely practical and unrelated: their *translation* practice. For, as Michel de Certeau first identified and we have traced from the beginning of this study, what separates medieval mystic movements from the early modern version is, above all, the latter's focus on *language*: the centring of a mystic practice not just at the heart of the human interior but in the heart of words, language, and representation. The first friars in Mexico were not "just" translators of Spanish to Nahuatl and back; they were, in collaboration with their native allies and pupils, inventors of a new language: Christian Nahuatl. It seems plausible that the shift from ascetic messianism to a language-centred mysticism, first within the Franciscan order and then spreading outward, arose from the Franciscan order's direct engagement with a project of rethinking the exact parameters of every word in the vocabulary of Christian doctrine, a necessary step in their massive project of translation, codification, and invention of Mexican Christianity.

Rather than expecting native Mexicans to learn Castilian and Latin and then Christian doctrine, the Franciscans proposed to teach them Christianity in their own language. This corresponded to the Franciscan ideal of a universal church, one not bound by particularities of race or language but available and accessible to all. However, the reality of the "accessibility" of Christian doctrine to Nahuatl-speakers (or speakers of other indigenous American languages) was not so simple: Nahuatl vocabulary was shaped to express Mexican religion and spirituality. In a very short period of time, Franciscans (soon joined by Dominicans, Augustinians, and a bit later, Jesuits), had to: learn the contours of Mexican spiritual concepts; invent a vocabulary in Nahuatl that could make Christian ideas available to Nahuatl speakers; and, finally, teach that vocabulary (as well as the concept of an alphabetic language and the Latin alphabet) and hence that cosmology, to their native pupils. It should be emphasized that this was not a one-way process, with European clergy operating in isolation and imposing their knowledge on the Nahua. Because the Europeans, at first contact, understood as little of Nahuatl as the Mexicans understood of Castilian or Latin, the groups had to work in tandem, sensing out the contours of each other's worlds and words, proposing neologisms and definitions and testing out their reception, always attentive to possible misunderstandings and misappropriations. In the process – or perhaps it would be better to say, the process itself consisted of – the production of thousands of texts: letters and *memoriales*, bilingual dictionaries, parallel bilingual texts, Nahuatl translations and adaptations of Christian texts (prayers, hymns, parables, catechisms, sermons), and original Nahuatl works. And this is where we may look to suss out a process by which Spaniards, in the process of translating terms that had over the centuries settled into stable meaning, into a language whose own system of meaning was entirely foreign to them, revitalized their own spiritual language.

Finding Mexican Mysticism

Unfortunately for our purposes, of the thousands of texts mentioned above, products of this effervescence of linguistic and cultural translation, almost none are *explicitly* concerned with translation. Alan Durston, who has worked on early Christian *quechua*, laments the "paucity and opacity of explicit statements concerning linguistic and translation policies, which often went unremarked or were glossed over" (23).[17] I am furthermore limited by my own formation as a peninsularist who does not read or speak any indigenous American language. I am, obviously, not the ultimate person equipped to bring these discourses out from the shadows. However, in recent decades, there has been a proliferation of studies by polyglot colonial Mexicanists, and I will draw on their work with respect to a few key terms to suggest a link between the translation project and Spanish mysticism, one that hopefully other more qualified scholars than I can develop (or reject).

Even in the early years of the Colegio de Santa Cruz, centre of the most ambitious, optimistic project for Franciscan indigenous education, there was never an explicit discussion of translating or publishing mystic texts, nor do we find explicit communication about how European metaphors and symbols could be translated into a mystic Nahuatl. However, by looking at changes in the definitions and translation choices for words central to the mystic vocabulary, we can sense some of the underlying discussion over how to represent these abstract concepts in and with a new language. Several studies of the translation choices for the word "alma" (soul), as well as the strategies for translating other concepts that cannot but implicate the paradoxes of mysticism – corporeal vs. incorporeal, presence vs. absence, representation vs. the ineffable – point to a new and inevitable focus on these paradoxes among Franciscan missionaries in New Spain.[18] Although the original contexts of translation may not have been directly related to mystic practice or representation, I will suggest that the attention to the paradoxes themselves would have produced the shift in discursive stability that inaugurates the new language of mysticism among European counterparts.

A second avenue through which we can uncover a current of engagement with mysticism in early colonial Mexico is by stepping aside from the catalog of *printed* works and looking at what Louise Burkhart has identified as a "sort of literary underground." Although most evidence of this activity occurs in the later sixteenth century, there is evidence of a process of *samizdat* translation going back to the 1530s, when, "with or without the collusion of sympathetic priests, Nahuas literate in their own language were passing texts among themselves, copying them, and adapting them for their own use" (Burkhart "Voyage" 50). David Tavárez's work on a partial translation of the *Imitatio Cristi* is a crucial piece of evidence linking Mexican colonial translation and European mysticism.

Mystic Body and Soul

As has been discussed throughout this work, Christian mystic experience is paradoxical because of the Catholic dualism between matter and spirit, body and soul. The interiorized experience of the divine is a union of spirits – the piece of the divine inside connecting with the divine beyond – but it can only be experienced through the body and the bodily senses. Because the body is seen as antithetical to the spirit, this experience is paradoxical. Many of the mystic images we have examined throughout this study are unsettling precisely because they combine a vocabulary of the body with that of the spirit, interiors with exteriors, in ways that were unfamiliar or new. But the unsettling power of such images depends on a shared understanding between speaker and audience of a clear separation between body and soul, exterior and interior. In a cultural context where the body–soul dualism were not present, or were configured differently, there would be no paradox and the combination would be unremarkable. For instance, let us use the well-known example of Teresa de Ávila's transverberation, which involves a "supernatural" being taking material form and piercing the human exterior to the heart and even further, to the "entrañas," yet still producing a sensation that "no es dolor corporal, sino espiritual, aunque no deja de participar el cuerpo algo, y aun harto" (*Libro de la vida* 384; ch. XXIX sec. 13) ("is not a physical pain, but a spiritual pain, though the body has some share in it – even a considerable share" [210]). The symbolic valences of *entrañas* (a physical, corporeal essence), heart (intermediate – a physical organ but almost exclusively understood in terms of moral, emotional, and spiritual connotations), and the soul/spirit, must be clear, and clearly different, for the image to be legible.

The Nahua also placed great symbolic importance on the heart, but the contours of the symbolic implications were distinct and ultimately could not be legibly inscribed into a Christian universe. As Osvaldo Pardo notes, "in Nahua culture, the heart was associated with vital energy, understanding, and will" (119). However, whereas Christian discourse has no place for the *literal* heart, native Mexicans did offer literal hearts as sacrifice (and probably such sacrifices loomed larger and more prominently in the European concept of the Nahua culture than in their actual practice). The heart in the heart sacrifice ritual is not *only* literal – obviously, its great symbolic importance is the reason it is chosen for sacrificial offering. However, whereas Christian priests needed to perform a sacrament to convert metaphoric blood (symbolically associated with the heart) into literal blood (the blood of Christ), no such transition was required before the Mexican sacrifice because the fundamental dualism between the literal and symbolic body that makes the Eucharist a sacrament is not present in Nahua thought. When it came to translating prayers and texts that referred to the "heart" and the "soul" – sometimes as synonyms, sometimes in opposition – the friars had to find a way to emphasize the associations they wished to promote while banishing the symbolic associations with Mesoamerican sacrifice and animism.

A number of scholars have traced the development of translations of "heart" and "soul" into Nahuatl. Louise Burkhart, drawing on López Austin, writes, "The word that most closely corresponded to the Christian notion" of soul "was the – *yolia*, a life force housed in and closely associated with the heart (*yollotl*)" (Burkhart "Death" 30). Still, Jill Furst explains, "the yolia differed substantially from the Christian soul. The Mexica said that it also took the form of the breath, a shadowy double of the body, and a precious gemstone. Released from the flesh, the yolia was even embodied as a bird" (22). The fluid movement of the life force reflected the non-dualism in Nahua thought between the sacred and the natural, as is implied in the very title of Furst's book: *The Natural History of the Soul in Ancient Mexico* (a more accurate title would be *The Natural History of the Things-that-Europeans-Ascribe-to-the-Soul*). Furst examines in detail the various linguistic strategies the friars used to attempt to create a word that would disturb Nahua associations without breaking off communication entirely. The options were threefold: introduce Latin terms and run the risk of incomprehension, use old terms and run the risk of fostering non-Christian associations, or attempt a compromise via the creation of hybrid terms. Alonso de Molina's *Vocabulario en lengua castellana y mexicana*, the most important bilingual dictionary of the period, shows that all strategies were employed.[19] Between *alma* and *ánima*, he lists six options: *teanima, teyolitia, teyolia, tetonal, totonal,* and *toyolia*. As Furst explains,

> the considerable number of words reduces to four roots with two modifying prefixes … The first is a combination of the Spanish and indigenous elements: *te-*, a Nahuatl prefix denoting a non-specific, human object (Karttunen 1983:215) and *ánima*, a Spanish word for soul …
>
> The second, *teyolitia*, yields a slightly different meaning. It consists of *te-*, indicating a human object, and *yolitia*, meaning "to give life to another."
>
> The related *teyolia* and *toyolia* signify *te-* (a human) or *to-* (our), and *yolia*, a word that does not occur alone in Molina's dictionary but that apparently refers to the heart. Thus, the soul apparently is, or resides in, that organ. (14–15)

Tetonal and *totonal* draw on a root word that expands the chain of associations even further. In the Nahuatl to Spanish portion, neither is defined as "soul": "*Totonal* is defined as 'the sign, under which one is born, or the soul and spirit', whereas *tetonal* is explained as a 'portion of someone, or a thing given by another'" (15). And, in fact, as Furst draws back further and looks at Nahuatl words with "yoli" and "tonal" as roots, the web of associations broadens and becomes less and less congruous with the Christian concept of either soul or heart. Etymology is not destiny, and words may become unmoored from the sacred or natural connotations of their etymological roots. Yet as long as the root word remains recognizable, its meaning is latent, and these latent or alternate meanings are precisely what poets and mystics activate in their task of making language new again. The word "transverberation," for example, is a neologism that stems from the Latin *verberare*, or "to strike," but also reactivates a latent (or perhaps even coincidental, spurious) association with *verbum*: the word made flesh.

The multiple and overlapping options given in Molina's dictionary for "soul" suggests that different speakers and writers made lexical choices depending on the aspects of the soul they wished to emphasize or de-emphasize in a given context. Indeed, an examination of sermons and manuscripts from the period shows a wide variation in lexical choices. Suzanne Klaus, in an extensive study of Nahuatl and bilingual sermons, notes that Sahagún and his colleague Juan Bautista, both use "*anima* or *yollotl* for designating the soul ... Generally *anima* and *yollotl* have the same meaning and the terms are exchangeable" (103, 145). She contrasts this lack of differentiation with the contemporary Spanish (in Castilian, for Spaniards) *Sermonario* of Felipe Díez, in which "heart" is used for emotions and "soul" for the theological principle. This corresponds to a larger difference between the sermon cycles: where Díez uses vivid pictorial imagery and emotional language, Sahagún and Bautista "in contrast strove for avoiding any emotions in order to make objective statements" (181). She surmises that this was because the friars writing in Nahuatl:

> feared misinterpretation or confusion by the Indians, and also by those missionaries who used the sermons as models because of their insufficient command of the language. They therefore fell back to a wording which they considered unambiguous and innocuous ... The parallelism of *soul* and *heart* appears more strenuously in the sermons by Sahagún and Juan Bautista than in the texts written by Diez, because in the Nahuatl sermons feelings were mostly excluded, and they consequently do not play a role in comments referring to *yollotl* (heart). (182)

Sahagún and Bautista preferred not being understood to being misunderstood, to introducing a heart that was too close to a sacred, beating organ. However, in the process of defining/inventing the "correct" Nahuatl term for *soul*, the early missionaries were exposed to heretofore unknown associations of hearts, souls, and natural imagery. Perhaps all those incursions into the resonances of *teanima, teyolitia, teyolia, tetonal, totonal,* and *toyolia* pushed Spaniards towards the rich, unsettling associations that define Spanish mystic writing.

Klaus and Louise Burkhart have also studied the Franciscans' preoccupation and lack of consensus with regard to the translation of another fundamental mystic symbol: light. Light is essential to mystic discourse, not just because the Bible is replete with resplendent angels, stars in the East, and luminous symbolism, but also because it is a substance that lies between spirit and matter; like the divine vision, it makes an impression on the senses, but in itself is not seen (it allows us to see other things) and has no corporeal substance (at least not until Einstein). The complexities of reflection and refraction also lend themselves to conveying the unreality and paradox of the divine experience. The Franciscan Saint Bonaventure's *Mística teología,* printed twice in sixteenth-century Mexico (in Spanish) uses the various properties of light as an extended metaphor for each stage of mystic union.[20] As with the heart, then, we find in mystic discourse a play with various levels of literal, metaphoric, and symbolic light, and as with the heart, the translation of the discourse to a culture that assigned divinity to the sun forced translators to invent etymologies and neologisms that could convey the desired meanings and discard those associated with idolatry. Louise Burkhart's article "The Solar Christ in Nahuatl Doctrinal Texts of Early Colonial Mexico" contains a detailed analysis of Bernardino de Sahagún's delicate navigation of the difference between a God of light and a sun-god in three Christmas sermons. Sahagún's sermon for the Christmas Eve Midnight Mass opens with a direct response to possible confusion between sun-symbols and sun-gods. He instructs parents to tell their children:

> Notlaçopiltzine ma vel ximozcali, ma ytech timotlapololti y tonatiuh, aic ticmoteotiz aic tictlatlauhtiz: ca ca tlanextli amo yoli amo tla-caqui, amo tlachia amotle quimati: ca ca tocouh totlavil, in titlaca otechmomaquili in totecuiyo dios, inic techtlanextiliz techtlauiliz.

> Do not be confused about the sun. You will never take it as a deity, you will never pray to it, for it is just illumination, it is not alive, it does not hear, it does not see, it does not know anything. For it is just our torch, our light, which our lord God gave to us people so that it would illuminate us, it would light us. (242)[21]

Sahagún distinguishes between torches that, by metaphoric extension, light the way (*tlahuilli, tlanextli*) and the sun-god (*tonatiuh*), which in the Nahua discourse was associated with warmth rather than light (238). Having set out the proper metaphorical distinction between these two Nahua words in Christian thought, Sahagún then introduces the Latin term *anima*: 'tonatiuh yn itech povi t*anima*" ("the sun to which our souls pertain"). The new word has been defined, inserted into a newly realigned map of Nahua light associations, and for the rest of the sermon, Sahagún evidently "feels free to use the sun as a metaphor for Christ" (242). Both Burkhart and Klaus focus on the insufficiency of such a cursory doctrinal/etymological prelude for clearly establishing the contours of Christian light imagery, and speculate on the possible interpretations that the linguistic ambiguities could have produced among Nahua audiences. What is important for the purposes of this argument is to note the clear concern on the part of Europeans writing in Nahuatl for the metaphoric and literal properties of their newly appropriated or newly coined words. In the absence of texts that expressly discuss the rationale behind choosing or avoiding certain translations, these texts that address metaphoric and literal meanings of Nahua terms in a Christian universe are the best evidence we have that the task of translation forced these early Franciscans to examine the contours of their own symbols and metaphoric language.

Another striking example of intersection between Christian and Nahuatl mysticism occurs around the symbol of the mirror. In the *Florentine Codex*, Tezcatlipoca, literally Smoking Mirror, was a central deity, child of the god of duality. Fitting this lineage, Tezcatlipoca is protean, splitting into pairs and doubles. The emphasis in the Nahuatl is on the dualism of the mirror, symbolic of the dualism of the Nahuatl gods, although Tezcatlipoca's smoking mirror not only reflects his dualism but is, according to various legends, a magic mirror capable of killing enemies. This is, of course, foreign to the Trinitarian Christian cosmos, where there are no literal mirrors. Smoking or revealing mirrors, for a Christian reader, inevitably provoke a series of biblical and mystical associations, most derived from 1 Corinthians 13:12 ("through a glass darkly"). The duality of the Christian mirror symbol rests in its capacity to reveal or distort truth, but the question of distortion or revelation is pertinent to humanity's partial comprehension of divinity, not of the divine itself. However, it would seem that when European friars learned the etymology of Tezcatlipoca or came upon phrases such as "*tezcatlanextia*" ("the mirror that makes things appear"),[22] they were struck by the overlap with the Christian symbol and, I would suggest, prompted to think further of the sacred in terms of mirrors and paradoxes of light.

Proof of the chord struck can be found by turning to a small but important *corpus* of theological texts written or translated into Nahuatl, either before such labours were explicitly prohibited or afterwards, in secret. David Tavárez recounts the progressive regulations and restrictions on such projects from 1555 onward but also to the survival of a corps of "Nahua intellectuals" working independently or in collaboration with Europeans through the late sixteenth century.[23] Crucially for our study, many of their projects involved translations or commentaries on the *Imitatio Cristi*, that same book with which we began this study and identified as a turning point in the interiorization of Christianity. Because these collaborations were secret, or at least the role of native translators was hidden, it is hard to know the precise circumstances of their elaboration, such as the relationship between native and Spanish translators or the dates of any portion of work. Typically, we have only a *termino ad quem*, such as the 1570 date of the *Imitatio* attested to by Mendieta in his *Historia eclesiástica*. He writes here that he brought a *Contemptus mundi* (alternate title of the *Imitatio*) "translated into the Mexican language and written by an Indian scribe in well-formed, even, and gracious lettering" to show Juan de Ovando, president of the Council of Indies, in that year. The manuscript, which ended up in El Escorial, is much more than a direct translation. Tavárez calls it a "nonliteral Nahuatl gloss … with added commentary that includes metaphors, similes, and idioms directed toward a Nahua readership" (218). While there is no signed author, Tavárez offers two likely candidates: Antonio de Molina and Luis Rodríguez.[24] Molina was born in Spain in 1513 or 1514 and came to New Spain as a child in 1522; thus, we might suppose him to be working actively on translation projects anywhere from the 1530s onward. We have less precise biographical information for Rodríguez, but he was a provincial official in New Spain by 1562 (Tavárez 214) and thus presumably already an adult in the decade or two preceding. These dates are important if we are to think of directions of influence; as discussed in chapter one, the *Imitatio/Contemptus Mundi* was a *starting point* for interiorization but did not push language in new directions and is not mystical in the sense we are using in this work. This next step occured in Spanish texts in the 1530s and 1540s and passed from prose to poetry in the 1560s and 1570s. If we are to suppose that Franciscan projects of translation in the New World were influential in this shift and not merely reflective of it, we must (and I believe we can) place them in the intervening decades.

In addition to the El Escorial copy of the *Imitatio*, Tavárez identifies another, incomplete *Imitatio* mansucript in the John Carter Brown collection. The relationship between the two is unclear. Both are "non-literal glosses" of the *Imitatio*, but "while the Escorial *Imitatio* is a highly polished, final manuscript version with no marginalia, the JCB *Imitatio* has all the hallmarks of a working draft, as it features various interlinear and marginal Spanish glosses of the Nahuatl main text" (216). For our purposes, then, this is the more interesting text, as the glosses provide incontrovertible evidence of Franciscans collaborating back and forth from Latin to Nahuatl *through Spanish*. And once we look at the text, we see that the movement from Latin to Nahuatl involves a push towards symbols and linguistic strategies that we identify with mysticism.[25]

The JCB manuscript opens quoting John 8:12 in Latin: "Ego sum lux mu[n]di q[ui] sequitur me non ambulat in tenebris. sed habebit lumen vite: I am the light of the world, whoever follows me does not go about in darkness" (qtd. in Tavárez 219). The voice then shifts to a Nahua speaker addressing "my dear child" and cọunselling him to "listen to, take, and hold" the Word of the Lord, or, as Tavárez's literal translation renders it: "the breath of the Owner of the Near and the Nigh, our lord Jesus Christ, which is painted in this book" (219).[26] We can easily see the combination of traditional indigenous structures and terms for speaking of the world ("in tloque in navaque," a classic Nahuatl expression to represent the cosmos, heaven and earth, nigh and near)[27] with Christian proper names (Jesucristo). The text continues in a prose that reads like poetry, not just because of the denaturalizing effect of any translation but because of the abundance of metaphor, symbol, word inversion, repetition, and metonymy. In Tavárez's English translation, the holy word is "very dear ... like a gold necklace, like a precious stone necklace that he places on you. Here you take and hold it, for you will put it on tomorrow or the next day [very soon]. It will soon come to stay on your belly, on your neck" (219).[28] A few lines later, the "dear child" is told he should place the Word of God "inside himself" and "wear it like a jewel ... May it drip into your flesh and bowels" (219).[29] It may not have been unusual for a Nahua speaker to think of divine substance "dripping" into flesh and bowels (indeed, the Nahua posited the cosmos as a cycle of consumption), but the literality of the body inserted into a Christian lesson about spiritual teachings makes the language fresh, disquieting, and potent. Something that in Kempis is a commonplace (that Christ's teaching should be taken "to heart") becomes fresh; the paradoxical unity and conflict between body and soul re-emerges, just as it does in Teresa and other poetry and prose narratives of mystic union.

Along with body imagery, the dominant symbol in the opening sections of the *Imitatio* is light. The light symbolism is complex – the Word of God is "the brightness and the torch,"[30] but like a tree, it also provides shelter and shade ("a tree canopy, or something that throws or makes a shadow; people go under its shadow and shelter") (221).[31] Here, shade and shadow have a positive association with tranquility and protection, but in the next section, "clouds and fog" and "darkness or shadow" (222)[32] represent ignorance, and God's light (again "the brightness and the torch" but now the author adds to the original *difrasismo* "the dawn, the sun ray"[33]) breaks out from behind them, "a ray of sun atop the mirror" (221).[34] Christ's word is also repeatedly characterized as a "a wide mirror polished on both sides," using the same Nahua phrase "tezcatl necoc xapo" that, in the *huehuetlatolli* (speeches) and *cuicatl* (songs) is used to describe Tezcatlipoca. When Tavárez calls this "a provocative rhetorical strategy" (224), he presumably refers to the provocations the linguistic syncretism might elicit among church officials who feared it masked the persistence of idolatrous practices. (Indeed, the reactions so "provoked" are almost certainly what explains the manuscript's incomplete, anonymous status.) But I believe we can think of other "provocations" arising from the translations and glosses of which the *Imitatio* is but one eloquent example, including the provocation to think of doctrine in poetic language. For as we noticed in chapter one, the *Imitatio* begins a shift towards interiorization, but it never problematizes representation; the interior is narrated in the same way as the exterior, from an omniscient perspective, with direct language or clear similes and descriptions. The Nahua translators gloss the *Imitatio* precisely by "translating" the direct language to a figurative, poetic, register, emphasizing paradox, ambiguous symbols, and the difficulty of representing the transcendent. The Nahua *devotio moderna* texts are few in number and presumably had limited circulation in the period, but the effect on the Spanish Franciscans working with the native Mexicans may well have been to push them from representing interiority "through a glass clearly" towards the reactivation of a poetically dense, poetic register that had roots in the Christian tradition going back to the Old Testament but had been latent in the theological tomes of the late medieval period.

We commented in chapter two on the anachronism of supposing that poetry is necessarily mystic. In fact, the *religious* poetry of the late medieval period in Spain was decidedly unmystical: tending towards simple expressions of praise or expositions of doctrine. Perhaps because of European assumptions about the content of complex poetry, the missionaries in Spain did not perceive Nahua oral traditions as necessarily transmitting idolatry. Most of the pre-Columbian codexes were destroyed on the assumption that religion was the province of the book, but the missionaries actively sought to preserve native oral speech, ironically by writing it down. Sahagún, Mendieta, Bautista, Olmos, and others were all interested in pre-Christian Nahua thought and expression, and regardless of their motives in doing so, they sought to access that pre-contact world through its linguistic legacy.[35] The Nahua had a complex and culturally vital tradition of ritualized discourse, divided principally into the *tlatolli* (prose, including the *huehuetlatolli*, formal prose admonitions) and *cuicatl* (songs) – that provide evidence of the indigenous Nahua use of language, symbol, and metaphor. The most important collection of *cuicatl* is the *Cantares mexicanos*, an anthology of Nahua poems individually recorded in the sixteenth century, although the specific circumstances of transcription are mostly unknown.[36] Still, we know from Sahagún's notes that he and his native assistants at the Colegio de Tlatelolco were transcribing native oral discourse, and it is most likely that the *Cantares* were a result of this project.[37]

What is immediately striking in his analyses is the degree to which his descriptions of Nahua poetic expression resemble a description of European mystic poetry, both formally and conceptually. One of Sahagún's informants testified to the sacred nature of poetry; the artist, he testified, has a *yoltéotl*, literally a "corazón endiosado" (qtd. in León Portilla *Filosofía náhuatl* 144) ("heart filled with God"), an expression which fits perfectly with the Christian mystical idea of an interior union with the divine. The true nature of the universe cannot be represented in prose, with the usual techniques of description and speech. Instead, a complex grammatical and symbolic world must be invented to "get at the very marrow of that which exceeds all vulgar experience" (146). In León Portilla's reading, the question of "what is true?" underlies these song cycles, and the Nahua answer, he argues, is neither Aristotelian nor sceptical. Instead:

> true poetry implies a particular way of knowing, fruit of an authentic interior experience, or, if one prefers, the result of an intuition. Poetry thus becomes a hidden and veiled expression that, on the wings of symbol and metaphor leads man to stammer and draw out from within himself what he has, in a mysterious and sudden way, what he has come to perceive. The poet suffers because he feels he will never manage to say what he yearns to; but in spite of this, his words can become an authentic revelation (143–4) … it is in this sense that flower and song [i.e. poetry] is the language in which a dialogue between man and the divine is established. (147)

Nahua poetry, in León Portilla's reading, is the problematized expression of the human experience of the divine. In other words, it is a mystic discourse, or at least it is a discourse that that, to a Christian audience, would *seem* mystical, given their own presuppositions about body–soul and matter–spirit dualism. It is entirely possible that León Portilla reads symbols and metaphors, or suffering and struggle, in expressions that meant something else to a pre-Columbian Nahua poet. But this only emphasizes the degree to which these texts, when composed by Franciscans precisely in the early years of the "golden age" of Spanish mystic poetry, would have both resonated with Christian mystic discourse and suggested new avenues for poetical expression.

El Coloquio Místico

I wish to close with one final example that, to my mind, is the most convincing evidence of this "missing" link, the effect of translation *on Spanish*. Unlike the *Cantares* or collections of *huehuetlatolli*, this is not a recreation of a pre-Hispanic text but instead a text that enacts translation: of bodies across oceans, of languages, of worldviews. I refer to Sahagún's recreation of the "Coloquio de los doce," the supposed first conversation between the Franciscan emissaries led by Martín de Valencia and Nahua leaders. Sahagún claims to have worked off notes ("papeles y memorias") from the Twelve he found at the Colegio de Santa Cruz. Since he arrived in New Spain in 1529, he also would have known the majority of the Franciscans present, and perhaps some of the Nahua, personally. There is much debate as to the historical accuracy of Sahagun's version.[38] It is undoubtedly not what a tape recorder in 1524 would have picked up, but for our purposes, the degree of verisimilitude is less important than the window offered into the effect that translation and transcription might have had on Spanish religious language.

Sahagún's "Coloquio" can be divided into two different types of discourse: the Spaniards' speech to their Nahua interlocutors, and the responses of the indigenous interlocutors to the presentation by the Franciscans. While Sahagún's manscript gives side-by-side versions of the text in Nahua and Castilian, there is obviously a difference between the "original" language of these two sections.[39] The Franciscans' speech would have been in Spanish and translated by a native (presumably someone who had learned Spanish from the earlier contact with *conquistadores*); the Nahuas' speech would have been originally in Nahuatl and translated into Spanish. The difference between the style of the two sections, and the similarity of the "response" chapters to other examples of pre-Columbian indigenous speech (such as the *Cantares*), testifies to a baseline of authenticity in the transcribed speech. While chapters VI and VII may not reflect *exactly* what the Nahua "principales" (chapter VI) and "sabios" (chapter VII) said, they do seem to reflect pre-contact discursive patterns and concepts.[40] If we compare these two hybrid discursive forms (European Christian words in Nahuatl, indigenous Nahua words in response to European Christians) with the discourses they negotiate – on the one hand, pre-contact Spanish expressions of Christian doctrine and, on the other, pre-contact indigenous speech – we can get a sense of the effect of the encounter on language.

Sahagún's text is entirely in prose. Chapters I–V, which contain the Franciscans' self-presentation and brief presentation of Christian doctrine, do not seem particularly "foreign" in terms of the language or concepts espoused. León Portilla, in his annotated edition, provides notes that connect certain expressions of the Franciscans' exposition to pre-Hispanic terms and idioms.[41] This could either correspond to the intervention of the native translator who sought to make the concepts familiar to a native audience, or, as León Portilla hypothesizes, "Sahagún, with his many years of experience as a missionary and Nahuatl expert, introduced terminology that had only become frequent with the passage of time" (*Estudio introductorio* 22). However, our interest is in showing an effect of the encounter on Spanish religious language or thought, and this is little apparent in the Spanish transcription/creation of the Franciscans' speech.[42] While the proper names and references to historical events clearly marks the unprecedented circumstances producing the document, the language of evangelization is similar to what we might find in Paul's letter to the Romans or Talavera's sermons for the *moriscos*.

This changes in chapter VI, when the text switches to the "voice" of the indigenous leaders. Even in Sahagún's prose translation, the text becomes rich in poetic language. The "señores principales" thank the Franciscans for their message:

> parécenos avéis abierto un cofre de riquezas divinas del Señor del cielo, y de las riquezas del gran Sacerdote que es Señor de la tierra … avéis mostrado todos los géneros de piedras preciosas, puríssimas, resplandecientes, sin mancha ni raza alguna, gruesas y redondas, saphiros, esmeraldas, rubíes y perlas; avéisnos mostrado plumajes nuevos, ricos y de gran valor. (86; ch. VI)

> It seems you have opened for us a chest of divine riches from the Lord of the Sky, and the riches of the great Priest who is Lord of the earth … you have showed us all manner of precious stones, so pure, shining, entirely

> without defects or threads, thick and round, saphires, emeralds, rubies and pearls; you have showed us new feathers, rich and of great value.

The "señores principales" pass the Franciscans' message along to the "sátrapas," who respond with a formal speech. The parallelism noted in the Franciscans' address now is employed not as simple coupling of synonyms but in full-fledged *difrasismos*, such as we noted in the *Imitatio* and indeed all Nahua poetry and ritual prose. The Spaniards came, in the words of the Nahua priests, "por la mar entre las nubes y nieblas" ("by sea between the clouds and the sky"). The Nahua are humbled to receive such a message since "por hierro nos a puesto nuestro Señor en las esquinas de su estrado y silla" (88; ch. VII) ("with iron our Lord has placed us in the corner of his dais and throne"). There is also a repeated use of literal body parts where Spanish would not specify them: "Embiáos Dios entre nosotros por ojos, oydos y boca suya, el que es invisible y spiritual en vosotros se nos muestra visible y oymos con nuestras orejas sus palabras" (88; ch. VII) ("God sends you among us as his eyes, ears and mouth, He who is invisible and spiritual is made visible through you and we hear with our ears your words"). León Portilla's direct translation of the Nahuatl renders these effects even more notable, with the Spaniards coming "en medio de nubes, en medio de nieblas,/ del interior del agua inmensa habéis venido a salir./ A vosotros os hace ojos suyos, a vosotros os hace oídos suyos,/ a vosotros os hace labios suyos el Dueño del cerca y del junto" (147; ch. VII) ("in the midst of clouds, in the middle of fog,/ from the interior of the great water you have come to leave./ He makes of you his eyes, He makes of you his ears, He makes of you his lips, the Lord of near and far"). Sahagún's "esquinas de su estrado y silla" is, in the poetic translation, "la punta de su estera, la punta de su sitial" ("the point of his dais, the point of his throne") and León Portilla comments that it is a "a well-known *difrasismo* that denotes authority" (149; ch. VII, note 7).

All these protestations of humility and acceptance of the Franciscans' words are quickly revealed to be generic obligations of courtesy, as the *sabios* move on to respond with polite but complete rejection of the Franciscans' monotheism.[43] "No recibáis pena, señores nuestros, por que con delicadeza y curiosidad queremos examinar los divinos secretos, bien ansí como sin temeridad a hurto quisiésemos entreabrir el cofre de las riquezas para ver lo que está en él" (88; ch. VII) ("Do not be afflicted, our Lords, if with delicacy and curiosity we wish to examine the divine secrets, just as if we, without recklessness, wished to secretly peek into the chest of riches to see what is inside"). The call to open a secret treasure, to peer inside at the divine mysteries almost like thieves, cannot but echo the mystery at the heart of mysticism. It is not hard to imagine that this metaphor resonated with the Franciscan interlocutors (and Sahagún's cohorts a generation later) *because* it echoes medieval mystic discourse. Indeed, if we compare Sahagún's translation with the literal rendering of León Portilla – "Pero tranquilícense vuestros corazones, vuestra carne,/ señores nuestros,/ porque romperemos un poquito,/ ahora un poquito abriremos,/ el cofre, la petaca, del Señor Nuestro" ("But rest your hearts, your flesh/ our lords/ if we break a little/ now we open up a little/ the chest, the *petaca*, of Our Lord") – we can already see Sahagún moulding the strange structure and symbols of Nahua poetry to a recognizable language (149; ch. VII). *Petacas* did not have a Catholic resonance, but the "cofre de riquezas" filled with "divinos secretos" did.

Dana Bultman has gone the furthest in linking Osuna's contemplative practices to "Nahua/Spanish dialogue" although, despite her call to put "Nahuatl terms first as the central framework for evaluating contact between Franciscan and Nahua conceptual and linguistic fields," she still imagines that what needs to be unearthed is the "the influence of Osuna's contemplative training on missionary cultural production": Europe's influence on America. But because of the near-simultaneity of the phenomena of the early years of linguistic contact and the authorship of the *Abecedarios,* I see no reason to assume that in this dialogue, the influence did not go both ways. Bultman summarizes the numerous "suggestive resonances one can find between Nahua and Franciscan concepts of 'soul,'" including "an understanding of interior animating forces as composite in nature … the heart as a central receptacle of divine fire, the relationship of heat and light with intelligence, and the intellect's connection to the natural energy of the sun" (311). I do not think (nor does Bultman claim) that the Franciscan brothers' beliefs changed substantially through contact with Nahua religion. The Franciscans did not come to the Americas with an "open mind" about their faith or doctrine, but they came with open minds – indeed, blank slates – when it came to their beliefs about the Mexican languages. And it is there that syncretism occurred: not initially on the level of doctrine, but on the level of representation. For the Nahua informants who sought to or were compelled explain the contours of their language to the Franciscans, the birds, winds, blood, etc. that defined their spiritual universe may or may not have been metaphors or symbols. The Franciscans "met" their interlocutors at the point of contact of recognizable symbols. For them, hearts, birds, and winds had power as metaphors and symbols, and if immediately they employed and emphasized these symbols to make Christianity legible to the native Mexicans, they also inevitably reiterated Christianity in metaphoric, visual, corporeal terms for themselves. It is this emphasis of the corporeal or natural world in the representation of immaterial, spiritual experience that they passed back to their brothers in Europe and that energized a European spiritual community which, for many other factors intrinsic to the history of Renaissance Europe, was already experiencing a spiritual revolution.

Final Thoughts

Imitations, translations, revolutions, circulations: this is the story of this book. I have attempted to trace the transformations of a discourse of interiorized mystic union as it traversed continents, genres, and institutional settings. The archaeology of discourse attempts to identify moments when words and ideas cohere into solid textual forms, but as this study has shown, a discourse that is about the irruption of transcendence is never truly settled or stable: when it settles, it is no longer transcendent. Manuals of contemplative prayer, mystic poems, and *vidas espirituales* are themselves negotiated texts, in which authors innovate against a backdrop of known, shared codes of meaning, and in doing so transform those very codes. We have considered how, in Counter-Reformation Spain, institutional pressures worked to fix those meanings and how individuals, many also affiliated with those same institutions, "colaron" through such attempts (to borrow a phrase from María Pizarro, the would-be mystic discussed in chapter three). Institutions as diverse as the Inquisition and the theatre can be linked together as forming and reforming according to an impulse, not so much to impose any one doctrine on the Spanish public but to guarantee their right to fix meaning, to confirm their authority over the words used to approximate the Word. There are very real people with real intentions behind these struggles, and this study has sought to respect their agency and individuality at the same time that it recognizes that the reason these words-approaching-the-Word are so transformative is because the ultimate ineffability of the Word means their meaning can always escape those intentions. In the context of other social and technological transformations, such as those we find at the dawn of the modern era in Spain, that slippage becomes uniquely fraught and uniquely potent and can be traced through the "interior" of processes as diverse as missionary translation, prayer treatises, mystic poetry, convent autobiography, Inquisition transcripts, and theatre scripts. Interpretation and enunciation of the ineffable becomes the mysterious lance that reverberates, *trans*verberates, across the early modern Spanish world.

Notes

Introduction

1 See *Marxism and Literature* Ch. 8.
2 James, William. *The Varieties of Religious Experience.*
3 Katz, Steven. *Mysticism and Philosophical Analysis.* Katz returns to this question in the later *Mysticism and Language.*
4 Particularly in the last thirty years, there has been a spate of historically contextualized, language-based studies of the works of Santa Teresa de Jesús and, to a lesser extent, San Juan de la Cruz. What is lacking, and what this book seeks to provide, is the return to a moment *before* Santa Teresa and San Juan were elevated above and separated from their fellow (would-be) mystics and writers on mysticism, and an analysis of these other voices and how their words intersected, influenced, and engaged the canonical mystics.
5 Most, but not all, scholars of mysticism agree that ineffability is a fundamental characteristic of mysticism. There is a tradition of prophetic, visionary spirituality that does not seem to struggle in its expression in language (see Don Cupitt, *Mysticism After Modernity*, for the argument for its inclusion in the category of "mysticism"). My exclusion of such visionary narratives in my study does not reflect a belief that they are less valid or less worthy of historical study. However, as I hope to show, it is specifically a struggle over language that links the developments in spiritual practice with the social and institutional changes specific to early modern Spain. A study of visionary prophets in early modern Spain (such as María de Santo Domingo, Juana de la Cruz, Lucrecia de León, and María de Ágreda) would be just that: a series of analyses of successive individuals and a symbolic analysis of their visions. It would not reveal transformations in subjectivity, law, and social structures. For biography, textual analysis, and further bibliography of María de Santo Domingo, see

Sanmartín Bastida and Curto Hernández; for Juana de la Cruz, Surtz; for Lucrecia de León, Kagan or Jordán Arroyo; María de Ágreda, Fedewa.

6 I am paraphrasing; de Certeau's actual distinction, which does not work in English, is between *lo místico* (mystic as adjective) and *la mística* (mystic as noun).

7 De Certeau here quotes J. Baruzi "Introduction a des recherches sur le langage mystique" en *Recherches philosophiques*, 1931–2, 75.

8 "Movement was essential. It was characterized both by a *shift of the subject* within the meaning space circumscribed with words and by a *technical manipulation* of these words in order to mark the new way in which they were being used … It denatured language: it distanced it from the function that strove after an imitation of things" (140–1).

9 The scholarship on early Christian and medieval mysticism is vast, but for a general introduction and further bibliography, see Bernard McGinn's magisterial series *The Presence of God* (a lifelong project that, as of 2020, consists of six volumes and eight separate titles).

10 Denys Turner is right to protest the tendency to represent "affirmative and negative theologies are alternative theological strategies" or "successive" stages of mysticism (hierarchically or chronologically). He is correct that even a "dead metaphor" is a metaphor, and "the tensions between affirmation and negation within all theological speech are, precisely, what determine it to be theological speech, and to be, in the only worthwhile sense of the term, 'mystical.'" ("Darkness of God and the Light of Christ" 147) We may accept that the literary strategies of negation that prevail in "apophatic" mystic works are not truly negative (a lack of strategies) and still recognize the linguistic, literary difference between the abstract, neo-Platonist writings of pseudo-Dionysius and the exuberant, erotic mysticism of Julian of Norwich or Catherine of Siena.

11 For instance, Giles Constable in *The Reformation of the Twelfth Century* 266, Martin and Barresi, *The Rise and Fall of Soul and Self* 90.

12 Hillgarth, *Encyclopedia of Philosophy*. Not all Llull scholars share this opinion.

13 See Fort i Cogul; Lea *History of the Inquisition in the Middle Ages*, Vol. II, 162–80 for the Tribunal in Aragon.

14 See Asin Palacios y López Baralt, *Sadilies y alumbrados*, López Baralt *San Juan de la Cruz y el Islám*.

15 "These include interiority; metaphors of light; wine, and architectural space; the hidden, arcane, and always elusive meaning of the text; mystical union; mystical drunkenness; sudden, even violent onslaughts of mystical ecstasy (*arrebatamiento*); mystical transformation; divine wisdom or illumination (*alumbramiento*) visited upon the mystic in a sort of lightning bolt (*relámpago*); the piercing of the heart or soul with 'swords of love.'"

16 See Andrés Martín's essay "Alumbrados, Erasmians, 'Lutherans' and Mystics" for an account of the "common denominator" between *alumbrados*, Erasmians, Lutherans, and mystics, as well as the inconsistencies in categorization.

17 Rafael García Pérez examines in detail the print and circulation history of the works highlighted by Melquíades Andrés Martín in *La imprenta y la literatura espiritual castellana en la España del Renacimiento*. Although he opens the study by asking some of the same questions that guide this work regarding the space and role of books of interior spirituality within a larger cultural matrix (14) – in the end, the strict focus on the books as physical objects themselves limits his ability to perceive wider circulation and transformation of phrases, ideas, and dynamics.

18 For more on Cisneros's textual patronage, see Ch. 8 "La producción religiosa y hagiográfica," in Gómez Redondo, especially 832–8. For Cisneros's role in supporting female spirituality, see Howe.

19 As Sarah Nalle writes in a thorough study of the question, "despite the very important differences in [seven prior] studies' methodologies, the results form a consistent picture … The popularity of reading first increased between 1407 and 1458 … During the sixteenth century reading appears to have spread into the lower classes of Spanish society, so that levels of literacy were much higher in early modern Spain than scholars have estimated previously" (67–9). Of relevance for this book are two additional studies of female literacy levels during the period: Anne Cruz's "Reading over Men´s Shoulders" and Darcy Donahue's "Wondrous Words," dedicated to secular and religious women, respectively. Both are to be found in the edited volume *Women's Literacy in Early Modern Spain and the New World*.

20 Using Foucault's concepts, we might point here to an evidence of how institutions/disciplines shape interpretation at the most fundamental level. Secular academia may read the same texts as a theologian (who is, in this case, also an academic), but we are not applying the same standards of analysis.

21 See Weber "The Three Lives."

22 See Keitt *Inventing the Sacred*; Sluhovsky *Believe Not Every Spirit*.

23 The most monumental of these is Álvaro Huerga's five-volume *Historia de los alumbrados (1570–1630)* (Madrid: Fundación Universitaria Española, 1978). Studies of particular groups of *alumbrados* or facets of *alumbradismo* include Sarrión Mora, Keitt, Hamilton, Andrés Martín ("Alumbrados, Erasmians, 'Lutherans' and Mystics").

1. Prayer Manuals

1 Due to the importance of language-based arguments to this book, I have left all original source quotes in the original Spanish, while all secondary

sources are presented in English. Unless otherwise noted, translations are my own.

2 Since the fifteenth century, the authors' identity has been a matter of debate. In addition to Kempis, other candidates are Jean Gerson, St. Bernard of Clairvaux, Ludolph of Saxony, and Giovanni Gersen. J. van Ginneken asserts that the work had no single author. For more on the authorship debate, Von Habsburg 3–5.

3 For catalogue information of known translations of the *Imitatio Christi* between 1470 and 1650, see von Habsburg. For a discussion of the Spanish translations, see Andrés Martín, "Alumbrados, Erasmians, 'Lutherans' and Mystics." All quotes from the *Imitatio* are from the Creasy translation.

4 See Von Habsburg ch. 9.

5 To sense the lack of "true" dialogue in the *Imitatio*, one might read *I colloqui* of Maria Maddalena de'Pazzi, an Italian mystic whose conversations with a variety of spiritual beings during raptures were transcribed by fellow nuns. Although at times Saint Teresa and others approximate the experience of rapture in their written word, as we will see in chapter three, Maddalena's *Colloqui* are the only example I know in which the entire text is a verisimilar recreation of mystic dialogue between the "self" and a Holy Spirit. Maria Maddalena de' Pazzi's *Colloqui* are magnificently analysed in Maggi's *Uttering the Word*.

6 See, for example, *Carro de dos vidas* Part I, Chapter XLVI (183–5) and the extended use and rejection of comparisons with earthly light, or Chapter LIV (203), where a swirl of prepositions disengages from any easily imaginable, spatial referent. Both of these strategies will reappear, and in more extreme and concentrated form, in Osuna and Laredo, the treatises whose analysis occupies the bulk of this chapter.

7 The textual phenomena that interest me are not limited to these two texts, but out of the corpus cited by Andrés Martín (*Historia de la mística de la Edad de Oro*), these are the two in which the narration of mystic union as interior process most consistently produces linguistic disruption and innovation. Furthermore, both texts are cited by the canonical Spanish mystics (Santa Teresa, San Juan de la Cruz), evidence of the circulation and influence of their ideas and words.

8 For individual biographies of Osuna and Laredo, see Pacho (for Osuna, 408–15, for Laredo, 486–90 and Boon *The Mystical Science of the Soul* ch. 2).

9 For more on the chronology and structure of the six *Abecedarios*, see Calvert 14–18. Here, we are concerned principally with the third and fourth *Abecedarios*, dedicated respectively to "recogimiento" and the "ley de amor." Similar phenomena to those analysed can be found in the others, but it is in the third and fourth that Osuna focuses most intensely on the achievement of mystic union and hence where the textual phenomena that interest us are most pronounced.

10 All quotes from the *Tercer abecedario espiritual* give the book, chapter, and page number in the López Santidrián edition. English translations of the *Tercer Abecedario* are from the Giles translation and give the corresponding page number. Translations from the other *Abecedarios* are my own.

11 For example, Dionysius the Areopagite provides an analysis of the etymologies of "cherubim" and "seraphim" in *The Celestial Hierarchy* ch. 7. Hugh of St. Victor also provides commentary on the same (see Kirchberger). The importance of etymology can be seen in the very title of the Areopagite's most influential work, *On the Divine Names*, repeatedly translated and commented by medieval exegetes. For more on the textual transmission of the Areopagite through the medieval period, see Harrington 1–44. Along with the commentaries on *The Song of Songs*, this is the most common topic for mystical commentary running into the early modern period.

12 The more intellectual exegetical tradition is also present in early modern Spain, as in Fray Luis de León's *De los nombres de Cristo*, in which he draws heavily on his knowledge of classical and Semitic languages for etymological exegesis, without returning every meaning to interiority itself.

13 The question is repeated various times in the chapter.

14 I refer throughout this chapter to medieval practices of scriptural allegory. While medieval Christian authors certainly differ in their particular applications of allegorical exegesis, the method of four-level scriptural exegesis (literal, moral, allegorical, anagogical) is laid out in Cassian (c. 350 CE–c. 435 CE) and Augustine and practiced with some consistency through Aquinas. For a clear enunciation of the theory and practice of late classical/early Christian allegory, see Turner "Cambridge Companion to Allegory" 71–2 (the examples of Nicholas of Lyra and Cassian). The example from Nicholas of Lyra of the fourfold reading of the word Jerusalem provides a perfect counterpart to Osuna: for Lyra, the "allegorical sense" is Jerusalem as "church militant" and the "anagogical sense" is "the Church triumphant": in both cases, the referent is external and grows broader.

15 Additional examples: a reading of Psalm 146:2 "Building up Jerusalem, the Lord will gather together all the exiles of Israel" that Osuna interprets to mean "Jerusalen es tu pacífica voluntad; Israel, tu entendimiento luchador inquiriendo; al cual se promete la vision de Dios" (I.3.140) ("Your Jerusalem is an undisturbed will and your Israel is the warrior understanding thirsting for the vision of God that is promised it" [57]). Solomon's temple, with its inner patio of three types of stone (3 Kings 6:36) prefigures three powers of the soul: "el pacífico Rey y Señor nuestro edifica el patio interior de nuestra ánima con estas tres ordenadas jerarquías, que se llaman piedras porque nos hacen estables, y polidas porque nos

hacen muy polidos y claros en el amor y conocimiento de lo que amamos" (VII.3.258–9) ("The peaceful King and Our Lord also builds the interior patio of our souls with these three ordered hierarchies, which like polished stones make us resolute and shining and clear in love and knowledge of our Beloved" [186]).

16 The *Cuarto Abecedario* is also known as the *Ley de amor*. All references are to the *Místicos franciscanos españoles* edition. All English translations of the *Abecedarios* other than the third are my own.

17 For example, he draws out from the *Cantares* the interiority of seeds in fruit: "ésta dice el Espíritu Sancto que está escondida, como se esconden los granos de la granada debajo de la corteza y de las telicas delgadas que están dentro" (*Tercer Abecedario* II.5.127) ("the Holy Spirit says that it is hidden, like pomegranate seeds beneath the rind and slender membranes within" [82]); he reads a passage about Elizabeth in the Bible and notes that "Elisabet quiere decir septenario de Dios, y significa los siete dones del Espíritu Sancto que en la contemplación se reciben" (II.7.135) ("Elizabeth signifies God's septenarius and refers to the seven gifts of the Holy Spirit granted in contemplation" [91]).

18 Richard of St. Victor was a twelfth-century Scottish monk. Although all his works touch on contemplation, perhaps the most important for later mystics is *De arca mystica* (1494), also known as the *Benjamin Major*. In the Spanish context, St. Richard's influence is most evident in Gómez García's *Carro de dos vidas*.

19 This history is synthesized in Gavrilyuk and Coakley, eds., *The Spiritual Senses*.

20 For the sixteenth-century vocabulary of emotions, see Elena Carrera, "The Emotions in Sixteenth-Century Spanish Spirituality."

21 In the *Cuarto Abecedario*, Osuna writes of the "verdadera ciencia de amor" ("true science of love") which, he goes on to say, consists in "ver a Jesucristo en la conciencia" (451) ("seeing Jesus Christ in your conscience"). Again, a science is proposed and defined in terms that are indefinite, incompatible with science.

22 I have eliminated the BAC edition's in-text references to specific Bible books, as they are inconsistent. The "fornaz" is a reference to 3 Daniel; Eliseo's "cámara secreta" is in 2 Reyes 6; the garden of King Asuero (also known as Xerxes) is in Esther.

23 Mystical commentaries, particularly those centred on the *Song of Songs* (*Cantar de los cantares*), have always dealt with the relation between corporeal and spiritual manifestations of love. Osuna is drawing on an existing tradition, but because he is writing in the vernacular, and as we see, his writings eventually escape the circle of men who have professed celibacy, this corporeal and often sensual language takes on new

connotations. For more on the tradition of exegesis of the *Song of Songs*, see Astell, *The Song of Songs in the Middle Ages* and E. Ann Matter, *The Voice of My Beloved*.

24 In her first chapter of *Heretical Mixtures*, Dana Bultman emphasizes Osuna's unusual (for a Catholic theologian) willingness to engage the body in the perfection of the spirit (29–55).

25 See Gavrilyuk and Coakley.

26 I have slightly adjusted the published translation to match the original verb mode.

27 In "Doing it for God," Paul Whitehill uses the term to denote the relationship Osuna proposes between *recogimiento* and the life of Christ. However, I would extend it to denote Osuna's view of the relationship between interiors and exteriors in general. While his theology does not necessarily differ from the medieval model of the "great chain of being," his focus and his writing style is circular rather than linear – the cosmos reflects the "mundo menor" as much as the process functions in reverse.

28 In an article published as this book was in press, Estelle Garbay-Velazquez catalogues the various spatial metaphors in Osuna, Bernaradino de Laredo (discussed later in this chapter), and fellow Franciscan Bernabé de Palma. See Garbay-Velázquez, "Representaciones del espacio interior e intimidad espiritual."

29 In another notable passage from the *Tercer Abecedario*, he proposes the similarity between the soul and a vessel and continues for pages extending the properties of the vessel to the soul: "Y hemos de derramar del corazón todo criado pensamiento, como le derrama el agua sin de ella ninguna cosa quedar, para que así sea lleno del divino licor y agua viva de la gracia del Señor. Esta evacuación es muy al revés de las otras que el Sabio dice ser hechas en los corazones de los malos que, según dice, son vasos quebrados que no pueden tener en sí la sabiduría, de los cuales dice: Las gracias de los locos serán derramadas. Estas vacuaciones se hacen por estar los vasos quebrados, mas las de los justos no, sino por estar sus vasos enteros y llenos del fuego del espíritu del amor, que los enciende tanto, que por el gran fervor echan de sí todo lo criado y no lo sufren; donde para figura de aquesto todos los vasos del templo de Dios habían de ser purificados con fuego, para que del todo quedasen perfectamente apurados" (IV.5.175–6). ("Like water, we are to pour out all creaturely thought from the heart, leaving nothing within, so that it will be filled with divine liquid and the living water of the Lord's Grace. This emptying is very much the opposite of other kinds that the wise man says are effected in the hearts of the wicked who, according to his explanation, are broken vessels that cannot hold wisdom and about whom he says: 'The graces of the foolish are spilled out.' These emptyings occur because they are broken glasses, but

those of the just occur because their glasses are whole and full of the fire of the spirit of love, which burns so intensely that their great fervor will not tolerate anything creaturely and casts it out. This image suggests that all vessels in God's temple must be purified with fire until they are perfectly cleansed of everything" [135]).

30 See also Cargogni 224–8.

31 See Huerga. Alonso de la Fuente and the *alumbrados* will be discussed in detail in chapter four.

32 I have adjusted the published translation to match the original more precisely.

33 The internal quote is from José Luis Pardo, *La intimidad*, Valencia, Pre-Textos, 1996, 301.

34 He remains within the accepted position of the Church that salvation via vocal prayer and good works is possible, but he is not ambiguous in stating that – again, for his assumed monasterial audience – mental prayer and *recogimiento* is superior.

35 All references are to the book, chapter (or, in this case, the preliminary section title), and page number in the *Fundación universitaria española* edition. I have modernized spelling. English translations from the first two books are my own. For the third book (the only one for which there exists a published translation), translations are by E. Allison Peers.

36 Francisco de Osuna makes the argument in the *Tercer Abecedario* that "saber" (to know) is etymologically related to "sabor" (taste) (VI.2).

37 Laredo paraphrases pseudo-Dionysius here, in a typical expression of apophatic mysticism.

38 To cite only one of many instances.

39 There is no shortage of viscerally graphic medieval narratives, and there also exist medieval Latin treatises on the nature of Christ's body and blood, such as those written in the aftermath of a miraculous bleeding host in Wilsnack, in early fifteenth-century Germany and analysed by Caroline Walker Bynum in *Miraculous Blood*, 36–43.

40 Boon notes that Laredo's meditations seem to suppose a circulatory theory before it was proposed by Miguel Servet, traditionally acknowledged as the first European to make such a claim (115). It seems to me unlikely that Laredo is thinking of any literal process in his treatise, given his free re-combination of body parts and processes in other aspects of the meditation. This seems more of a case of life-imitating allegory.

41 Laredo continues with an etymological argument, tracing the meanings of *espíritu* and *mente* to arrive at the conclusion that "de aquí viene que la contemplación quietísima, y reposada, y muy pura llámase oración mental, que quiere decir oración de sola el ánima en su pura substancia esencial, ajena de sus potencias inferiores" (305) ("thus we conclude that the

quietest, settled, very pure contemplation is called mental prayer, which means prayer by the soul alone in its pure essential substance, divorced from the inferior faculties" [72]).

42 The wordplay and fine etymological distinctions of this section are impossible to maintain in translation.

43 Again, the etymological wordplay cannot be preserved in translation.

44 *Madre* is mother, there is no way to maintain this etymology, or the sound echo of *mar* (sea) and *madre* in English.

45 A note indicates that the translator has changed *poder* in the original for *poner*.

46 I have modified the translation slightly to maintain the prepositional parallelism with the original.

47 This ranges from single sentences to a section that covers three chapters (III, 35–8, 400–8) and is taken directly from Enrique Suso's *Horologio de la sabiduría eterna* (Henry of Suso, *Horologium sapientiae*).

48 Although those readers who look only for doctrinal clarity have done so. Eulogio Pacho, for example, complains of the "abundance of repeated explanations, the lack of a complete and ordered analysis of the book's central narrative" (534) and the "arbitrarily prolonged and overly forced allegories" (491). He has a similar critique of Osuna's *Abecedarios* (436–8).

49 Pego Puigbó: "The tradition of exercises of mental prayer … would crystallize in Counter Reformation spirituality through Ignatius of Loyola's book, which converted meditation into an application of the faculties to Scripture, to the point of later facilitating the systematic presence of the visual as the element that configures literary discourse" (58).

50 In "Loyola's Spiritual Exercises and the Modern Self," Moshe Sluhovksy provides an excellent analysis of the transition in the use and interpretation of the *Exercises* over the second half of the sixteenth century, and the compromises that permitted their survival in the period of Inquisitorial persecution of mystics. "The history of Loyola's *Spiritual Exercises* is thus a history of both the emergence of a new sense of modern individual subjecthood and of the anxiety this novelty brought with it … The Jesuits escaped the silencing and repression of *alumbradismo* lay spirituality during the first half of the sixteenth century, but by 1600 the individualized subject-formation the *Exercises* had originally cultivated was restricted significantly" (228). For more on the development of the Jesuit order, see O'Malley *The First Jesuits*.

51 In *Mysticism and the Golden Age of Spain*, McGinn synthesizes the change in Loyola's reputation as a mystic: "The historical image of Ignatius of Loyola (1491–1556) has changed dramatically over the past seven decades. For almost four centuries Ignatius was viewed as the prime soldier of

the Counter Reformation, the stern ascetic, the iron-willed founder of the Society of Jesus, and the creator of the rigid Ignatian method of prayer … Renewed study of Ignatius's *Spiritual Exercises*, as well as the reflections about his life down to 1538 that he dictated to one of his followers between 1553 and 1555, the *Acts* (*Acta*), have helped shift the modern view of Ignatius firmly in the direction of his mysticism." Several of the essays in the Brill *Companion to Loyola* deal with the changes in Loyola's reputation and his relationship to mysticism, particularly Roldan Figueroa's essay relating Loyola to Juan de Ávila. See also Darcy Donahue "The Mysticism of Saint Ignatius de Loyola" in *A Companion to Jesuit Mysticism*.

52 Emilio Orozco Díaz *Poesía y mística* 135.

53 In his *Autobiography*, Loyola mentions having read the *Vita Christi* while recovering from his battle injury. See O'Reilly 2012, 642–5 for the influence of the *Vita Christi* on the *Exercises*.

54 Roland Barthes perceptively links the *Exercises* and *Diario* as part of a "structure made up of relays" between a transmitting agent and a receiving agent (43). He identifies distinct chains of transmission superimposed within the *Exercises* themselves: Loyola to the retreat director; the retreat director to the retreatant; the retreatant to God; and God to the retreatant. The *Diario* closes the circle, placing the original "author"/creator (Loyola) in the position of receiver. Unfortunately, there is no facsimile or accessible copy of the manuscript, held in Rome but apparently severely deteriorated. The Biblioteca de Autores Cristianos edition attempts to reproduce the irregular notes, deletions, and symbols of the original.

55 This dilemma is most clearly stated within the *Diario* on day 1:8, "no tener renta alguna" ("to have no income at all"). See Mendizábal "Introducción" 179–85 for more on this choice.

56 Mendizábal, regarding the "loqüela": "We will probably never know precisely the nature of this gift that Ignacio certainly values so much. Of course it is not similar to the interior or exterior locutions described in the authors of spiritual treatises" (199).

57 The <> symbols represent words that were crossed out by Loyola in the original manuscript. The BAC edition preserves or, where this is typographically impossible, recreates via symbolic substitutions, the original manuscript in all its idiosyncrasy (unlike S. Thió's "corrected" version in *La intimidad del peregrino*), although the editors are inconsistent in noting deletions in the text or as footnotes. I have restored all cross-outs to the text itself, between the <> symbols. The deletions are evidence of the layers of textual modification that Loyola went back and read his own text, and the obvious process of self-editing that in some unclear way accompanied his own process of self-reading and self-making.

58 According to Mendizabal, the Virgin and Jesus Christ.

59 For all translations of the *Diario*, I have done my best to reproduce the level of linguistic irregularity, the balance between sense and non-sense, of the original.

60 The abbrevations "a," "l," and "d" indicate whether the tears came "antes" (before), "a lo largo" (during), or "después de" (after) the mass.

61 Because the *Exercises* is not a text primarily meant to be read, there is no definitive manuscript nor is the precise word choice of great importance, as it was for the mystic manuals discussed previously in this section. For this reason, I will cite only the Ganss English translation.

62 Sluhovsky rightly highlights the importance of Loyola's innovation of the insertion of a spiritual director between the text and the practitioner, both for expanding the circle of contemplative practice but also for guaranteeing orthodoxy ("Loyola's Spiritual Exercises" 220–3).

63 Barthes also emphasizes this contrast between the mystics and Loyola. Unlike the mystics for whom language is a necessary obstacle in the goal to transcend language, "What he [Loyola] is striving to obtain is more the sign of God than knowledge of Him or His presence; language is his definitive horizon and articulation an operation he can never abandon in favor of indistinct – ineffable – states" (53).

64 And additionally in the insertion, near the very end of the *Exercises*, of 18 "Rules for Thinking With the Church" (points 352–370). O'Malley notes that these can be interpreted as "balancing the rest of the text" or more directly as "an 'antidote' to the heretics of the day," both Lutherans and *alumbrados* (49–50).

65 In the Index of 1551, there figures only one *libro de oración*. In the famous Valdés Index of 1559, there are more titles in the section of "libros espirituales" than any other section, except for books by heretics: 13 Latin works and 25 in Spanish, including Fray Luis de Granada, Juan de Ávila, Bernabé de Palma, and Francisco de Borja (Andrés Martín *Historia de la Mística* 315).

66 I have slightly modified the translations to match the original.

67 Speaking to "otra persona muy mucho aventajada en las cosas espirituales … me dijo que algunas veces se le ofrecía en estos tales puntos padecer tanta violencia, que le parecía apartársele unas de otras las costillas y que creía ser aquello; porque hay tiempos en los cuales todo el cielo se le haría al ánima lugar estrecho para la poder caber, y querría ensanchar los límites de su enterramiento" (601) ("another person very far advanced in spiritual things … told me that sometimes these motions were so violent that the very ribs seemed to be torn asunder, and that the person who experienced them believed that this was happening to him. For there are times when the whole of the heavens would be too narrow to

contain the soul, so that it would try to enlarge the limits into which it had withdrawn" [265]).

68 "Aunque en nuestros tiempos haya muchas personas visitadas de Dios con abundancia de gracia, también hay muchos tan ajenos della, que viendo en otros por algunas señales exteriores lo que no ven en sí, ténenlos por locos y engañados o endemoniados" (V.2.185) ("Although there are many people these days whom God visits with a plenitude of grace, there are also many others far removed from grace who, when they see outward evidence in others of what they themselves lack, consider them demented, deceived, or demonized, or at the very least, hypocritical" [144]).

69 The injunction to discern spirits ("believe not every spirit") goes back to the Bible (John 4:1), but in the early modern period it became for the first time a central preoccupation of theologians, confessors, and everyday Catholics. The first important treatises in this "science" are Jean Gerson's *De probatione spirituum and De distinctione verarum visionum a falsis*, but it is after the Council of Trent that the topic truly becomes an obsession in Spain, with a corresponding proliferation of theological and practical treatments of the question. For a concise history of the shift and a bibliography of the key works, see Keitt ch. 3, Sluhovsky *Believe Not Every Spirit* pt. III.

70 In fact, Loyola uses the term "discernment of spirits" for the process of self-identification of the signs of God's will, but this is an entirely separate concept.

71 For titles of prayer manuals written and published between 1560 and 1650, see Andrés Martín, *Historia de la mística* 165–85. Among the most popular authors publishing new works in this category, as measured by print runs and translations, are Diego de Estella, Luis de Granada, Diego Pérez de Valdivia, Juan de los Angeles, Leandro de Granada, Jerónimo Gracián de la Madre de Dios, and Juan Eusebio Nieremberg. It should be noted that these pages form part the better part of a catalog of 1,200 distinct "obras espirituales" (a category from which he excludes saints' lives, sermons, theatre, and "Scholastic treatises except in cases of extreme importance" [152]) *published* in the Spanish Empire between 1492 and 1720, the vast majority originally in Castilian. See 153–201 for the entire list, which includes details on publication and translation.

72 See Virgilio Pinto Crespo "Control ideológico" and Angel Alcalá Galve "Control de espirituales," both in *Historia de la Inquisición*, for a thorough discussion of the Inquisition's censorship of works of interior prayer, and Melquiades Andres Martin 621–9 in *La teologia espanola del siglo XVI* vol. 2, which also provides the full list of titles on the 1559 Index. A facsimile of the 1559 Valdés Index is at: http://fotos.patrimonionacional.es/biblioteca/ibis/pmi/Indice_1559/index.html.

2. Mystic Poetry

1 According to Orozco Díaz, the mystic transcends "perceptible reality, achieving direct knowledge of the divine essence," while the secular poet "penetrates reality by intuition, in a synthetic vision, discovering the hidden and mysterious relations between things" (59). For Helmut Hatzfeld, "The mystic and the poet have categorically similar experiences. In the first place, both grope in the dark for what they alone cannot produce; then, in an instant, they receive an 'illumination' that allows them to perceive intuitively, rather than analytically, a reality that is hidden to the ordinary man" (15, translation mine). Or, from the back cover of Colin Wilson's *Poetry and Mysticism*, "The mystic's moment of illumination shares with great poetry the liberating power of the deepest levels of consciousness ... Poetry, Wilson argues, is a contradiction of the habitual prison of daily life and shows the way to transcend the ordinary world through an act of intense attention-and intention. The poet, like the mystic, is subject to sudden 'peak experiences' when 'everything we look upon is blessed.'"

2 The authorship and origins of this book of the Bible are unknown and debated (the attribution to King Solomon is probably specious). It shares a style with much ancient Near Eastern love poetry, probably transmitted orally before being written. In different ancient translations in different languages (Greek, Aramaic), it is represented as lyric or dramatic poetry. It was incorporated into the Old Testament Bible in approximately 70 CE. It enters the Latin canon through Origen, although he was not the first to translate it. See *The Oxford Companion to the Bible* ("Song of Solomon" entry) for the ancient history; see Matter ch. 2 for the early Latin history of the book.

3 Because it is both seemingly unrelated and incompatible with the rest of the Bible, the Cantar has, since the beginning of Christian exegesis, been a focal point for allegorical exegesis (Origen's *In Canticum Canticorum* is probably the earliest). While not all allegorical interpretations of the text are mystical in nature, the twelfth-century mystics almost all wrote or used this text in their own writings: most notably Bernard of Clairvaux, Hugh of St. Victor, Richard of St. Victor. See Astell ch. 3, Matter ch. 5 on the medieval mystical exegesis of this book.

4 Bruce Wardropper's *Historia de la poesía lírica a lo divino en la cristiandad occidental* is the definitive study of this process. See especially chapter VIII for the Spanish Renaissance. The best-known work on a particular example is Dámaso Alonso's study of the motif "vivo sin vivir en mí" in *La poesía de San Juan de la Cruz.*

5 English translation by Henry Sullivan.

6 "Mystical practices, to the extent that they become separate from the poem, the shadow of which delineated a space for them, drifted away to become autonomous sources of interminable discourse, destroying the very unity for which they had furnished the principle. These detached procedures would perform their tasks in other fields, especially literary ones" (*Mystic Fable* 77).

7 The *amor cortés* poetry of the *cancionero*, for example, uses paradox and "juegos verbales" but relatively little natural or sensorial imagery, while the Italianate sonnets of a Garcilaso or Boscán abound in the latter but are not generally characterized by the former.

8 English translations of Fray Luis de León's poems are from Barnstone.

9 There are exceptions, of course, particularly in the case of the Beguines, who lived in lay communities. See McGinn *The Presence of God* vol. 3, Ven Engen *Sisters and Brothers of the Common Life*.

10 The digital revolution has provided us with no shortage of analogous examples, as people adjust old assumptions about voice and audience to new digital realities that project our words instantaneously to everyone with an Internet connection.

11 Helmut Hatzfeld classifies the genealogies of San Juan's symbols as follows: "ahistorical, synthetic, secular, Arabic and Germanic" (35). Hatzfeld reviews the previous theories, not to challenge the practice of genealogical reading itself but only to propose two new sources: Raimundo Llull and Jan van Rusybroeck. Hatzfeld's approach is in fact exemplary of the assumption that literary criticism is genealogy: "Since the literary critic is, above all, a literary historian, he ought to distinguish between symbols that imitate or are derived from previous sources, and symbols created by each particular author" (28).

12 See Oxford Dictionary of Literary Terms, 3rd ed. "Poetry: Language sung, chanted, spoken, or written according to some pattern of recurrence that emphasizes the relationships between words on the basis of sound as well as sense: this pattern is almost always a rhythm or metre, which may be supplemented by rhyme or alliteration or both. The demands of verbal patterning usually make poetry a more condensed medium than prose or everyday speech, often involving variations in syntax, the use of special words and phrases (poetic diction) peculiar to poets, and a more frequent and more elaborate use of figures of speech, principally metaphor and simile." The first part of the definition is particular to *poetry*, the latter to *poetic language*.

13 A paradigmatic example of a non-mystical nature poem would be the nineteenth-century Anglican hymn by Cecil Frances, "All Things Bright and Beautiful."

14 Much ink has been spilled on the question of whether Fray Luis was a mystic or not. Fray Luis himself wrote that he had never experienced mystic union. Certainly, his commentary on the *Cantar* involves reading of the mystical sense of Scripture in the classical sense (one of the four levels of allegorical exegesis), and his preoccupation with the proper language for God (esp. in *Los nombres de Cristo*) touches on many of the same issues that trouble mystic expression, but this is akin to the negative mysticism of psuedo-Dionisio, rather than the affective and, crucially, *interior* experience of God that is the subject of this book. See Márquez for the synthesis of previous scholarship on the question of Fray Luis's mysticism (Dámaso Alonso, E. Allison Peers, and Rafael Lapesa each share the overall judgment expressed here) as well as his own dictum that Fray Luis "was not a mystic, but instead nostalgic for mysticism" (294).

15 Because San Juan's works were never published in his lifetime and there exist multiple manuscripts, critical editions vary slightly, none in ways relevant to the argument in this book. I have used the Asún transcription for the poems, and the Biblioteca Castro edition for the prose commentaries.

16 All English translations of San Juan de la Cruz are from Kavanaugh and Rodríguez.

17 I have changed Kavanaugh's "surely" to "certain" as in the original it is an adjective modifying light rather than an adverb.

18 "Symbol" *Oxford Dictionary of Literary Terms*, 2008.

19 Poem XI, 8–39. All references to the poems of Teresa of Ávila as well as their translations are from the Vogt bilingual edition. Vogt states in his preface that he relied "primarily on the Spanish text of St. Teresa's complete works prepared by Luis Santullano" in consultation with other Spanish editions.

20 The opening verse of Garcilaso de la Vega's, Soneto XXIII (1533), the best-known lyrical poem of the Spanish Renaissance.

21 References to the *Comentarios* provide the "Cántico" verse and commentary chapter, followed by the page numbers corresponding to the Biblioteca Castro edition.

22 See Mancho Duque and Baruzi for more on the dynamic nature of the symbol in San Juan.

23 For a study of Luis de León's translation of the *Cantares* and persecution, see Fernández Álvarez, Thompson *The Strife of Tongues*.

24 Díaz Cerón, 679–81. "No Figure in my Mind" (Arenal and Schlau 176). All English translations and page numbers are from Arenal and Schlau. Cecilia de Nacimento (1570–1646) was a Carmelite nun and poet. Since Arenal and Schlau highlighted her work in chapter 2 of *Untold Sisters*, she has been

the subject of a number of important critical studies, including Donnelly and Sider's bilingual edition of her works, Weber and Rhodes's respective essays in *Studies on Women's Lyric Poetry*, Mujica's *Women Writers*, and Toft in *A New Companion to Hispanic Mysticism*.

25 Cecilia del Nacimiento, spiritual and poetic disciple of San Juan de la Cruz, uses the same expressions in her "Liras de la transformación del alma en Dios" (in Díaz Ceron 49).

26 See *La poesía de San Juan de la Cruz (desde esta ladera)*, 78.

27 Because these are neologisms, it is nearly impossible to find translations.

28 In the 1726 *Diccionario de autoridades*, "agudeza" is defined as "2. Metaphoricamente: la sutileza, prontitúd y facilidád de ingénio en pensar, decir ò hacer alguna cosa" ("2. Metaphorically, the subtlety, readiness and ease of the wits to think, say or do something"). Baltasar Gracián enshrines it as *the* paradigmatic rhetorical device of the Baroque in his *Agudeza y arte del ingenio*.

29 I have modified the published translation to maintain the difference between the Spanish imperfect and preterite.

30 Not all of San Juan's poems are "depersonalized." He has, in fact, his own gloss on the same phrase – "Vivo sin vivir en mí" ("Coplas del alma que pena por ver a Dios"), which has been amply analysed in comparison with the more famous Teresan adaptation (see Hatzfeld 210–52). My reading of the pronouns in Saint Teresa's version largely applies to San Juan de la Cruz's poem as well. It seems likely that the canonization of San Juan's more "impersonal" works and Teresa's first-person ones corresponds to preconceptions of masculine and feminine spirituality.

31 In "Transgendering the Mystic Voice," Anne Cruz considers the particular openness of mystic expression to the assumption of a "yo" whose gender is not that of the author.

32 See López Baralt in *Mujeres de Luz, la mística femenina y lo femenino en la mística*, 235–67.

33 As Racha Kirakosian writes, "Accounts of mystical lives are inextricably linked to music" (122). The most extensive integration of music and mystical vision is found in the works of Hildegard of Bingen. The International Society of Hildegard von Bingen Studies provides a useful introduction to her works and bibliography on their website: http://www.hildegard-society.org/p/music.html. See also Holsinger, Kirakosian. The fifteenth-century theologian Jean Gerson wrote extensively on the allegorical properties of music; for more on Gerson and music, see Joyce.

34 For example, in chapter VII of *Conceptos de Amor de Dios VII*, Teresa writes that: "sé de una persona que estando en oración semejante oyó cantar una buena voz, y certifica que, a su parecer, si el canto no cesara

que iba ya a salirse el alma, del gran deleite y suavidad que nuestro Señor le daba a gustar" ("I know of a person who, while similarly in prayer heard a good voice singing, and who swears that, it seemed to them that if the song did not cease, their soul would escape due the great delight and gentleness that Our Lord allowed them to enjoy" [Translation mine. I have used the plural, as it is not clear whether the person is female or male]).

35 "Coplas del alma que pena por ver a Dios" is the title of San Juan's gloss on "vivo sin vivir en mí"; "Véante mis ojos" appears in "El cántico espiritual" (v. 48).

36 *Untold Sisters: Hispanic Nuns in Their Own Works.*

37 It seems that one need only scratch the surface of a convent's archives to find poetry, whether original or copied, integrated into other textual forms or perhaps set to music, integrated into other texts or on its own. Inmaculada Osuna Rodríguez, in her research on one Sevillan convent, uncovers a "microcosmos" of poetic activity, including the writing of Constanza Osorio (1565–1637), who authored a 300-page commentary on the Psalms which included her own poetic version of nine of them, and also her *Huerto del celestial esposo* ("Garden of the Heavenly Bridgroom"), a commentary on the Song of Songs, also including an original poem. As theology or poetry, they may be unremarkable, but it is the very fact that so many nuns in Counter Reformation Spain were obviously exposed to and were motivated to respond creatively to these two foundational mystic texts, that is remarkable. The less remarkable each individual discovery, the more remarkable the phenomenon.

38 For example, many of Cecilia de Nacimiento's poems were long attributed to San Juan de la Cruz.

39 According to the count of Patrocinio García Barriuso in *La monja de Carrión*. As he discusses, the majority are copies or adaptations of poems by other authors, including several from Lope.

40 "Poemas 'sanjuanistas' fuera del Carmelo" en la Revista *Estudios* no. 137, abril-mayo 1982, 149–98.

41 For example, Estefanía de la Encarnación (fol. 92r-93v), or the anonymous Dominican nun discussed in chapter three (BN Mss 5807).

42 See both Weber's and Rhodes's essays in Olivares.

43 Letter dated 28 October 1605. Carta 8 in the *Obras completas.*

44 Letter dated 22 April 1605. Carta 10 in the *Obras completas.*

45 The process and experience of mystic union acquired the sort of social currency and function that pictures of food do today – no picture of food captures the taste of a dish, but by sharing these pictures through diverse media platforms, people today sustain relationships, transmit ideas, and carve out identities.

46 See García Barriuso for the correspondence between Felipe III and Sor Luisa de la Ascención. See Cueto Ruiz, Puyol Buil for Felipe IV's correspondences with visionary nuns, particularly Sor María de Ágreda.
47 Colin Thompson concludes that, in all likelihood, San Juan wrote the first thirty or thirty-one stanzas in prison and then smuggled the manuscript out with him on his escape, although he does not discount the possibility that he did not actually begin writing the words down until after his escape (*Poet and the Mystic* 50).
48 Asún, Raquel. "Introducción" a San Juan de la Cruz, *Poesía completa y obras en prosa*.
49 See Weber "Could Women Write Mystical Poetry?" 191–2 for a succinct review of the various theories and opinions of the "genetic relationship between Juan's poems and commentaries."
50 In Aldo Ruffinatto's words, San Juan rejects the option of providing a "a scientific (heuristic) model of the artistic model" and instead chooses "consciously or unconsciously, a different path, that of constructing an artistic model of the artistic model" (155).
51 The page numbers correspond to the Biblioteca Castro edition of the Commentaries.
52 As with the "Cántico" commentaries, parenthetical references to the "Noche oscura" commentaries give chapter and page number in the Biblioteca Castro edition. The translators have chosen "conduct" for *modo* here, and later they use "way" (296); I find "method" more useful in the analysis that follows.
53 The phrase comes from the title of Toft's contribution to *The Oxford Companion to Hispanic Mysticism*.
54 The reference, drawing on San Juan's own description of the boundary between the heavens and the earth as a "ladera," is to the secular side or shore.

3. Spiritual Autobiography

1 "Como comencé a leer las Confesiones, paréceme me veía yo allí; comencé a encomendarme mucho a este glorioso santo. Cuando llegué a su conversión, y leí, como oyó aquella voz en el huerto, no me parece sino que el Señor me la dio a mí, según sintió mi corazón." (171; ch. 9 sec. 7). "When I began to read the *Confessions* I seemed to see myself portrayed there, and I began to commend myself frequently to that glorious saint. When I came to his conversion, and read how he heard the voice in the garden, it seemed exactly as if the Lord had spoken to me" (69). All further quotations from the *Libro de la Vida* will follow the chapter, section, page

number format. Spanish quotations are from the Steggink edition, English page numbers are from the Cohen translation.

2 I will use the lower case *vida* to refer to the genre, *Vida* to refer to specific works.

3 The inconsistent enforcement of Catholicism among the *moriscos* who remained after the expulsion of Muslim rulers meant that in practice this was not entirely true. However, none of the *moriscos* who remained and continued to practice Islam more or less unmolested in the decades between the expulsion and Felipe II's crackdown on these communities wrote a spiritual autobiography.

4 The visions, particularly the "vision at Ostia" narrated in Book IX.9, is undeniably mystical. Yet in the totality of his *oeuvre*, Augustine dedicates little space to the cultivation of mystic experience. The main exception, aside from the chapters of the *Confessions*, is *De Genesi ad litteram* XII. Here he lays out a theory of three types of visions – corporeal, spiritual, and intellectual – that became Church dogma and that we will see applied throughout chapters three and four by mystics and sceptics alike. The schema emerges out of Augustine's exegesis of 2 Corinthians 12, in which Paul recounts his rapture to paradise, and Augustine emphasizes that such visions are exceedingly rare. Despite his own experience, he does not suggest ways that an "ordinary" Christian might cultivate such an experience, nor does he recount any visionary experience not already attested to in Scripture. See Kenney, *The Mysticism of Saint Augustine* for a detailed analysis of the visions in *The Confessions*.

5 The best-known example of the *autobiografía por petición* would be San Ignacio de Loyola's *Autobiografía* (not to be confused with his *Diario*, considered in chapter one). Despite the title under which it has been published (not a term ever used by Loyola), the *Autobiografía* does not properly fall into the category considered in this chapter, as it is written in third person and adheres more closely to the generic norms of the hagiographic biography, with little speculation into psychological processes or subjective experience. See O'Malley, McManamon for more on the "autobiografía," O' Rourke Boyle for why it should not properly be categorized as such.

6 A discussion of the relationship with confessors is inevitably a part of all studies of Santa Teresa and her work. For a summary of past scholarship on the relationship as well as a subtle and convincing argument, see Weber "The Three Lives of the *Vida*." In "Confessors, Penitents, and the Construction of Identities," Jodi Bilinkoff also gives a useful broader perspective on the mutual benefit that confessors and spiritually gifted penitents could provide each other.

7 references to Garcilaso de la Vega, Soneto X ("dulces prendas por mi mal halladas" ["Oh lovely gifts, by me too fatal found!"]) and the Égloga III.

8 "Visto he, con mucha atención, este libro en que Teresa de Jesús ... da relación llana de todo lo que por su alma pasa, a fin de ser enseñada y guiada por sus confesores, y en todo él no he hallado cosa que a mi juicio sea mala doctrina, antes tiene muchas de gran edificación y aviso para personas que tratan de oración ... Resuélvome en que este libro no está para que se comunique a quienquiera, sino a los hombres doctos y de experiencia y discreción cristiana. Él está muy a propósito del fin para que se escribió, que fue dar noticia esta religiosa de su alma a los que la han de guiar, para no ser engañada." The "Censura" is included as an appendix in the Steggink edition of *El libro de la vida*, 557–61. ("I have examined, with great attention, this book in which Teresa of Jesús gives a full account of everything her soul experiences, with the goal of being taught and guided by her confessors, and throughout I find nothing that in my judgment is bad doctrine – quite the contrary, it contains many things that are of great edification and caution for those who practice [mental] prayer. My determination is that this book is not to be communicated with just anyone, but only with learned men, with experience and Christian discretion. The book is quite well tailored for the purpose for which it was written, which was to give an account of this religious woman's soul to those who are to guide her, so she not be deceived." Translation mine.)

9 See my article "Incoherent Subjects, Incomplete Lives" in *Religions* for more on the diversity of spiritual autobiographies beyond the canon of printed, edited texts.

10 This practice of constant and dispersed narrative is the norm among early modern mystic women. The writings of María Vela y Cueto, examined in this chapter, follow a similar pattern. Susan Laningham reports, in her Introduction to the English version of Cueto y Vela's *Vida*, that Sor María recorded the "raw materials" of her visionary experiences in notebooks for her confessor, starting in 1598. At this point, her claims were met with "increasing speculation, rumor, resentment, and fear." The *Libro de las Mercedes* and María herself were scrutinized and subject to tests, and in 1603 she was reported to the Inquisition. However, the Inquisitor's decision not to proceed against her, as well as a new confessor who believed her, implied a change in her fortunes as an individual and as an author. The new confessor, Manuel González Vaquero, ordered her to write her *vida* and returned to her the accounts of *mercedes* for her to consult. There are points of overlap between the two works, both of which remained unedited until Margaret Rees's editions of 2007, but the accounts of the *mercedes* are clearly written without a larger project in mind and in a context of doubt and anguish, whereas the *Vida* integrates the past doubts

into a confident narrative that has already achieved approval and legibility. Between Vela y Cueto's death in 1617 and the twenty-first century, another version of Vela y Cueto's life circulated: the biography written by her confessor González Vaquero, obviously written in consultation with the two autobiographical accounts, but in the confident third-person voice of a male confessor arguing for his protégé's sanctity.

11 Indeed, the editor of the recent critical edition of these accounts, Salvador Ros, calls them a "verdadera autobiografía" ("true autobiography").

12 María Vela y Cueto's *Vida* was buried with her, and only discovered six years later when she was disinterred as part of a canonization process (Laningham 1). In other cases, we have only hints of *vidas* that were truly lost: in the *proceso* of Isabel de Briñas, a widow and *beata* in Madrid in the 1630s, she replies to an accusation of falsely circulating visions that "el confesor que tenía antes del padre Daza le había mandado que escribiera algunas cosas que la pasaban de su vida y ansí lo hizo y habrá 3 años poco mas que los quemó, porque oyó una razón a dicho padre Daza de que él no consintiera que se escribiese nada, y que no se acuerda de nada de lo que tenía escrito." ("the confessor she had prior to Father Daza had ordered her to write some of the things that happened to her in her life and she did so, and about 3 years ago she burned it, because she heard Father Daza say that he did not consent that she write anything, and she does not remember anything that she had written"). AHN Inq. leg. 102, exp. 5.

13 The content and form of these vary widely, and not all of them contain mystic visions.

14 The *vida espiritual* is a Counter-Reformation phenomenon and appears throughout Catholic Europe. Nicholas Paige has done a magisterial study of the genre in France. To my knowledge, there is no single study of the genre in Italy, but Gabriela Zarri provides a useful overview in two separate studies: "L'autobiografia religiosa negli scritti di in Camilla Battita da Varano" and "La scrittura monástica." The editions and critical studies of individual "autobiographies" from outside Spain are too numerous to include here, but the series The Other Voice is the leader in recent scholarship and publication on early modern women's autobiographies and spiritual writings. The quantity of Spanish examples far outnumbers those produced elsewhere. Furthermore, Spanish examples will be qualitatively different, as Spanish religious writers were more directly subject to levels of censure and control. Indeed, the French and Italian studies reveal more diverse and less conflictive contexts of production of accounts of revelation, and in several instances there is no *vida* tied to the account of the visions, precisely because the author is not defending her life. For such examples, see Maggi *Uttering the Word*, Haraguchi "Vita di Eleonora."

15 Stephen Haliczer found that "35.5 percent of the women in my sample saw her in visions, making her the most frequently seen of all the women saints" (60). This rather understates the phenomenon; as far as I can tell, no other woman saint appears with any frequency in the visions, and of male saints who are not also biblical figures, the only repeat appearances are the founders of the respective orders.

16 For instance, in the preface to a 1697 published edition of the *vida espiritual* of María de la Antigua (discussed later in this chapter), the unnamed author authorizes the text to follow by noting that "Siguieron un mismo camino interior Santa Teresa de Jesús y la V. Madre Maria de la Antigua ... que mas parece identidad de espiritus, que semejanza. Los Libros de Santa Teresa de Jesus y estos Escritos de la V. Madre Maria de la Antigua son testimonio demonstrativo de esta verdad." ("The Venerable Mother María de la Antigua and Saint Teresa of Jesus followed the same inner path ... it seems more a case of spiritual equivalence than similarity. Saint Teresa's books and the Venerable Mother María de la Antigua's writings are evident testimony of this fact.") The logic is rather circular, as the *Desengaño* itself narrates María de la Antigua's constant deliberate self-styling in the Teresan model. From a secular point of view, one could say that María's strategy of authorization through imitation works perfectly.

17 Patrocinio García Barriuso reports that Sor María's superiors in the convent recovered 1375 *pliegos* (240). The text beneath an anonymous stamp of Sor María which shows her transcribing a divinely dictated book says that "pasan de 3 mil cuadernos que en año y medio escribió" ("her writing over a year and a half exceeds 3000 notebooks"). Even taking into account the hagiographical tendency to exaggerate, the author must mean 3,000 sheets of paper rather than 3,000 notebooks.

18 Sor Luisa was renowned in her day for her piety and revelations and was consulted by both the Duke of Lerma and Felipe III before falling under suspicion. The Inquisition investigation lasted fourteen years and was closed, after her death, with a formal exoneration.

19 Sor Luisa's biographer, Patrocinio García Barriuso, asserts based on references in letters that she did write a *vida* but that it was lost in a fire. See also Rico Collado. For more on the relationship between the two nuns, see García Barriuso 239–41.

20 There is no further indication of who the "Your Grace" addressed is. These notes are found in the manuscript, not the printed edition.

21 Although the translation of María de la Antigua is my own, I have used the Kavanaugh translation of San Juan de la Cruz for the poem.

22 All English translations of Ana de San Bartolomé are from the Donahue edition.

23 This is one of many examples in which Teresa de Jesús María hears an inner voice of Scripture, predominantly from the Song of Songs. The quote is from Songs 2:10.
24 The quote is from Songs 2:1–2.
25 For further bibliography on eucharistic visions, see Bynum ch. 5 of *Holy Feast, Holy Fast*, esp. 172–80, on communion in the visions of Catherine of Siena. The centrality of communion in the religious imagination only became more widespread with the Counter-Reformation emphasis on the sacrament through the promotion of the Festival of Corpus Christi and the *autos sacramentales*.
26 John 12:32.
27 Songs 1:3.
28 References to the *Life of Catherine* are in the form book, chapter, page number in the Harvill Press edition.
29 In "Ecstasy, Prophecy, and Reform," Ahlgren considers whether Teresa would have read a translation of Capua's *Life* or come to know Catherine's legend through collections of saint's lives. She interprets a reference in a 1579 letter as proof of the former, but for our purposes what is essential is that neither Teresa nor her fellow Spanish visionaries knew the first-person letters, only the second- and third-hand, third-person versions.
30 The most notable changes are the chronological adjustment – in Catherine's letters, the vision occurs as she is lying near death, whereas Raymond retroactively places it "immediately prior to Catherine's apostolic travels" – and the whole-cloth invention of an exchange. In Watt's reading, the effect is to represent all of Catherine's "controversial activity" as, in fact, "God's action on Earth," with Catherine as merely "a fragile human shell for the divine will" (815).
31 15 February 1380. All references are to the Noffke translation and edition.
32 While Catherine's is the best-known example of a mystical transfer of hearts, it was a common trope among mystic visionaries, particularly women, from the High Middle Ages onward. See Wendy Wright 188–90.
33 The scriptural quotes in Latin are from, in order of appearance, Songs 1:2, Luke 1:38, Psalms 39.
34 In her book *Jesus as Mother*, Caroline Walker Bynum examines the medieval history of the representations of Christ and other male saints "bleeding" or giving milk, especially in the works of Bernard of Clairvaux. See 113–35.
35 The passage is from a letter dated 11 January 1671. The page numbers correspond to the BN manuscript, but the numeration is not consistent or always consecutive (it restarts at various times within the manuscript).
36 There continued to be a robust tradition of prophecy throughout the early modern period, of course, but this is not what we find in the *vidas* (and

when we do, it is in those that provoked censure, as we shall see in the following chapter).

37 "Relación que hace una monja de su modo de oración y mercedes que en ella recibía y no dice su nombre- ni en qué convento" ("A nun's account of her method of prayer and the mercies she received and it does not say her name or convent") (BN Mss 5807). I deal with this manuscript, although in a different framework, in "Incoherent Subjects, Incomplete Lives."

38 The poem is listed under this title in the Vogt bilingual edition, although it is often cited as "Muero porque no muero."

39 BN Mss 5807.

40 I have inserted punctuation only where I felt the intention was evident. The prose is even less clear in Spanish, where the flexibility of word order allows greater ambiguity.

41 BN MSS 5807.

42 It is unclear to what "primera y segunda" refer. There seems to be a "cuando" missing after "leía," although it is not entirely clear.

43 In chapter 10 of *the Darkness of God* (226–51) Turner argues that the critical tendency to read St. John's "dark night" as the experience of depression is a modern mistake, based on post-Enlightenment ignorance of the medieval tradition of negative (apophatic) mysticism. The anonymous nun's manuscript shows that this "mistaken" identification was already being made by St. John's near contemporaries.

44 I have slightly modified the translations to match the original.

45 This is the thesis of *Teresa of Ávila and the Rhetoric of Femininity*. It has been largely accepted among later scholars working on Teresa, particularly those in gender studies.

46 Josefina Ludmer has termed the strategic use of humility as a strength the "tretas del debil" ("tricks of the weak"). Although her analysis is of Sor Juana, not a mystical writer, the category is useful for analysing the *vidas* as well.

47 See, for example, Ahlgren *Teresa of Avila and the Politics of Sanctity* chapter 3, esp. 68–83.

48 Included in the *Obras completas*. Cecilia de Nacimiento also wrote a *Vida*, but it has been lost. The Carmelite historian Fr. Manuel de San Jerónimo cites fragments in the sixth volume of *Reforma de los Descalzos de Nuestra Señora del Carmen* (1710).

49 Fray Antonio has slightly misremembered the quote, which comes from the *Sermo ad Catechumenos*. It is "pavor ipse."

50 The meaning is not entirely clear in some of these phrases, particularly with the punctuation, but as it is a printed text, I have retained the original even when a logical reading would suggest minor changes.

4. Mysticism before the Inquisition

1 Obviously, some confessors were more sympathetic to the *devotio moderna* than others, but by the late sixteenth century most confessors were familiar with the language of interior contemplation, and for their part confessants with mystical leanings proved remarkably adept at seeking out and finding confessors who were amenable to their spiritual practices.

2 Joseph Pérez notes, accurately, that "It was not the Enlightenment reformers who abolished the Inquisition, but rather Napoleon Bonaparte." The constitutional delegates at Cádiz in 1812 were divided on the issue (the vote was 90–60 in favour of abolition), and many opposed the tribunal because they wanted Inquisitorial powers returned to the bishops, rather than out of a belief in religious freedom. Still, the terms of opposition quickly shifted after the restoration of the monarchy. See Moreno, 109–24, for the role of liberal reformers in the abolition of the Inquisition and Escudero, 371–410, for the debates at the *Cortes*.

3 For more on the origins of the inquisitional procedure, see Langbein, 131–8; Berman, 151–9, 187–9; von Caenegem, 85; Elliott ch. 4 (119–79).

4 The same would be true of Islam by the mid-sixteenth century.

5 Homza 19.

6 The case is excerpted and translated in Homza 16–25. Even more strident, and typical of a defense against an accusation of Judaizing, was his denial of eating leavened bread: "unleavened bread is such a foreign thing to me, it's as likely I ate it as it is that Muhammed ate pork" (19).

7 Archivo Histórico Nacional (hereafter AHN), Inq. Leg. 115 Exp. 2. (Her name is also given as María Pizarra in the *proceso*). Although the use of the terms was hardly consistent, in general an *iluso* was someone "passively misled by the devil's illusions," while an *iludente* "designated someone who had actively misled others into believing her illusions." Jaffary, 35–6.

8 Huerga vol. 5, cap. II, 45–71.

9 Erasmus's status in Spain was still in a state of transition in the early 1530s; there had been no official condemnation of his work, and he still had admirers among King Charles V's inner circle, but by the 1530s anti-*erasmistas* had begun a sustained persecution of his devotees. Cazalla prudently responded to the questions that she had never praised Luther, and while she had once admired Erasmus, she had since been corrected.

10 Quotes from Cazalla's *proceso* are from María Ortega-Costa's published edition. All translations from María Cazalla's *proceso* are my own.

11 In this way, they echo the shift we identified in chapter one in the Franciscan prayer manuals, with their equation of etymology for theology.

12 The end goal of torture, a confession, is ultimately a linguistic utterance, but it consists of a simple "confieso" rather than any speech act that must (or can) be analysed for shades of meaning.

13 Alison Weber also makes this point and distils the history of Alonso de la Fuente's interventions in "Demonizing Ecstasy."

14 All included in volume I of Huerga's *Historia de los Alumbrados*, 329–473. The volume has an exhaustive study of his biography and interventions in Extremadura, and he reappears in subsequent volumes. All citations from de la Fuente are from Huerga. Translations are my own.

15 In another section he elaborates "Es efecto de esta secta mudar a los hombres y hacerlos malcasados … de todo esto se olvidan poniendo hacienda, libertad y estado en manos de los maestros" (385). ("One effect of this sect is to transform men and make them unhappy in their marriages … they forget all this and place their estate, their liberty and station in the hands of their masters").

16 It is impossible to reproduce the ambiguity of the terms "sentimiento" and "sentido" in English, which can refer to feelings, meaning, sensory perceptions, and bodily sensations.

17 The quote is from John 3: 20–2. This "calificación teológica" of the alumbrados' "proposiciones" was written by Hernando del Castillo and included by de la Fuente as the first section of the *Memorial* to Felipe II.

18 This can lead to almost surreal conversations between Inquisitors, functionaries, and priests about stool quantity and quality. For example, in the case of María Pizarro, the *comisario* writes, "Preguntéla si tenía excrementos quando no comía ni bebía. Respondióme que no: otro día me dijo que cuando bebía tenía orina. Y otro día me dijo que cuando bebía, se le corrompía el estómago, y espelía como un humor" ("I asked her if she defecated when she did not eat or drink. She responded, no: another day she told me that when she drank she urinated. And another day she told me that when she drank, her stomach experienced corruption and expelled something like a humor"), and later, in the *audiencia*, she reported that "bebiendo mucho se corrompía y echaba algunos excrementos aunque todo era agua" ("when she drank a lot, there was corruption [digestion] and she produced some excrement, although it was all water"). Another case with extensive discussions of excrements is that of Francisca Ruiz (Archivo Diocesano de Cuenca, Leg. 446, Exp. 6245 and Leg. 450, Exp. 6265). See Sarrión Mora, 293–304.

19 His case is discussed at length by Andrew Keitt in *Inventing the Sacred*.

20 AHN Leg. 106, Exp. 2. Mateo Rodríguez's case, along with several others cited in this chapter, is treated extensively in Keitt. I am grateful to Andrew for providing me with his notes and partial transcriptions of the *procesos*

for Rodríguez, María de la Encarnación, Isabel de Briñas, and María Bautista.

21 As stated by Augustine in *On Christian Doctrine* 1.6.6. "if I have spoken, I have not said what I wished to say. Whence do I know this, except because God is ineffable? If what I said were ineffable, it would not be said" (10–11) and commented in Eckhart Sermon 53 (203–5).

22 AHN Inq. Leg. 7, Exp. 8, 1648–56.

23 AHN leg. 113, Exp 5. 3 December 1575. Haliczer cites several other examples of Inquisitors' insistence/assumption of rational criteria when interrogating mystical or miraculous claims. He does not quote directly, however, or draw attention to the linguistic impasse at the heart of the conflict. Furthermore, he has a tendency to echo the Inquisitors' tone and perspective (e.g., Francisca "deftly parried" the Inquisitors' objection), 139–41.

24 AHN Inq. Leg. 104, Exp. 2.

25 AHN Inq. Leg. 102, Exp. 5.

26 María de la Encarnación.

27 Isabel de Briñas.

28 In common usage, the verb means "to pass through," "to filter," "to strain."

29 María Bautista testifies in the *audiencias* to a lifetime of writing her spiritual experiences for confessors, although the papers are lost. There is, however, within the proceso, a *vida* she wrote while in prison (to my knowledge, the only extant example of such a document), and which I have analysed more fully as evidence of a "failed" *vida* in "Incoherent Subjects, Incomplete Lives."

30 At another point in her file, a *calificador* noted that "dijo ella al confesor que le parecía que la cortaban la cabeza, y que la hacían pedazos el cuerpo y luego los tornaban a juntar, cosa fuera de razón" ("she said to her confessor that it seemed to her that her head was being cut off, and that her body was being smashed into pieces and then put back together, which is beyond reason").

31 The Inquisitors could sentence those accused to one of two classes of abjuration: *de levi* or *de vehementi*. The criteria between light or vehement suspicion was quite subjective, but only the latter sentence required that any further convictions be treated as a relapse (with the consequent augmentation of punishment). See Lea, 121–35, for an overview of Inquisition punishments. It is impossible to cite any statistics on this point because the terminology of the charges is so inconsistent. However, of the cases considered in this chapter, the trial duration and sentences were as follows: Mateo Rodríguez, 1633–6, *abjure de levi, con méritos*, in a public *auto*, 200 lashes in Madrid and 100 in Toledo, exiled from Toledo

and Madrid for six years; María Bautista, 1639, gravely reprimanded in the *sala* of the Inquisition and advised to keep quiet about any visions she might have or have had, as well as not to write any further, given a specific confessor (a *calificador* of the Inquisition) for two years; Isabel de Briñas, 1639–41, reprimanded in the *sala* of the Inquisition, required to remain in Toledo for two years and confess only with a confessor they specify (a Dominican); María de la Encarnación, 1639–41, penanced in an auto and exiled from Madrid for four years; María Pizarro, 1635–41, sentenced in *auto público con méritos*, exiled from Siruela, confined to a convent or hospital in Toledo for four years to receive instruction, limited to taking communion three times a year for two years, prohibited from returning to her prior confessor; Juan de Yegros, 1648–56, they find him to be "leso en el juicio y entendimiento" ("suffering from cognitive damage") and sentence him to return to his convent and to be treated with much caution, with very moderate penitences and a good diet. Both the cases of Pizarro and Yegros involved repeated votes *in discordia*.

32 Stephen Haliczer provides a statistical picture of the inverse correspondence between a visionary's class and the authorities' scepticism of her visions. Within his sample group of approximately forty-five cases, "the most fundamental difference between the group of women mystics whose lives were the subject of officially approved biographies or autobiographies and the women who were arrested by the Holy Office on charges of 'false sanctity' concerns social status. While 70 percent of the approved mystics came of aristocratic families, none of the 'pretended' mystics could boast of social status greater than that of having a husband who was a struggling commission merchant" (81).

33 An unsigned Inquisition guide to discernment offers eleven "reglas" of discernment. The fifth rule is that: "la facilidad y frecuencia de extaticarse, principalmente en lugares públicos y libres para el curso de las gentes, sin que el sujeto se resista al éxtasis, ni procure esconderse, funda bastante sospecha de que tal acto es parte de la naturaleza o de la diabólica malicia" ("the ease and frequency of achieving ecstasy, principally in public places where people circulate freely, and with no resistance on the part of the subject, nor any attempt to hide, is grounds for significant suspicion that such an act is natural or from diabolic malice"). AHN Inq. Lib 33. Fol. 290–4.

34 AHN Inq. Leg. 102, Exp. 2. Stephen Haliczer discusses the episode in *Exaltation and Infamy*, and as noted previously, with a tone that rather disturbingly echoes that of the Inquisitors ("this potential collapse of her fantasy world … impelled her to try one last desperate gamble to convince the inquisitors" [141]).

35 Kallendorf "The Rhetoric of Exorcism," 214.

36 There are many other studies of exorcism, although de Certeau's in *Possession at Loudun* and Maggi's *Satan's Rhetoric* stand out for their attention to language. De Certeau cites theologian Ismael Bouilliau's rejection of the validity of the devil's speech and points out that even in Urban Grandier's conviction for witchcraft in Loudun, "in reality the 'depositions of the devils' enter neither into the reasons adduced nor into the legal proofs for the condemnation pronounced by the judges" (*Possession* 147).

37 AHN Inq. Leg. 115, Exp. 3.

5. Mysticism on Stage

1 Huerga vol. 5, cap. II, 45–71. For our purposes, the definition of the three stages is less important than the identification of a progressive theatricality in the later seventeenth century *alumbrados*, as opposed to the mysticism of the first "radical" group, led by Cazalla.

2 For a comparative study, see Cañadas chapters 1 and 2.

3 It should be noted that the majority of attacks on the theatre in Spain did not argue that it was heretical in theory but only that it was amoral in practice: the audience got too rowdy, the actors had too much freedom to violate codes of gender and sex, it distracted from more pious pastimes, etc. See Cotarelo y Mori for the opposition to the theatre, Vitse for the different positions taken within the Church.

4 John J. Allen makes this point and supports it with maps showing the locations of theatres in London vs. the Madrid in *Los teatros comerciales*, 183–4.

5 See Díez Borque *Los espectáculos del teatro y la fiesta* (191–246) and Ferrer Valls on paratheatre. See Diez Borque "Sombras de la documentación" for the relation between textual *relaciones* and the festive events they relate.

6 Unless noted, all translations of works of theatre in this chapter are my own. Spanish theatre of the early modern period is written in verse; I have sacrificed all pretensions to artistry and provided the most literal prose translation possible.

7 *Obras escogidas* vol. 3, p. 23. The edition does not have verse numbers.

8 The "maya" is a beautiful young woman chosen to preside over a local spring festival.

9 Some of the Old Testament *autos* employ the language of the Canticle in a more straightforward way but without emphasizing the mystic elements (as de Certeau understands the term). See Arellano *Estructuras dramáticas* 81–3 for examples.

10 Alexander Parker, whose overall argument is in defense of the artistic sophistication and skill of the *autos*, singles out *La humildad coronada*

(discussed below) as one of the *autos* in which the allegory "can be so elaborate that sometimes Calderón seems to indulge in it for the sake of its complication only" and for which the "the only inducement he could have had to employ" the allegory was "the desire to offer his audience new intellectual surprises and excitement" (96).

11 On the creation of "mystic spaces" in Calderón's *autos*, see Arellano *Estructuras dramáticas* 153–7. Also relevant is his discussion of "oniric and thaumaturgical spaces," 185–9. Arellano explores the "funcionamiento místico" in Calderón's *autos* further in "Doctrina y espectáculo," although he uses the term "mystic" in a much broader sense than this study, as a synonym for allegorical or the antithesis of mimetic.

12 All quotes of *La hidalga del valle* are from the Mary Lorene Thomas edition.

13 "pues el músico y poeta/ es el Espíritu Santo./ ¿Qué trae consigo este día/ que todo el orbe es contento,/ es música todo el viento,/ es todo el valle alegría,/ toda la tierra armonía,/ todas las nubes colores,/ belleza todas las flores,/ risa todos los cristales,/ paz todos los animales,/ todos los cielos favores?/ Pues, mariposas aladas,/ infinitos niños bellos/ suben y bajan a ellos/ con alas tornasoladas,/ las frentes traen coronadas/ flores de otra primavera./ ¡Quién uno coger pudiera!" (701–19) ("the musician and poet is the Holy Spirit. What does this day bring, on which all the globe is happiness; all the wind is music; all the valley is joy; all the earth, harmony; all the clouds, colors; beauty all the flowers; laughter all the crystals; peace all the animals; all the heavens, favours? Infinite beautiful Christ children, the winged butterflies rise and descend to them with sun-dappled wings, their foreheads adorned with flowers of another Spring: oh, if only one could pick one!").

14 Also known as *La humildad coronada de las plantas*.

15 All types of trees. For the allegoric symbolism of each, see Arellano 2002, 9–13.

16 Certain books of the Old Testament were consistently cited in mystical poetry (Song of Songs, Psalms) and it would certainly be possible for Baroque playwrights to retroactively dress Old Testament devotion in new spiritual forms, but I find no evidence of this occurring.

17 See Dassbach chapter 3 "El mártir" in *La comedia hagiográfica*, 59–68.

18 There are three plays about Teresa attributed to Lope. The only one whose authorship we can be certain of, because Lope mentions it in the catalogue of his work inserted in *El peregrino en su patria*, is *La Madre Teresa de Jesús*, and no known copy exists. The two other works, titled, respectively, *La bienaventurada Madre Santa Teresa de Jesús* and *Vida y muerte de Santa Teresa de Jesús*, exist only in damaged copies and cannot be ascribed to Lope for certain. This article uses the second of the three plays, known as *Santa Teresa de Jesús* since Menéndez y Pelayo published it in 1890 under that title

and published with critical apparatus in *A New Anthology of Early Modern Spanish Theater*. See Mujica 170.

19 For more on Augustine's theories of visions, see Keskiaho 9–14 and chapter 4, and Sluhovsky *Believe Not Every Spirit* 174 and note 9.

20 In her article "Staging mysticism," Susan Paun de García describes a scene in José Canizares's 1717 *comedia* about Saint Gertrude, *La más amada de Cristo*, in which Gertrude is seen writing as a dove flutters above and around her desk. A spectacular vision interrupts the tableaux and neither the text nor the act of writing is discussed in the play, which conforms more to the treatment of visionary sanctity (not mystic at all, in the de Certeau definition we are using) that we find in the Teresa, Juana, and Santa Rosa plays I analyse later in this chapter.

21 See Case, Thomas. "Metatheater and Worldview …" 132.

22 While I consulted spelling and punctuation with Sainz de Robles, I have retained the verse numbers from the Teatro Español del Siglo de Oro (TESO) online edition, as Sainz de Robles does not provide them.

23 In *Técnicas de representación en Lope de Vega*, Teresa Kirschner proposes four categories of complex staging (staging beyond the literal representation of events): symbolic staging, articulatory staging, spectacular staging, and totalizing staging. Symbolic staging involve exteriorization of "the mental processes of dreaming or thinking by representing on stage what is dreamed or imagined by his characters." (52–3). While her study is focused on Lope, there is no reason her categories cannot be applied to the *comedia* in general. See also Dassbach chapter 5, De la Granja "Espacios del sueño," and Fernández Rodríguez "Imagenería sacra."

24 I use the word "pre-modern" here to characterize the prophetic revelation that we find relatively unchanged from the Old Testament through the popular apparitions in Castile analysed by William Christian and in distinction with the *devotio moderno*. The staging techniques of such visions are entirely modern (Baroque).

25 The Spanish plays on the double meaning of *fuente* as wound and fountain.

26 The wordplay between *verse* and *vestirse* (to see and to wear, respectively) is impossible to reproduce in English.

27 It is impossible to reproduce the wordplay with "forms" (which in Spanish also refers to the Communion host) in English.

28 I am uncertain as to whether he invents the scene or is drawing on a hagiographic legend. Augustine certainly has plenty to say about the devil and temptation in his *Confessions*, but he never imagines the pull towards sin in an externalized physical form.

29 See chapter 3 of *Possession at Loudun*. This is inevitably a function of the speech of the exorcist. Almost all official exorcism manuals cautioned against entering into open-ended conversations with demons but

advocated asking "the possessing spirit for its name, the cause of the possession, the presence of additional demons within the demoniac's body and about possessions of other individuals" (Sluhovsky *Believe Not Every Spirit* 75). For a fascinating discussion of the use of proper names in the *Thesaurus Exorcismorum*, a widely distributed anthology of exorcism manuals in the period, see Maggi *Satan's Rhetoric* 112–16.

30 Dassbach analyses the use of offstage voices and revealed visions in Lope's *comedias de santos*. "Visions are more spectacular than voices, if and when, of course, they are staged and not simply narrated. Notwithstanding they are generally simple set pieces, not requiring complicated stage devices or *tramoya*. They are, rather, plastic tableaux that can be presented by drawing a curtain at the back of the stage in the space for apparitions, and revealing an image painted on canvas or a statue; alternately, they present a more complicated scene, with one or several characters creating a plastic tableaux that appears on high, either on a wooden cloud or one of the balconies at the back, above the stage. Nevertheless, and due to the intimate nature of this kind of experience, the visions above all lend themselves to discreet stagings that re-inforce the intimate character of this phenomenon." (101–2).

31 The description mixes several common iconographic representations of Augustine: El Greco's "Saint Augustine of Hippo" shows the staff and church, while the fifteenth-century altarpiece of the church of Sant Agustí Vell in Barcelona features the most famous scene of "Saint Augustine Disputing With the Heretics."

32 See especially pp. 139–41 of the article.

33 All Spanish quotes from the play are from the Mujica edition; English translations are mine.

34 Indeed, Mujica notes in her introduction to the play that "there is no evidence in *Santa Teresa de Jesús* that Lope ... actually read Teresa's own writing" ("The Sacred and the Political" 171).

35 *Ahumada* means smoked/burnt but is also Teresa's second surname.

36 The directions are inserted between verses 1157 and 1158 (Act II).

37 This occurs between verses 1170 and 1171 (Act II).

38 The directions are between 2644 and 2645 (Act III).

39 There are numerous scholarly biographies of Rosa de Lima, as well as much recent scholarship on her life in the context of gender studies. There are also numerous hagiographies; the best known and most influential is Hansen. For more on the first hagiography and the passage from life to legend, see Millar Carvacho. For more on the mystical elements of her life, see Graziano. For her writing – or lack thereof – see Báez Rivera chapter 3 pp. 101–58.

40 Although the play is published under Moreto's name, Moreto in fact died after writing the first two acts. The third was composed by his contemporary Pedro Francisco Lanini y Sagredo (Castañeda 48–9). There is no modern critical edition of the play. I am using the digital edition based on the 1676 manuscript, but I have modernized spelling. All English translations are my own.
41 Dassbach: "prophecies and celestial voices, although as expressions of the supernatural they are less scenically spectacular than others, are often presented as a first step to establish the first contact between the saint and the world beyond" (99–100).
42 The play on words with *en seco* is impossible to reproduce in English. Bodigo is confused because he can only imagine pleasure as coming from food.
43 The directions directly follow v. 1189 in Act III.
44 The directions follow v. 1219.
45 Cohen uses "snapping fingers" for "dar higas," but the gesture is much stronger.
46 For example, see chapter XXV. While the overall emphasis of the chapter is on the possibility of self-discernment, she also narrates her own difficulties: "Pues estándome sola, sin tener una persona con quien descansar, ni podía rezar ni leer, sino como persona espantada de tanta tribulación, y temor de si me había de engañar el demonio, toda alborotada y fatigada, sin saber qué hacer de mí. En esta aflicción me vi algunas, y muchas veces, aunque no me parece ninguna en tanto extremo. Estuve ansí cuatro o cinco horas, que consuelo del cielo ni de la tierra no había para mí, sino que me dejó el Señor padecer, temiendo mil peligros" (338–9; ch. XXV sec. 17). ("Now when I was alone, with no company to give me relaxation, I could neither pray nor read, but was as if stunned by all these trials and by fear that the devil might be deceiving me. I was utterly disquieted and exhausted, and did not know what to do. I have several times – indeed, often – been in this sort of state, but never, I think, in such distress as then. I would remain in this condition for four or five hours on end, and there was no comfort for me, either in heaven or on earth: Our Lord left me to suffer my fear of a thousand dangers" [180]). The emphasis on her doubts may be part of a strategy of humility rather than a "true" representation of her confidence at the time, but it is nonetheless telling that Lope erases this doubt – performative or genuine – from his Teresa.
47 The stage directions are in Act II, immediately following verse 1359.
48 While medieval exorcism practices were not standardized, the post-Trent period saw an appropriation of the power of exorcism by officially designated clergy, and the standardization of practice in the 1612 *Ritual*

romanum. See Caciola 231–73, Clark *Thinking With Demons* chapters 26–28, and Sluhovsky *Believe not Every Spirit* 61–94.

49 For more on Juana de la Cruz, see Surtz 1990, McGinn (*Mysticism in the Golden Age of Spain* 15–24). She is best known for her work as an abbess in the reformation of the Franciscan convents and for her sermons, supposedly delivered while "arrobada" and collected in the *Libro del conorte*, recently translated into English and published in Toronto's Other Voice series as *Mother Juana de la Cruz: Visionary Sermons*. Despite the ecstatic state in which these sermons were said to have been proclaimed, in themselves they bear few of the marks of mystic discourse. They are written in third-person omniscient voice and consist mostly of clear doctrinal exposition. Mary Giles, contrasting Madre Juana's *Libro* with the spiritual autobiography of another nun, writes that "the omniscient narrative voice of Madre Juana … tells the story, interprets events, and comments on meaning … Madre Juana's voice is disembodied, coming from off stage, as it were, narrating, describing and explaining" (287). See Mary Giles "Spanish Visionary" in *Performance and Transformation*.

50 All references in this chapter are to the first play in the trilogy, unless otherwise noted. All quotes are from the Aguilar edition, with page numbers followed by act, scene, and verse numbers.

51 See Hughes 46–69 for basic summary and analysis of the trilogy.

52 For a similar scene, see Agustín Moreto *Los siete durmientes* fol. 105–7w.

53 For more on the early modern discernment of miracles, see Daston (and the further development of these ideas in Daston and Park) and Harrison.

54 In *Santa Rosa del Perú*, the gracioso Bodigo performs various "miracles" which range from purely comic misunderstandings to deliberately fraudulent impostures. As Natalia Fernandez Rodriguez explores in "Veneno mortal para la juventud," it was precisely the comic treatment of miracle, or more broadly the trivialization of the sacred, that drew the ire of theologians against the *comedia de santos* in general and led to the prohibition of several, starting with *Santa María Egipcíaca*, banned in 1785 and various times (and with different justifications) in successive years. See also del Río Barredo for more on the motivations behind censorship of the *comedia de santos*, esp. 285–96.

55 There is no critical edition of *Santa María Egipcíaca*. I have modernized spelling but otherwise followed the text and punctuation of the 1756, indicating act and page numbers in parenthesis. Translations are mine.

56 (Audiencia 22–12–1650, from the *proceso* of Juan Egujo). It is commonplace for scribes to summarize that a defendant, in his/her responses "desatinaba y hablaba cosas fuera de propósito" ("he spoke nonsense and talked about things that nothing to do with anything") (n.d., n.p., *proceso* of Esteban Cárdenas); "dijo otras muchas locuras e desatinos" ("he said

other crazy things and nonsense") (*proceso* of Andrés Hernández Tejero, audiencia 9–13–1543), etc. Perhaps the most remarkable example of a scribe's omission being made visible is in the case of Bartolomé Sánchez, subject of Sara Nalle's monograph *Mad for God*.

57 To cite just one of many examples, in the *auto* in Sevilla, it was announced that the leader of the Seville alumbrados, Catalina de Jesús, was "declarada por embustera" ("declared a fraud") and condemned for "embuste y fingimiento de virtud y santidad" ("fraud and feigned virtue and sanctity") to six years of reclusion in "el convento o hospital que le fuere señalado … y confiese con el confesor que el Santo Oficio le señalare … y que se recojan por edictos públicos cualesquier cosas de su persona o vestido que se hayan dado por reliquias … y que no salga de esta ciudad por el tiempo de los dichos seis años" ("the hospital or convent to which she may be assigned … and she shall confess with the confessor from the Holy Office who is assigned to her … and by public edict any items of her person or attire that were given as relics be gathered up … and that she not leave the confines of this city for the said six yeas") (Huerga 511; vol. 4). The other ringleader, Juan de Villalpando, retracted his past pretensions to sanctity and declared all his previous claims fraudulent.

58 See John J. Allen "El público: La nobleza y el vulgo" in Ruano de la Haza and Allen, *Los teatros comerciales*, 182–96.

59 "Relación de las personas testificadas en el Santo Oficio de la Inquisición de Sevilla en materia de alumbrados fuera de los que han sido castigados, suspensos y libres, de la gravedad y substancia de sus causas" ("Account of the persons denounced before the Holy Office of the Inquisition of Seville in the matter of *alumbradismo*, outside those who have been punished, freed, or had their cases suspended, on the seriousness and substance of their cases") (quoted in Huerga 529–35; vol. 4).

60 Many *beatas* were unattached to any order, but others, while still living outside the convent and not subject to the same level of authority and control as enclosed nuns, were affiliated with one or another order. See Sarrión Mora.

61 In addition to the countless examples of divine and human lovers demonstrating turbación, suspensión, etc. on stage, Agustín de la Granja cites several examples of meta-suspensión: actors preparing roles or non-lovers feigning love by *performing suspensión, turbación, frenesí*, etc. ("Los actores del siglo XVII ante La vida es sueño").

6. The Missionary Impulse

1 This distinction is clearly drawn by Fray Bernardino de Sahagún in the Introduction to his *Historia general de las cosas de Nueva España*, in which he

compares his project of studying native religious practices to that of the doctor who studies disease to eliminate it.

2 In his influential *The Spiritual Conquest of Mexico*, Robert Ricard argued that the Church was "successful" in destroying native religions. In recent decades, critical scholarship has pushed back against this thesis, drawing attention to areas of resistance and syncretism as well as the limits of the Church's reach. See Christensen for a summary of recent challenges to this "traditional Eurocentric narrative that prominently portrays the victorious acts of Spaniards in conquering and settling the Americas" ("Recent Approaches" 39).

3 A slight exception to the trend I have noted is found in the final chapter of Steven Turley's *Franciscan Spirituality and Mission in New Spain*, which examines the effects of the missionary experience on peninsular spirituality and concludes that "it is impossible to determine a net effect" (172). The section is brief and very narrowly focused on the lives of the returned missionaries. In general, the book focuses on the establishment and reform of institutions, emphasizes asceticism and poverty over contemplation in Franciscan identity, and gives little consideration to language.

4 See Grafton 3–6 for a summary of the two narratives (the triumph of empiricism vs. the persistence of tradition).

5 Elliott himself acknowledges that "the evidence for this assertion [the lack of interest in sixteenth-century Europe for the Americas] unfortunately lacks the firm statistical foundation which it should properly possess" (12).

6 For medieval Franciscan mysticism, see Cusato, McGinn *The Flowering of Mysticism*.

7 Phelan's interpretation has its detractors. Gómez Canedo, for instance, finds the Franciscans' writings and practice in the New World to be in keeping with their regular practice in Europe and in earlier centuries, which certainly had an apocalyptic bent but did not necessarily see the Second Coming as imminent. My reading of the Franciscan missionary mindset does not depend on the Franciscans believing they were living in the very last days, however, only that they saw the New World conversions as part of a utopian promise of salvation.

8 In fact, they were not quite the first, as three Franciscans from the Netherlands (part of the Habsburg Empire) had arrived the year before, in 1523. But precisely because of the symbolism of an envoy of *twelve*, this first envoy was immediately subsumed in the narrative of the "first twelve" who arrived from Spain a year later.

9 Quoted in Morales. The *Decreto* can be found in Mendieta, *Historia eclesiástica Indiana*, bk. 3, ch. 10 1: 344.

10 Translations mine.

11 These are impossible to translate elegantly but are roughly equivalent to "excess," "overdoing the spirit of God," and "transport without grace."
12 La Beata del Barco refers to María de Santo Domingo (also known as La Beata de Piedrahita), a Dominican mystic whose revelations and teachings were collected in the *Libro de la oración*. While there exist numerous witnesses to María's raptures and stigmata, she does not represent these experiences in the text; the *Libro* (dictated, rather than written by María herself) is a mostly clear exposition of revealed doctrine, centring on the Passion. There is little problematization of representation or exploration of subjectivity. See Sanmartín Bastida and Curto Hernández.
13 "En exceso," literally "in excess," suggests the spirit overflowing the rational self.
14 Mendieta's *Historia eclesiástica indiana* was written towards the end of the sixteenth century but not published in its entirety until 1870, due to censorship. John Phelan's thesis about the Franciscan attitudes in the New World draws largely on Mendieta.
15 W. Michael Mathes has recreated the catalogue of the library. The theological works are almost all in Latin; vernacular works are dictionaries and histories of Mexico. There is little mystical content, the exception being numerous works by Dennis the Carthusian, and a title or two from Osuna and Luis de Granada, although all in Latin and not their most important mystic works. The fortunes of the Colegio mirror in many ways that of the missionary project in Mexico at large: a brief initial period of utopianism which was quickly undermined by disease and decline in support from the Crown. For a good general introduction to the Colegio, see Cortés.
16 Dana Bultman speculates that the Inquisition's interest in possession of Osuna's works stemmed from the prohibition of a separate Osuna work on the Eucharist (297).
17 Durston contrasts this with the many "sources available to students of nineteenth- and twentieth-century missionization," where translators speak explicitly about choices and weigh alternatives. The difference is due to the development, between the sixteenth and nineteenth centuries, of a *science* of linguistics, and an understanding of the universal vs. particular structures of language. I would suggest that the position of the early missionaries to Mexico in the development of this science is akin to their position in the development of the science of cultural anthropology or ethnology. A first "wave" of descriptive and relatively unsystematic texts forms the basis through which a system becomes visible.
18 See Bultman "Winds, Hearts, and Heat" 302–4.
19 Molina, a Franciscan friar, was born in Spain but moved to New Spain at a young age. His *Vocabulario* was published in Mexico in 1555 (the first

dictionary published in the New World) and in Spain, in an expanded version, in 1571.

20 See Burkhart "The Solar Christ" 236 for more on sun and light imagery in the Old and New Testaments and medieval sacred writing.

21 Translation by Burkhart.

22 León Portilla *La filosofía nahuatl* 156–7, 390.

23 See also Nesvig, Part II.

24 See Tavárez 213–15 for the reasons to support each possible candidate.

25 I am relying on the portion of David Tavárez's translation published in this first article; the translation of the entire manuscript is still in progress. Fol 2–3r of the Escorial *Imitatio* in Nahuatl is reproduced in Tavárez, 219–22, with the side-by-side translations I am using here.

26 "Notlaçopiltçine tla xicmocaquilti xiccui tla xicana in iyyotçin tloque navaque to.o i. xo. in nica[n] amoxpan icuiliuhtoc."

27 Angel Garibay termed this technique of "the coupling of nouns with different symbolic connotations to create a complex, unified symbol" *difrasismo* and notes its prevalence across Nahua discourse (*Llave del nahuatl* 112). See Montes de Oca Vega, esp. chapter 1, for an extended discussion of the definitions of *difrasismo* and its relation to metaphor, parallelism, and other European poetic devices.

28 "in iuhq[ui]ma teocuitlacozcatl in iuhq[ui]ma chalchiuhcozcatl mitzmapanilia yn nican ticcui in nican ticana. Ca yeuatl ic timapantiaz in moztlatiz y[n] viptlatiz moxillan motozcatlan onactiaz in que[n]manian"

29 "ma vel monacazco onchipini ma vel moyollocaltitlan"

30 "in tlauilli in ocotl": the same *difrasismo* used in Sahagún's Christmas sermon, discussed above.

31 "in iuhqui malacayoticac cehualloticac ecauhyoticac iceuallotitlan iyecauhyotitlan necacalaquilo"

32 "in mixtitlan ayauhtitlan"; "amo tlayouayan amo <mix>tecomac in yatiuh"

33 "in tlauilli in ocotl in tlauizcalli tona<m>eyotl"

34 "in ye toconmaviçoua in tlavili in ocotl in ye tontlachiaz in tezcac in imiyauayoca[n] tonameyotl."

35 For a summary of different scholars' perspectives on these motives, as well as a useful introduction to the role of the Catholic Church in both destroying and preserving native Mexican texts, see Arbagi. It is worth noting, although outside the scope of this study, that the condition for preserving Mexican "archives" seems to have been their domestication through representation in European alphabetic script and representational formats. Sahagún and his collaborators did *not* preserve native codices; they preserved the *content* of those texts by recreating them in Nahuatl, but in an alphabetic Nahuatl that, while accompanied by illustrations

whose semiotics draw more from European visual traditions than pre-Columbian ones. While Sahagún and the Franciscans were mostly (re) creating texts destroyed by others, it is noteworthy that there was no parallel Franciscan initiative to preserve *original* materials, only their content.

36 The transcribed *Cantares* were discovered in 1889 as part of a larger manuscript of diverse materials written or transcribed in sixteenth-century Mexico. They were first published (with Spanish translation) by Angél María Garibay in *Poesía nahuatl*, and in a more recent edition by León Portilla. There is suggestive resonance in the title *cantares mexicanos* with *El Cantar de los Cantares*. A "cantar" is simply a song, of course, but the archaism (instead of "canciones") cannot but call to mind the text known as *the* Song.

37 According to León Portilla ("Estudio introductorio" 19), Sahagún's notes made towards the end of his life (in 1577) indicate that in 1547 "while in the convent of Tepepulco, he repeatedly interviewed indigenous wise men who showed him old books (codexes) and allowed him to transcribe examples of their 'Ancient word," *Huehuehtlahtolli*, and that this was the beginning of a twenty-year project of recording every aspect of pre-Columbian Nahua culture, all culminating in *La historia general de las cosas de Nueva España*.

38 See the "Estudio introductorio" 23–6 for a discussion of the controversy.

39 All references to the "Coloquio" are from León-Portilla's beautiful edition, which offers a facsimile of Sahagún's original manuscript as well as a print transcription of the Castilian prose, and then a transcription of the Nahuatl as poetry, with a new and more literal Castilian translation (also represented in poetry). Because my interest is in the translation, and because there is no "true" original (the entire dialogue being a creation/ recollection of a Spanish author), I have chosen not to cite the Nahuatl here. All English translations are my own.

40 It is understood that the "señores principales" are the political leaders, whereas the "sátrapas" are the priests.

41 For instance, he notes that the introduction by the Franciscans of the authority of the Pope, although conventional in the Spanish, employs in the Nahuatl words which native informants use to describe Quetzalcoatl in the *Códice Florentino* (libro III, cap. IX) (109; note 1).

42 Of course, if we believe the Spanish does reflect exactly what the Franciscans said in 1524, any influence of indigenous thought would be impossible. However, if we believe Sahagún's intervention is evident in the Nahuatl, it is reasonable to think he might have had an active editorial role in the Spanish. Indeed, there is a tendency in his Castilian to pair synonyms which, as discussed in this chapter, is an essential feature of

Nahua discourse. However, formal Spanish is also prone to redundant parallelisms, and the effect does not stand out unless one is looking for it.

43 Sadly, the majority of the books that supposedly contained the back and forth between the "sátrapas" and Franciscans are lost or perhaps were not completed. The "voice" is returned to the Franciscans, and they reply with a brief introduction to doctrine. Of the thirty chapters Sahagún outlined in his introduction to the never-published text, only thirteen and part of the fourteenth were present in the manuscript discovered in 1628.

Bibliography

Archival Sources

Bautista, María. Archivo Histórico Nacional (AHN), Sección Inquisición, Legajo 102, Expediente 2.1639–40.

Briñas, Isabel de. AHN, Inq. Leg. 102, Exp 5.1639–41.

Cárdenas, Esteban. Archivo Diocesano Cuenca (ADC), Leg. 224/2780.1561.

Egujo, Juan. AHN, Inq. Leg. 99, Exp. 6.

Estefanía de la Encarnación. *La vida de Sor Estefanía de la Encarnación, monja profesa en el Monasterio de religiosas Franciscas de Nuestra Madre Santa Clara, en esta villa de Lerma*. Biblioteca Nacional de España (BNE) Mss. 7459. Biblioteca Digital Hispánica, http://bdh-rd.bne.es/viewer.vm?id=0000145512&page=11631. Accessed 13 July 2021.

Francisca de los Apóstoles, testimony in AHN, Inq. Leg. 113, Exp 5.1575.

Hernández Tejero, Andrés. AHN, Inq. Leg. 38, Exp. 6.1543.

María de la Antigua. *Desengaño de religiosos y de almas que tratan de virtud*. BNE Mss. 6674. Sig. XVII.

María de la Encarnación (María Maseda y Legarda). AHN, Inq. Leg. 104, Exp. 2.1639–41.

Pizarro (also Pizarra), María. AHN, Inq. Leg. 115, Exp. 2.1636–41.

"Relación que hace una monja de su modo de oración y mercedes que en ella recibia y no dize su nombre- ni en que convento." BNE, Mss. 5807. Sig. XVII.

Rodríguez, Mateo. AHN, Inq. Leg. 106, Exp. 2.1633–6.

Ruiz, Francisca. ADC, Inq. Leg. 446, Exp. 6245 and Leg. 450, Exp. 6525.1630s/40s.

Salgado, Agustina. AHN, Inq. Leg. 115, Exp. 3.1712–16.

Teresa de Jesús María. "Autobiografía y relación de las mercedes divinas recibidas." 1636. BNE, Mss. 8482. Biblioteca Digital Hispánica, http://bdh-rd.bne.es/viewer.vm?id=0000145888&page=1. Accessed 13 July 2021.

Yegros, Juan de. AHN, Inq. Leg. 7, Exp. 8.1648–56.
Untitled Guide to Discernment of Revelations. AHN, Inq. Lib 33, folios 290–4.

Printed Sources

Ackerman, Jane. "John of the Cross, the Difficult Icon." *A New Companion to Hispanic Mysticism*, edited by Hilaire Kallendorf, Brill, 2010, pp. 148–73.

Ahlgren, Gillian T.W. "Ecstasy, Prophecy, and Reform: Catherine of Siena as a Model for Holy Women of Sixteenth-Century Spain." *The Mystical Gesture: Essays on Medieval and Early Modern Spiritual Culture in Honor of Mary E. Giles*, edited by Robert Boenig, Ashgate, 2000, pp. 53–66.

–. *Teresa of Avila and the Politics of Sanctity*. Cornell UP, 1996.

Alcalá Galve, Ángel. "Control de espirituales." *Historia de la Inquisición en España y America*, vol. 1, edited by Joaquin Pérez Villanueva and Bartolomé Escandell Bonet, Madrid, 1984–2000, pp. 780–842.

Alexander, Cecil Frances. *Hymns for Little Children*. J. Masters, 1848.

Allen, John J. "Los teatros comerciales en el Siglo XVII." *Los teatros comerciales del siglo XVII y la escenificación de la comedia*, Edited by José María Ruano de la Haza and John Jay Allen, Editorial Castalia, 1994.

Alonso, Dámaso. *La poesía de San Juan de la Cruz. (Desde esta ladera)*. Aguilar, 1958.

Ana de San Bartolomé. *Autobiografía*. Editorial de la Espiritualidad, 1969.

–. *Autobiography and Other Writings*. Translated by Darcy Donohue, University of Chicago Press, 2008.

Andrés Martín, Melquíades. "Alumbrados, Erasmians, 'Lutherans' and Mystics: The Risk of a More 'Intimate' Spirituality." *The Spanish Inquisition and the Inquisitorial Mind*, edited by Angel Alcalá, Social Science Monographs, 1987, pp. 457–94.

–. *Historia de la mística de la Edad de Oro en España y América*. Biblioteca de Autores Cristianos, 1994.

–. *La teología española en el siglo XVI*. La Editorial Católica, 1976. 2 vols.

Arbagi, Michael. "The Catholic Church and the Preservation of Mesoamerican Archives: An Assessment." *Archival Issues*, vol. 33, no. 2, 2011, pp. 112–20.

Arellano, Ignacio. "Doctrina y espectáculo: Escenografía mimética y escenografía mística en los autos de Calderón." *Dramaturgía y espectáculo teatral en la época de los Austrias*, edited by Judith Farré. Biblioteca Aurea Hispánica, 59, Iberoamericana, Verveurt, 2009, pp. 21–45.

–. *Estructuras dramáticas y alegóricas en los autos de Calderón*. Universidad De Navarra, Edition Reichenberger, 2001.

–. Introducción. *La humildad coronada*, by Pedro Calderón de la Barca, edited by Ignacio Arellano, Universidad de Navarra, Reichenberger, 2002.

Arenal, Electa, and Stacey Schlau, editors. *Untold Sisters: Hispanic Nuns in their Own Works*. U of New Mexico P, 1989.

Asín Palacios, Miguel. *Sāḏilīes y alumbrados*. Preliminary study by Luce López Baralt, Hiperión, 1990.

Astell, Ann. *The Song of Songs in the Middle Ages*. Cornell UP, 1990.

Astorch, María Ángela. *Mi camino interior*. Edited by Lázaro Iriarte, Hermanos Menores Capuchinos de la Provincia de Navarra-Cantabria-Aragón, 1985.

Asún, Raquel. Introducción. *Poesía completa y obras en prosa*, by San Juan de la Cruz, Planeta, 1989.

Augustine, of Hippo, Saint. *Confessions*. Translated by Carolyn J.-B Hammond, Harvard UP, 2014. 2 vols.

–. *The Literal Meaning of Genesis*. Vol. II, Books 7–12, translated by John Hammond Taylor, Newman Press, 1982.

–. *On Christian Doctrine*. Translated by D.W. Robertson Jr., Liberal Arts Press, 1958.

Báez Rivera, Emilio Ricardo. *Las palabras del silencio de Santa Rosa de Lima o la poesía visual del inefable*. Universidad de Navarra, Iberoamericana, Vervuert, 2012.

Baranda Leturio, Nieves, and María Carmen Marín Pina. "Prólogo: El universo de la escritura conventual femenina: deslindes y perspectivas." *Letras en la celda. Cultura escrita de los conventos femeninos en la España moderna*, edited by Nieves Baranda Leturio and María Carmen Marín Pina, Iberoamericana, Verveurt, 2014, p. 11–48.

Barthes, Roland. *Sade/Fourier/Loyola*. Translated by Richard Miller, Farrar, Straus, and Giroux, 1976.

Baruzi, Jean. *San Juan de la Cruz y el problema de la experiencia mística*. Junta de Castilla y León, 1991. (Translation of *Jean de la Croix et le problème de l'expérience mystique*. Presses Universitaires de France, 1924.)

Bécquer, Gustavo Adolfo. *Rimas*. Ediciones Cátedra, 1983.

–. *The Poems of Gustavo Adolfo Bécquer: A Metrical, Linear Translation*. Translated by Henry Sullivan, Spanish Literature Publications, Inc., 2002.

Berman, Harold J. *Law and Revolution: The Formation of the Western Legal Tradition*. Harvard UP, 1983.

Bernabé de Palma. *Via spiritus*. Biblioteca de Autores Cristianos, 1998.

Bilinkoff, Jodi. "Confessors, Penitents, and the Construction of Identities in Early Modern Avila." *Culture and Identity in Early Modern Europe (1500–1800)*, edited by Barbara B. Diefendorf and Carla Hesse, U of Michigan P, 1993, pp. 83–100.

Boon, Jessica A. Introduction. *Mother Juana de la Cruz, 1481–1534: Visionary Sermons*, edited by Jessica A. Boon, translated by Ronald E. Surtz,

Iter Academic Press, Arizona Center for Medieval and Renaissance Studies, 2016.

–. *The Mystical Science of the Soul: Medieval Cognition in Bernardino de Laredo's Recollection Method*. U of Toronto P, 2012.

Brown, Peter Robert Lamont. *Augustine of Hippo; a Biography*. U of California P, 1967.

Bultman, Dana. *Heretical Mixtures: Feminine and Poetic Opposition to Matter-spirit Dualism in Spain, 1531–1631*. Albatros Ediciones, 2007.

–. "Winds, Heart, and Heat in Premodern Franciscan and Nahua Concepts of 'Soul'." *Colonial Latin American Review*, vol. 27, no. 3, 2018, pp. 296–315.

Burkhart, Louise. "Death and the Colonial Nahua." *Nahuatl Theater: Death and Life in Colonial Nahua Mexico*, edited by Barry Sell, Louise Burkhart, and Gregory Spira, U of Oklahoma P, 2004, pp. 29–54.

–. "The Solar Christ in Nahuatl Doctrinal Texts of Early Colonial Mexico." *Ethnohistory*, vol. 35, no. 3, July 1988, pp. 234–56.

–. "The Voyage of Saint Amaro: A Spanish Legend in Nahuatl Literature." *Colonial Latin American Review*, vol. 4, no. 1, 1995, pp. 29–57.

Bynum, Caroline Walker. *Holy Feast and Holy Fast: The Religious Significance of Food to Medieval Women*. U of California P, 1987.

–. *Jesus as Mother: Studies in the Spirituality of the High Middle Ages*. U of California P, 1982.

–. *Wonderful Blood: Theology and Practice in Late Medieval Northen Germany and Beyond*. U of Pennsylvania P, 2007.

Caciola, Nancy. *Discerning Spirits: Divine and Demonic Possession in the Middle Ages*. Cornell UP, 2003.

Calderón de la Barca, Pedro. *La hidalga del valle*. Edited by Mary Lorene Thomas, Universidad de Navarra, Reichenberger, 2013.

–. *La humildad coronada*. Edited by Ignacio Arellano. Universidad de Navarra, Reichenberger, 2002.

Calvert, Laura. *Francisco de Osuna and the Spirit of the Letter*. U of North Carolina Dept. of Romance Languages, 1973.

Cañadas, Iván. *The Public Theaters of Golden Age Madrid and Tudor-Stuart London: Class, Gender, and Festive Community*. Ashgate, 2005.

Cargogni, Costanzo. "Houses of Prayer in the History of the Franciscan Order." *Franciscan Solitude*, edited by André Cirino and Jose Raischl, Franciscan Institute, 1995, pp. 211–64.

Carrera, Elena. "The Emotions in Sixteenth-Century Spanish Spirituality." *Journal of Religious History*, vol. 31, no. 3, September 2007, pp. 235–53.

Case, Thomas. "Metatheater and World View in Lope's 'El divino africano.'" *Bulletin of the Comediantes*, vol. 42, no. 1, Summer 1990, pp. 129–42.

Castañeda, James A. *Agustín Moreto*. Twayne, 1974.

Castro, Américo. "Una comedia de Lope de Vega condenada por la Inquisición." *Revista de filología española*, vol. 9, no. 3, 1922, pp. 311–14.

Catherine of Siena, Saint. *The Letters of Catherine of Siena*. Edited and translated by Suzanne Noffke, Arizona Center for Medieval and Renaissance Studies, 2000.

Cazalla, María de. *Proceso de la Inquisicion contra Maria de Cazalla*. Edited by Milagros Ortega-Costa, Fundación Universitaria Española, 1978.

Cecilia del Nacimiento. *Obras completas*. Edited by José M. Díaz Cerón, Editorial de Espiritualidad, 1971.

–. *Journeys of a Mystic Soul in Poetry and Prose*. Edited and translated by Kevin Donnelly and Sandra Sider, The Other Voice in Early Modern Europe: The Toronto Series, 18, Centre for Reformation and Renaissance Studies, 2012.

Certeau, Michel de. *The Mystic Fable. Vol. I: The Sixteenth and Seventeenth Centuries*. Translated by Michael B. Smith, U of Chicago P, 1992.

–. *The Possession at Loudun*. Translated by Michael B. Smith, U of Chicago P, 2000.

Christensen, Mark. *Nahua and Maya Catholicisms: Texts and Religion in Colonial Central Mexico and Yucatan*. Stanford UP, 2013.

–. "Recent Approaches in Understanding Evangelization in New Spain." *History Compass*, vol. 14, no. 2, 2016, pp. 39–48.

Christian, William. *Apparitions in late Medieval and Renaissance Spain*. Princeton UP, 1980.

Clark, Stuart. *Thinking With Demons: The Idea of Witchcraft in Early Modern Europe*. Oxford UP, 1997.

–. *Vanities of the Eye: Vision in Early Modern European Culture*. Oxford UP, 2007.

Colón, Cristobal. "Carta a Luis de Sangangel." Research at King's College London: Early Modern Spain: Electronic Texts, http://www.ems.kcl.ac.uk /content/etext/e021.html. Accessed 13 July 2021.

Constable, Giles. *The Reformation of the Twelfth Century*. Cambridge UP, 1996.

Cortés, Rocío. "The Colegio Imperial de Santa Cruz de Tlatelolco and Its Aftermath: Nahua Intellectuals and the Spiritual Conquest of Mexico." *A Companion to Latin American Literature and Culture*, edited by Sara Castro-Klaren, Blackwell Publishing, 2008, pp. 86–105.

Cotarelo y Mori, Emilio. *Bibliografía de las controversias sobre la licitud del teatro en España*. Est. De La "Rev. De Archivos, Bibl. Y Museos," 1904.

Cruz, Anne. "Reading Over Men's Shoulders: Noblewomen's Libraries and Reading Practices." *Women's Literacy in Early Modern Spain and the New World*, 2nd ed., edited by Anne J. Cruz and Rosilie Hernández, Routledge, 2016, pp. 41–58.

–. "Transgendering the Mystical Voice: Angela de Foligno, San Juan, Santa Teresa, Luisa de Carvajal y Mendoza." *Echoes and Inscriptions: Comparative*

Approaches to Early Modern Literatures, edited by Barbara Simerka and Christopher Weimer, Bucknell UP, 2000, pp. 127–41.

Cueto Ruíz, Ronald. *Químeras y sueños: las profetas y la monarquía católica de Felipe IV.* Universidad, Secretariado de Publicaciones, 1994.

Cupitt, Don. *Mysticism After Modernity*. Blackwell Publishers, 1998.

Cusato, M. F. "Mysticism in the Spiritual Franciscan Tradition." *The Wiley-Blackwell Companion to Christian Mysticism*, edited by Julia A. Lamm, John Wiley & Sons, 2012, pp. 311–28.

Dassbach, Elma. *La comedia hagiográfica del Siglo de Oro español: Lope de Vega, Tirso de Molina y Calderón de la Barca*. Peter Lang, 1997.

Daston, Lorraine. "Marvelous Facts and Miraculous Evidence in Early Modern Europe." *Critical Inquiry*, vol. 18, no. 1, Fall 1991, pp. 93–132.

Daston, Lorraine, and Katharine E. Park. *Wonders and the Order of Nature, 1150–1750*. Zone Books, 1998.

Deleuze, Gilles. *The Fold: Leibniz and the Baroque*. Translated by Tom Conley, U of Minnesota P, 1993.

Díez Borque, José María. "Las sombras de la documentación y el valor informativo." *Teatros y vida teatral en el siglo de oro a través de las fuentes documentales*, edited by Luciano García Lorenzo and J.E. Varey, Tamesis, 1991.

–. *Los espectáculos del teatro y de la fiesta en el Siglo de Oro español*. Ediciones del Laberinto, 2002.

Donahue, Darcy. "The Mysticism of Saint Ignatius Loyola." *A Companion to Jesuit Mysticism*, edited by Robert Maryks, Brill, 2017, pp. 6–35.

–. "Wondrous Words: Miraculous Literacy and Real Literacy in the Convents of Early Modern Spain." *Women's Literacy in Early Modern Spain and the New World*, 2nd ed., edited by Anne J. Cruz and Rosilie Hernández, Routledge, 2016, 105–22.

Durston, Alan. *Pastoral Quechua: The History of Christian Translation in Colonial Peru, 1550–1650*. U of Notre Dame P, 2007.

Eckhart, Meister. *The Essential Sermons, Commentaries, Treatises, and Defense*. Translated by Edmund Colledge and Bernard McGinn. Paulist Press, 1981.

Egginton, William. *How the World Became a Stage: Presence, Theatricality, and the Question of Modernity*. SUNY Press, 2003.

Egido, Aurora. "La fábrica de un auto: Los encantos de la culpa." *Estudios sobre Calderón*, edited Javier Avaricio Maydeu, vol. II, Istmo, 2000, pp. 11–134.

Elliott, Dyan. *Proving Woman: Female Spirituality and Inquisitional Culture in the Later Middle Ages*. Princeton UP, 2004.

Elliott, J. H. *The Old World and the New: 1492–1650*. Canto Edition, Cambridge Studies in Early Modern History, Cambridge UP, 1992.

Escudero, José Antonio. *Estudios sobre la Inquisición*. Marcial Pons, 2005.

Fedewa, Marilyn. *María of Ágreda: Mystical Lady in Blue.* U of New Mexico P, 2009.
Fernández Álvarez, Manuel. *El fraile y la Inquisición.* Espasa, 2002.
Fernández del Castillo, Francisco. *Libros y libreros en el siglo XVI.* Tip. Guerrero, 1914.
Fernández Rodríguez, Natalia. "Imagenería sacra y espacios pictóricos en las comedias de santos de Lope de Vega." *Ehumanista,* vol. 30, 2015, pp. 83–98.
–. "Veneno mortal para la juventud: público y censura ante las pecadoras penitentes de la comedia nueva." *Bulletin of Hispanic Studies,* vol. 88, no. 8, December 2011, pp. 911–30.
Ferrer Valls, Teresa. "La fiesta en el Siglo de Oro: en los márgenes de la ilusión teatral." *Teatro y fiesta del Siglo de Oro en tierras europeas de los Austrias,* edited by José María Díez Borque, SEACEX, 2003, pp. 27–37.
Fort i Cogul, Eufemià. *Catalunya i la inquisició.* Aedos, 1973.
Foucault, Michel. *The Archaeology of Knowledge and the Discourse on Language.* Translated by A.M. Sheridan Smith, Pantheon Books, 1972.
–. *The Order of Things: An Archaeology of the Human Sciences.* Pantheon Books, 1970.
Furst, Jill. *The Natural History of the Soul in Ancient Mexico.* Yale UP, 1995.
Garbay-Velázquez, Estelle. *La circulación manuscrita de los poemas alfabéticos de Francisco de Osuna: El caso del manuscrito "MSS/74" de la Biblioteca Nacional de España.* Mélanges de la Casa de Velázquez, Casa de Velázquez, 2013, pp. 197–221.
–. "Representaciones del espacio interior e intimidad espiritual en los tratados de tres franciscanos recogidos (Francisco de Osuna, Bernabé de Palma y Bernardino de Laredo)." *E-Spania,* vol. 37, October 2020.
García, Gómez. *Carro de dos vidas.* Edited by Melquíades Andrés Martín, Universidad Pontificia de Salamanca, Fundación universitaria española, 1988.
García Barriuso, Patrocinio. *La monja de Carrión: Sor Luisa de la Ascensión Colmenares Cabezón: (aportación documental para una biografía).* Self-published, 1986.
García Pérez, Rafael. *La imprenta y la literatura espiritual castellana en la España del Renacimiento, 1470–1560.* Ediciones Trea, 2006.
Garibay K., Angel María. *Llave del nahuatl.* Porrua, 1989.
–, ed. *Poesía nahuatl.* Universidad Nacional Autónoma de Mexico, 1964.
Gavrilyuk, Paul, and Sarah Coakley, editors. *The Spiritual Senses.* Cambridge UP, 2012.
Gerson, Jean. *On Distinguishing True from False Revelations. Jean Gerson: Early Works,* translated by Brian Patrick McGuire, Paulist Press, 1998.
–. *On the Proving of Spirits. The Concept of Discretio Spirituum in John Gerson's "De probatione Spirituum" and "De Distinctione Verarum Visionum a Falsis,"* translated by Paschal Boland, Catholic University of America Press, 1959.

Giles, Mary E. "Spanish Visionary Women and the Paradox of Performance." *Performance and Transformation*, edited by Mary A. Suydam and Joanna E. Ziegler, St. Martin's Press, 1999, pp. 273–98.

Gómez Canedo, Lino. *Evangelización, cultura y promoción social: Ensayos y estudios críticos sobre la contribución franciscana a los orígenes cristianos de México (siglos xvi-xviii)*. Editorial Porrua, 1993.

Gómez Redondo, Fernando. *Historia de la prosa de los Reyes Católicos: el umbral del Renacimiento*. 1a ed., Cátedra, 2012.

Gracián y Morales, Baltasar. *Agudeza y arte de ingenio*. Edited by Evaristo Correa Calderón, Editorial Castalia, 1969.

Grafton, Anthony. *New Worlds, Ancient Texts: The Power of Tradition and the Shock of Discovery*. Harvard UP, 1992.

Granja, Agustín de la. "Los actores del siglo XVII ante *La vida es sueño*: De la técnica de la turbación a la práctica de la suspensión." *Bulletin of Hispanic Studies*, vol. 77, no. 1, January 2000, pp. 145–71.

–. "Los espacios del sueño en el corral de comedias." *El espacio y sus representaciones en el teatro español del Siglo de Oro: Homenaje a Frédéric Serralta*, edited by Françoise Cazal, Christophe González, and Marc Vitse, Biblioteca Aurea Hispánica, 17, Iberoamericana, Vervuert, Universidad de Navarra, 2002, pp. 259–312.

Graziano, Frank. *Wounds of Love: The Mystical Marriage of Saint Rose of Lima*. Oxford UP, 2004.

Greenblatt, Stephen. *Shakespearean Negotiations: The Circulation of Social Energy in Renaissance England*. U of California P, 1988.

Haliczer, Stephen. *Between Exaltation and Infamy: Female Mystics in the Golden Age of Spain*. Oxford UP, 2002.

Hamilton, Alastair. *Heresy and Mysticism in Sixteenth-century Spain: The Alumbrados*. U of Toronto P, 1992.

Hansen, Leonard. *Vita mirabilis et mors pretiosa venerabilis sororis Rosae de S. Maria*. 2 vols., translated into Spanish from the Latin by Jacinto Parra as *Vida admirable de Santa Rosa de Lima*, Patrona del Nuevo Mundo, 1671.

Haraguchi, Jennifer. "Vita di Eleonora: A Unique Example of Autobiographical Writing in Counter-Reformation Italy." *I Tatti Studies in the Italian Renaissance*, vol. 17, no. 2, September 2014, pp. 369–97.

Harrington, L. Michael. Introduction. *A Thirteenth-Century Textbook of Mystical Theology at the University of Paris*, edited and translated by L. Michael Harrington, Dallas Medieval Texts and Translations 4, Peeters, 2004, pp. 1–44.

Harrison, Peter. "Miracles, Early Modern Science, and Rational Religion." *Church History*, vol. 75, no.3, 2006, pp. 493–510.

Hatzfeld, Helmut. *Estudios sobre la mística española*. Gredos, 1955.

Hillgarth, Jocelyn Nigel. "Lull, Ramón (c. 1232–1316)." *Encyclopedia of Philosophy*, edited by Donald M. Borchert, 2nd ed., vol. 5, Macmillan

Reference USA, 2006, pp. 609–11. Gale Virtual Reference Library. Accessed 2 July 2019.

Holsinger, Bruce W. *Music, Body, and Desire in Medieval Culture: Hildegard of Bingen to Chaucer.* Stanford UP, 2001.

Homza, Lu Ann, editor. *The Spanish Inquisition, 1478–1614: An Anthology of Sources.* Hacket Publishers 2006.

Howe, Elizabeth Teresa. "Cisneros and the Translation of Women's Spirituality." *The Vernacular Spirit: Essays on Medieval Religious Literature,* edited by Renate Blumenfeld-Kosinski, Duncan Robertson, and Nancy Bradley Warren, Palgrave, 2002, pp. 283–96.

Huerga, Alvaro. *La historia de los alumbrados (1570–1630).* Fundación universitaria española, 1978–92. 5 vols.

Hughes, Ann Nickerson. *Religious Imagery in the Theater of Tirso de Molina.* Mercer UP, 1984.

International Society of Hildegard von Bingen Studies, http://www.hildegard-society.org/p/home.html. Accessed 14 July 2021.

Irwin, Joyce. "The Mystical Music of Jean Gerson." *Early Music History,* vol. 1, 1981, pp. 187–201.

Jaffary, Nora E. *False Mystics: Deviant Orthodoxy in Colonial Mexico.* U of Nebraska P, 2005.

James, William. *The Varieties of Religious Experience; a Study in Human Nature; Being the Gifford Lectures on Natural Religion Delivered at Edinburgh in 1901–1902.* Longmans, Green, 1902.

Jiménez, Francisco. "Vida de Fray Martín de Valencia." Included as an Appendix in Antonio Rubial García, *La hermana pobreza: El franciscanismo: de la Edad Media a la evangelización novohispana.* Facultad de Filosofía y Letras, UNAM, 1996.

Jímenez de Cisneros, García. *Exercitatorio de la vida espiritual* [1500]. Cervantes Virtual, http://www.cervantesvirtual.com/obra/garcia-jimenez-de-cisneros-obras-completas-ii-exercitatorio-de-la-vida-spiritual--0/. Accessed 14 July 2021.

Jordán Arroyo, María. *Entre la vigilia y el sueño: Soñar en el Siglo de Oro.* Iberoamericana, Verveurt, 2017.

Juan de la Cruz, San. *The Collected Works of St. John of the Cross.* Translated by Kieran Kavanaugh and Otilio Rodríguez, Institute of Carmelite Studies, 1979.

–. *Poesía completa y comentarios en prosa.* Edited by Raquel Asún, Planeta, 1989.

–. *Poesías. Subida del Monte Carmelo. Noche oscura. Cántico espiritual. Llama de amor viva.* Edited by Francisco Javier Díez de Revenga, vol. II of *Mística del Siglo XVI,* Biblioteca Castro, 2009.

Juana de la Cruz, Sor. *Mother Juana de la Cruz, 1481–1534: Visionary Sermons.* Edited by Jessica A. Boon, translated by Ronald E. Surtz, Iter Academic Press, Arizona Center for Medieval and Renaissance Studies, 2016.

Kagan, Richard. *Lucrecia's Dreams: Politics and Prophecy in Sixteenth-Century Spain*. U of California P, 1995.

Kallendorf, Hilaire. *Exorcism and its Texts: Subjectivity in Early Modern Literature of England and Spain*. U of Toronto P, 2003.

–. "The Rhetoric of Exorcism." *Rhetorica*, vol. 23, no. 3, Summer 2005, pp. 209–37.

Karttunen, Frances E. *An Analytical Dictionary of Nahuatl*. U of Texas P, 1983.

Katz, Steven T. *Mysticism and Language*. Oxford UP, 1992.

–. *Mysticism and Philosophical Analysis*. Sheldon Press, 1978.

Keitt, Andrew W. *Inventing the Sacred: Imposture, Inquisition, and the Boundaries of the Supernatural in Golden Age Spain*. Brill, 2005.

Kenney, John Peter. *The Mysticism of Saint Augustine: Rereading the* Confessions. Routledge, 2005.

Keskiaho, Jesse. *Dreams and Visions in the Early Middle Ages: The Reception and Use of Patristic Ideas, 400–900*. Cambridge UP, 2015.

Kirakosian, Racha. "Musical Heaven and Heavenly Music: At the Crossroads of Liturgical Music and Mystical Texts." *Viator*, vol. 48, no. 1, 2017, pp. 121–44.

Kirchberger, Clare. "Hugh of Saint Victor on the Celestial Hierarchy of Denys the Areopagite." *Life of the Spirit*, vol. 11, no. 123, September 1956, 132–8.

Kirschner, Teresa. *Técnicas de representación en Lope de Vega*. Tamesis, 1998.

Klaus, Susanne. *Uprooted Christianity: The Preaching of the Christian Doctrine in Mexico Based on Franciscan Sermons of the 16th Century Written in Nahuatl*. Saurwein, 1999.

Langbein, John H. *Prosecuting Crime in the Renaissance: England, Germany, France*. Harvard UP, 1974.

Laningham, Susan Diane. Introduction. *Autobiography and Letters of a Spanish Nun*, by María Vela y Cueto. Translated by Jane Tar, Iter Press, 2016.

Laredo, Bernardino de. *Subida del Monte Sión*. Fundación universitaria española, Universidad Pontificia de Salamanca, 2000.

–. *The Ascent of Mount Sión: being the third book of the treatise of that name*. Translated by E. Allison Peers, Faber and Faber, 1952.

Lea, Henry Charles. *The History of the Inquisition in the Middle Ages*. Harper & Brothers, 1887. 3 vols.

León, Luis de. *De los nombres de Cristo*. Edited by Javier San José Lera, Galaxia Gutenberg, 2008.

–. *Poesías completas*. Edited by Cristobal Cuevas, Castalia, 2001.

–. *The Unknown Light: The Poems of Fray Luis de León*. Translated by Willis Barnstone, SUNY Press, 1979.

León-Portilla, Miguel. *Coloquios y doctrina cristiana: con que los doce frailes de San Francisco, enviados por el Papa Adriano VI y por el Emperador Carlos V, convirtieron a los indios de la Nueva España: en lengua mexicano y española.* UNAM: Fundación de Investigaciones Sociales, 1986.

–. *La filosofía nahuatl estudiada en sus fuentes.* Universidad Nacional Autónoma de México, 1956.

López Austin, Alfredo. *Cuerpo humano e ideología: las concepciones de los antiguos Nahuas.* Universidad Nacional Autonoma De Mexico, Instituto De Investigaciones Antropologicas, 1980.

López Baralt, Luce. "La amada nocturna en San Juan de la Cruz se pudo haber llamado Layla." *Mujeres de Luz, la mística femenina y lo femenino en la mística,* edited by Pablo Beneito, Trotta, 2001.

–. *San Juan de la Cruz y el Islám: estudio sobre las filiaciones semíticas de su literatura mística.* 1a ed., Colegio de México, Centro de estudios lingüísticos y literarios, Universidad de Puerto Rico–Recinto De Río Piedras, 1985.

López Durán, Fernando. *Un cielo abreviado: Introducción crítica a una historia de la autobiografía religiosa en España.* Fundación Universitaria Española, 2007.

Loyola, Ignacio de. *Autobiografía y Diario espiritual.* Edited by Luis María Mendizábal, Biblioteca de Autores Cristianos, 2011.

–. *La intimidad del peregrino: Diario espiritual de San Ignacio de Loyola.* Edited by Santiago Thió de Pol, Ediciones Mensajero, 1980.

–. *The Spiritual Exercises of Saint Ignatius: A Translation and Commentary by George E. Ganss, S.J.* The Institute of Jesuit Sources, 1992.

Ludmer, Josefina. "Las tretas del débil." *La sartén por el mango: Encuentro de escritoras latinoamericanas,* edited by Patricia Elena González. Puerto Rico: Huracán, 1985, pp. 47–54.

Ludolph von Sachsen [Ludolph of Saxony]. *The Life of Jesus Christ.* [English translation of *Vita Christi*]. Edited and translated by Milton T. Walsh, Cistercian Publications, Liturgical, 2018.

Maggi, Armando. *Satan's Rhetoric: A Study of Renaissance Demonology.* U of Chicago P, 2001.

–. *Uttering the Word: The Mystical Performances of Maria Maddalena de' Pazzi, A Renaissance Visionary.* SUNY Press, 1998.

Mancho Duque, María Jesus. *Palabras y símbolos en San Juan de la Cruz.* Fundación Universitaria Española, 1993.

Maravall, José Antonio. *The Culture of the Baroque: Analysis of a Historical Structure.* Translated by Terry Cochran, U of Minnesota P, 1986.

María de la Antigua, Sor. *Desengaño de religiosos y de almas que tratan de virtud.* 3a impresión, por Joseph Llopis, 1697.

María Maddalena de' Pazzi, Santa. *I colloqui. Vol. II, III* of *Tutte le opere.* Centro Internazionale del Libro, 1961.

Márquez, Antonio. "De mística luisiana: ser o no ser." *Fray Luis de León: Historia, humanismo y letras,* edited by Víctor García de la Concha and Javier San José Lera. Universidad de Salamanca, 1996, pp. 287–98.

Martin, Raymond, and John Barresi. *The Rise and Fall of Soul and Self: An Intellectual History of Personal Identity*. Columbia UP, 2006.

Maryks, Robert, editor. *Companion to Ignatius of Loyola: Life, Writings, Spirituality, Influence*. Brill, 2014.

Mathes, W. Michael. *Santa Cruz de Tlatelolco, la primera biblioteca académica de las Américas*. Secretaria de Relaciones Exteriores, 1982.

Matter, E. Ann. *The Voice of My Beloved: The Song of Songs in Western Medieval Christianity*. U of Pennsylvania P, 1990.

McGinn, Bernard. *The Flowering of Mysticism: Men and Women in the New Mysticism (1200–1350)*. Vol. III in *The Presence of God: A History of Western Christian Mysticism*, Crossroad Publishers, 1998.

–. *Mysticism in the Golden Age of Spain (1500–1650)*. Vol. VI, pt. 2 in *The Presence of God: A History of Western Christian Mysticism*, Crossroad Publishers, 2017.

McManamon, John. *The Texts and Contexts of Ignatius Loyola's "Autobiography."* Fordham UP, 2013.

Mendieta, Gerónimo de. *Historia eclesiástica indiana*. Edited by Joaquín García Icazbalceta, Editorial Salvador Chavez Hayhoe, 1945. 4 vols.

Mendizábal, Luis María. Introducción. *Autobiografía y Diario Espiritual*, by Ignacio de Loyola, Biblioteca de Autores Cristianos, 2011.

Millar Carvacho, René. "Rosa de Santa María (1586–1617): Génesis de su santidad y primera hagiografía." *Historia*, vol. 1, no. 36, 2003, pp. 255–73.

Molina, Alonso de. *Vocabulario en lengua castellana y mexicana y mexicana y castellana*. 2nd ed., Editorial Porrua, 1977.

Molina, Tirso de. "El divino colmenero." *Autos sacramentales I*, edited by Ignacio Arellano, Blanco Oteiza, and Miguel Zugasti, Instituto de Estudios Tirsianos, 1998.

–. "La Santa Juana. Primera, Segunda, y Tercera Parte." *Obras dramáticas completas*, edited by Blanca de los Ríos, Aguilar, 1946.

Morales, Francisco. "New World Colonial Franciscan Mystical Practice." *A New Companion to Hispanic Mysticism*, edited by Hilaire Kallendorf, Brill, 2010, pp. 71–101.

Moreno Martínez, Doris. *La invención de la Inquisición*. Marcial Pons, 2004.

Moreto, Agustín. "Santa Rosa del Perú." *Segunda parte de las Comedias de Don Agustin Moreto*, En la Imprenta de Benito Macè, 1676. Digital edition. TESO (Teatro del Siglo de Oro).

–. Los siete durmientes y más dichosos hermanos." Santander: Ayuntamiento; Alicante: Biblioteca Virtual Miguel de Cervantes, 2012, http://www.cervantesvirtual.com/nd/ark:/59851/bmc1r7c4. Accessed 14 July 2021.

Mujica, Barbara. "The Sacred and the Political." *A New Anthology of Modern Spanish Theater*, Yale UP, 2013, pp. 170–78.

–, editor. *Women Writers of Early Modern Spain: Sophia's Daughters*. Yale UP, 2004.

Nalle, Sara. "Literacy and Culture in Early Modern Castile." *Past & Present*, vol. 125, November 1989, pp. 67–96.

–. *Mad For God: Bartolomé Sanchez, the Secret Messiah of Cardenete*. UP of Virginia, 2001.

Nesvig, Martin. *Ideology and Inquisition: The World of the Censors in Early Mexico*. Yale UP, 2008.

O'Malley, John W. *The First Jesuits*. Harvard UP, 1993.

O'Reilly, Terence. "Early Printed Books in Spain and the Exercicios of Ignatius Loyola." *Bulletin of Spanish Studies*, vol. 89, no. 4, 2012, pp. 635–64.

–. "Meditation and Contemplation: Monastic Spirituality in Early Sixteenth-Century Spain." In *Faith and Fanaticism: Religious Fervour in Early Modern Spain*, edited by Leslie Twomey, Routledge, 1997, pp. 37–60.

O'Rourke Boyle, Marjorie. *Loyola's Acts: The Rhetoric of the Self*. U of California P, 1997.

Orozco Díaz, Emilio. *Poesía y mística: Introducción a la lírica de San Juan de la Cruz*. Ediciones Guardarrama, 1959.

Osuna, Francisco de. *Cuarto Abecedario. Místicos franciscanos españoles*, Tomo I, vol. 38, edited by Juan Baustista Gomis, Biblioteca de Autores Cristianos. Digital edition. Princeton Theological Seminary Library, https://archive.org/details/misticosfrancisc01gomi. Accessed 14 July 2021.

–. *Tercer abecedario espiritual. Místicos franciscanos*, Tomo II, edited by Saturnino López Santidrián, Biblioteca de Autores Cristianos, 1998.

–. *The Third Spiritual Alphabet*. Translated by Mary Giles, Classics of Western Spirituality, Paulist Press, 1981.

Osuna Rodríguez, Inmaculada. "Poesía intramuros: Creación y recepción poética." *Letras en la celda. Cultura escrita de los conventos femeninos en la España moderna*, edited by Nieves Baranda Leturio and María Carmen Marín Pina, Iberoamericana, Verveurt, 2014.

–. *Oxford Companion to the Bible*. Edited by Bruce M. Metzger and Michael David Coogan. Oxford UP, 1993.

–. *Oxford Dictionary of Literary Terms*. 3rd ed., edited by Chris Baldick, Oxford UP, 2008.

Pacho, Eulogio. *El apogeo de la mística cristiana: Historia de la espiritualidad clásica española (1450–1650)*. Monte Carmelo, 2008.

Paige, Nicholas. *Being Interior. Autobiography and the Contradiction of Modernity in Seventeenth-Century France*. U of Pennsylvania P, 2001.

Pardo, Osvaldo. *The Origins of Mexican Catholicism: Nahua Rituals and Christian Sacraments in Sixteenth-Century Mexico*. U of Michigan P, 2006.

Parker, Alexander. *The Allegorical Drama of Calderon: Introduction to the Autos Sacramentales*. Dolphin Books, 1943.

Pastore, Stefania. *Una herejía española*. [*Un'eresia spagnola*]. Marcial Pons, 2010.

Paun de García, Susan. "Cañizares's *La más amada de Cristo, Santa Gertrudis la Magna*." *Religious and Secular Theater in Golden Age Spain: Essays in Honor of Donald T. Dietz*, edited by Susan Paun de García and Donald R. Lawson, Peter Lang, 2017, pp. 91–104.

Pego Puigbó, Armando. *El Renacimiento espiritual: introducción literaria a los tratados de oración españoles (1520–1566)*. Consejo Superior de Investigaciones Científicas, 2004.

Pérez, Joseph. *La Inquisición española*. Ediciones Martínez Roca, 2005.

Pérez Montalbán, Juan. "La gitana de Menfis Santa María Egypciaca: comedia famosa." en la imprenta de Antonio Sanz, en la plazuela de la calle de la Paz, 1756. Fondos digitalizados Universidad de Sevilla.

Phelan, John. *The Millennial Kingdom of the Franciscans in the New World*. U of California P, 1970.

Pinto Crespo, Virgilio. "Control ideológico: censura e 'Indices de libros prohibidos.'" *Historia de la Inquisición en España y América*, vol. 1, edited by Joaquín Pérez Villanueva and Bartolomé Escandell Bonet, Biblioteca de Autores Cristianos, 1984, pp. 648–61.

Poutrin, Isabelle. *Le voile et la plume: Autobiographie et sainteté féminine dans l'Espagne moderne*. Casa De Velázquez, 1995.

Pseudo-Dionysius, the Areopagite. *The Divine Names and the Mystical Theology*. Translated by C.E. Rolt, Society for Promoting Christian Knowledge, The Macmillan, 1940.

–. *The Mystical Theology, and the Celestial Hierarchies of Dionysius the Areopagite: With Commentaries by the Editors of the Shrine of Wisdom and Poem by St. John of the Cross*. 2nd ed., Shrine of Wisdom, 1965.

Puyol Buil, Carlos. *Inquisición y política en el reinado de Felipe IV: los procesos de Jerónimo de Villanueva y las monjas de San Plácido, 1628–1660*. CSIC, 1993.

Raymond of Capua. *The Life of Catherina of Siena*. [*Legenda maior*]. Translated by George Lamb, Harvill Press, 1960.

Real Academia Española. *Diccionario de Autoridades. (1726–1739)*. Digital edition. http://web.frl.es/DA.html. Accessed 14 July 2021.

Rhodes, Elizabeth. "Gender in the Night. Juan de la Cruz y Cecilia del Nacimiento." *Studies on Women's Lyric Poetry of the Golden Age. Tras el espejo la musa escribe*, edited by Julián Olivares, Tamesis, 2009, pp. 202–17.

–. *The Unrecognized Precursors of Montemayor's Diana*. U of Missouri P, 1992.

Ricard, Robert. *The Spiritual Context of Mexico: An Essay on the Apostolate and the Evangelizing Methods of the Mendicant Orders in New Spain: 1523–72*. Translated by Lesley Byrd Simpson, U of California P, 1966.

Richard of St. Victor. *Selected Writings on Contemplation*. Edited by Clare Kirchberger, Faber and Faber, 1957.

Rico Collado, Francisco Luis. "La Inquisición y las *visionarias* clarisas del siglo XVII: el caso de sor Luisa de la Ascensión." *Bulletin of Spanish Studies*, vol. 92, no. 5, 2015, pp. 771–90.

Río Barredo, María José del. "Censura inquisitorial y teatro del 1707–1819." *Hispania Sacra*, vol. 38, no. 78, January 1986, pp. 279–330.

Robinson, Cynthia. *Imagining the Passion in a Multiconfessional Castile: The Virgin, Christ, Devotions, and Images in the Fourteenth and Fifteenth Centuries.* Penn State UP, 2013.

Roldán Figueroa, Rody. "Ignatius of Loyola and Juan de Ávila on the Ascetic Life of the Laity." *A Companion to Ignatius of Loyola*, edited by Robert Maryks, Brill, 2014, pp. 159–78.

Ros García, Salvador. Introducción. *Experiencias Místicas: Relaciones y cuentas de conciencia. Santa Teresa de Jesús*, by Santa Teresa de Jesús, edited by Salvador Ros García, Biblioteca de Autores Cristianos, 2014.

Ruffinatto, Aldo. *Sobre textos y mundos: Ensayos de filología y simbiótica hispánicas.* Translated by José Muñoz Rivas, Universidad de Murcia, 1989.

Ryan, Michael. "Assimilating New Worlds in the Sixteenth and Seventeenth Centuries." *Comparative Studies in Society and History*, vol. 23, no. 4, October 1981, pp. 519–38.

Sahagún, Bernardino de. *Coloquios y doctrina cristiana: con que los doce frailes de San Francisco, enviados por el papa Adriano VI y por el emperador Carlos V, convirtieron a los indios de la Nueva España: en lengua mexicano y española.* Edited by Miguel Ángel León Portilla, Universidad Nacional Autónoma de México: Fundación de Investigaciones Sociales, 1986.

–. *Historia general de las cosas de la Nueva España.* Edited by Ángel María Garibay Kintana, Porrua, 1956.

Sanmartín Bastida, Rebeca, and María Victoria Curto Hernández. *El libro de la oración de María de Santo Domingo: Estudio y edición.* Iberoamericana, Verveurt, 2019.

Sarrión Mora, Adelina. *Beatas y endemoniadas: mujeres heterodoxas ante la Inquisición, Siglo XVI a XIX.* Alianza, 2003.

Shuger, Dale. "Incoherent Subjects, Incomplete Lives: The Limits of Spiritual Autobiography in Spain." *Religions*, vol. 8, no. 12, November, 2017, pp. 277–93.

–. "The Language of Mysticism and the Language of Law in Early Modern Spain." *Renaissance Quarterly* 68, no. 3 (2015): 932–956.

Sluhovsky, Moshe. *Believe Not Every Spirit: Possession, Mysticism, & Discernment in Early Modern Catholicism.* U of Chicago P, 2007.

–. "Loyola's *Spiritual Exercises* and the Modern Self." *Companion to Ignatius of Loyola: Life, Writings, Spirituality, Influence*, edited by Roberty Maryks, Brill, 2014, pp. 216–31.

Surtz, Ronald. *The Guitar of God: Gender, Power, and Authority in the Visionary World of Mother Juana de la Cruz (1481–1534).* U of Pennsylvania P, 1990.

Tavárez, David. "Nahua Intellectuals, Franciscan Scholars, and the *Devotio moderna* in Colonial Mexico." *The Americas*, vol. 70, no. 2, October 2013, pp. 203–35.

Teresa of Ávila, Saint. *The Complete Poetry of St. Teresa de Ávila: A Bilingual Edition*. Edited and translated by Eric W. Vogt, UP of the South, 1996.

–. *Experiencias místicas: Relaciones y cuentas de conciencia*. Edited by Salvador Ros García, Biblioteca de Autores Cristianos, 2014.

–. *The Life of Saint Teresa de Ávila: By Herself*. Translated by J. M. Cohen, Penguin Books, 1957.

–. *Libro de la vida*. Edited by Otger Steggink, Castalia, 1986.

Thomas, á Kempis. *Thomas à Kempis: The Imitation of Christ: A New Reading of the 1441 Latin Autograph Manuscript*. Translated and edited by William C. Creasy, Mercer UP, 1989.

Thompson, Colin P. *The Poet and the Mystic: A Study of the Cántico Espiritual of San Juan de la Cruz*. Oxford UP, 1977.

–. *The Strife of Tongues. Fray Luis de León and the Golden Age of Spain*. Cambridge UP, 1988.

Toft, Evelyn. "Cecilia del Nacimiento: Second Generation Mystic of the Carmelite Reform." *A New Companion to Hispanic Mysticism*, edited by Hilaire Kallendorf, Brill, 2010, pp. 231–53.

Turley, Steven E. *Franciscan Spirituality and Mission in New Spain, 1524–1599*. Ashgate Press, 2014.

Turner, Denys. "Allegory in Christian late antiquity." *The Cambridge Companion to Allegory*, edited by Rica Copeland and Peter T. Struck, Cambridge UP, 2010.

–. "The Darkness of God and the Light of Christ: Negative Theology and Eucharistic Presence." *Modern Theology*, vol. 15, no. 2, 1999, 143–58.

–. *The Darkness of God: Negativity in Christian Mysticism*. Cambridge UP, 1995.

Valdés, Fernando. Cathalogus libroru[m] qui prohibe[n]tur mandato Illustrissimi & Reuerend. D. D. Ferdinandi de Valdes Hispalen. Archiepi, Inquisitoris Generalis Hispaniae (Índice de libros prohibidos), 1559. Real Biblioteca, digital facsímile, http://fotos.patrimonionacional.es/biblioteca/ibis/pmi/Indice_1559/index.html. Accessed 14 July 2021.

Vázquez, Luis. "Poemas 'sanjuanistas' fuera del Carmelo." *Estudios*, no. 137, April–May 1982, 149–98.

Van Caenegem, R. C. *Legal History: A European Perspective*. Hambledon Press, 1991.

Vega, Garcilaso de la. *Obras Completas: con comentario*. Edited by Elias L. Rivers, Editorial Castalia, 1974.

Vega Carpio, Lope de. "El divino africano." *Obras escogidas. Teatro*, Tomo III, edited by Federico Carlos Sainz de Robles, Aguilar, 1969, pp. 206–37.

–. "El divino africano." Teatro Español del Siglo de Oro (TESO). Digital edition.

–. "La maya." *Obras escogidas. Teatro,* Tomo III, edited by Federico Carlos Sainz de Robles, Aguilar, 1969, pp. 19–33.

–. "Santa Teresa de Jesús: Monja Descalza de Nuestra Señora del Carmen." *A New Anthology of Modern Spanish Theater,* edited by Barbara Mujica, Yale UP, 2013.

Vela y Cueto, María. *Libro de las Mercedes and Vida,* edited by Margaret Rees, Mellen Press, 2007.

Van Engen, John. *Sisters and Brothers of the Common Life: The Devotio Moderna and the World of the Later Middle Ages.* U of Pennsylvania P, 2008.

Vitse, Marc. "Teoría y géneros dramáticos en el Siglo XVII." *Historia del teatro español Vol. 1,* edited by Javier Huerta Calvo, Gredos, 2003, pp. 717–55.

Von Habsburg, Maximilian. *Catholic and Protestant Translations of the Imitatio Christi, 1425–1650: From Late Medieval Classic to Early Modern Bestseller.* Ashgate, 2011.

Wardropper, Bruce W. *Historia de la poesía lírica a lo divino en la cristiandad occidental.* Revista de Occidente, 1958.

Webb, Heather. "Catherine of Siena's Heart." *Speculum,* vol. 80, no. 3, July 2005, pp. 802–17.

Weber, Alison. "Could Women Write Mystical Poetry?: The Literary Daughters of San Juan de la Cruz." *Studies on Women's Poetry of the Golden Age: Tras el espejo la musa escribe,* edited by Julián Olivares, Tamesis, 2009, pp. 185–201.

–. "Demonizing Ecstasy: Alonso de la Fuente and the *alumbrados* of Extremadura." *The Mystical Gesture: Essays on Medieval and Early Modern Spiritual Culture in Honor of Mary E. Giles,* edited by Robert Boenig. Ashgate, 2000, pp. 147–65.

–. *Teresa of Avila and the Rhetoric of Femininity.* Princeton UP, 1990.

–. "The Three Lives of the *Vida:* The Uses of Convent Autobiography." *Women, Texts and Authority in the Early Modern Spanish World,* edited by Marta Vicente and Luis Corteguera, Ashgate, 2003, pp. 107–26.

Whitehill, Paul. "Doing It for God: Renaissance Rhetoric and the Beginnings of Spanish Mystical Writing." *Hispanófila,* vol. 152, no. 1, 2008, pp. 39–52.

Williams, Raymond. *Marxism and Literature.* Oxford UP, 1977.

Wilson, Colin. *Poetry and Mysticism.* City Light Books, 1969.

Wright, Wendy M. "Inside My Body Is the Body of God: Margaret Mary Alacoque and the Tradition of Embodied Mysticism." *The Mystical Gesture: Essays on Medieval and Early Modern Spiritual Culture in Honor of Mary E. Giles,* edited by Robert Boenig, Ashgate, 2000, pp. 185–92.

Yepes, Diego de. *Vida, virtudes y milagros de la bienaventurada virgen Teresa de Jesús*. Por Ángel Tauanno, 1606. Biblioteca Digital Hispánica, http://bdh-rd.bne.es/viewer.vm?id=0000078113&page=1. Accessed 14 July 2012.

Zarri, Gabriella. "L'autobiografia religiosa negli scritti di in Camilla Battita da Varano: 'La vita spirituale' (1491) e le 'Istruzione al discepolo' (1501)." *In quella parte del libro de la mia memoria: verita e finzioni dell'"io" autobiografico*, edited by Francesco Bruni, Fondazione Giorgio Cini, 2003, pp. 133–58.

–. "La scrittura monastica." *Letras en la celda. Cultura escrita de los conventos femeninos en la España moderna*, edited by Nieves Baranda Leturio and María Carmen Marín Pina, Iberoamericana, Verveurt, 2014.

Index

Toronto Iberic

1 Anthony J. Cascardi, *Cervantes, Literature, and the Discourse of Politics*
2 Jessica A. Boon, *The Mystical Science of the Soul: Medieval Cognition in Bernardino de Laredo's Recollection Method*
3 Susan Byrne, *Law and History in Cervantes'* Don Quixote
4 Mary E. Barnard and Frederick A. de Armas (eds), *Objects of Culture in the Literature of Imperial Spain*
5 Nil Santiáñez, *Topographies of Fascism: Habitus, Space, and Writing in Twentieth-Century Spain*
6 Nelson Orringer, *Lorca in Tune with Falla: Literary and Musical Interludes*
7 Ana M. Gómez-Bravo, *Textual Agency: Writing Culture and Social Networks in Fifteenth-Century Spain*
8 Javier Irigoyen-García, *The Spanish Arcadia: Sheep Herding, Pastoral Discourse, and Ethnicity in Early Modern Spain*
9 Stephanie Sieburth, *Survival Songs: Conchita Piquer's* Coplas *and Franco's Regime of Terror*
10 Christine Arkinstall, *Spanish Female Writers and the Freethinking Press, 1879–1926*

11 Margaret Boyle, *Unruly Women: Performance, Penitence, and Punishment in Early Modern Spain*
12 Evelina Gužauskytė, *Christopher Columbus's Naming in the* diarios *of the Four Voyages (1492–1504): A Discourse of Negotiation*
13 Mary E. Barnard, *Garcilaso de la Vega and the Material Culture of Renaissance Europe*
14 William Viestenz, *By the Grace of God: Francoist Spain and the Sacred Roots of Political Imagination*
15 Michael Scham, Lector Ludens*: The Representation of Games and Play in Cervantes*
16 Stephen Rupp, *Heroic Forms: Cervantes and the Literature of War*
17 Enrique Fernandez, *Anxieties of Interiority and Dissection in Early Modern Spain*
18 Susan Byrne, *Ficino in Spain*
19 Patricia M. Keller, *Ghostly Landscapes: Film, Photography, and the Aesthetics of Haunting in Contemporary Spanish Culture*
20 Carolyn A. Nadeau, *Food Matters: Alonso Quijano's Diet and the Discourse of Food in Early Modern Spain*
21 Cristian Berco, *From Body to Community: Venereal Disease and Society in Baroque Spain*
22 Elizabeth R. Wright, *The Epic of Juan Latino: Dilemmas of Race and Religion in Renaissance Spain*
23 Ryan D. Giles, *Inscribed Power: Amulets and Magic in Early Spanish Literature*
24 Jorge Pérez, *Confessional Cinema: Religion, Film, and Modernity in Spain's Development Years, 1960–1975*
25 Joan Ramon Resina, *Josep Pla: Seeing the World in the Form of Articles*
26 Javier Irigoyen-García, *"Moors Dressed as Moors": Clothing, Social Distinction, and Ethnicity in Early Modern Iberia*
27 Jean Dangler, *Edging toward Iberia*
28 Ryan D. Giles and Steven Wagschal (eds), *Beyond Sight: Engaging the Senses in Iberian Literatures and Cultures, 1200–1750*
29 Silvia Bermúdez, *Rocking the Boat: Migration and Race in Contemporary Spanish Music*
30 Hilaire Kallendorf, *Ambiguous Antidotes: Virtue as Vaccine for Vice in Early Modern Spain*
31 Leslie Harkema, *Spanish Modernism and the Poetics of Youth: From Miguel de Unamuno to* La Joven Literatura
32 Benjamin Fraser, *Cognitive Disability Aesthetics: Visual Culture, Disability Representations, and the (In)Visibility of Cognitive Difference*
33 Robert Patrick Newcomb, *Iberianism and Crisis: Spain and Portugal at the Turn of the Twentieth Century*

34 Sara J. Brenneis, *Spaniards in Mauthausen: Representations of a Nazi Concentration Camp, 1940–2015*
35 Silvia Bermúdez and Roberta Johnson (eds), *A New History of Iberian Feminisms*
36 Steven Wagschal, *Minding Animals In the Old and New Worlds: A Cognitive Historical Analysis*
37 Heather Bamford, *Cultures of the Fragment: Uses of the Iberian Manuscript, 1100–1600*
38 Enrique García Santo-Tomás (ed), *Science on Stage in Early Modern Spain*
39 Marina Brownlee (ed), *Cervantes'* Persiles *and the Travails of Romance*
40 Sarah Thomas, *Inhabiting the In-Between: Childhood and Cinema in Spain's Long Transition*
41 David A. Wacks, *Medieval Iberian Crusade Fiction and the Mediterranean World*
42 Rosilie Hernández, *Immaculate Conceptions: The Power of the Religious Imagination in Early Modern Spain*
43 Mary Coffey and Margot Versteeg (eds), *Imagined Truths: Realism in Modern Spanish Literature and Culture*
44 Diana Aramburu, *Resisting Invisibility: Detecting the Female Body in Spanish Crime Fiction*
45 Samuel Amago and Matthew J. Marr (eds), *Consequential Art: Comics Culture in Contemporary Spain*
46 Richard P. Kinkade, *Dawn of a Dynasty: The Life and Times of Infante Manuel of Castile*
47 Jill Robbins, *Poetry and Crisis: Cultural Politics and Citizenship in the Wake of the Madrid Bombings*
48 Ana María Laguna and John Beusterien (eds), *Goodbye Eros: Recasting Forms and Norms of Love in the Age of Cervantes*
49 Sara J. Brenneis and Gina Herrmann (eds), *Spain, World War II, and the Holocaust: History and Representation*
50 Francisco Fernández de Alba, *Sex, Drugs, and Fashion in 1970s Madrid*
51 Daniel Aguirre-Oteiza, *This Ghostly Poetry: Reading Spanish Republican Exiles between Literary History and Poetic Memory*
52 Lara Anderson, *Control and Resistance: Food Discourse in Franco Spain*
53 Faith Harden, *Arms and Letters: Military Life Writing in Early Modern Spain*
54 Erin Alice Cowling, Tania de Miguel Magro, Mina García Jordán, and Glenda Y. Nieto-Cuebas (eds), *Social Justice in Spanish Golden Age Theatre*
55 Paul Michael Johnson, *Affective Geographies: Cervantes, Emotion, and the Literary Mediterranean*

56 Justin Crumbaugh and Nil Santiáñez (eds), *Spanish Fascist Writing: An Anthology*
57 Margaret E. Boyle and Sarah E. Owens (eds), *Health and Healing in the Early Modern Iberian World: A Gendered Perspective*
58 Leticia Álvarez-Recio (ed), *Iberian Chivalric Romance: Translations and Cultural Transmission in Early Modern England*
59 Henry Berlin, *Alone Together: Poetics of the Passions in Late Medieval Iberia*
60 Adrian Shubert, *The Sword of Luchana: Baldomero Espartero and the Making of Modern Spain, 1793–1879*
61 Jorge Pérez, *Fashioning Spanish Cinema: Costume, Identity, and Stardom*
62 Enriqueta Zafra, *Lazarillo de Tormes: A Graphic Novel*
63 Erin Alice Cowling, *Chocolate: How a New World Commodity Conquered Spanish Literature*
64 Mary E. Barnard, *A Poetry of Things: The Material Lyric in Habsburg Spain*
65 Frederick A. de Armas and James Mandrell (eds), *The Gastronomical Arts in Spain: Food and Etiquette*
66 Catherine Infante, *The Arts of Encounter: Christians, Muslims, and the Power of Images in Early Modern Spain*
67 Robert Richmond Ellis, *Bibliophiles, Murderous Bookmen, and Mad Librarians: The Story of Books in Modern Spain*
68 Beatriz de Alba-Koch (ed), *The Ibero-American Baroque*
69 Deborah R. Forteza, *The English Reformation in the Spanish Imagination: Rewriting Nero, Jezebel, and the Dragon*
70 Olga Sendra Ferrer, *Barcelona, City of Margins*
71 Dale Shuger, *God Made Word: An Archaeology of Mystic Discourse in Early Modern Spain*

www.ingramcontent.com/pod-product-compliance
Lightning Source LLC
LaVergne TN
LVHW090150080826
844660LV00013B/753/J

* 9 7 8 1 4 8 7 5 2 8 8 0 5 *